Radicals in America

Radicals in America is a masterful history of controversial dissenters who pursued greater equality, freedom, and democracy – and transformed the nation. Written with clarity and verve, *Radicals in America* shows how radical leftists, while often marginal or ostracized, could assume a catalytic role as effective organizers in mass movements, fostering the imagination of alternative futures.

Beginning with the Second World War, *Radicals in America* extends all the way to the present, making it the first comprehensive history of radicalism to reach beyond the sixties. From the Communist Party and the Black Panther Party for Self-Defense, its coverage extends to the Battle of Seattle and Occupy Wall Street.

Each chapter begins with a particular life story, including a Harlem woman deported in the McCarthy era, a gay Japanese-American opponent of the Vietnam War, and a Native American environmentalist, vignettes that bring to life the personal within the political.

Howard Brick is the Louis Evans Professor of History at the University of Michigan. He is the author of *Daniel Bell and the Decline of Intellectual Radicalism* (1986), *Age of Contradiction: American Thought and Culture in the 1960s* (1998), and *Transcending Capitalism: Visions of a New Society in Modern American Thought* (2006).

Christopher Phelps is associate professor of American history at the University of Nottingham. He is the author of *Young Sidney Hook: Marxist and Pragmatist* (1997) and articles in the *Journal of American History*, *The Nation*, *The Financial Times*, and other periodicals. He has received several awards for his historical and political writing.

Cambridge Essential Histories

Series Editor

Donald Critchlow, *Arizona State University*

Cambridge Essential Histories is devoted to introducing critical events, periods, or individuals in history to students. Volumes in this series emphasize narrative as a means of familiarizing students with historical analysis. In this series leading scholars focus on topics in European, American, Asian, Latin American, Middle Eastern, African, and World History through thesis-driven, concise volumes designed for survey and upper-division undergraduate history courses. The books contain an introduction that acquaints readers with the historical event and reveals the book's thesis; narrative chapters that cover the chronology of the event or problem; and a concluding summary that provides the historical interpretation and analysis.

Titles in the Series

Radicals in America

The U.S. Left since the Second World War

HOWARD BRICK

University of Michigan

CHRISTOPHER PHELPS

University of Nottingham

CAMBRIDGE
UNIVERSITY PRESS

CAMBRIDGE
UNIVERSITY PRESS

32 Avenue of the Americas, New York, NY 10013-2473, USA

Cambridge University Press is part of the University of Cambridge.

It furthers the University's mission by disseminating knowledge in the pursuit of education, learning, and research at the highest international levels of excellence.

www.cambridge.org
Information on this title: www.cambridge.org/9780521731331

© Howard Brick and Christopher Phelps 2015

First published 2015

Printed in the United States of America

A catalog record for this publication is available from the British Library.

Library of Congress Cataloging in Publication Data
Brick, Howard, 1953–
Radicals in America : the U.S. Left since the Second World War / Howard Brick
(University of Michigan, Ann Arbor), Christopher Phelps (University of Nottingham).
pages cm. – (Cambridge essential histories)
Includes bibliographical references and index.
ISBN 978-0-521-51560-3 (hardback) – ISBN 978-0-521-73133-1 (paperback)
1. Social movements – United States – History – 20th century. 2. Social movements –
United States – History – 21st century. 3. Radicalism – United States – History.
4. Political activists – United States – History. 5. Dissenters – United States – History.
6. Liberalism – United States – History. 7. Right and left (Political science) – United
States – History. 8. United States – Politics and government – 1933–1945. 9. United
States – Politics and government – 1945–1989. 10. United States – Politics and
government – 1989– I. Phelps, Christopher, 1965– II. Title.
HN57.B653 2015
303.48'4–dc23 2015005774

ISBN 978-0-521-51560-3 Hardback
ISBN 978-0-521-73133-1 Paperback

In memory of
Karl W. Pohrt (1947–2013)
and with gratitude and love for
Carol, Emma, Nowell, and Rosa

Contents

Introduction

Margin and Mainstream in the American Radical Experience

"Please be informed that I am ready to serve in any unit of the armed forces of my country which is not segregated by race," wrote Winfred Lynn to his local draft board in 1942 after learning of his conscription into the United States Army. The 36-year-old landscape gardener from Jamaica, Queens, New York City, loathed Nazi Germany, fascist Italy, and Imperial Japan but vowed to go "to prison or to die, if necessary, rather than submit to the mockery of fighting for democracy in a Jim Crow army." Only when his lawyers concluded that his case against the Selective Service would be stronger were he in uniform did Lynn submit to conscription. He saw duty in the Pacific, made the rank of corporal, and watched his case reach the Supreme Court, which declined to hear it on January 2, 1945, dashing what one black newspaper, proclaiming Lynn "Hero of World War II," termed "the most important legal battle to challenge segregation in the armed forces." Only the Second World War's end in 1945 brought him an honorable discharge and the outcome he had sought for three long years: freedom.[1]

Worrying that Lynn's stance was too radical, even unpatriotic, the nation's leading civil rights organization, the National Association for the Advancement of Colored People (NAACP), had declined to support his case. His first attorney was his younger brother, Conrad Lynn, who

[1] Dwight Macdonald and Nancy Macdonald, *The War's Greatest Scandal: The Story of Jim Crow in Uniform* (March on Washington Movement, n.d.), p. 5; "Winfred Lynn Reports on Jim Crow in Army," *Socialist Call*, 5 November 1945, p. 3; "Harlem Awaits With Big Welcome Winfred Lynn, Hero of World War II," *Arkansas State Press*, 26 October 1945, p. 1.

had been expelled from the Communist Party in 1937 for supporting Trinidadian workers' strikes, contrary to the Party's conciliatory Popular Front line. Next to join the defense was another radical, Arthur Garfield Hays, a civil libertarian who had represented anarchists Nicola Sacco and Bartolomeo Vanzetti, evolutionist John T. Scopes, and the Scottsboro Boys. The chief supporter of Lynn outside the courtroom was a militant trade union, the Brotherhood of Sleeping Car Porters, comprised mostly of black train workers inclined to fight for race equality as well as economic gain.

Winfred Lynn's disregard of wartime pressures out of insistence upon equality bore the militancy of the Brotherhood, whose leader A. Philip Randolph was graced with imperturbability, a courteous bearing, and a mellifluous voice. Randolph visited the White House repeatedly as chief race spokesman of the 1940s, striving to prevent a resurgence of the European colonialism and lynching that followed the First World War. "This is not a war for freedom," he held in 1944. "It is not a war for democracy. It is not a war to usher in the Century of the Common Man. . . . It is a war to continue 'white supremacy,' the theory of *Herrenvolk,* and the subjugation, domination, and exploitation of the peoples of color. It is a war between the imperialism of Fascism and Nazism and the imperialism of monopolistic capitalistic democracy." Randolph organized a 1943 Harlem mass meeting on Lynn's behalf and signed a letter lamenting "the sight of a Jim Crow American army fighting against Nazi racialism."[2]

With Randolph as the spearhead, this left-led black freedom movement of the 1940s made two signal breakthroughs: it widened access to jobs and compelled desegregation of the armed forces. Randolph had formed a March on Washington Movement around those demands, planning a rally of tens of thousands at the Lincoln Memorial on July 1, 1941. As a socialist, he considered racism the product of economic insecurity and competition and held that "our present political and economic capitalist order is unable to satisfy the needs of modern man" because under it "one section of the population appropriates a part of the product which others have produced without giving any equivalent exchange." In the spring of 1941 the March on Washington Movement swelled with poor

---

[2] A. Philip Randolph, "March on Washington Movement Presents Program for the Negro," in *What the Negro Wants,* ed. Rayford W. Logan (Chapel Hill: University of North Carolina Press, 1944), p. 135; A. Philip Randolph, Willard S. Townsend, Norman Thomas, and Roy Wilkins, "A Worthy Cause," *Los Angeles Tribune,* 3 January 1944, p. 9.

and working-class blacks, although the small black middle class viewed it as an irresponsible provocation and the Communist Party objected out of fealty to the Non-Aggression Pact between Joseph Stalin's Soviet Union and Adolf Hitler's Nazi Germany. All the same, the March on Washington Movement was impressively effective. Worried about the "international embarrassment" that would result from a demonstration against segregation in the nation's capital, as *Fortune* magazine put it, President Franklin Delano Roosevelt agreed to issue Executive Order 8802, which established a Fair Employment Practices Committee (FEPC) to monitor defense contractors, just in time for Randolph to call off the protest march. It was the most significant federal civil rights advance since Reconstruction.[3]

In the years that followed, Randolph forgot neither armed forces deseg-regation nor "the famous Winfred Lynn case," as he called it in Congres-sional testimony in 1948. Jim Crow units had endured menial, humil-iating work during the Second World War, and black Americans saw the military as a national institution with millions of employees whose desegregation would weaken the racial caste system. When Democratic President Harry S. Truman proposed universal military training and con-scription as the Cold War set in, Randolph visited the White House to inform Truman that his own "frank, factual survey" found that "Negroes are in no mood to shoulder a gun for democracy abroad so long as they are denied democracy here at home." If a draft were instituted while dis-crimination persisted, Randolph announced, he would "advise Negroes to refuse to fight as slaves for a democracy they cannot possess and cannot enjoy": "Negroes are just sick and tired of being pushed around, and we just do not propose to take it, and we do not care what happens." This threat of mass draft resistance was radical – "treasonable," said Georgia Senator Richard Russell – but sufficiently credible to disconcert Truman, who faced an election year as well as an accelerating Cold War strug-gle with the Soviet Union over Africa, Asia, and Latin America, whose peoples already were inclined to look askance at U.S. claims to repre-sent the "free world" given American racial segregation. When Truman issued Executive Order 9981 in 1948, abolishing racial segregation in the

---

[3] Herbert Garfinkel, *When Negroes March: The March on Washington Movement in the Organizational Politics for FEPC* (1959; New York: Atheneum, 1973), pp. 17, 64; Cornelius L. Bynum, *A. Philip Randolph and the Struggle for Civil Rights* (Urbana: University of Illinois, 2010), p. 57.

FIGURE 0.1. The March on Washington Movement organized by the black social-ist labor leader A. Philip Randolph, which called on the U.S. military to abandon its racist practices during the Second World War. 1943. *Authors' collection.*

military, Randolph called off the civil disobedience campaign, having once again applied popular pressure to wrest a stunning civil rights victory by federal executive order.[4]

That might mark the end of the story were it not for one final twist. Truman's executive order was so vague about the timetable for military desegregation that some radicals saw it as postponing, rather than fulfilling, justice. Among them was Winfred Lynn, who joined a small band of radicals led by pacifists A. J. Muste and Bayard Rustin who vowed to carry the civil disobedience campaign forward. Their Campaign to Resist Military Segregation – with Lynn the gardener as its treasurer – urged "Negro and white youth to refuse induction into segregated military establishments." Just as A. Philip Randolph had honored Lynn's wartime resistance in his testimony to Congress, so Lynn was following a credo first articulated by Randolph: "These rights will not be given. They must be taken."[5]

What is a radical? The word *radical* comes from the same Latin word as *radish*. Both describe objects that are red, zesty, and sometimes found underground, but their real etymological connection is in their shared derivation from *radix,* the Latin word for *root.* As any gardener knows, radishes are root vegetables, and radicals seek the roots of social problems. When Thomas Paine, an artisan radical of the eighteenth century, rebutted the conservative Edmund Burke's condemnation of crowd violence in the French Revolution, he pointed to the bloodthirsty example that monarchy had set. "Lay, then, the axe to the root," he wrote, "and teach governments humanity."[6]

By positing a need to go to the root, radicals suggest that mere pruning will invite social problems to sprout forth with renewed vigor. That is why radicals have not opposed particular wars alone but often have set

---

[4] Senate Committee on Armed Services, *Universal Military Training: Hearings Before the Committee on Armed Services,* 80th Cong., 2nd sess., 1948, pp. 687–688; Jervis Anderson, *A. Philip Randolph: A Biographical Portrait* (1973; Berkeley: University of California, 1986), p. 239; Senate Committee on Armed Services, *Universal Military Training,* p. 689; William C. Berman, *The Politics of Civil Rights in the Truman Administration* (Columbus: Ohio University Press, 1970), p. 119.

[5] "Resist Military Segregation Goes On After A. Philip Randolph Abandons It," *Arkansas State Press,* 27 August 1948, pp. 1, 8; A. Philip Randolph, "Keynote Address," in *March on Washington Movement: Proceedings of Conference Held in Detroit September 26–27, 1942,* p. 5.

[6] Thomas Paine, *Rights of Man: Being an Answer to Mr. Burke's Attack on the French Revolution* (London: Printed for J. S. Jordan, 1791), p. 33.

out to eliminate militarism, state expansion, and empire – or even, among pacifists, violence and domination themselves. Likewise, it is why radicals have not stopped at attempts to reduce poverty through charity but sought to replace the very system of concentrated private ownership and capital accumulation that generates vast inequalities in income and wealth. To be sure, radical activism frequently leads to lesser adjustments, along the lines of the old adage that by demanding the whole loaf one may secure half. Ultimately, however, radicals have tended to be sustained by the view that a great range of social problems are tied together and must be addressed holistically.

Because they do not accept the status quo's legitimacy, radicals have often adopted tactics and strategies considered irregular or beyond the pale. Some methods – marching in demonstrations, signing petitions, setting up picket lines, or running candidates independent of the major parties – may seem innocuous exercises of basic democratic rights, but to conventionally minded Americans such activity can seem weird or risky. Radicals have often been tarred as dangerous, reckless, extremist, or subversive, especially if they advocate tactics such as disruptive civil disobedience or armed self-defense, but that does not necessarily prevent them from being effective. As Nathaniel Hawthorne once put it, "The world owes all its onward impulses to men ill at ease."[7]

The terms *left* and *right* are often used in conventional political discourse to describe positions on the contemporary U.S. political scene, with liberalism and the Democratic Party referred to as "the left" and conservatism and the Republican Party as "the right." Radicals have defined the left more robustly. In the French Revolution of 1789, when left and right were first used to designate contending political blocs, "the left" meant revolution: the overturning of existing social relations, the eradication of the *ancien régime* of feudalism and monarchy. The quintessential slogan of the French Revolution – *liberty, equality, fraternity* – is as good a place as any to start in understanding the radical left, especially if *solidarity* is substituted for the last of the three terms, to make it gender neutral. *Liberty, equality, solidarity*: the radical left has sought to expand personal freedom, establish greater social, political, and economic equality, and widen the scope of mutuality by recognition of the inherent dignity of all. The role of the left has been to point to a future society governed by self-determination and cooperation, pitting it against both the elitism of

---

[7] Nathaniel Hawthorne, *The House of the Seven Gables; and the Snow Image* (1851; Boston: James R. Osgood, 1871), p. 330.

traditional society with its top-down ranking of humankind and modern ultra-competitive society with its survival-of-the-fittest ethics.

The conviction that power should be distributed on a vastly more participatory basis – that every gardener may govern, to adapt an old formulation – has led the radical left to dissent from conventions that many take to be natural. The left has tended, if not with total consistency, to oppose the division of people into superior and inferior castes or groups, whether by social class (wealthy, poor, intermediate), gender (male and female), or race ("whites" over African Americans, Latinos, Native Americans, and other people of color). Some past social structures of division, such as slavery and state-mandated racial segregation, have succumbed to radical challenges, but even today privileges accorded on the basis of class, gender, and race remain the focus and target of radical action, supplemented by concerns such as promoting peace, environmental sustainability, and freedom of sexual orientation. What makes left-wing criticism radical is the conviction that freedom, equality, democracy, and solidarity will demand changing the existing order of social life in fundamental ways – supplanting, for example, the power of multinational corporations – and devising new egalitarian ways of social interaction and political engagement. In this way the radical left differs profoundly from the so-called "radical" right, which works to reinforce class, gender, and racial privileges, if often in the guise of liberty, patriotism, populism, tradition, or merit. The radical left has always been a minority current in an American society that is reluctant to entertain possibilities of dramatic change. Indeed, U.S. culture has seen implacable, enduring hierarchies despite the country's founding declaration that "all men are created equal." Nevertheless, the left has propelled major changes and frequently given shape to what Americans broadly take as the nation's core traditions.

This comprehensive history of American left-wing radicalism since the Second World War will cover the left's surge right after the Second World War, adversity in the McCarthy era, growth in the 1960s and 1970s, and precariousness in more recent decades. The waxing and waning of radical fortunes across this entire period are best understood by apprehending *margin* and *mainstream* as the constitutive duality of the American radical experience. Radicals must exist in estrangement from society, in opposition to the whole established order, as when the Black Panther Party condemned a white-dominated "Babylon" or radical feminists opposed "the patriarchy." Radicals oppose existing society, placing them on the outside, but at the very same time desire a future in which their values are made the basis of a restructured society. Toward that end, they must strive to transform, by whatever means available to them, the culture and society they oppose, which requires engaging larger currents that can issue in victories. The task of maintaining ardent opposition to the status quo, as outsiders if need be, while also seeking solidarity with strong social forces, here and now, that might be capable of changing it root and branch poses a dialectic of margin and mainstream. That dialectic entails a tension between two commitments: the willingness to hold fast for a minority view and the struggle to imagine and help fashion a new majority. Such a tension can be, at different times, fruitful in generating new strategies and tactics of change or disabling as it tempts leftists in either direction, toward unjustified pride in their isolation or toward an appeal to popularity that sacrifices their radical goals. Margin and mainstream, together, provide the fulcrum of our analysis of the history of American radicalism.

So characteristic of the radical experience is this duality that it dates to American radicalism's formative phase, prior to the Civil War, when to advocate immediate freedom for all slaves was a *radical* idea embraced by a prophetic minority, an idea that made one a pariah. Wendell Phillips, one such pariah, is an exemplary case study in how margin and mainstream works powerfully as a descriptor of the condition of radical commitment. A well-bred Boston attorney, Phillips risked comfort and found himself relegated to the margins when he decided to give full measure to his beliefs when he saw another abolitionist attacked by a conservative mob. As a result, Phillips became "the first and greatest American agitator," even the "inventor" of the "method of agitation," according to his first biographer, and as a result was compelled to suffer "the decree of social outlawry."[8]

If a rebel, however, Phillips was not alone. The decades before the Civil War saw abolitionism spill over, stimulating other egalitarianisms. Communal experiments in socialism mushroomed. The early labor movement challenged onerous working conditions and poor pay. Experimental freethinking flourished against the restraining orthodoxies of established religion, public opinion, and custom. Radical women of the late eighteenth and early nineteenth centuries – Mary Wollstonecraft, Fanny Wright, Margaret Fuller, Elizabeth Cady Stanton, Susan B. Anthony, Sojourner Truth, Victoria Woodhull, and others – were regarded as scandalous for

---

[8] Carlos Martyn, *Wendell Phillips: The Agitator* (New York: Funk & Wagnalls, 1890), pp. 105, 179.

their advocacy of equal rights for women, abolition, and freethinking about religion and marriage. These combined campaigns shocked and outraged the American public even if they presaged many social and cultural changes later widely accepted. They give enduring clues as to the sensibility of American radicalism, for radicals ever since have repeatedly acknowledged them as forerunners, as when A. Philip Randolph said of the "New Negro radicals" of his generation, "We stood upon the shoulders of the civil rights fighters of the Reconstruction era, and they stood upon the shoulders of the black abolitionists."[9]

Wendell Phillips understood full well that the abolitionist cause he had joined was that of a distinct and beleaguered minority subject to vitriolic opprobrium, as he stated in 1853: "The press, the pulpit, the wealth, the literature, the prejudices, the political arrangements, the present self-interest of the country, are all against us.... The elements which control public opinion and mould the masses are against us. We can but pick off here and there a man from the triumphant majority." Simultaneously, his radicalism rested on a deep belief in the cause of democracy, the rule of the majority among a self-governing people. In the very same year as his unblinking recognition of his marginality, he said, "The convictions of most men are on our side, and this will surely appear, if we can only pierce the crust of their prejudice or indifference." He was committed to change by means of moral suasion, because he believed the democratic age required "a government of brains, a government of ideas. I believe in it – in public opinion." In these words, Phillips made clear the tension between the necessity of accepting marginality as a principled oppositionist, even to the point of inviting scorn and persecution, while simultaneously orienting toward, indeed *believing in*, the people at large.[10]

How did Phillips hold to opposition in the face of overpowering hostility while claiming democracy was on his side? Only by a powerful sense of futurity: a confidence that today's persecuted minority would in the long run forge popular sentiment. Radicals by necessity tack back and forth between the aspiration to represent a broad popular constituency and the actual status of being a political minority engaged in agitation, persecuted by authorities, and abhorred by much of popular opinion. Small bands of radicals can reshape the mainstream when, given the right

---

[9] Anderson, *A. Philip Randolph*, p. 21.
[10] Wendell Phillips, *The Lesson of the Hour*, ed. Noel Ignatiev (Chicago, Ill.: Charles H. Kerr, 2001), pp. 46, 70, 80.

combination of changing circumstances and wise and creative strategy, the agitators' ideas and ambitions succeed in mobilizing sufficient numbers to demand great change, whether by electoral means or mass protest outside the doors of formal legislatures, compelling new policies and popular majorities.

A democratic dilemma arises insofar as opposition to the status quo places agitators in a literal or figurative stance of outlawry. Disobeying existing conventions, they often must face a reactionary, resistant mainstream – not only among constituted authorities but much of the public too. For a radical politics, then, "democracy" cannot mean whatever majority opinion holds at any particular moment but must speak to the promise that masses of people will at some point prove amenable to radical ideas, whether consciously or not. At the same time, the radical left must expect and be prepared for rapid changes in circumstances, so its agitators must address themselves not to routine government and party competition but cultivate readiness for "extraordinary politics," revolutionary situations that are not in any strict sense predictable or well scripted. Phillips recognized this, declaring in 1853, "Politics is but the common pulse-beat, of which revolution is the fever-spasm." The latter could be found in those exceptional moments when marginal agitators suddenly gain access to mainstream sentiment and in crises that demand dramatic improvisations. Thus even though Phillips began as a pacifist, he proved ready to change his tactics and strategy as the Civil War broke out. He and the escaped slave Frederick Douglass bent all their agitation toward compelling the reluctant Republican Party leadership to make abolition of slavery the Union's cause of arms. The fact that war provided the occasion for Abraham Lincoln to issue the Emancipation Proclamation on January 1, 1863, and ride to reelection in 1864 on a platform endorsing a new Constitutional amendment for an absolute end to slavery in the republic – ideas far outside the mainstream only a few years before – proved Phillips's revolutionary anticipation correct. The antislavery crusade remains one of the clearest cases in all American history of how forbidden, vilified radical opinions and organizing can suddenly propel dramatic and almost completely unexpected new futures.[11]

For black abolitionists and the most radical of white abolitionists, the eradication not only of slavery but also of racism was the aim. Beyond that profoundly radical objective, abolitionism gave rise to all manner of

[11] Phillips, *Lesson of the Hour*, p. 73.

ferment, from women's rights to resistance to imperialism and war, thus giving birth to the modern American radical left. These varied currents did not always coalesce, and sometimes they even clashed (many women's suffrage advocates were white supremacists, for example, and socialists could be too), but many individual radical thinkers did combine all of the most egalitarian of these demands. The ensemble that emerged was truly a "movement of movements," to use a phrase that would gain ground at the end of the twentieth century to convey the range of protests for freedom, autonomy, social justice, and collective self-determination in the United States and the world.

Following the Civil War, "the Labor Question" became a central focus of the American left. The nineteenth-century phraseology would not survive, but the constellation of issues of property, work, and class that it summoned very much remained at the center of radical thought and action up through the Second World War. The older radicalism against slavery was not immaterial to that development. Although many abolitionists hewed to the bourgeois belief that "free labor" lay in freedom of contract, abolition seemed radical in its day precisely because it proposed to confiscate property without compensation – for slaves had been, after all, valuable owned property. Some opponents of chattel slavery sought also to surmount "wage slavery": the condition of workers within the modern order of private property, production for profit, and capital accumulation. Radicals faulted capitalism for its glaring inequalities of power and wealth, for exploitation of wage labor, for a headlong rush of market-oriented life that perpetuated such hierarchies as the Victorian subordination of women to men, and for fostering extreme individualism in personal accumulation of wealth, attenuating ethical responsibility to others. Many looked to Europe as harbinger of new societies to come. When the Paris Commune of 1871 erupted, Wendell Phillips proclaimed, "There is no hope for France but in the Reds." His fellow veteran of abolitionism, Theodore Tilton, held, "The same logic and sympathy – the same conviction and ardor – which made us an Abolitionist twenty years ago, make us a Communist now."[12]

Criticism of capitalism and bourgeois life came in two forms. One, social, assailed inequalities of wealth and power; the other, artistic,

---

[12] Quoted in Timothy Messer-Kruse, *The Yankee International: Marxism and the American Reform Tradition* (Chapel Hill: University of North Carolina, 1998), p. 103, 106.

valued autonomy above stifling custom, prejudice, or tradition.[13] Both were present in the writings of capitalism's best-known opponents, Karl Marx and Friedrich Engels, nineteenth-century German revolutionaries who lived in exile in England organizing an International Workingmen's Association and corresponding extensively with Americans, especially German-American émigrés. In their *Communist Manifesto* (1848), they announced that the working class should "win the battle of democracy" by taking the reins of social power. This proletarian revolution would topple the exclusive control over investment and planning by owners of private capital and create a new order in which productive property would be held in common, class antagonism would disappear, and there would arise "an association, in which the free development of each is the condition for the free development of all." Popular self-determination would create freedom and abundance, goals that the rule of wealth, despite its habitual gloss of free-market liberty and prosperity, denied to the mass of working poor.[14]

Other radical doctrines competed with this kind of revolutionary socialism in the nineteenth century, notably anarchism, which claimed to oppose coercive government more vigorously. Both socialists and anarchists sought an egalitarian and self-governing society of common property through working-class self-activity, but there were sharp differences between them over whether to pursue elections or legislation (which socialists favored and anarchists disdained) or carry out individual acts of violence against corporate and political rulers (which some anarchists practiced and socialists opposed, favoring education and political action instead, culminating in mass insurrection). By the dawn of the twentieth century, most American radicals had concluded this debate in favor of Marx's resolution of the problem of margin and mainstream. As the development of capitalism expanded the ranks of wage earners, workers would be pressed to take collective action against their employers and develop a commitment to shared ownership. The new society lay within the old; the radical opposition, hounded and reviled in its own time, looked forward to a socialist future. If this prospect of an eventual working-class breakthrough inspired early twentieth-century radicals, the course of world events in the following century would complicate that prognosis, given

---

[13] Luc Boltanski and Eve Chiapello, *The New Spirit of Capitalism*, trans. Gregory Elliott (London: Verso, 2005).

[14] Karl Marx and Friedrich Engels, *Manifesto of the Communist Party* (New York: Monthly Review Press, 1998), pp. 39, 40.

both capitalism's resilience and undemocratic developments in countries where capitalism was displaced, such as the Soviet Union. The result was much introspection and searches for new conceptualizations of the radical project.

A key variable intersecting with radicalism's history in the first half of the twentieth century was liberalism, which had attained substantial intellectual and policy sway by the Second World War. Once a laissez-faire doctrine of minimal government, liberalism had shifted in favor of active government intervention in the economy through regulation and social expenditure, seeing such policies as essential to sustaining the objective of individual freedom for all that was the philosophical essence of liberalism, given widespread acknowledgment that starvation, destitution, and homelessness rendered citizens incapable of pursuing their own futures. Franklin Delano Roosevelt's New Deal of the 1930s built upon the first inroads of the Progressive Era, and was in turn built upon by Lyndon Baines Johnson's Great Society of the 1960s.

Despite the radical left's peak strength in those same decades, radicals and liberals often looked upon one another warily, existing here in mutuality, there in tension. Liberals often found radicals wild-eyed or impractical, whereas to radicals, liberals could seem gutless. As Edmund Wilson wrote, "The surest way to shake an American reformer, the surest way to make him back down, has always been to accuse him of socialism." More basically, where liberals tended to see social problems as aberrations to be fixed in an otherwise chiefly healthy society, the radical left has insisted that they are produced by a system that must be supplanted. Radical agitators working on a single problem may appear to have reformist aims, as in the quest to eliminate legal segregation so that African Americans might attain full citizenship. Yet such protests often materialize with the core involvement of those, such as socialists, who are motivated by much larger egalitarian aims. Furthermore, struggles to enact simple reforms often radicalize movement participants, pushing them toward greater militancy in aims and tactics and toward new views of the depth and breadth of social change needed to achieve freedom, equality, and solidarity. Likewise, pressures exerted within social movements by their left wings can enlarge liberals' ambitions and urge them on to reforms that might not otherwise occur. The connection between conscious radical groups, usually very small, and vibrant and large social movements is the lifeblood of radical political development. The balance between margin and mainstream – the outsider status of the radical and the ambition to assemble majorities capable of wresting change – is constantly played out in causes ranging from labor to antiwar, from queer liberation to global justice.[15]

The margin–mainstream duality also explains the "un-American" stigma imposed on radicalism, a trope that has outlasted McCarthyism. The charge that radicals are not true Americans is a bid to sear them with marginality. It is also a misapprehension, for even radicals of the farthest left have spoken with American inflection. Some radicals, to be sure, have sought to leapfrog over their marginality by identifying with over-seas movements and states, seeking to draw upon their power, resources, and prestige. That occurred when Communists followed the Soviet Union blindly, leaving them vulnerable to McCarthyism. It also occurred when the Weatherman faction of Students for a Democratic Society coined the expression "fight the people," a self-defeating estrangement from Amer-ican life, in the belief that it positioned them well to serve Third World interests. If foreign examples and ideologies have in this way been a very deep pitfall, it bears notice that an internationalist sensibility has equally informed radical skeptics who have been opposed to copy-cat emulation of foreign states, parties, and leaders. In the 1940s, such radical dis-senters encouraged Soviet workers to restore democracy; in the 1960s they heeded Vietnamese revolutionaries who advised American radicals to build the largest possible coalitions to stop the Vietnam War rather than alienate the public by carrying out bombings. This kind of interna-tionalism has enabled paths to the American mainstream, not alienation from it.

American radicals since the Second World War, in seeking solidarity across borders to fix problems no single nation can resolve, have been "citizens of the world," a favored self-description of their revolutionary ancestor Thomas Paine, who spent a life moving freely between Britain, America, and France. Relatively immune from the parochial "exception-alist" view that the only valid solutions to American problems are found within a single nation's political culture, radicals have been more likely than other Americans to see their activity in a world context and rec-ognize that other societies sometimes achieve better outcomes, evident in varied measures of health and happiness. Since the middle of the twentieth century, radicals have acted in recognition that America is an unsurpassed military hegemon, starting with its nuclear monopoly and continuing to its unipolar military dominance in the twenty-first century. Radicals have viewed any one country's quest for world supremacy as

---

[15] Edmund Wilson, *The American Earthquake* (London: W. H. Allen, 1958), p. 277.

unstable, undesirable, and unattainable, and their radicalism has been leavened by developments abroad, from the Hungarian uprising of 1956 to the French general strike of 1968, from the 1959 revolution by Cuba's "bearded ones" to the Zapatista rebellion in Mexico in the 1990s. Just as the Indian anticolonial movement led by Mohandas Gandhi inspired A. Philip Randolph to undertake his mass protest campaigns in the 1940s, many subsequent radicals have been inspired by examples in Africa, Asia, Latin America, and Europe.

Often this internationalist confluence has been mutual. In 2009, Bradley Manning, a young Oklahoma-born Army private who experienced antigay bullying by other military personnel, decided to express his opposition to the war in Iraq, where he was stationed, by leaking hundreds of thousands of secret U.S. government cables to a whistle-blowing website, WikiLeaks, launched by Julian Assange, an Australian radical. In February 2010, WikiLeaks published the releases, which included State Department cables with abundant evidence of the corrupt, dictatorial nature of the Tunisian regime supported by the United States. On December 17, 2010, a poor Tunisian street vendor, Mohamed Bouazizi, doused himself in paint thinner and lit a match in an act of self-immolation. His death sparked mass demonstrations fueled by the WikiLeaks revelations, toppling Tunisia's government. The result was the Arab Spring of 2011. As Egyptians occupied Cairo's Tahrir Square and felled their own dictatorship, the cascading series of Middle Eastern revolts inspired young protestors in Spain to occupy Madrid Square to protest unemployment and austerity in the Great Recession. When the radical Canadian media critics Adbusters took to the Internet to suggest an analogous movement in the United States, protestors took over Manhattan's Zuccotti Park to object to financial-sector malfeasance. This Occupy Wall Street movement was denounced as "un-American" by conservatives, but with the slogan, "We are the 99 percent!" the movement succeeded, at least for a time, in focusing broad public attention on the upward redistribution of wealth that benefited the top 1 percent of the population almost exclusively. These flashpoints of 2010–11 show how radical perspectives can and do circumnavigate the world, with contagious effects.

Against such a global tableau, this book will chronicle American radicalism since the Second World War. The first chapter, "War and Peace, 1939–1948," describes the bright hopes of a radical left led largely, though not exclusively, by the Communist Party during and after a war that saw the defeat of the fascist powers. "All Over This Land, 1949–1959" catalogues the Communist-led left's defeat in the Cold War era but also sketches a radical revival whose fuller flourishing is detailed in "A New Left, 1960–1964." The quickening and proliferation of sixties radicalism, with the black-led freedom movement and opposition to the Vietnam War at its core, resulted in a vibrancy of possibility conveyed in "The Revolution Will Be Live, 1965–1973." Left-wing aspirations for sweeping change continued to remain strong into the 1970s, with a new attentiveness to class politics, told in "Anticipation, 1973–1980." The election of Ronald Reagan to the presidency was a shock for the left, but the following decade still saw significant protest mobilizations against the nuclear arms race and in solidarity with Central America and South Africa, detailed in "Over the Rainbow, 1980–1989." After the fall of the Berlin Wall, American radicalism entered its great doldrums and drift, never quite cohering or regaining force despite many innovations in environmental and global justice, as is described in "What Democracy Looks Like, 1990 to the Present." Each of these chapters provides analysis of the character, strengths, and weaknesses of a specific phase of American radicalism striving to break free of marginality. Each opens with a biography of a life – typically, an unsung life – that in some way illustrates key themes of the radicalism of that period, without any chimerical pursuit of "representative" status. Taken together, these portraits show the vast diversity of American radicals' lives of commitment.

As radicalism oscillates between margin and mainstream, its usual position is as outlier. That does not make American society impervious to it. Synthesizing the key principles of freedom, equality, and solidarity has always been a steep challenge, but the left has often succeeded in mobilizing impulses for solidarity and equality within a society that valorizes individualism, and has defended freedoms that American conservatives and liberals have disregarded despite their stated admiration for liberty. At times, radicals have advanced their project through social movements that generate excitement well beyond the left's own ranks, as when Wendell Phillips set out on his abolitionist quest or when Winfred Lynn and A. Philip Randolph, at first virtually alone, confronted racist segregation in the 1940s. Despite being small in numbers, castigated, and belittled, left-wing radicals have often spurred important movements, won wide hearing for their ideas, and affected policy. As one cause leads to another, as one activist cohort yields to a new generation, visions of radical transformation are refashioned – and American society with them.

I

War and Peace, 1939–1948

In January 1946, a council of 240 delegates in the Philippines representing more than 10,000 U.S. soldiers chaired by Sergeant Emil Mazey (Sub-Base R, Batangas, Luzon) lodged a protest with the War Department against the slow pace of troop demobilization. The war was over. American troops had clasped hands with Red Army soldiers at the River Elbe in April 1945; Berlin fell in May, Japan in August. Why were they not yet home? Continued occupation of the Philippines was needless, for the Filipinos were friendly. Guerrillas in the Hukbalahap – the People's Anti-Japanese Army – had helped secure the islands. Since the Huks were initiated by the Communist Party of the Philippines, however, the U.S. Army Counter-Intelligence Corps (CIC) was overseeing their suppression by measures including summary execution. In this context, GI resistance was not just about going home; it was an act of solidarity with Filipinos. When two Senators visited Luzon, Emil Mazey stood in a room full of generals risking court martial to testify that the Army had burnt surplus shoes, blankets, and jackets that could have gone to Filipinos. The occupation, he held, was laying the groundwork for peacetime conscription and a permanent military presence in Asia.

As part of a worldwide U.S. troop "bring us home" movement, the Philippines rebellion was connected in myriad ways to a 1945–1946 working-class upsurge in the United States, where pent-up resentment about an inflation-pinched standard of living and vast wartime corporate profits resulted in the largest strike wave in American history. Millions struck in one sector after another: oil, coal, lumber, glass, textiles, trucking, meatpacking, and steel. The epicenter was auto, where the United

Automobile Workers (UAW) – whose factory-occupation sit-down strikes in 1936–1937 propelled the rise of the Congress of Industrial Organizations (CIO) – walked out at General Motors (GM), the nation's largest corporation. "Open the books!" declared Walter Reuther, director of the union's GM department, demanding that the company boost pay without increasing consumer prices – or lay bare its ledgers to prove it could not. That was a page taken from Leon Trotsky, who had envisioned factory committees saying, "Show us your books; we demand control over the fixing of prices." Soon GM granted a large wage increase, though without keeping prices down.[1]

Mazey, the son of Hungarian immigrants raised in Michigan, had worked in Detroit's auto plants before entering the armed services. Radicalized by the Depression, he joined the Proletarian Party and helped win union recognition at Briggs Manufacturing, where he was elected president of UAW Local 212 in 1937. When the war arrived, Mazey, by then a Socialist Party member, opposed the plan for "incentive pay" backed by management and the Communist Party, considering it piecework. He led the 1943 UAW convention fight against the no-strike pledge, objecting to a Communist delegate's call for "a truce in the class struggle" by saying, "The class struggle has not been stopped during the war – it has been intensified!" When 7,000 Briggs workers halted production of Navy plane wings, Mazey said, "I don't blame them for their action and I would want to do the same thing if I were in the plant."[2]

Drafted into the Army, Mazey survived malaria and combat to organize a weekly "World Event Forum" at his base in the Philippines. In autumn 1945 he spoke on "Why Labor Unrest?" Once the GI rebellion broke loose, the Army transferred him to Okinawa, Japan – "the Army's Siberia," Mazey complained – but plenty of other khaki-clad dissidents remained. In Manila, infantrymen cabled Washington, "We ask the simple question: Why have we not been returned?" In Frankfurt, Germany, four thousand G.I.s and WACs converged on U.S. headquarters, chanting, "We want to go home!" A Hawaii protest of 15,000 servicemen at Hikham Field led Gen. Dwight D. Eisenhower to direct commanders to send home any personnel not needed. In spring 1946, with Mazey still stranded in Japan, his discharge impending, he was elected to the UAW

---

[1] Leon Trotsky, *The Transitional Program for Socialist Revolution* (1938; New York: Pathfinder, 1973), p. 87.

[2] "Unionist-Soldiers Urged Keeping Up Battle for Workers' Rights, Mazey Revealed in Rapping No-Strike Pledge," *Socialist Call*, 26 November 1943, p. 9; "7,000 on Strike in Plant Making Navy Plane Wings," *Dallas Morning News*, 26 February 1944, p. 3.

national executive by the same union convention that propelled Walter Reuther to the UAW presidency. The intrusions into the railroad and coal strikes by President Harry S. Truman and his suggestion that the Democratic Congress pass a law allowing the military to draft strikers against the government did not sit well with Mazey. Buoyed by the British Labour Party's landslide victory over Winston Churchill's Conservative Party in 1945, Mazey gave an address to the Michigan Commonwealth Federation, advocating a "social order in which democratic economic planning and control will supersede unregulated private enterprise and monopoly." It was time, Mazey declared, for an American labor party: "The New Deal is dead."[3]

Emil Mazey's radical journey from auto unionism to combat and back is emblematic of an entire left-wing generation's experience. Most of the radical left of the time shared Mazey's tenets that capitalism is unfair and unreliable, that an active labor movement is the fulcrum of change, and that social transformation requires a political party with a socialist program. This set of radical postulates, brimming with confidence and premised upon party and class, seemed validated by a postwar strike wave that confirmed American workers' capacity for militant action. In retrospect, however, the year Mazey returned home – 1945 – stands out as a very different dividing line, a year when the dropping of atom bombs on the Japanese cities of Hiroshima and Nagasaki initiated the nuclear age, when premonitions were felt of a coming Cold War, and when the death of Franklin Delano Roosevelt put a coda on New Deal liberalism. The watershed was not obvious to contemporaries who entered the period with vivid memories of the 1930s, when industrial workers, the unemployed, sharecroppers, tenants, farmers, and students were all on the move – organizing, striking, marching. Proud of fascism's defeat, radicals came out of the war meaning to revive the great alliances of the left, labor, and liberals. Instead, they faced mounting headwinds as manufacturers launched a counteroffensive against labor, Republicans retook Congress in 1946 for the first time since the 1929 stock market crash, and the Cold War began. A seasoned left with crusading ambitions still existed, but in

---

[3] Emil Mazey, "Unionists on Luzon," *Socialist Call*, 26 November 1945, p. 10; "CIO Says GI Exiled by Army to Okinawa," *Times-Picayune*, 27 February 1946, p. 2; "Stranded Troops Issue Protest," *Sunday Oregonian* 11 November 1945, p. 6; "All Army Men Not Needed to Be Discharged: Eisenhower Acts as Troops Protest in Germany, Japan," *Rockford Morning Star*, 10 January 1946, p. 1; "Time for New Party is Now, Mazey Says," *Socialist Call*, 18 November 1946, p. 1; *Michigan Commonwealth Federation* (n.p., n.d. [1944]), p. 1.

the postwar years – especially after 1947 – liberal-left partnerships frayed rather than advancing as in the 1930s.

Until 1945 the Communist Party of the United States of America (CPUSA) had maintained its status as the predominant organization on the left despite regular criticism of it from an array of radicals such as Emil Mazey, who saw it as less about communism than "Stalinism," the bureaucratic dictatorship in the Soviet Union. In 1939, the CPUSA had shown its loyalty to the Soviet Union by embracing its agreement with Nazi Germany, disgusting many liberals, but once the Nazis invaded the Soviet Union in 1941 the Grand Alliance between the Soviet Union, Britain, and the United States allowed the party to reach an all-time high of some 80,000–100,000 members. That began to wane in the postwar period as the Communists' subordination to the Soviet Union placed them under a cloud of public suspicion. Their relative clout on the left inhibited more democratic concepts of socialism from gaining traction. By 1948 several different third-party movements arose to challenge Truman's conservative liberalism, each ending in defeat. Even as those failures portended crisis for the traditional labor- and party-centered left, a new style of radicalism began to stir, dedicated to antiwar principles; skeptical that the modern state, as an agent of total war, could make a better world through welfare provision; and committed to nonviolent civil disobedience against racial segregation. The late 1940s, therefore, saw the initial shoots of a reorientation of radicalism that would not become visible to most of the American public until the flourishing of the New Left in the 1960s.

In the decades before the Second World War, the greatest divide within the radical left appeared between groups that in some way laid claim to the Marxian heritage. The flagship left-wing organization at the beginning of the twentieth century was the Socialist Party of America, which reached its pinnacle in the presidential campaigns of Eugene V. Debs, a legendary railway labor leader whose electoral high-water mark came in 1912. Favoring public ownership of the commanding heights of the economy, the Socialists elected several Congressmen and hundreds of state and local officials, from Oklahoma to Pennsylvania. They adamantly protested U.S. participation in the First World War, suffering the consequences in the suppression of their organizations and publications and the jailing of their leaders. By the 1930s, under the leadership of Norman Thomas, a former Presbyterian minister and conscientious objector, the Socialists regained a footing but would never again generate the electoral success they enjoyed before the First World War, in part because the New Deal borrowed many policies they had long advocated, such as old-age pensions and unemployment insurance. While Socialists were sometimes dismissed as milquetoast by radicals further to the left, the democratic socialist ideal tied to a gradual reform politics animated a fair portion of leaders in the new industrial union movement, including Sidney Hillman of the Clothing Workers, Alex Rose of the Hatters, and David Dubinsky of the Garment Workers. After the Second World War, these opinion-makers remained to the left of President Truman but were hopeful that a coming tide of improvement would lead to a more humane society, even in the face of total war's horrific devastation.

A more prominent, forceful component of the left during the Depression and Second World War was comprised by the Communists. Emerging after the First World War in 1919 out of the Socialist Party's left wing, Communists initially positioned themselves as more revolutionary than Socialists. They disdained an electoral-legislative approach and identified with the 1917 insurrection in Russia depicted in John Reed's *Ten Days that Shook the World* (1919). To them, the moderate European social-democratic parties of 1914 had cast aside the motto "workers of the world, unite" and the workers' anthem "The Internationale" to march straight into nationalist fratricide, a betrayal that contrasted unfavorably with the Bolsheviks (meaning "Majority" in Russian), who had pulled all Russian troops out of the First World War after overthrowing the czarist autocracy. The Russian Revolution created "soviets," or councils, of factory workers, soldiers, and peasants. These decision-making bodies were described by Bolshevik leader Vladimir Lenin in his pamphlet *State and Revolution* (1917) as the basis of an entirely new system of governance. "All Power to the Soviets," the Bolshevik slogan, promised to bring democracy to a higher level than the "bourgeois" parliaments of Western countries, even if it was also to act as a "dictatorship of the proletariat" capable of subduing violent counterrevolution. American Communists joined the Communist International, or Comintern, led by the Soviet Union and sought to mold a highly disciplined party ready for action. By 1928–1933, as Joseph Stalin consolidated control of the Soviet state, Communists spoke of a "Third Period," excoriated socialist competitors as "social fascists," and forecast imminent revolution. Even as the 1929 crash discredited capitalism, triggering a downward spiral of joblessness, bankruptcies, and foreclosures, this hyperradical Third Period strategy generally proved ineffective and divisive, though Communists did organize fairly successful Unemployed Councils.

The Communist Party of the United States of America (CPUSA) – as Communists named their organization in 1930 – achieved much greater influence between 1935 and 1939 under the People's Front, or Popular Front, initiated in response to the 1933 Nazi seizure of power in Germany, a debacle that revealed the mistakenness of go-it-alone Third Period arrogance. The Popular Front, simultaneously adopted in Spain, France, and elsewhere, entailed Communists building broad-based coalitions with liberals and socialists to promote shared progressive-democratic objectives. In the United States, dozens of Popular Front organizations opposed fascism's rise in Europe, helped build industrial labor unions, fought oppression of blacks and Mexican Americans, and sought to address poverty and economic inequality. Yiddish readers could still choose between the Socialist *Forverts* or the Communist *Freiheit* as rival dailies, but Socialists and Communists often collaborated in the Popular Front, as when they formed the American Labor Party in New York in 1936 to allow voters to support the New Deal without voting for the corrupt Tammany Hall machine, or when A. Philip Randolph, a Socialist, agreed to head the Communist-created National Negro Congress.

The CPUSA reshaped the culture of the left, particularly because of its emphasis on interracial unity. The Party's militant defense of nine young men falsely accused of rape in Scottsboro, Alabama, attracted such talented black members or allies as novelist Richard Wright and blues-folk singer and guitarist Lead Belly. Billie Holiday's haunting "Strange Fruit" (1939), a challenge to lynching, was written by Communist schoolteacher Abel Meeropol. More broadly, intellectuals, professionals, novelists, and artists from Dashiell Hammett to Theodore Dreiser were drawn to an international movement that linked them to the French poet Louis Aragon, the Russian author Maxim Gorky, and the Spanish painter Pablo Picasso. Old firebrands Elizabeth Gurley Flynn and Ella Reeve Bloor served as labor elders in the movement, while writers Meridel Le Sueur, Mary Inman, and others proposed women's equality. The party ran symbolic candidates for office, but mainly denounced Republican reaction, tacitly supporting Roosevelt's New Deal. Communists organized an Abraham Lincoln Brigade to fight in the Spanish Civil War of 1936–1939, in which a democratically elected Popular Front government battled to stave off General Francisco Franco's rebels supported by large landowners, the Catholic Church, and the fascist powers. At the peak of the Popular Front, the CPUSA claimed to represent the best of the American democratic tradition dating back to

FIGURE 1.1. When the Communist Party of the United States of America (CPUSA) held its convention in Chicago, Illinois, in 1938, portraits of Lincoln, Lenin, and Stalin flanked the stage while the Party's leader Earl Browder spoke. *Chuckman's photos on Wordpress: Chicago Nostalgia and Memorabilia.*

Thomas Jefferson, going so far as to claim "Communism is Twentieth Century Americanism" – a claim epitomized by "Ballad for Americans" (1939), an anthem composed by Communist songwriter Earl Robinson and sung by Paul Robeson, a former All-American college football player, concert singer, star of stage and screen, and activist for racial equality.

Other, smaller bands of radicals contested the Communist claim to the Marxist heritage. They held that the optimal road to transformation lay in autonomous working-class militancy and internationalism forged "from below," not a left-liberal version of American nationalism that gave political support to the Soviet state. As a lively minority on the left, these radicals posited that the Soviet Union under Stalin had become a dictatorship *over* the proletariat, ruled from the top down. While these radicals included Socialists in some unique formations, such as that grouped around the labor radical A. J. Muste, they were mainly concentrated among followers of Stalin's archenemy, the Russian exile Leon Trotsky, who took up residence in Mexico in 1936. Such revolutionary socialists faulted American Communists for corrupting Marxist theory to conform to the interests of a bureaucratic state. They opposed capitalism and Stalinism alike and advocated a labor party, viewing the Democratic Party as a hodgepodge beholden to powerful Southern segregationists and Wall Street bankers who short-circuited the interests of urban workers, immigrants, and blacks.

Radicals of anti-Stalinist persuasion, however, were unable to unify – and all too often lacked interest in doing so, reveling in polemics over doctrine, analysis, and strategy. The Bolshevik model's valorization of correct leadership and programmatic homogeneity contributed to repeated schisms as ever-tinier grouplets named after their leading theorists – Trotskyists, Lovestoneites, Musteites, Oehlerites, Stammites, Fieldites, Marlenites – laid claim to being the proletariat's true vanguard, debating one another in mimeographed bulletins or in the pages of freewheeling periodicals such as the *Modern Monthly*, *Common Sense*, and *Partisan Review*. At times anti-Stalinist Marxist groups did find grounds for cooperation, but even if taken as a whole their ranks were vastly outnumbered by official Communism, and they tended to fracture. At the outset of the Second World War the largest of these groups, the Socialist Workers Party (SWP), split down the middle.

As for the CPUSA, its size and dynamism were mutually reinforcing. It grew from fewer than 10,000 in 1930 to more than 75,000 members by the end of the decade. Initially, admiration of the Soviet Union benefited Communists. Soviet industrial development under the Five-Year Plan was widely admired in contrast with the West's economic paralysis, proof even to many social democrats and liberals of planning's superiority. To Communists, the Soviet Union was the very repository of historical destiny, and to most liberals the Soviet Union seemed at least the antithesis of fascism. The Popular Front focus on fascism as the threat of the day made it difficult for anti-Stalinist leftists to get others to recognize or acknowledge the Soviet state's forced collectivization, show trials, and purges, or the ruthless suppression of anarchists and independent Marxists by Communists in Spain. Tourists returned from the Soviet Union to report on it glowingly, and Communists disparaged "Trotskyite wreckers," claiming anti-Stalinists were in league with fascists. The embattled anti-Stalinist Marxist left did preserve the idea, taken for granted in the day of Debs, that without democracy there can be no socialism, but their factionalism and small numbers made for an uphill fight. Popular Front claims to represent "the people" – delivered in a Kansan prairie twang by Earl Browder, the CPUSA's general secretary – held sway as Communists celebrated the Soviet constitution of 1936 as the most democratic in the world. The Party's reach extended into niches many Americans barely perceived, as when the Chinese Hand Laundry Alliance and the Chinese Anti-Imperialist Alliance of America were organized in the Chinatowns of New York and San Francisco.

Radicalisms of more idiosyncratic sorts existed too. Dorothy Day's anarchist *Catholic Worker* encouraged pacifist community organizing. Christian reformists inspired by Gandhian noncooperation joined with socialists to organize annual college student strikes against war. Seekers of black freedom, whether integrationist or black nationalist, objected to segregation and European domination of Africa. Irreligious freethinkers were sprinkled among all radical currents. Plenty of independents – writers, artists, shop-floor union militants, and participants in regional campaigns such as Upton Sinclair's End Poverty in California (EPIC) – collaborated with anyone, helping to spark a labor sensibility that altered the values of millions. As one *New Yorker* writer recalled about the 1930s, "The ancient American shibboleths of success – save your money, keep your shoes shined and get to work on time – were being replaced by newer precepts: never pass a picket line, in unity there is strength, and other variations of the statement that individual success can only be attained by collective struggle. The word *union* acquired a new significance and a new dignity."[4]

The left's great point of commonality in the 1930s was its hatred of fascism. As the Nazi counterrevolution suppressed German labor and the left, making Jews, gypsies, homosexuals, and the disabled into scapegoats for capitalist crisis, radicals warned of the growing menace. What they – Communists, in particular – did not anticipate was the Soviet signing of a nonaggression pact with Germany in 1939, carving up Poland and much else between them. The result was fateful. To liberals and radicals critical of the Communists, the Hitler–Stalin Pact confirmed Stalinism's malignity, permanently damaging Communist influence in the American Federation of Teachers and other left-liberal bastions. Most American Communists, however, swallowed and rationalized the new line. The Soviets had

---

[4] Richard O. Boyer, *The Dark Ship* (Boston: Little, Brown, 1947), pp. 104–105.

no choice, they said, given that the West opted for Munich appeasement over "collective security," Stalin's proffered antifascist alliance. Still, left-liberals were appalled. They had worked alongside Communists in the American League Against War and Fascism, the American League for Peace and Democracy, the League of American Writers, and other Popular Front groups, believing Communists to be staunch foes of fascism. They were stunned to see Communists switch to an abstentionist position – "The Yanks Are Not Coming" – to forestall American entry into the conflict. Although Communists launched new organizations such as the American Peace Mobilization to try to recapture solidarity with liberals, the pact forever damaged the moral prestige they had attained in Spanish Civil War days. The obvious origin of the reversal in Soviet foreign policy left many New Deal liberals, once Popular Front believers, permanently wary of Communists.

The CPUSA's new antiwar position spoke to a traditional American reluctance to get involved in "foreign entanglements," as George Washington famously put it, as well as memories of the First World War's senseless carnage. That, however, vied with the clear and present danger presented by fascism in 1939–1941. Many liberals declared that the United States should recognize its responsibility as a major world power to check Germany and Japan. Others, including both radical leftists and conservatives, thought the United States should resist being drawn into another European war of atrocity and destruction that, to judge by the outcome of the last, would not resolve the problems of dictatorship, militarism, and empire. The Communists were hardly alone in opposing intervention, since many Socialists, pacifists, and revolutionary anti-Stalinists did too. The radical left reprised its familiar position, expressed in Lenin's *Imperialism: The Highest Stage of Capitalism* (1916), which saw capital's search for investment outlets as the root of empire. In this understanding, internationalism demanded noninterventionism in opposition to wars fought by workers on behalf of empires that mainly benefit the wealthy and privileged.

It was difficult, however, to sustain left unity on anti-imperialist grounds given the special circumstances of the Second World War. Particularly after the fall of France, which possessed colonies but practiced republican democracy at home, many leftists grew worried by the prospect of a Nazi Britain. For American Communists the dilemma was solved when Germany invaded Russia on June 22, 1941, bringing the Soviets and British into alliance; the CPUSA performed an about-face to demand American intervention. Such flip-flopping was scorned and mocked by anti-Stalinist radicals, as in the song "Our Line's Been Changed Again" (to a chorus of "I knows it, Browder"):

> *We're now a party with finesse;*
> *Our line's been changed again.*
> *With bourgeois groups we'll coalesce;*
> *Our line's been changed again.*[5]

Many Communists, however, had never really left the Popular Front behind in their hearts and were happy to toss aside the awkward Nazi–Soviet pact for a renewed alliance with liberals against fascism at a moment when interventionist sentiment was on the rise. Trotskyists, anarchists, and Socialists who opposed fascism and capitalism alike found the coming of war cause for quandary and irresolution, and insofar as they aligned with pacifists to criticize the war they assumed a pariah – even outlaw – status. Eighteen leaders of the SWP were convicted under a 1940 law, the Smith Act, that made it a crime to advocate overthrowing the government. The Communist Party, by then fully for the war, welcomed the verdict and the banning of the SWP newspaper, *The Militant*, from U.S. postal privileges.

Once Japan struck the Pearl Harbor naval base on December 7, 1941, bringing the nation into the war, public opinion was resolved. Communists cast themselves in the American mainstream as a wartime Popular Front ensued. They hailed Soviet heroism as Stalingrad became the war's pivotal battle; called for opening a "second front" in western Europe, which eventually materialized on D-Day in 1944; and promoted Allied unity under the leadership of the Big Three: Roosevelt, Stalin, and Churchill. As thousands of American Communists served in the armed forces, they felt part of the "Century of the Common Man" declared by Vice President Henry Wallace as an alternative to conservative publisher Henry Luce's call for an "American Century." In this liberal–radical confluence, attention to ordinary citizens' economic welfare was judged the common premise of the New Deal and Soviet Communism. Pro-Soviet fervor obscured how Stalin's purges had decimated the Soviet military

---

[5] "Our Line's Been Changed Again" was written by Alton Levy (1916–65) and later recorded by Joe Glazer and Bill Friedland on *Ballads for Sectarians* (Labor Arts, 1952). Levy joined the Young People's Socialist League (YPSL) in 1931, was an organizer for the International Ladies Garment Workers Union, and in 1943 was court-martialed and sentenced to prison for four months for objecting to discrimination against black soldiers on his Nebraska Army base, a verdict protested by labor unions who urged FDR to intervene.

command and left the country unprepared for the Nazi onslaught, giving Germany an immense advantage at the outset of the war. The wartime Popular Front partly restored luster to the Communist Party's reputation, however, and generated a considerable antifascist political culture, including themes of a common American democratic identity lent musical expression in composer Aaron Copland's "Fanfare for the Common Man" (1942) and folksinger Woody Guthrie's "This Land is Your Land" (first recorded 1944).

As A. Philip Randolph's March on Washington Movement illustrated, national unity would not be simple, nor was dissent from the war limited to socialists and pacifists dumbfounded at the sight of Communists selling war bonds. As African Americans initiated a "Double V" campaign calling for the victory of democracy at home and abroad, the National Association for the Advancement of Colored People (NAACP) attracted hundreds of thousands of new recruits in northern cities ready to mount mass protest action. Similarly, many rank-and-file workers expected the national effort to be predicated on equality of sacrifice if they were to accept the proposal of Roosevelt and most union leaders – the chief exception being United Mine Workers' leader John L. Lewis, a stentorian Republican patriarch – that they surrender the strike tactic for the war's duration. Here was the paradoxical flipside of the demand for unity and order: the war, by exciting expectations for democracy and shared commitment, actually spurred agitation for change, which in turn sparked a conservative backlash in favor of shoring up class and racial hierarchies. Conflict, then, was unavoidable. Many white workers resisted the increased numbers of black Americans on the mass-production shop floor brought about by the Fair Employment Practices Committee, waging spiteful walkouts and engaging in racist rioting in Detroit in 1943. In Los Angeles, white sailors rampaged against young Chicanos and blacks wearing flamboyant zoot suits. Soon followed a riot of African Americans in Harlem, New York, outraged by the reported police shooting of a black serviceman at a dancehall. Toward war's end in 1944–1945, however, working-class outbursts took interracial form in walkouts defiant of the no-strike pledge, enraging the political right, which considered unionism in itself subversive of managerial authority. Thus the epic class contests of the postwar years were set in motion.

Whereas in the 1930s Communists sought to sharpen popular grievances, during the war they sought to dampen discontent. They saw dissenters from the war as defeatists, sinister "fifth columnists" doing the work of the fascists by undermining domestic morale. This rubric of unity could be used to challenge ethnic and religious bigotry in the name of a common Americanism, as in the Popular Front film written by Albert Maltz, *The House I Live In* (1945), with Earl Robinson's title song crooned by Frank Sinatra. But Communists often saw campaigns against racism as divisive, a distraction from all-out production. Thus they opposed Jim Crow and the poll tax but at the same time opposed the March on Washington Movement, vilified Randolph, and supported the mass internment of Japanese-Americans and annihilation of Hiroshima and Nagasaki. Unions controlled by Communists and their allies, often designated "left-led," became the firmest enforcers of no-strike contracts. This duality permitted Communists to denounce hate strikes by white workers as disruptive while slandering as "pro-Nazi" the interracial mineworkers' strike of 1943 and opposing the spontaneous wildcat strikes of 1944–1945. "American workers in this period faced many riddles," recalled Stan Weir, a wartime merchant seaman and anti-Stalinist socialist, "but none more bewildering than the one posed by the Stalinists. All that most unionists had ever heard about the Communists, whether in the labor or daily press, told them that the CP represented 'revolution,' but during the war they were such postured patriots that it would have been comic if they had not had so much official power over unionists' lives."[6]

In April 1945, the theoretical organ of the French Communist Party (PCF), *Cahiers du communisme*, carried an article under the byline of Jacques Duclos, with profound ramifications for the American Communist movement. The PCF had emerged from the liberation of France in 1944 with immense size and prestige since Communists had been the backbone of the French Resistance. The Duclos letter, however, clearly emanated from Moscow. At issue was American Communist leader Earl Browder's so-called Tehran line. In Iran in 1943, Stalin, Churchill, and Roosevelt had arrived at common protocols in their first face-to-face meeting, prompting Browder to predict postwar peace and the coexistence of socialism and capitalism. Taking his cue from Stalin's 1943 dissolution of the Communist International, Browder disbanded the CPUSA in 1944, reconvening it as the Communist Political Association (CPA). Downgrading the Communist Party into a mere organization had allowed Communists to work as Democrats for Roosevelt's reelection in 1944.

[6] Stan Weir, "American Labor on the Defensive: A 1940s Odyssey," *Radical America* 9 (July-August 1975), pp. 174–175.

For the postwar future, Browder forecast a full-employment expansion, a healthy welfare state, and a labor–capital accord. Advising Communists to accept "the perspective of a *capitalist* United States" and vowing to clasp hands with financier J. P. Morgan if necessary, Browder announced he had no objection to the phrase "free enterprise." His Tehran line was the maximal form of the Popular Front desire to meld with the American mainstream, wholly blunting radicalism's oppositional role. "Sure, I believed it!" recalled the Alabama Communist steelworker Hosea Hudson. "I thought the bosses going to lay down with the workers, the wolves and the lambs going to lay together. I was teaching that . . . in the union and everywhere." Browder's line reflected the American Communist tendency to heed Stalin's lead in all matters, but in this case Browder's political instincts let him down, as Stalin's direction took a sudden sharp turn in 1945.[7]

The rank-and-file Communist – the schoolteacher in Cleveland, the seaman in the National Maritime Union, the secretary in Seattle – did not read *Cahiers du communisme*. Even mid-level party functionaries were only likely to have known about the Duclos article when a translation of it appeared in *The Daily Worker* of May 24, 1945. Although he signaled willingness to engage in self-abasement, Browder was rapidly removed from leadership and then expelled from the organization he had led for fifteen years. The top echelon of American Communists exorcised "Browderism," now cast as "revisionism" and "opportunism." The CPA was abandoned, the CPUSA reconstituted, and the helm taken by William Z. Foster, a former syndicalist who led the steel strike of 1919. Given to rigid doctrinal orthodoxy, Foster announced that Browder had abandoned Marxism for "right-wing bourgeois liberalism." Foster promised a return to class struggle.[8]

While this abrupt leftward lurch would cost the party some 20,000 members within a few years – including *Daily Worker* editor Louis F. Budenz, who in late 1945 converted to Catholicism – initially the Communists sought to combine their new line with continued alliances with New Deal liberals such as Sen. Claude Pepper of Florida, who told a Madison Square Garden crowd celebrating the fall of Berlin in 1945 that the victory traced to "one of the greatest names in history, Joseph

---

[7] Earl Browder, *Teheran: Our Path in War and Peace* (New York: International Publishers, 1944), p. 69; Nell Irvin Painter, *The Narrative of Hosea Hudson: His Life as a Negro Communist in the South* (Cambridge: Harvard, 1979), p. 307.

[8] William Z. Foster, "The Struggle Against Revisionism," *Political Affairs*, September 1945, p. 782.

Stalin," and that "in Soviet–American unity freedom lives and tyranny is dead." As Roosevelt's death led to Harry Truman's presidency, the post-war CPUSA still sought to knit together Communists and left-liberals in Popular Front fashion, although this increasingly took the form of opposition to, rather than alliance with, the current administration. Prospects for a renewed left–liberal–labor alliance seemed propitious. In 1946, general strikes in midsized cities – from Rochester, New York, to Oakland, California – called not only for better wages but public policies, such as lower streetcar rates, that could help all working people. Talk abounded of a new "social unionism" by which workers could assume a political voice in the nation's affairs. Ardent liberals and socialists of many stripes began to talk of a new labor-based third party to carry the banner. When Truman used his authority to quash a 1946 railroad strike, many labor activists resolved to campaign against his reelection, and A. Philip Randolph and others called for socializing the great monopolies through an independent labor party. In this way, the Communists' leftward swing was in step with a fairly broad left–liberal–socialist constituency who wanted to go beyond vanquishing fascism to challenge capitalism.[9]

The Communist Party emerged from the war a powerhouse, with two dailies (*The Daily Worker* and a West Coast counterpart, *The People's World*), a theoretical journal (*Political Affairs*), and an array of institutions comprising a complete social world, particularly in New York City. Party members could live in the Allerton Coops in the Bronx, obtain life insurance from the International Workers Order, march in annual May Day parades to Union Square, buy inexpensive copies of the Marxist classics or novels by Howard Fast at the Workers Book Shop, read the latest issue of *The New Masses* featuring poetry of Langston Hughes and charcoal drawings by William Gropper, take classes in history, typing, or "dialectical materialism" at the Jefferson School of Social Science, and pack their children off to summer camps such as New Jersey's Wo-Chi-Ca, whose name, though seemingly Native American, was a contraction of "Workers Children's Camp." They could vote for Peter V. Cacchione of Brooklyn or Benjamin Davis, Jr., of Harlem, the two Communists on New York's city council. The party was structured from the top down, with a line set by the central committee on the ninth floor of its headquarters at 35 East 12th Street, but the almost nightly activities of branch units and mass organizations gave members a feeling of fostering popular-democratic values against a callous commercial society. The basis

---

[9] Sen. Claude Pepper, "Reply to the Russia-Haters," *New Masses*, 12 June 1945, p. 6.

of this left-wing culture was "the people." Folk balladeers such as Woody
Guthrie, Pete Seeger, Tom Glazer, and Josh White reclaimed work songs
and traditional tunes from the Appalachian mountains, Deep South, and
Dust Bowl while setting to music fresh topical material in songs like "Voting Union," "A Dollar Ain't a Dollar Anymore," and "Talking Atom."
As party members and friends clapped and sang along at hootenannies
and rallies, left-wing politics seemed to harmonize – literally – with the
common folk.

Despite cultivating such a close-knit enclave and claim to American
revolutionary traditions, the CPUSA was under increasing strain as postwar uncertainty gave way to Cold War antagonism. Communists enjoyed
some new support from liberals unnerved by the atom bomb or dedicated
to racial equality, but many viewed the Communists with deepening suspicion. This distrust largely traced to what had once been the Communists' great asset, their connectedness to the Soviet Union. Just as many
Americans were vexed by Soviet expansion into Poland, Finland, and the
Baltic states in 1939–1941, so from 1945 to 1948 Soviet foreign policy
raised ire and anxiety. In good part this was the Soviets' own making,
but not entirely, since Stalin's initial objectives were mainly regional. In
fending off the Nazi invasion, the Soviet Union had sustained 23 million
dead and massive damage (compared to less than half a million American dead). After the war, Stalin aimed to erect a buffer zone in Eastern
Europe to guard against future invasion from the West. That was cold
comfort to nations such as Poland and Romania, but the hardening of
Communist control in Eastern Europe hardly proved a design for world
domination. By contrast, the United States emerged from the war mostly
unscathed, with its global reach unambiguous. Its foreign policy was
shaped by sophisticated strategists who sought unimpeded access to a
free world market, a condition that meant the United States could never
again let rivals such as Germany or Japan get close to contesting U.S.
military preeminence. That stipulated an aggressive policy of keeping the
only conceivable rival, the Soviet Union, perpetually on the defensive,
however weak it might currently be. The United States took the lead in
shaping the economic and financial basis of the world order, convening
allies at Bretton Woods, New Hampshire, in 1944 to create organs for
a stable but flexible monetary exchange system (the International Monetary Fund) and economic aid for poorer countries (the World Bank) so
as to avoid another prolonged Great Depression. World affairs ranked at
the top of American elite opinion as never before, as embodied in Henry
Luce's concept of an "American Century."

At first it was not evident just how treacherous foreign affairs would be for a left-wing opposition like the CPUSA, since Popular Front activity was sustained for a time by world developments. This was particularly the case in black aspirations for decolonization. At war's end, the black press, from the *Chicago Defender* to the *Pittsburgh Courier,* warned against the United States conceding to the desire of Britain and France to reclaim their colonies in Asia and Africa or, worse, stepping into their shoes as a colonial power. Such sentiment surged in 1945 when a strike of Nigerian railroad workers was followed by a Pan-African Congress in Manchester, England. Over the next year or two, American solidarity with Africa was spearheaded by the Council on African Affairs (CAA), begun by Communists in the late 1930s and filled with new energy, particularly in support of the African National Congress in South Africa. Directed by Max Yergan, a Howard and Harvard graduate with a PhD from New York University, the CAA attracted non-Communist liberals and socialists such as educator Mary McLeod Bethune and sociologist E. Franklin Frazier. Even moderate NAACP leader Walter White joined the CAA in 1946, fearing that the severe escalation of Cold War rhetoric in Winston Churchill's "iron curtain" speech would divert the United States from support for worldwide self-determination, a goal symbolized by the founding of the United Nations in San Francisco in 1945. Also combining internationalism and radicalism was the Civil Rights Congress (CRC), convened in 1946 after a rash of brutal southern lynchings. Headed by William Patterson, the CRC in 1951 submitted *We Charge Genocide*, a dossier presenting American racial oppression as a human rights issue, to the United Nations. That followed earlier messages to the UN by the National Negro Congress in 1946 and the NAACP's 1947 *Appeal to the World,* drafted by W. E. B. Du Bois, dean of black intellectuals and by then increasingly pro-Soviet in large part due to his anticolonial views. Each of these three petitions of black Americans to the United Nations reflected a left-wing consciousness that saw campaigns against American apartheid and world colonialism as indissoluble.

Another postwar Popular Front linkage between international events and domestic reform appeared with the 1946 founding of the Congress of American Women (CAW), under the slogan, "Ten women anywhere can organize anything." CAW sought both to promote women's interests and to counteract rising anti-Soviet hostility, relying in part on maternalist arguments that women as nurturers of children were most inclined to peace. The Social Register supplied some of its leaders, including department-store heiress Elinor Gimbel and Cornelia Bryce Pinchot, wife

of Pennsylvania's former governor, but CAW also reflected the wartime
"Rosie the Riveter" influx of women into industry. Combating the postwar ideology that a woman's place is in the home, it addressed working
women's issues from wages to housework; challenged what one leader
called "ideas of male superiority," including within the Communist Party;
called for equal pay for comparable work; sought to end discrimination
against women without overturning protective legislation on behalf of
women workers; and promoted public housing with cafeterias and 24-
hour childcare to "free women from housekeeping," as a CAW report by
Susan B. Anthony II, great-niece of the famous suffragist, put it. Devoting
unusual attention to black women's inequality, CAW demanded extension of the fair labor standards and social-security coverage to agricultural
and paid domestic workers.[10]

Despite such efforts, the postwar Popular Front never achieved lift-
off. Popular Front coalitions between Communists and liberals proved
very hard to sustain, as when the Southern Conference for Human Welfare and Southern Negro Youth Congress, key interracial efforts opposed
to segregation, both collapsed in 1948. What most hampered prospects
for a Popular Front, especially after 1947, was the intensifying Cold
War. While friction between the United States and Soviet Union was
inevitable given the innate differences between the systems – especially
after 1945, given that Europe lay divided, East from West, in rival blocs –
American Communists and their sympathizers had some basis for their
characterization of the Cold War as a policy development that primarily
served military-industrial interests seeking to secure an open world market against any potential rivals. In an address to Congress on March 12,
1947, Truman announced his intention to defend "free peoples" against
"totalitarian regimes" by providing military aid to Greece, which faced
a Communist-led insurgency, and neighboring Turkey. That same year,
the National Security Act created the Central Intelligence Agency, the
National Security Council, and the Department of Defense. A Cold War
was on, despite cautionary establishment voices – the columnist Walter
Lippmann among them – who warned that by making the United States
policeman of the world, Truman's containment policy failed to discrimi-
nate between vital and peripheral national interests.

[10] CAW report: Kate Weigand, *Red Feminism: American Communism and the Making of
     Women's Liberation* (Baltimore: Johns Hopkins, 2001), p. 57; "Ideas of male superior-
     ity": Margaret Cowl in *The Daily Worker*, quoted in House Committee on Un-American
     Activities, *Report on the Congress of American Women*, 81st Cong., 2d sess., 1949,
     p. 86.

American Communists continued their encomiums for Stalin and the Soviet model, with the *New Masses* in 1945 holding that "the Soviet Union is the highest form of democracy," but liberals were increasingly caustic about such claims. Harvard historian Arthur M. Schlesinger, Jr., 28 years old, was among the first to articulate the new mood, penning an article for Luce's *Life* magazine in summer 1946 that rendered Communist Party membership pathological. Communist causes, he wrote, filled "the lives of lonely and frustrated people, providing them with social, intellectual, even sexual fulfillment they cannot obtain in existing society." To repudiate the Popular Front by demarcating social reform from Communism, Schlesinger and others – Eleanor Roosevelt, theologian Reinhold Niebuhr, and attorney Joseph Rauh among them – formed Americans for Democratic Action (ADA) in January 1947. The ADA was meant to answer both conservative redbaiting of liberalism and all Communist attempts to bend liberal initiatives to Soviet interests. Republicans had just gained a majority in both houses of Congress in November 1946, in an election registering discontent with strikes and inflation and new traction for Republican charges that Democrats were soft on Communism. In March 1947, Truman himself sought to neutralize that Republican ploy by instituting his own loyalty oath in federal employment, initiating scrutiny into the political associations and beliefs of millions of federal employees.[11]

This Cold War liberal attempt to uphold liberalism by emphatically distinguishing it from Communism failed to blunt redbaiting's new efficacy in rolling back social reform. The late 1940s would see the stymieing of social-democratic efforts to extend the New Deal by introducing national health insurance; the rejection of "socialized medicine" would leave health care insurance in the United States a matter handled by employers, with many workers not covered at all. In Congress, Republicans directed their new clout toward eviscerating the Wagner Act, the key New Deal measure assuring union rights. Ohio Senator Robert Taft and New Jersey Representative Fred A. Hartley, Jr., put forward a National Association of Manufacturers wish list as a labor relations bill. Taft-Hartley in effect banned sympathy strikes, mass picketing, and secondary boycotts (all important solidarity tactics in unions' strike battles); expanded the scope for antiunion propaganda in workplaces; and required union officers to sign an oath stating they had no Communist

---

[11] David Zaslavsky, "The One Party System," *New Masses*, 13 November 1945, p. 17; Arthur M. Schlesinger, Jr., "The U.S. Communist Party," *Life*, 29 July 1946, p. 85.

affiliation if their union wished to enjoy protection of the National Labor Relations Board. Organized labor unified to oppose both the restrictions on strike action and anti-Communist affidavits, but in June 1947 the Republican Congress passed Taft-Hartley over Truman's veto – a symbolic gesture by a president who knew the measure would pass but hoped to win back union voters. (In the years following, Truman nonetheless invoked Taft-Hartley repeatedly to intercede against strikes.)

Republican electoral gains also lent new power to the House Committee on Un-American Activities (HUAC), which held closed hearings in Los Angeles in May 1947 and then issued subpoenas to Hollywood figures to testify in Washington that fall. Created in 1938 as a rearguard action against labor and the New Deal, HUAC was made up of right-wing Republicans and segregationist Democrats who sought to ferret out "subversive" activity, often with oafish execution, as in this exchange between Alabama Rep. Joe Starnes and Federal Theatre Project director Hallie Flanagan:

MR. STARNES: You are quoting from this Marlowe. Is he a Communist?

MRS. FLANAGAN: I am very sorry. I was quoting from Christopher Marlowe.

MR. STARNES: Tell us who Marlowe is, so we can get the proper reference, because that is all that we want to do.

MRS. FLANAGAN: Put in the record that he was the greatest dramatist in the period of Shakespeare, immediately preceding Shakespeare.[12]

HUAC's reputation for philistinism lingered as it concentrated upon Communist influence on motion pictures in 1947. Many stars initially objected to the hearings as a baseless inquisition. Katherine Hepburn, Lauren Bacall, Humphrey Bogart, Judy Garland, Spencer Tracy, Rita Hayworth, and others participated in "Hollywood Fights Back," a radio broadcast of the Committee for the First Amendment that denounced HUAC for fanning hysteria and menacing artistic freedom. They mustered more star power than HUAC's friendly witnesses, such as Ginger Rogers's mother or B-list actor Ronald Reagan, although HUAC did draw Gary Cooper. Around the country, newspapers scoffed at HUAC's supposition that left-wingers had seized Hollywood and inserted radical messages in

---

[12] House Committee on Un-American Activities, *Investigation of Un-American Propaganda Activities in the United States: Hearings*, 75th Cong., 3rd sess., 1938, vol. 4, p. 2857; "Hunting Hollywood Reds," *Repository* [Canton, Ohio], 16 May 1947; cartoon from *Akron Beacon-Journal* reproduced in *New York Times*, 26 October 1947; "Where to Draw the Line," *Oregonian*, 29 October 1947.

movies. "Not one subversionist has been trapped beside his swimming pool," observed one newspaper. An editorial cartoon showed Mickey Mouse and Donald Duck cowering as a Congressman shouted, "What about you?" A newspaper in the Pacific Northwest editorialized that HUAC "ought to be discontinued," since it "has helped the Communists far more than it has hurt them." Even Motion Picture Association of America president Eric Johnston – an industry mouthpiece – criticized HUAC.[13]

The Cold War was a dramatically new context, however, and Hollywood a juicy target. A vibrant Popular Front had existed there when screenwriters and stars lent their names, money, and élan to the Hollywood Anti-Nazi League in the 1930s. During the war, Communist screenwriters had typically worked on ultrapatriotic scripts such as *Sergeant York* (1941), *Objective, Burma!* (1945), and *Pride of the Marines* (1945), but Hollywood war-propaganda films such as *Mission to Moscow* (1943), *North Star* (1943), and *Song of Russia* (1944) also prettified the Soviet ally to a degree of gross historical distortion. HUAC was egged on by the leader of the right wing in Hollywood's craft unions, Roy Brewer, who resented his Communist-led competitors. A turning point came when eleven left-wing screenwriters, directors, and producers, with John Howard Lawson in the lead, denounced HUAC, shouting over the pounding gavel of Chairman J. Parnell Thomas of New Jersey and declining to answer whether they had belonged to the Screen Writers Guild or the CPUSA. Young screenwriter Ring Lardner, Jr., who lost one brother to the Spanish Civil War and another to the Second World War, answered the question, "Are you now or have you ever been a member of the Communist Party?" by saying, "I could answer it, but if I did I would hate myself in the morning." Even while faulting HUAC for its rude treatment of witnesses deemed "unfriendly," the press criticized such defiance as unseemly. German-born playwright Bertolt Brecht fled the country after testifying. HUAC, using information supplied by the Federal Bureau of Investigation, produced evidence of the involvement of the remaining Hollywood Ten in Communist initiatives. As Congress cited the Ten with contempt in November 1947 for refusing to answer its questions, fifty movie moguls met at the Waldorf-Astoria hotel in New York City, center of film finance. Anxious not to incur a right-wing boycott that

[13] "Hunting Hollywood Reds," *Repository* [Canton, Ohio], 16 May 1947; cartoon from *Akron Beacon-Journal* reproduced in *New York Times*, 26 October 1947; "Where to Draw the Line," *Oregonian*, 29 October 1947.

would damage box-office receipts, they suspended the Hollywood Ten
without pay, declaring, "We will not knowingly employ a Communist."
The blacklist had begun.[14]

Government investigations and internal house-cleanings were soon to
follow in many other fields: radio, television, universities, schools, industry. The Attorney General's List of Subversive Organizations, announced
in 1947 under Truman's loyalty oath program, served as a checklist of
groups that would mark a federal employee who belonged to one as
a security risk subject to dismissal. Private employers also frequently
consulted the Attorney General's list, making it the basis for a national
blacklist. With Popular Front groups recast as "red fascist" façades –
even the star-studded Committee for the First Amendment was dubbed "a
recently created Communist front" by the California state government's
un-American committee – liberals beat a retreat. Humphrey Bogart wrote
a 1948 article terming himself and other Hollywood stars "American
dopes" for protesting HUAC, vowing they would no longer be "used as
dupes by Commie organizations."[15]

Such developments alarmed those liberals who thought racism, monopolies, and militarism more in need of federal redress than American Communists. For leadership they looked to New Deal liberalism's standard-
bearer, Henry A. Wallace, an outspoken Iowa native who made his
fortune in hybrid corn before joining FDR's cabinet as Secretary of
Agriculture in the 1930s and serving as Vice President from 1941 to
1945. Roosevelt replaced Wallace with Truman on the ticket in 1944
but appointed him to a cabinet-level position as Secretary of Commerce;
Truman kept him on in that capacity until 1946, when Wallace spoke
out against the administration's hardening line toward the Soviet Union,
prompting Truman to dismiss him. Wallace became senior editor at the
New Republic, where he mirrored Freda Kirchwey's policy at the other
liberal flagship periodical, the *Nation,* in criticizing the Cold War turn in
foreign policy. Backed by the Progressive Citizens of America (PCA), the
ADA's left-leaning rival, Wallace announced he would run for President
at the head of a new Progressive Party in 1948.

---

[14] House Committee on Un-American Activities, *Hearings Regarding the Communist Infil-
    tration of the Motion Picture Industry*, 80th Cong., 1st sess., 1947, p. 482; Fourth
    Report, Senate Fact-Finding Committee on Un-American Activities, *Communist Front
    Organizations,* Sacramento, 1948, p. 210; "Movies to Oust Ten Cited for Contempt of
    Congress," *New York Times,* 26 November 1947, p. 27.
[15] Humphrey Bogart, "I'm No Communist," *Photoplay*, March 1948.

Early endorsements from New York Mayor Fiorello LaGuardia and "brain truster" Rexford Tugwell lent respectability to Wallace's promise to reinvigorate New Deal reform. As the deep bass voice of Paul Robeson rang out at campaign events, Wallace generated enthusiasm on college campuses and spoke to packed stadiums. Initial projections of 8 to 15 million votes inspired hope for a significant protest ballot and the Progressive Party's emergence as a permanent alternative. In the Southwest, Mexican Americans formed Amigos de Wallace, and when Wallace traversed the South he addressed mixed audiences of blacks and whites, calling for Jim Crow to end. When his running mate, U.S. Senator Glen Taylor of Idaho, was arrested in May 1948 for entering at the "Negro" door of a Birmingham, Alabama, church, Wallace blasted "the hypocrisy of spending billions for arms in the name of defending freedom abroad, while freedom is trampled on here at home."[16]

A religious mystic with scientific inclinations, Wallace was far from a socialist, calling himself an advocate of "progressive capitalism" that would combine free enterprise, government administration of natural resources and public utilities, and "statesmanship" to moderate the business cycle. Tied to a cordial relationship with the Soviet Union, this vision was close to what Earl Browder imagined as a "people's capitalism." While the CPUSA had repudiated Browderism, it embraced Wallace in 1948 as an opponent of the Cold War. Wallace's Communist support divided the broad left. Many agreed with Wallace that American bellicosity was provoking Soviet intransigence but lamented his apologetics for Soviet actions. A. Philip Randolph instead backed Socialist candidate Norman Thomas, while most social democrats and liberals yielded to ADA entreaties to stick by Truman. By the end of 1948, anti-Communist liberals were wedded ever more tightly to Cold War politics, anti-Stalinist socialists were almost wholly marginalized, and Communists were increasingly seen, in the words of journalist Murray Kempton, as "seceding from American political reality." The American left was in profound crisis – so soon after its great postwar hopes.[17]

Truman had alienated liberals early in his administration, but as the 1948 campaign approached, he courted them assiduously. Adopting much of Wallace's domestic program, he dubbed his policy the Fair Deal, announced desegregation of the military to fend off Randolph's

[16] Curtis D. Macdougall, *Gideon's Army* (New York: Marzani and Munsell, 1965), p. 7.
[17] James Waterman Wise, *Meet Henry Wallace* (New York: Boni and Gaer, 1948), p. 391; Murray Kempton, *A Part of Our Time* (1955; New York: Dell, 1967), p. 76.

FIGURE 1.2. Former Vice President Henry Wallace, candidate of the Progressive Party in 1948, passes Birmingham, Alabama, refusing to speak there after local authorities denied him permission to address an integrated black and white audience. *ACME Telephoto / New York World-Telegram and the Sun Newspaper Photograph Collection (Library of Congress) / Corbis.*

threatened resistance, convened a Committee on Civil Rights that led to an ADA-promoted Democratic platform plank calling for an end to Jim Crow, and promised expanded Social Security benefits, national health insurance, more low-income public housing, and federal commitment to maintain full employment while opposing Taft-Hartley and sponsoring the Marshall Plan for economic reconstruction in Western Europe as the benign face of U.S. foreign policy. As Truman made his "give 'em hell" left turn – little of which, apart from the Marshall Plan, he acted on once elected – the press and Democrats kept up a drumbeat of accusations against the Progressives as Communist pawns. The charge was unfair in that Wallace and most of his supporters started from independent convictions, but the Progressive Party did bear a Communist imprint. A young Communist speechwriter drafted most of Wallace's addresses. Across summer and autumn of 1948, popular support for Wallace evaporated as he criticized U.S. policy but failed to forthrightly condemn a blatant Communist coup in Czechoslovakia and the Soviet blockade of West Berlin. Tugwell and other liberals peeled away as Wallace declined to distance himself from his Communist supporters.

The 1948 campaign pushed a good part of American liberals, social democrats, and labor into the Cold War camp, just as Marshall Plan aid worked to dissolve postwar alliances of liberals and socialists with Communists in Europe. In the unions, still the gravitational center of American radicalism, left-liberals and social democrats increasingly gained strength against Communists. After Walter Reuther won the UAW presidency in 1946, a victory in his long fight against the opposed faction that included Communists, Emil Mazey was named secretary-treasurer. The Reuther leadership objected to Taft-Hartley but then took advantage of it to poach 17,000 workers at Caterpillar's tractor works from the Communist-led Farm Equipment union – claiming that if the UAW did not, more conservative unions would. Many like Reuther and Mazey long sought an independent party of the left but felt unable in 1948 to support the Progressive Party given Wallace's softness toward the Soviet Union. A Truman defeat, they anticipated, might make another kind of third party possible, one premised on the labor unions, but as ordinary CIO voters cast ballots for Truman he won a surprise victory over his Republican opponent, Thomas Dewey. Wallace was trounced, his tally only slightly over one million votes, most of them in New York and California. Even Dixiecrat Strom Thurmond, who bolted the Democrats to protest the civil rights plank, obtained more votes and carried four states where Wallace carried none. The defeat of the Progressive Party, whose dissent had been premised primarily on foreign policy, thus had discouraged the emergence of the independent labor party whose prospect had been bandied about in the immediate postwar years. The close association of mainline unions and the Democratic Party was sealed for decades, with profound effects on American politics. Labor, the movement that early twentieth-century radicals considered the fulcrum for social change, was increasingly disposed to accept the standards of mainstream politics in a Cold War context – and not to rock the boat.

A decidedly marginal stance was assumed by another, much smaller part of the left in the years from 1945 to 1948, its nucleus being left-wing pacifists who struggled to keep antiwar sentiment alive during the Second World War, many of them jailed for refusing to cooperate with the Selective Service system. Almost alone among Americans, these radical pacifists denounced the firebombing of Dresden and nuclear destruction of Hiroshima and Nagasaki. The prospect of global nuclear war lent pacifism new appeal among youth, as did the moral power of the successful civil disobedience campaigns led by Mohandas Gandhi in South Africa and India. "We may attack measures and systems," he said. "We may not, we must not, attack men. Imperfect ourselves, we must be tender toward others and be slow to impute

motives."[18] In the United States, the Cold War brought radical pacifists
into dialogue and cooperation with radical democratic socialists swimming against the tide. Together, this strand of the left practiced tactics of
nonviolent civil disobedience, promoted racial equality, and warned of
the danger of concentrated power in bureaucratic forms both in Stalin's
Soviet Union and in Western "democracies." Here working-class struggle often ceded centrality on the grounds that the mass industrial unions
had settled into bureaucratic routine. In the distance between Progressive
Party hopefulness in progress and this left's more pessimistic prognosis lay
a gulf between the mainstream and margin that often frustrated aspiring
radicals.

Like the radical pacifists, the anti-Stalinist Marxist left had opposed
the aims of the main combatants in the Second World War, whether
Germany and its quest for European domination, Japan and its designs
in Asia, Britain and its intention to preserve its empire, or the United
States and its aspirations for worldwide economic sway. But it split apart
when the Socialist Workers Party – no longer guided by Trotsky, victim of a Stalinist agent in 1940 – divided in half over how to view the
Soviet Union's wartime conquests. SWP leader James P. Cannon upheld
Trotsky's classic view that the Soviet Union's nationalized property meant
it should be defended against the encircling capitalist system until its Stalinist bureaucracy could be overpowered by workers' revolution. By this
measure, even if the Soviet Union was a "degenerated workers' state," its
war advances were progressive in that they supplanted capitalist property relations. A contrary faction led by Max Shachtman left to form a
new Workers Party (WP), soon holding that Trotskyist theory needed
recalibration because the Soviet system had congealed into a new oppressive class order of "bureaucratic collectivism." This tendency held that
neither Moscow nor Washington warranted support, placing Soviet domination over Poland, Finland, and the Baltic states in a category every bit
as imperialist as American domination over Latin America. Neither the
SWP nor the WP possessed numbers or weight to enact its positions, but
many other radicals and intellectuals followed their debates with interest.
Both parties told their members during the war to serve if drafted, while
refusing to support the war politically or blunt working-class militancy
on the shopfloor.

Pacifists, like the Trotskyists, held little hope that the Second World
War would bring about the "people's century," that phrase of Henry

---

[18] Louis Fischer, *The Life of Mahatma Gandhi* (New York: Harper, 1950), p. 195.

THE NEW INTERNATIONAL
A MONTHLY ORGAN OF REVOLUTIONARY MARXISM

VOLUME VI   APRIL 1940   NUMBER 3

For the Third Camp!

FIGURE 1.3. The anti-Stalinist left imagined a workers' democracy or "third camp" independent of both the dictatorial fascist and Communist powers (shown together here on the left at the time of the Nazi-Soviet pact) and the capitalist powers (on the right). *Authors' collection.*

Wallace's so redolent of the Popular Front. To pacifists, the highly technological and industrial character of modern total war, with its deliberate destruction of economic targets and civilian lives, demanded moral refusal. Dwight Macdonald, a witty prose stylist, was the most prominent voice of this current. Initially a Trotskyist, he renounced both of its factions by 1941. After the Second World War he observed the failure of Trotsky's prognostication that this world war would, like the first, end in revolutionary upheaval. Trotsky had posited that popular uprisings would occur among colonized peoples, in the capitalist countries, and in resistance to Russia's Stalinist bureaucracy, but while anticolonial movements did accelerate throughout Asia and Africa in the decade after the war, in the capitalist world only a brief explosion of strike activity and an impulse toward social-democratic politics, not socialist revolution, emerged, while in the Soviet bloc the rule of dictatorship was total. The liberation of Nazi extermination camps, with their skeletal survivors, amply justified the crushing defeat of Germany, but for Macdonald it awakened deeper and more agonizing questions about how such depravity could possibly emerge from modern civilization. Other radicals' disenchantment with labor mirrored Macdonald's skepticism that the working class, the traditional agency of the left, could check powerful trends toward bureaucratization and inhumanity. "As labor unions have become strong, wealthy, fat, and respectable, they have behaved more and more like organized business," wrote the Chicago organizer Saul Alinsky, who in *Reveille for Radicals* (1946) proposed something of a recast Popular Front that would mobilize the citizenry in "people's organizations," not self-interested groups, and organized by neighborhood, not party.[19]

Alinsky's roseate progressive politics contrasted with Macdonald's *politics*, a magazine founded in 1944, although Alinsky shared its skepticism about unions. Macdonald said labor had "quite lost touch with the humane and democratic ideals it once believed in," ordinary workers having shown themselves to be "as brutally and rabidly nationalistic – *in their capacity as organized workers* – as their own ruling classes are." Macdonald sought a standpoint around which to rally radicals unsatisfied with leftist orthodoxies. He drew attention to the anarchosocialist pacifism of the most militant of the war's conscientious objectors in Civilian Public Service facilities – dubbed "American-style concentration camps" by young Yale alumnus David Dellinger – or in prison for refusing to register or serve at all. Subject to ostracism by relatives, friends, and neighbors for ostensible lack of courage, bravery, or patriotism, COs required stamina. Macdonald gave voice to their antiwar resistance in a mood so downbeat and jaded it bordered on resignation. The world's leading powers – defeated and victorious – had come to resemble each other, he wrote: the New Deal, Nazi Germany, Stalinist Russia, and European social democracy all favored highly centralized states wedded to militarism and empire, denying any real prospect for left-wing goals of justice, equality, solidarity, and democratic self-government. "War and the preparation of war has become the normal mode of experience of great nations," held Macdonald. "The power of the State has never been

[19] Saul Alinsky, *Reveille for Radicals* (1946; New York: Vintage, 1969), p. 27.

greater, the helplessness of the great mass of citizens never more extreme." Macdonald distinguished "radicals" prepared to face this new, grim state of affairs squarely from "progressives" who assumed that history, science, or production would bring freedom and democracy. Macdonald's radicals were "as yet few individuals – mostly anarchists, conscientious objectors, and renegade Marxists like myself – who reject the concept of Progress... and who therefore redress the balance by emphasizing the ethical aspect of politics." For Macdonald, bands of marginal outsiders who placed conscience above the state and held out for a new world offered the only way to pursue libertarian, socialist, and pacifist aspirations. This outlook drew courage from French existentialist philosopher Albert Camus's call for radicals to view themselves as "neither victims nor executioners," upholding a "relative Utopia" as "the only realistic choice," and repudiating the left's conviction of historical necessity.[20]

Radical pacifism was concerned with race just as much as war. Its most effective practical expression was the Fellowship of Reconciliation (FOR), a small, decades-old pacifist organization led by A. J. Muste, a tall, gaunt former Congregational pastor turned militant labor advocate in the 1920s who led a cluster of anti-Stalinist Marxists in the 1930s before reverting to faith-based pacifism on the eve of the war. In 1942, the FOR Chicago field organizer, seminarian, and war resister George Houser, with encouragement from Muste and FOR national race relations secretary James Farmer, launched the Congress of Racial Equality (CORE), which sought to embody, not merely advocate, racial equality. During the war CORE activists in Chicago and other cities carried out "sit-ins" at restaurants known to refuse service to blacks, calmly occupying tables in youthful interracial groups until they were served or police evicted them. This spirit was pacifist insofar as it sought to end the violence embedded in oppression but not at all "passivist," as Dellinger put it. That sentiment was echoed by Roy Finch of the FOR's secular counterpart, the War Resisters League: "We want more and not less militancy, more controversy, more negativism, more open conflict."[21]

[20] Dwight Macdonald, "The Responsibility of Peoples," *politics*, March 1945, p. 29; "Amnesty for Army Prisoners and C.O.'s," *Direct Action* 1:1 (Autumn 1945), pp. 10–14; Dwight Macdonald, "The Root is Man," *politics*, April 1946, pp. 101–2; Albert Camus, *Neither Victims Nor Executioner* (Berkeley: World Without War Council, 1968), p. 10.
[21] Dellinger quoted in John D'Emilio, *Lost Prophet: The Life and Times of Bayard Rustin* (Chicago, Ill.: University of Chicago, 2003), 84; Finch quoted in James Tracy, *Direct*

To Muste, resisters who went to prison were "the shock troops of pacifism." In 1940, even before U.S. entry into the Second World War, Dellinger and seven other Union Theological Seminary students declined the religious exemption to which they were entitled. In prison, they fought racial segregation, endured solitary confinement, and embarked on a hunger strike to protest harsh discipline and censorship of inmates' mail. In 1943, Jim Peck, another imprisoned resister, organized a 135-day strike at Danbury, Connecticut, against segregated dining in the penitentiary, successfully using press coverage to compel desegregation. Bayard Rustin, a young black pacifist radical raised in Pennsylvania as a Quaker who was briefly a Communist between 1938 and 1941 before becoming sorely disillusioned, and then joined FOR and CORE, went to prison in 1944; his challenges to racial discrimination prompted a white inmate to beat him severely with a wooden club. After the war, in 1947, Rustin, Peck, Houser, and other young CORE members – eight white, eight black – undertook a "Journey of Reconciliation" to test a Supreme Court ruling against racial discrimination in interstate travel. On commercial buses through Virginia, North Carolina, Tennessee, and Kentucky, the whites sat in the back, the blacks in front, upending segregationist norms. Rustin and Peck were arrested in Durham, North Carolina, then Rustin again in Chapel Hill, where Peck was hit on the head by white taxi drivers. Rustin served out his 22-day sentence on a North Carolina chain gang, writing about it for the *New Republic*.[22]

After the war, Dellinger was part of an obscure circle of radical pacifists who attempted to build their own community based on shared land ownership and farming in western New Jersey – an example of the small-scale libertarian socialist initiatives Macdonald hailed as the alternative to "progressive" mass movements. From his farm, Dellinger printed a short-lived magazine devoted to "an American revolution by non-violent methods" called *Direct Action*, launched in 1945. In addition to, as its name suggests, advocating challenges to authority at the very point where oppressive power is exercised, *Direct Action* envisioned a "decentralized" socialism, called for amnesty for war resisters, and declared that prisons, as keystones of a violent, oppressive society, must be dismantled. Dellinger's group was unafraid to adopt a blatantly marginal stance of absolute opposition, arguing that "the fear of unpopularity,

    Action: Radical Pacifism from the Union Eight to the Chicago Seven (Chicago, Ill.:
    University of Chicago, 1996), p. 3.
[22] Muste quoted in D'Emilio, *Lost Prophet*, 73.

imprisonment, or death should not hold us back any longer." *Direct Action*'s view – in marked contrast to the Popular Front – was that "henceforth no decent citizen owes one scrap of allegiance (if he ever did) to American law, American custom, or American institutions." This opting out of the mainstream, espousal of pacifism, repudiation of old left-wing forms of organization, and advocacy of rebellious fantasies would – while offering itself as a seedbed for a new American radicalism – prove to be self-marginalizing in the 1940s.[23]

Another strategic option for this wing of the left existed, namely the search for a potentially powerful mass constituency that would oppose both capitalism and Soviet-style Communism. Such an approach would have to reach out to rank-and-file workers even as the labor unions' organizational arteries hardened. Max Shachtman and his followers labeled the constituency of the powerless, dispossessed, exploited, and oppressed a "third camp" in world politics. Similar European efforts labeled it a "third force," allied with neither reformist social-democratic nor Stalinist Communist parties. Macdonald's *politics*, despite his own pessimism, paid close attention to such prospects, both at home and abroad, including a small but stirring French initiative, the Rassemblement Démocratique Révolutionnaire (RDR). The RDR, which sought independence from capitalism, social democracy, and Stalinism alike in the name of freedom, dignity, and revolution, was formed out of segments of the wartime Resistance to fascism. It included philosopher Jean-Paul Sartre, whose existentialism declared a humanist commitment to moral responsibility and freedom, and David Rousset, a Buchenwald death camp survivor who after the war published news of prison labor camps in the Soviet Union. These *engagé* intellectuals proposed a socialist Europe with a neutral course independent of both the United States and the Soviet Union. As the Cold War crystallized, however, their prospects withered. "One cannot create a movement" simply by willing it, admitted Sartre.[24]

The tension between margin and mainstream in the life of the radical left poses two opposite dangers. In the first case – sectarianism – marginal opposition creates hothouse environments where disputes over small distinctions of ideology feed narrow orthodoxies or stringent moral

[23] Dave Dellinger et al., "Call to a Conference: Preliminary Announcement," *Direct Action* 1, no. 1 (Autumn 1945), pp. 15–17; "Amnesty for Army Prisoners and C.O.s," *Direct Action,* 1, no. 1 pp. 10–14; [Dave Dellinger], "Declaration of War," *Direct Action,* 1, no. 1 pp. 6–8; Robert Duncan, "What to Do Now," *Direct Action,* 1, no. 1 pp. 35–39.

[24] RDR and Sartre quoted in Ronald Aronson, *Jean-Paul Sartre: Philosophy in the World* (London: Verso, 1980), pp. 162, 164.

codes limit popular appeal. In the second – opportunism – submersion
in the mainstream dilutes a radical program for the chimera of momen-
tary influence. If Browder's wartime Communists epitomized the second,
the small anti-Stalinist Marxist and pacifist left too often fell prone to
the first. Those searching for a radically democratic alternative found it
hard to extricate themselves from marginality despite their insight that
"progressive" politics was often a euphemism for a gauzy conception of
bureaucratic statism as progress. In 1948, both Norman Thomas's final
Socialist Party campaign and the first SWP presidential run by Teamster
veteran Farrell Dobbs fell utterly flat, even as symbolic gestures. By 1950,
the once-bold Walter Reuther was telling his comrade Emil Mazey that
continued membership in the Socialist Party was poor judgment, since
redbaiters would like nothing more than to tag the United Automobile
Workers as socialist. The postwar radical impulse had run its course.
Even Macdonald, who combined pacifism's moral conviction with bleak
realism, did not stay radical. In 1949, he closed down *politics*, stating
his profound confusion at the prospect of advocating unilateral nuclear
disarmament in the face of an atomic-armed Stalinism. By 1952, he cast
his lot with the Cold War, declaring "I Choose the West." Rousset and
Sartre in France also chose sides – opposite ones, with Sartre opting for
the French Communist Party and Rousset the ardently anti-Communist
Congress for Cultural Freedom. Although an idiosyncratic swathe of the
left had laid the moral and intellectual basis for what would later be
known as "sixties radicalism," it was far easier to imagine a socialism
independent of the two great camps than to sustain such a radicalism in
the most frigid phase of the Cold War.

2

All Over This Land, 1949–1959

> I'd hammer out danger
> I'd hammer out a warning
> I'd hammer out love between
> All of my brothers
> All over this land
>   – The Weavers,
>   "The Hammer Song"
>   (1949)

"The bourgeoisie is fearful," and "for good reason," wrote Claudia Jones in a 1949 article in *Political Affairs*, theoretical organ of the Communist Party, entitled "An End to the Neglect of the Problems of the Negro Woman!" Despite servile "mammy" stereotypes in film and radio, she wrote, "Negro women – as workers, as Negroes, and as women – are the most oppressed stratum of the whole population" and "the real active forces, the organizers and workers, in all the institutions and organizations of the Negro people." Jones's account of black female "degradation and super-exploitation" owed much to her mother's death at 37, as well as her own experiences in a dress factory and laundry. Her appreciation of black women's history of resistance sustained her own. On January 19, 1948, Jones was arrested by the Immigration and Naturalization Service in the apartment shared with her sisters at 504 West 143rd Street, Harlem. Born in the British West Indies as Claudia Cumberbatch, she had arrived from Trinidad with her parents as a child in 1923, becoming involved with radical causes after encountering the Scottsboro Boys campaign in Harlem as a teenager in 1935. Employed first as educational director of the Young Communist League and then as secretary of the CPUSA women's commission, Jones – a "negress," the Federal Bureau of Investigation reported – was now slated for deportation. "Subject was militant. Ridiculed being arrested," New York's FBI agents cabled J. Edgar Hoover. Released on bail, with hearings pending, Jones embarked on a national speaking tour, excoriating the American "political gestapo" for its fear of a "dangerous Red Negro woman."[1]

In that same year, 1948, another Trinidadian, C. L. R. James, was first contacted by immigration authorities anticipating his deportation. By year's end, James would publish "The Revolutionary Answer to the Negro Problem in the United States" in *The Fourth International*. James's article was a challenge to left-wing assumptions that class unity would solve racism. "The independent Negro struggle has a vitality and validity of its own," held James, who saw American blacks as having a "hatred of bourgeois society...greater than any other section of the population in the United States." Elegant in bearing, steeped in literature and philosophy, and speaking with an English accent, James arrived in the United States for a lecture tour in 1938 after six years in Britain. He tarried fourteen years, taking part in a series of American socialist groups, writing under pseudonyms (mainly "J. R. Johnson"), and marrying a model, Constance Webb, with whom he had a son. A chronicler of the black past in *The Black Jacobins* (1938) and *A History of Negro Revolt* (1938), James was at first a follower of Leon Trotsky, but his leftism deepened to the point of requiring a rupture with Trotskyist orthodoxy after he concluded the Soviet Union was no sort of "workers' state" but "the greatest example of barbarism that history has ever known." Envisioning "a world which makes no distinction at all between the sexes," James came to lead a tiny group, Correspondence, his chief collaborators being two women – Raya Dunayevskaya and Grace Lee, one Russian-born and Jewish, the other Chinese-American.[2]

Black Trinidadians, longtime residents of the United States, leaders of organized radical formations, and Marxists attuned to black resistance: James and Jones were virtually the same, yet they were wholly at odds. Jones cited Stalin admiringly and claimed that in the Soviet Union "full

---

[1] Claudia Jones, "An End to the Neglect of the Problems of the Negro Woman!" *Political Affairs* (June 1949): 51–67; Federal Bureau of Investigation, Claudia Jones File (100–72390); "Red Speaker Raps Stassen, Imperialism," *Oregonian*, 29 April 1948, p. 15.

[2] J. Meyer [pseud. of C. L. R. James], "The Revolutionary Answer to the Negro Problem in the United States," *Fourth International*, December 1948), pp. 242–251; C. L. R. James, *Mariners, Renegades and Castaways* (New York: C. L. R. James, 1953), p. 188.

enjoyment of equal rights by women is *guaranteed* by the very nature of the Socialist society, in which class divisions and human exploitation are abolished." To James, the Soviet Union was a dystopia: "By reading and instinct, I never for one single moment was anything but an enemy of the Communist Party and the Stalinist regime."[3]

America, too, they saw differently. Profoundly alienated by the depth of McCarthyism, Jones scolded the American mainstream in the antifascist idiom of the Popular Front. James, every bit as revolutionary, sought a renewal of the American democratic tradition. Prosecuted under the Smith Act and imprisoned alongside Elizabeth Gurley Flynn in Alderson, West Virginia, Jones perceived a "fascist drive on free speech and thought in our country" – not only in the persecution of Communists but in a mass culture that wished to relegate women to domesticity: "the fascist triple-K (*Kinder-Küche-Kirche*)." She faulted the federal government for "arresting the anti-fascists" instead of "prosecuting the Ku Klux Klan." To James, by contrast, American popular culture was strikingly democratic. He recounted his love for comic strips and gangster movies in his appreciation of an ever-changing society that Europeans too quickly dismissed as "Coca-Cola civilization." Locked on Ellis Island awaiting deportation, James penned a book on Herman Melville's *Moby Dick* that he sent to every member of Congress to illustrate his worthiness to remain in America. In James's reading, Captain Ahab's pursuit of the whale is a totalitarian obsession resisted by the lowly mariners, renegades, and castaways, whose resistance is sustained by a joyful shipboard work culture.[4]

Jones and James were islanders and castaways, forced into exile – James in 1953, Jones in 1955. Each sought haven in London, there to be separately immersed in the Caribbean diaspora and in solidarity with rising national liberation movements worldwide. Jones, a Communist to the end, published the *West-Indian Gazette*, initiated the London Carnival (later the Notting Hill Carnival), visited China, and died in 1964, buried just to the left of Karl Marx in London's Highgate Cemetery. In the very month Jones was deported, December 1955, Rosa Parks, a seamstress, was arrested in Montgomery, Alabama, for refusing to yield her bus seat to a white man. The boycott that followed was initiated by

---

[3] Claudia Jones, "International Women's Day and the Struggle for Peace," *Political Affairs*, March 1950, p. 41; James, *Mariners*, pp. 151, 187.

[4] *13 Communists Speak to the Court* (New York: New Century, 1953), p. 19; Jones, "International Women's Day," p. 34; "Missing Witness Delays Hearing for Woman Red," *The San Diego Union*, 14 September 1948, p. 2.

local women and relied on working-class riders' resolve. When the young Montgomery movement leader, Dr. Martin Luther King, Jr., and his wife Coretta Scott King visited London in 1957, they spoke to C. L. R. James, éminence grise of pan-Africanism, surely unaware of James's forecast, less than a decade before, of an independent black American movement for democratic rights, let alone Claudia Jones's anticipation that "the triply oppressed Negro women" would be in the forefront of black liberation.[5]

Three paradoxes characterize the history of American radicalism in the 1950s. First, opponents of the left were able to define radicalism as powerful and menacing precisely because it lacked power and could not effectively contest the terms of debate. After Henry Wallace's 1948 drubbing, the left's impotence rendered radicals vulnerable to the intense paranoia and repression now remembered as McCarthyism, which portrayed radicalism as an octopus affixing its tentacles to every facet of American life. A second paradox is that the red scare, however severe, did not finish off the Popular Front left. Only when American Communism *self*-destructed in 1956 did disillusionment disperse those Communist Party members who had clung on, steadfastly, against all odds. The third and final paradox is that the near-total collapse of the Communist Party did not end radical dissent – although initially it seemed it might – but rather cleared the way for a new radicalism, making the fear-filled fifties but a precursor to the radical sixties.

The red-scare repression had started as early as 1946, when HUAC subpoenaed leaders of the Joint Anti-Fascist Refugee Committee and charged them with contempt when they declined to turn over lists of their financial donors and European refugees, resulting in their conviction. The following year, HUAC targeted Hollywood. After Truman's victory in 1948, HUAC sought to use its power to discredit his administration, while trepidations about subversion surged. Red-scare momentum mounted in 1949, the year when Pete Seeger and Lee Hays of the Weavers penned "The Hammer Song" and first performed it at a benefit for Communist Party leaders on trial in New York City under the Smith Act, for conspiracy to advocate or teach the violent overthrow of the government. In that year, the Soviet Union's detonation of its first atomic bomb and the Civil War victory of the Chinese Communists exacerbated fears of a world dominated by Communism. Full-bore repression erupted the following year, when the junior Senator from Wisconsin, Sen. Joseph McCarthy, delivered a 1950 speech to a Republican women's club in

5 Jones, "International Women's Day," p. 44.

Wheeling, West Virginia, waving in the air a piece of paper he claimed listed 205 "card-carrying Communists" in Truman's State Department. His charge of treason among State Department employees had no basis, but the claim of internal subversion acquired urgency with the outbreak of the Korean War in June 1950. While McCarthyism focused with special ferocity upon the CPUSA, it stigmatized all forms of left-wing dissent and damaged basic civic freedoms of speech and association. Left-wing fears that a fascist state was imminent, however, proved to be an overreaction. As McCarthy overreached in attacking the Army for harboring Communists, the Senate censured him in 1954, and he retreated, disgraced, into an alcoholic fog. Between the deaths of the two Josephs – Stalin in 1953, McCarthy in 1957 – came a relative abatement of the most authoritarian phase of the Cold War, East and West.

A beleaguered core of Communist Party members persevered through what playwright Lillian Hellman called that "scoundrel time," their names kept on FBI lists as candidates for custodial detention in the event of a national security crisis. After 1956, Nikita Khrushchev confirmed that what critics had long said was true: Stalin's purges and forced labor camps killed more Communists than the bourgeoisie ever did. Then Khrushchev himself sent Soviet troops to halt a Communist reform process underway in Hungary, marking the limits of the post-Stalin thaw. Even as these developments sent American Communism into crisis, new shoots of dissent emerged in the United States as a mix of groups and causes, from the margin to the mainstream, began to dispel some of the repressive atmosphere. The critical breakthrough was the black-led movement against racial segregation in 1955–1956 in Montgomery, Alabama, organized with the aid and advice of small bands of veteran radicals, after which no one could any longer maintain, in Cold War fashion, that all mass movements must result in totalitarianism. Small groups of young people in the Socialist Party and other tiny groups kept radicalism alive, while a bohemian spirit against stifling normality was given voice by the Mattachine Society, a consciously gay organization. Pacifists resumed public campaigns to "Ban the Bomb." In all these ways, a prototypical "new left" was coming to life amidst the rubble of the old. Radicalism was recomposing, not dying, as revulsion against McCarthy-era repression, combined with the inspiration of the black-led freedom movement, began to produce fresh messages of hope and freedom, all over the land.

How political repression battered the Popular Front – and how recriminations weakened movement organizations' ability to withstand the barrage – may be seen in the fate of the Congress of American Women,

a group advocating peace and gender equality, which was placed on
Truman's Attorney General's subversive list in 1948 for its ties to the
Women's International Democratic Federation (WIDF) sponsored by
European Communist parties. In 1949, a HUAC report branded CAW
a "specialized arm of Soviet political warfare" and attacked its leaders,
including Nora Stanton Blatch Barney, granddaughter of the suffragist
Elizabeth Cady Stanton. Barney was not a member of the CPUSA but
had made the naïve statement upon returning from a peace conference
in Hungary that non-Communists "get better treatment there than the
Communists over here." The HUAC report stung sufficiently that Susan
B. Anthony II withdrew from CAW. As these blows fell, the Communist Party placed Claudia Jones on the CAW steering committee, where
she became, in CAW veteran Betty Millard's phrase, "the ideologue of
the movement," hammering CAW for insufficient recruitment of black
working women. Even Millard, a Communist, thought the castigation
unfair. Patience was advised for three reasons: work, children, and limited income presented obstacles to black women's participation; CAW
was unusual in its extent of black women leaders (including Dr. Charlotte Hawkins Brown, Ada B. Jackson, Vivian Carter Mason, and Thelma
Dale); and CAW had devoted itself to the fight to free Rosa Lee Ingram,
a Georgia widow accused of murdering a white neighbor she and her
sons attested had tried to rape her. As relations curdled within CAW,
women began dropping away. "We were done in first by McCarthyism,"
recalled Harriet Magill, another Communist CAW member, "and second
by the Party constantly giving us hell for not organizing working class
women." Although CAW cut its ties to WIDF, hoping to defuse charges
of foreign domination, the Justice Department demanded in 1950 that
CAW register as an agent of a foreign power. Facing a costly, probably futile, legal battle, CAW disbanded. Because of McCarthyism and
because CAW women criticized "feminism" – a term they reserved for the
National Woman's Party, whose Equal Rights Amendment they thought
would weaken labor protections – when the women's liberation movement surged in the 1960s many young feminist activists overlooked CAW,
thinking their nearest ancestors were the suffrage victors of 1920.[6]

---

[6] House Committee on Un-American Activities, *Report on the Congress of American
Women*, 81st Cong., 2nd sess., 1949, 1, p. 54; Amy Swerdlow, "The Congress of Amer-
ican Women: Left-Feminist Peace Politics in the Cold War," in *U.S. History as Women's
History: New Feminist Essays*, ed. Linda K. Kerber, Alice Kessler-Harris, and Kathryn
Kish Sklar (Chapel Hill: The University of North Carolina Press, 1995), pp. 308, 312;
Weigand, *Red Feminism*, p. 107.

Cold War repression in the United States was directed foremost at the Communist Party. It had many dimensions: legislation directed against "subversives"; imprisonment of leading Communists; Congressional and state-level investigations of Communist "infiltration," particularly by HUAC and the Senate Internal Security Subcommittee; loyalty oaths for government workers at federal and state levels; political deportations of immigrants; blacklists blocking employment; and the tapping of phones, bugging of rooms, and opening of mail by FBI agents who paid intimidating visits to the neighbors, relatives, and employers of suspected radicals. A constellation of figures and forces fanned the fear: J. Edgar Hoover, who got his start in the 1919 red scare; right-wing columnists and papers such as the *Chicago Tribune* and Hearst chain; the Catholic Church hierarchy; patriotic civic groups such as the Daughters of the American Revolution and Knights of Columbus; and veterans' organizations such as the American Legion and Veterans of Foreign Wars. Corporate interests spearheaded by the National Association of Manufacturers seized on the Cold War to check the power of labor and roll back the New Deal, and the Chamber of Commerce issued a flurry of early pamphlets including *Communist Infiltration in the United States* (1946), *Communists within the Government* (1947), and *Communists within the Labor Movement* (1947), which defined Communism as "a secret conspiratorial movement in the interests of a foreign power" and portrayed all "socialism" – including the New Deal's Department of Agriculture – as "essentially identical" to Communism.[7]

Such equation of liberalism with socialism and socialism with Communism was the hallmark of McCarthyism proper, a political style that peaked during the Korean War of 1950–53 and sought to discredit all left-of-center figures as agents in Stalin's Trojan Horse. Motivated by partisan electoral prospects, McCarthy and other Republican candidates and officials, hungry to make inroads against the Democratic coalition dominant in American politics since the 1930s, claimed that the Roosevelt and Truman administrations knowingly coddled Communists, and rebutted any and all critics in the press by comparing them to *The Daily Worker*.

In this pursuit, the words "Communist," "subversive," and "un-American" took on highly elastic meanings. "If someone insists that

---

[7] *Communists within the Labor Movement* (Washington: Chamber of Commerce of the United States, 1947), p. 4; *Communism: Where Do We Stand Today?* (Washington: Chamber of Commerce of the United States, 1952), p. 54.

there is discrimination against Negroes in this country, or that there is inequality of wealth, there is every reason to believe that person is a Communist," the Republican chairman of the Washington State Legislative Fact-Finding Committee on Un-American Activities, Representative Albert Canwell of Spokane, reportedly said. In the House of Representatives, Rep. John Rankin of Mississippi, a member of HUAC, alleged that the Committee for the First Amendment was not quite American: after all, he said (smearing American Jews) Danny Kaye's real name was David Daniel Kaminsky, Eddie Cantor's was Edward Iskowitz, and Edward Robinson's was Emmanuel Goldenberg. In 1948, Rankin referred to "this 'civil rights'" as a ploy of the "communistic movement" and insinuated Bolshevism was a Jewish plot by alluding to "a racial minority that has seized control, as members of the Politburo."[8]

The southern Dixiecrat bloc that Rankin epitomized joined with the Republican right as the conservative bulwark of McCarthyism. Even leading Democrats elsewhere often responded to the Communist issue by trying to outflank Republicans, not resist them. Nevada Senator Pat McCarran, a Democrat, proposed the Internal Security Act of 1950, which in planning for emergency detention for radicals required all subversive organizations to register with the Subversive Activities Control Board. That measure was approved by a Democratic Congress, and the same Senator sponsored the McCarran–Walter Act of 1952, used to accelerate deportation of radicals and block many international intellectuals from visiting the United States to speak – even as, at the very same time, the FBI and CIA were making it possible for many former Nazis to become citizens, given their utility as Cold War assets. Democratic Senator Hubert Humphrey, an ADA liberal and champion of racial equality from Minnesota, fashioned the Communist Control Act of 1954, which denied the Communist Party the rights of ordinary political parties.

The severity of such measures was justified by the alleged threat the Communist Party posed to American security, particularly in espionage. Many left-liberals and radicals long denied such activity, partly because accusers had obvious right-wing biases, and partly because so few American radicals – even CPUSA members – knew of such activity. In the period before 1945, however, Soviet intelligence did indeed cultivate

---

[8] Canwell quoted in Helen Lynd, "Truth at the University of Washington," *American Scholar* 18 (summer 1949): 350; House Committee on Un-American Activities, *Hearings Regarding Communist Espionage in the United States Government*, 80th Cong., 2nd sess. (Washington, 1948), pp. 534, 544.

several hundred American intelligence sources heavily drawn from Party circles. Sometimes the Soviet secret police, acting through its American operatives, engaged in nefarious activity. They killed a member of their own clandestine team, Juliet Stuart Poyntz, in 1937 when she vowed to defect after developing doubts about the Soviet Union; they monitored American anti-Stalinist socialist groups; and they helped orchestrate the murder of Leon Trotsky in Mexico in 1940. The espionage project expanded dramatically during the late 1930s and early 1940s among talented young college graduates in the Popular Front left and among CPUSA members who found work in Washington, D.C., as the federal bureaucracy expanded. Not all – perhaps not even most – of the Popular Front leftists who took part in such activity saw themselves as spies. Many did not understand, or only half-guessed, that the documents and gossip they passed along to the Party were being transmitted to Moscow. Invariably they acted out of antifascist idealism, accepting no monetary payment from their handlers. Insofar as they did know the information they were sharing would reach the Soviet Union, they acted because they believed it would be used to achieve the defeat of the fascist powers and thought they were building international trust by aiding a wartime ally. Since they were not aiding a hostile power, their intention may not have been treasonous, but distributing classified information in wartime was a criminal act potentially subject to capital punishment.

Not all Popular Front radicals complied when Soviet representatives asked them for classified information. The physicist J. Robert Oppenheimer, director of the Manhattan Project integral to the creation of the atomic bomb, was thoroughly involved in Popular Front causes on the West Coast and surrounded by Communists in his personal life, including his brother, wife, and landlord, but rebuffed invitations to pass on atomic secrets. Owen Lattimore, a State Department consultant blamed by McCarthy for espionage resulting in Communist advances in Asia, did not take part in anything of the kind. Many others, however, passed along privileged information: chief White House economist Lauchlin Currie; Duncan Lee and Maurice Halperin of the Office of Strategic Services; War Production Board economist Nathan Silvermaster; State Department officials Laurence Duggan and Noel Field; and others, including people within the Pentagon. Not all were "card-carrying members of the Communist Party," as McCarthy would say – once involved in passing information, they were directed to distance themselves from visible radical political activity, in any event – but Popular Front sensibilities motivated them all.

Most American citizens did not know anything about Soviet espionage in the United States until 1948, by which time the spy rings, ironically, were no more. In 1945, two key agents had defected from the Soviet cause: cipher clerk Igor Gouzenko at the Soviet embassy in Canada and American Communist underground leader Elizabeth Bentley, a Vassar graduate trained by her Ukrainian lover Jacob Golos (who died in 1943) to be the top American spy handler during the Second World War. The two defections did not become public news instantly, but the Soviets, understanding the magnitude of this security breach, immediately recalled their two top Russian spymasters from the United States and dissolved their American espionage networks in 1945. Only a few contacts soldiered on; Judith Coplon, a young Communist employed in the Department of Justice and recruited by the Soviets in 1944, was arrested in one of the last espionage cases of the period in 1949 as she tried to pass what she thought were FBI documents to a Russian official.

The public revelations of 1948 had unintended consequences from the standpoint of those Americans who had thought during the Depression and Second World War that information-sharing would foster more congenial relations between the United States and Soviet Union, advance the Communist cause, or help defeat an authoritarian right. Bentley and another former American Communist of the 1930s Party underground apparatus, Whittaker Chambers, by then a *Time* magazine editor, appeared before HUAC in 1948, naming many of their former clandestine contacts. There was reason to doubt their veracity. Bentley in particular would prove a handful for her FBI handlers, given her instability, alcoholism, and mendacity, while the pudgy, disheveled Chambers hardly inspired confidence. Considering the proceedings to be an election-year ploy, Truman famously dismissed them as a "red herring." Two especially shocking charges emerged, however. First, Bentley stated that Harry Dexter White, the highest-ranking economist in the Treasury under Roosevelt, a shaper of Bretton Woods, the World Bank, and the International Monetary Fund, had passed secrets to the Soviets during the war. Two weeks afterward, White testified, denying he was a Communist. Three days later, he died, age 55, from a heart attack. Chambers corroborated Bentley's statements about White, then dropped a second bombshell by claiming that Alger Hiss, a former high-level New Deal official, by then president of the Carnegie Endowment for International Peace, had been a Communist in the 1930s. When Chambers repeated his claim to the news media, Hiss sued him for libel, prompting Chambers to elaborate that Hiss, as a high-ranking State Department official in the 1930s, passed secrets to the Soviets. To prove it, Chambers brought reporters to his Maryland farm and pulled the allegedly purloined microfilm out of a hollowed-out pumpkin. Hiss was an elegant, polished, widely admired Harvard Law graduate, present at the wartime Dumbarton Oaks and Yalta conferences, a symbol of liberal internationalism. In 1950, since the statute of limitations had expired on espionage, a court convicted him of perjury for denying he had been a Communist. Decades later Hiss died still professing his innocence, but a preponderance of documentary evidence from Soviet cables and Soviet intelligence files indicates that he did pass information – and that Elizabeth Bentley was indeed a spy ringleader, as she averred.

The red hunters' charges, then, were accurate in that during the New Deal era – between 1935 and 1945 – perhaps as many as four or five hundred American Communists participated, with varying degrees of knowingness and motives, in espionage. At the same time, the red hunters were wildly inaccurate, to the point of demagogy, as to the operations' postwar scope. They made many unsubstantiated smears against specific individuals, and were irresponsible in maligning all dissent as "disloyal." By 1950, when McCarthy first made his dramatic entrance on the national stage claiming to have a list of "card-carrying Communists" in the State Department, there were in fact none. In 1951, when McCarthy alleged "a conspiracy so immense and an infamy so black as to dwarf any previous venture in the history of man," an internal Soviet KGB memo complained that its U.S. information was pathetic given a "lack of agents in the State Department, intelligence service, counterintelligence service, and all the other most important US governmental institutions."[9]

When Soviet espionage was later reestablished in the United States, its agents were secured by conventional means, such as money and black-mail, not idealistic radical politics, for those recruited that way had proven amateurish. The revelations, however, left the CPUSA profoundly vulnerable. Of the hundreds of thousands of Americans who passed through the Communist Party in the 1930s and 1940s, very few had any inkling whatsoever of any espionage, but the Party's leadership and apparatus, including Earl Browder himself, did help Soviet agents between 1935 and 1945 to identify government workers who could help obtain American state secrets. Once this use of political adherents and allies in espionage was disclosed, it put all Communists under suspicion. The basic template for

[9] Oshinsky, *Conspiracy*, p. 197; Allen Weinstein and Alexander Vassiliev, *The Haunted Wood* (New York: Random House, 1999), p. 300.

FIGURE 2.1. Senator Joseph McCarthy of Wisconsin took the national stage in 1950 with claims of Communist domination of the federal government, accelerating the suppression of many forms of American radical dissent. © *Bettmann/CORBIS.*

the ensuing red scare was expressed by HUAC member Richard M. Nixon in 1948: "Where you have a Communist you have an espionage agent."[10]

Having been attracted to the left out of concern for social justice, CPUSA members and their allies reacted to charges of espionage with disbelief. They considered the very suggestion a slander concocted by powerful interests with ulterior motives, out to stop Communists for their effectiveness as tribunes of the people. It took one to know one, they thought, when Whittaker Chambers stated, "Disloyalty is a matter of principle with every member of the Communist Party." To rank-and-file Communists, the real un-Americans jeopardizing the Bill of Rights were HUAC and the redbaiters. Popular Front culture, with its reverence for American tradition, made it easy for rank-and-file Communists to accept such statements as Eugene Dennis's that "the Communist Party of

---

[10]   William A. Reuben, *The Honorable Mr. Nixon* (1956; New York: Action Books, 1960), p. 78.

the United States is a purely American political party. It is the party of the American working class." That required considerable wishful thinking given the CPUSA's fidelity to Stalin's Soviet Union, but Party members who passed through the Depression and Second World War saw themselves not as traitors, subversives, or spies but as fighters for a fuller American democracy, economic justice, and racial equality.[11]

After the spy revelations of 1948, political hysteria began to mount. In 1949, as Mao took power in China and the Soviets tested their own atom bomb, fear rose that Moscow would achieve world domination. In Pittsburgh, Pennsylvania, a group calling itself Americans Battling Communism (ABC) attacked a Communist meeting in April. Late that summer, crowds in Peekskill, New York, violently attacked two successive Civil Rights Congress benefit concerts featuring Paul Robeson, who completed his passage from All-American to un-American when he said it was "unthinkable" that black Americans would serve in a war against the Soviet Union and that he loved the Soviet people more than those of "any other nation." The violence at Peekskill was blamed on the left, perversely; Communists, *Life* held, "hoped for just such a chance to become propaganda martyrs."[12]

The CPUSA's ability in this situation to appeal to Americans' democratic sense of fair play and tolerance was hampered by its own spotty civil liberties record, including support for suppression of Trotskyists under the Smith Act and Japanese-American internment during the Second World War. Developments in Eastern Europe were especially disastrous. During the industrial union drives in steel, coal, and meatpacking during the 1930s, immigrant workers in states such as Pennsylvania and Ohio had flocked to the American Slav Congress and subscribed to the Communist Party's foreign-language papers, giving it some influence in fraternal halls in immigrant neighborhoods. As the Soviet Union imposed single-party dictatorial regimes – or "people's democracies" – in East Germany, Romania, Hungary, Bulgaria, Albania, Czechoslovakia, and elsewhere in the postwar years, Lenin's expression about the "withering away of the state" under communism came to seem a cruel joke. In Yugoslavia, Partisan antifascist hero Joseph Tito parted ways from

---

[11] House Committee on Un-American Activities, *Hearings Regarding Communist Espionage in the United States Government*, 80th Cong., 2nd Sess., 1948, p. 565; Eugene Dennis, *I Challenge the Un-Americans* (New York: Communist Party, 1947), p. 4.

[12] "Robeson Assails Stettinius," *New York Times*, 21 April 1949; "Loves Soviet Best, Robeson Declares," *New York Times*, 20 June 1949; "Peekskill Battle Lines," *Life*, 29 September 1949, p. 52.

Stalin in 1948. In the rest of Eastern Europe, purge trials took place from 1948 to 1954 against "Titoist" or "Trotskyite" deviations, while in the Soviet Union, Stalin's last feverish purge, deeply anti-Semitic, claimed to suppress a fictitious "Doctor's Plot." Such news, combined with the influx of displaced and bitterly anti-Communist refugees, led to a sharp fall in support for the once-creditable CPUSA among Eastern European immigrants.

The difficulty of sustaining a Popular Front in the Cold War became clear in March 1949, when 800 artists, actors, musicians, and writers, including playwright Lillian Hellman, novelist Thomas Mann, and composers Aaron Copland and Leonard Bernstein, gathered for a Cultural and Scientific Conference for World Peace at the Waldorf-Astoria hotel in New York, welcoming Soviet visitors including composer Dmitri Shostakovich. Just as Wallace's 1948 campaign was the last major political challenge to the Cold War, the Waldorf-Astoria conference was its last serious cultural challenge. A number of formerly Marxist opponents of Stalinism, including Dwight Macdonald, Mary McCarthy, and Sidney Hook, worked out of a Waldorf bridal suite to frustrate the effort, asking provocative questions at the conference's major sessions that embarrassed the sponsors with constant reminders of the repression of intellectual freedom in Communist states. While such critics honored the left's long-held belief in a democratic culture, they also tended, over time, toward simple approval of U.S. Cold War policy. Their objections to Communism revealed little of the residual socialist principles they claimed to hold, thus signaling a trend toward deradicalization among formerly left-wing thinkers.

Some once-staunchly leftist anti-Stalinists, such as James Burnham, John Dos Passos, Max Eastman, and George Schuyler, went the full distance and became outright conservatives in the 1950s, but the more common trend was a shedding of Marxist ideas that resulted in a "non-Communist left" whose center of gravity was among liberals and social democrats who favored the United States in the Cold War. The Central Intelligence Agency (CIA), founded in 1947, was at first headed by worldly sophisticates who valued left-of-center contestation of Communist views. They spent millions of dollars to place operatives in organized labor, including ex-radicals Jay Lovestone and Irving Brown, and to subsidize periodicals from the *New Leader* to *Partisan Review*. Covert funding bolstered organizations such as the American Committee for Cultural Freedom (ACCF) and its international parent group the Congress for Cultural Freedom (CCF). A prominent CCF journal, *Encounter,* launched in London under the editorship of Irving Kristol, a former Trotskyist, and Stephen Spender, a former Communist, typified the turning of anti-Stalinist radicalism into liberal anticommunism. There were outright paid CIA agents in these fronts, such as Michael Josselson, Nicholas Nabokov, and Melvin Lasky, but few perceived the CIA's role, camouflaged by channeling the lavish outlays through wealthy individuals or philanthropic foundations. The Agency never insisted on total support for American policy since mildly dissident remarks merely sustained organizations' sense of themselves as "free" and "independent" in contrast to Soviet cultural straitjackets. Rather, the government support encouraged positive associations about American culture and storylines of "progress" on racial segregation, while seeking to blunt the appeal of neutralist dissent that would stand apart from both Cold War camps. Seeing themselves as the "responsible" left, ex-radicals played a role in discouraging any sharply adversarial criticism of American capitalism. "It is time for the American radical to grow up," said Arthur Koestler, author of *Darkness at Noon*, on a United States tour in 1948. Nonetheless, a crude rendition of their relationship to the CIA as one of puppets to puppeteer is mistaken. Many democratic minds felt spontaneous revulsion toward Stalin's Soviet Union, while the intervention of intelligence agencies was supplemented by other factors – McCarthyism, new heights of affluence, and the real ameliorations of the New Deal and Fair Deal – that engendered caution and moderation in political criticism.[13]

As if to confirm the analysis of its opponents on the left, the CPUSA under William Z. Foster became ever more authoritarian in the late 1940s, mimicking Soviet clichés and carrying out internal inquisitions to match the external ones besetting it. Party leaders browbeat screenwriter Albert Maltz in 1946 when he suggested in the *New Masses* that literature should not be judged by the politics of the author; launched a campaign against "white chauvinism" in 1948–1952 that put members on internal trial for trivial pretexts; perennially forecast crisis in obstinate denial of the reality of the postwar economic boom; adhered to the "scientific" Stalinist dogmatisms of Lysenko in biology and Zhdanov in art and literature; and polemicized crudely against philosophical pragmatism and psychoanalysis as "imperialist." This Stalinist salmagundi was rounded out by a number of defensible intellectual contributions, such as the research of Herbert Aptheker and Philip Foner into areas of black and labor history

---

[13] Koestler quotation in Frances Stonor Saunders, *Who Paid the Piper? The CIA and the Cultural Cold War* (London: Granta, 1999), p. 62.

neglected by conservative historians; a few party loyalists who wrote with
creative independence, such as the distinguished poet Thomas McGrath;
and talented black writers more or less close to Paul Robeson's Harlem
circle in the 1950s including Audre Lorde, Paule Marshall, Alice Chil-
dress, and Julian Mayfield. But the sum total, as the Red Scare set in, was
a massive loss of prestige for Communism among intellectuals and professionals. George Orwell's *1984* (1948) coined the word "doublethink,"
and *The God that Failed* (1949), a collection of essays by Richard Wright,
Louis Fischer, Ignazio Silone, and other ex-Communists, gave voice to dis-
illusion. Some Popular Front apostates – including Max Yergan of the
Council on African Affairs – went so far as to assist the FBI.

In the labor movement, Communists, once sparkplugs of insurgency
during the Depression, were badly on the defensive, as typified by steelworker Hosea Hudson's experience in Alabama. In the changing room
at his factory one day in 1948, a union local leader announced, "Mr.
Jackson said he don't want no more of these Communist newspapers
in this shop! Whoever fooling with them going lose they job!" Hudson's influence among his co-workers came to an abrupt end: "After that
announcement, all the guys fell away from me. I tried to get them to
meeting.... They wouldn't show up." Soon after, Hudson was expelled
from the Birmingham Industrial Union Council, fired from his job, and
removed from his office in United Steel Workers Local 2815, which he
had helped found. Communists in the labor movement tried to combat
the drive for their exclusion by claiming it was the work of employers and
war profiteers – the United Electrical films *Deadline for Action* (1946)
and *The Great Swindle* (1948), produced by Spanish Civil War veteran
Carl Marzani, are prime examples – but a formidable tide ran against
them.[14]

Some longtime union allies of the Communist Party, such as Joseph
Curran of the National Maritime Union, renounced the Communists
when they insisted that unions reject the Marshall Plan and endorse Henry
Wallace. Transit Workers Union (TWU) leader "Red Mike" Quill balked
when the Party demanded the TWU oppose a New York City transit fare
increase that would enable pay raises for his union's members. In 1949,
the Congress of Industrial Organizations (CIO) under Philip Murray,
who once worked in a bloc with the CPUSA, voted to expel its
Communist-led unions. Multiple factors explain the CIO's purge: worry

---

[14] Nell Irvin Painter, *The Narrative of Hosea Hudson: His Life as a Negro Communist in
the South* (Cambridge: Harvard, 1979), p. 312.

about noncompliance with Taft–Hartley; unease at the prospect of "guilt by association"; genuine opposition to Soviet totalitarianism; and salivation over weaker unions' membership. A small CP-led union representing 15,000 agents at Prudential Insurance, for example, was raided by the CIO's United Paperworkers in what Vicki Garvin, a black Communist and union official, called a "cannibalistic policy of raiding" accompanied by redbaiting that "paralleled in viciousness that waged by the Prudential." By 1950, United Electrical; the International Longshore and Warehouse Union (whose Australian-born leader Harry Bridges defeated many government attempts to deport him); the Mine, Mill, and Smelter Workers; the Marine Cooks and Stewards; and a number of smaller "left-led" unions were expunged. Once at the core of the CIO, these unions were often militant defenders of the interests of women, people of color, and the poor– such as Food, Tobacco, Agricultural (FTA) Local 22 in Winston-Salem, North Carolina, which represented R. J. Reynolds Tobacco workers. Justified as an inoculation against totalitarianism, the CIO purge diminished democratic rights for all union dissenters, contributed to the reversal of labor's postwar momentum, and was a factor leading to the labor unions' long-term bureaucratization and decline. Only a few expelled unions survived. The CIO gave up Operation Dixie, its plan to unionize workers in the South, and merged with the staid American Federation of Labor to form the AFL-CIO in 1955, by which time the great wave of postwar worker militancy was a faint memory.[15]

Throughout 1949, eleven top leaders of the Communist Party were tried under the Smith Act at Foley Square in New York City on charges of advocating the forcible overthrow of the United States government. No overt act or plan was specified. The CPUSA's renunciation of Browderism in 1945, argued the government, was a shelving of peaceful strategy, and its commitment to Marxism-Leninism meant fidelity to such passages as that of the *Communist Manifesto* of 1848 that stated Communists "openly declare that their ends can be attained only by the forcible overthrow of all existing social conditions." Most of the government's witnesses were FBI informants, including Herbert A. Philbrick, who infiltrated Massachusetts Communist groups from 1940 until the moment he testified in court. None provided evidence of violence, merely Machiavellian maneuvering. Louis Budenz, former *Daily Worker* editor,

---

[15] Vicki Garvin, untitled United Professional and Office Workers of America (UPOWA) speech, CIO national convention, 1949 (Vicki Garvin Papers, Schomburg Center for Research in Black Culture, New York, Box 3, Folder 6).

alleged that even if Communists denied advocating force and violence they used "Aesopian language" whose hidden meanings proved the contrary. Despite the defense's appeal to the First Amendment for protection of assembly and belief, the jury returned a guilty verdict. Additional trials resulted in convictions of another 108 Communist leaders around the country. When the judge sentenced Elizabeth Gurley Flynn in 1953, he offered her a chance to accept exile in the Soviet Union in place of imprisonment in the United States. "That's like asking a Christian if he wishes to go to heaven right away," she replied. Claudia Jones, sentenced in the same proceedings, said, "The only act which I proudly am guilty of is membership in the Communist Party which is not illegal." As the convictions showed, however, Communist Party membership had in effect become precisely that: illegal.[16]

Some liberals called this a "witch hunt." Arthur Miller's play *The Crucible* (1953) presented the Salem witch trials of 1692 as an allegory of contemporary intolerance. Unlike witches, Communists were not imaginary, but the analogy did speak to the intensification of alarmism. An admixture of superstition, ignorance, and malice took hold as proposals for water fluoridation were called Communist plots, books were removed from libraries, liberals were called "pinko," and McCarthy labeled the Democratic Party "the bedfellow of international Communism." Films such as *I Married a Communist* (1949) or *I Was a Communist for the FBI* (1951) portrayed all Communists as murderers, spies, deceivers, and saboteurs. In a bellwether 1950 Senate race, HUAC member Richard Nixon – made famous by his pursuit of Alger Hiss – prevailed in California over Democratic Congresswoman Helen Gahagan Douglas by printing up pink handbills on her House record.[17]

Some "old-fashioned American liberals," as C. L. R. James called them, believed that the crimes of Communists, if any, were best prosecuted by laws against specific acts, such as against espionage, rather than by criminalizing their beliefs and associations. Such liberals James appreciated in a new light: "Today it is not their limitations I am conscious of, but rather the enormous service they did to civilization, as decade after decade they struggled for the right of *habeas corpus*, freedom of assembly, freedom of speech, went to jail for them, died for them." Liberalism of that kind,

---

[16] Helen C. Camp, *Iron in Her Soul: Elizabeth Gurley Flynn and the American Left* (Pullman: Washington State University Press, 1995), xxvii; "Convicted Communists Snub Offer to Go to Russia instead of Prison," *New York Times*, 3 February 1953, p. 8.

[17] Oshinsky, *Conspiracy*, p. 111.

however, was increasingly rare as Cold War liberals sped Communism's criminalization. The Supreme Court under Chief Justice Fred Vinson, a Truman-appointed Kentucky Democrat, upheld the convictions in the Joint Anti-Fascist, Hollywood Ten, and Smith Act cases. Morris Ernst, general counsel of the American Civil Liberties Union, published articles such as "Why I No Longer Fear the FBI" (*Reader's Digest*, 1950). Sidney Hook, founder of the American Committee for Cultural Freedom, argued that a free society had to protect nonconformist *heretical* thought but owed no such protection to a subversive *conspiracy* such as the CPUSA. Given the Soviet menace, he called for denying any known Communist the right to teach in public schools, no matter their record of classroom comportment.[18]

Objectively, the American left had dwindled by the 1950s, a vulnerability that helps explain why the repression could mount to such a frenzied pitch. In Italy and France, where much larger Communist parties held considerable electoral clout, no thoroughgoing red scare like that in the United States took hold. The American panic was heightened by the arrival of the Korean War in 1950, when the Communist North invaded the South. As the United States intervened on the side of the South, presided over by a repressive strongman, and China stepped in to back the North, the war became a proxy for the two great world blocs and bogged down in stalemate. A frustrated American right indulged in the fantasy that "a conspiracy so immense" of Washington traitors, rather than a constellation of world forces and events, explained the impasse. Against this backdrop, an obscure New York couple, Julius and Ethel Rosenberg, were convicted for conspiring to pass secrets about atomic bomb design to a Soviet handler in 1945. Later revelations made clear Julius had indeed spied for the Soviet Union. Prosecutors had no solid evidence for their charge that Ethel was his accessory, however, and improprieties marred the trial as the judge engaged in *ex parte* communications with prosecutors. Blaming the Rosenbergs for the Korean War, he sentenced them to death. Campaigns for mercy and commutation proved futile. The execution of the Rosenbergs on June 19, 1953, left their two boys orphaned.

In the early 1950s, federal investigative committees roamed the country in search of subversion, landing in cities as small as Dayton, Ohio, and Lansing, Michigan, where hearings were front-page news. As a rule, they opened with ex-radical penitents, some of whom were inadvertently

[18] James, *Mariners*, pp. 199–200.

poetic in evoking their past, as when one said he joined the Communist Party "to make over the whole world into a more perfect sphere of beauty and goodness."[19] Unapologetic leftists faced a dilemma when subpoenaed. Proud affirmation of Party membership would obligate answering all other questions, thus betraying others and surrendering their freedom of association, or else face prison. Since the committees and courts refused to recognize the First Amendment as a legitimate basis for declining to answer, most witnesses – all but the "friendly" ex-Communist witnesses – invoked the Fifth Amendment and its protection against self-incrimination. Taking the Fifth drew attention to the bind that inquiries about CPUSA membership posed: since American courts in the Smith Act trials had ruled such affiliation a conspiracy to overthrow the government by force or violence, even admitting membership could make one vulnerable to indictment. To most Americans, however, taking the Fifth seemed a red flag, an admission of moral guilt. Innocent men, claimed Sidney Hook, need not hide behind silence. "Fifth Amendment Communists" were often fired by their employers for failing to cooperate with Congress's investigative committees and as a result often turned to work for themselves as owners of coin-operated laundromats, chicken farms, and other small businesses.

In time, a few left-wing witnesses began to test boundaries. "I cannot and will not cut my conscience to fit this year's fashions," Lillian Hellman declared in a letter to HUAC in 1952, offering to not take the Fifth and answer all questions about herself if the committee would agree not to ask her about others, since "to hurt innocent people whom I knew many years ago to save myself is, to me, inhuman and indecent and dishonorable." In 1955, Pete Seeger stood on the First Amendment's right to political speech and association, as did Arthur Miller the following year, eventually to be vindicated in court. In a separate twist, two ex-Communist witnesses, Harvey Matusow and David Brown, admitted in 1955 to having lied about hundreds of others, encouraged by the FBI. When HUAC called Paul Robeson to testify whether he was a member of the Communist Party in 1956, he answered, "Would you like to come to the ballot box when I vote and take out the ballot to see?" Robeson thundered, "You are the un-Americans and you ought to be ashamed of yourselves," to which HUAC's chairman replied, "I have endured all of this I can," declaring the proceedings adjourned. "I think," Robeson replied, "you should adjourn this forever, that is what I would say." Not until 1957

---

[19] House Committee on Un-American Activities, *Investigation of Unauthorized Use of United States Passports – Part 3*, 83rd Cong., 1st sess., 1954, p. 3269.

would the Supreme Court under Republican Chief Justice Earl Warren begin to unwind the McCarthy era by ruling that Congress must have a clear legislative purpose for subpoenaing witnesses before they may be found in contempt and by delimiting the Smith Act to actual incitement to violence.[20]

As many Americans in the 1940s and 1950s developed a protective disinclination to join *anything* out of fear of signing the wrong petition or taking the wrong periodical, even Stalinism's opponents on the left suffered loss of membership. The anarchosyndicalist Industrial Workers of the World (IWW) had won representation in more than a dozen industrial plants in Cleveland, Ohio, but that vanished after Taft-Hartley was implemented. Max Shachtman's Workers Party (renamed the Independent Socialist League in 1949) and the Socialist Workers Party (SWP) were both placed on the Attorney General's subversive list. Sidney Lens, a Chicago labor union leader and writer for *The Progressive*, had his passport revoked. The Congress of Racial Equality (CORE) divided over whether to permit Communists in its ranks, while the Fellowship of Reconciliation (FOR) led by A. J. Muste shrank during the Korean War.

Here and there holdouts preserved a tradition of creative Marxist inquiry. Even at the height of McCarthyism in 1953, the art historian Meyer Schapiro wrote that Marx's concepts of production and class if applied "in a true spirit of investigation" offered the best hope for a "unified theory" of culture and art. In *The Worldly Philosophers* (1953), economist Robert L. Heilbroner credited Marx for the "most penetrating examination the capitalist system has ever undergone." The anti-Stalinist left, though miniscule, was also better able than Communists to explain popular uprisings of the sort that took place 1953 in East Berlin. Such socialists saw official Communism as radical insofar as it favored abolition of capitalist property relations and interracial equality but retrogressive in failing to consistently uphold working-class democracy and political freedom. In 1950, Max Shachtman debated Earl Browder, the deposed CPUSA secretary general, with radical sociologist C. Wright Mills presiding before an audience of 1,200 in New York's Webster Hall on the topic, "Is Russia a Socialist Community?" Observing that purges had left the general secretaries of Communist parties in Hungary and Bulgaria "shot, or hanged, or garroted," Shachtman extended his arm toward Browder and intoned, "There – there but for an accident of geography

---

[20] Lillian Hellman, *Scoundrel Time* (Boston: Little Brown, 1976), p. 93; House Committee on Un-American Activities, *Investigation of the Unauthorized Use of United States Passports – Part 3*, 84th Cong., 2nd sess., 1956, pp. 4494, 4509.

stands a corpse!" At the same time, anti-Stalinist radicals were capable of surprising fair-mindedness, as when Irving Howe, reviewing *Invisible Man* for *The Nation* in 1952, faulted Ralph Ellison for portraying the Communists as "so stupid and vicious that one cannot understand how they could have attracted him" in earlier years. Periodicals such as the *American Socialist* (1954–1959), sponsored by a small group led by Bert Cochran, and Julius and Phyllis Jacobson's *New Politics* (born 1961), signaled the interest of anti-Stalinist leftists in breaking out of their marginality in the post-Stalin era and connecting up with a mainstream of political action. Perhaps the most successful of these in attracting intellectual talent was Irving Howe's *Dissent* (launched 1954), which had a radically democratic spirit and openness in its earliest years. "Socialism is the name of our desire," *Dissent* declared. That romantic panache would fade, however, as the moderate left around *Dissent* aged, and although the journal would always be somewhat heterogeneous its most binding force would be Howe's archly anticommunist reformism.[21]

In the most difficult circumstances imaginable, some new Popular Front initiatives emerged, too. With hits such as "Goodnight Irene" in 1950, the Weavers became a national sensation, selling millions of records and performing "The Hammer Song" and other left-wing folk music until excluded from radio and television in 1952. *UE News* cartoonist Fred Wright devised whimsical workaday everymen more in keeping with postwar American realities than thirties-era proletarian stereotypes. *The Salt of the Earth* (1954), an independent film based on a Mine-Mill strike in New Mexico steeled by Chicana women's resolve, was made by a blacklisted Hollywood director, screenwriter, and actors. Other blacklisted writers found work in France or Britain or wrote for American studios and television under pseudonyms; two of Dalton Trumbo's pseudonymous screenplays won Oscars while he was blacklisted. Progressives sympathetic to the "socialist world" but seeking independence from Party control took on the Cold War in the *National Guardian*, launched in 1948 (with novelist Norman Mailer in its first issue), and *Monthly Review*, begun in 1949 (with physicist Albert Einstein in its first issue).

[21] Meyer Schapiro, "Style," in *Anthropology Today*, ed. Alfred Louis Kroeber (Chicago, Ill.: University of Chicago Press, 1953), p. 311; Robert L. Heilbroner, *The Worldly Philosophers* (New York: Simon and Schuster, 1953), p. 160; "Is Russia a Socialist Community?" *The New International* 16 (May–June 1950): 167; Irving Howe, "A Negro in America," *Nation*, 10 May 1952, p. 454; Lewis Coser and Irving Howe, "Images of Socialism," *Dissent* 1 (April 1954), p. 122.

I. F. Stone, a radical journalist formerly close to the Popular Front, inaugurated his independent *Weekly* in 1953 (with articles such as "Time for a Deportation – To Wisconsin"). The commercial-free, listener-supported radio network Pacifica, its name taken because it was headed by pacifists, opposed McCarthyism on libertarian grounds and afforded some Communist spokespeople airtime; Pacifica began broadcasting in 1949 at KPFA in Berkeley, California, adding KPFK in Los Angeles in 1959 and WBAI in New York in 1960. The National Emergency Civil Liberties Committee defended Communists in the courts. Even some "Communist fronts" kept at it. The Civil Rights Congress hired attorney Bella Abzug to defend Willie McGee, a black delivery truck driver executed in Mississippi in 1951 for rape of a white woman although no convicted white rapist had ever faced the death sentence in that state. The National Negro Labor Council (1951–1956) and its executive secretary, Coleman Young, maintained small chapters in Harlem, Detroit, Cleveland, and Baltimore, advocating job equality for blacks and denouncing manufacturing's transfer to the low-wage South. The American Committee for the Protection of the Foreign Born resisted deportations. Black women in Sojourners for Truth and Justice picketed against South African apartheid in Washington.

The once-vibrant world of the Popular Front, however, had shriveled greatly. In New York City, the newspaper *PM* (1940–1948) was succeeded by the *Star* (1948–1949) and then *Compass* (1949–1952), finally giving way to silence. Many Popular Front institutions closed up shop as their finances, once used for organizing, became ensnared in court fees, attorney bills, and bail. The Chinese Workers' Mutual Aid Association, founded in 1937 to organize West Coast cannery workers, dwindled to twenty members and disbanded in 1954. In the Southwest, where Mexican and Mexican-American Communists had defended zoot suiters in the Sleepy Lagoon Defense Committee and workers' rights in the Mine-Mill union, Guatemala-born Luisa Moreno was deported, Josefina Fierro de Bright left for her native Mexico, and the Asociación Nacional México-Americana – created in 1949 to oppose the cheap labor terms of the Bracero program and advocate for the civil rights of "el pueblo olvidado" (the forgotten ones) – was extinguished after being listed as subversive in 1954. New York City denied permits for May Day parades after 1952, and the state's insurance regulators liquidated the International Workers' Order in 1954. Both the Progressive Party and American Labor Party were casualties as redistricting ended Popular Front independent politics with the 1950 defeat of Rep. Vito Marcantonio, longtime

Congressman for Manhattan's Puerto Rican barrio. In Hawaii, where the left-led Longshoremen's union had organized Japanese and Filipino sugar plantation workers, Party member Koji Ariyoshi, publisher of the *Honolulu Record* (1948–1953), was jailed with others under the Smith Act. A leader of the Portuguese left among Massachusetts textile workers, Eula Figuerido, was deported in 1954. The Civil Rights Congress dissolved in 1955. Numerous individual tragedies occurred, such as the suicide of Progressive Party supporter and Harvard University literature scholar F. O. Matthiessen in 1950, and the early death at age 42 in Seattle in 1956 of Filipino writer Carlos Bulosan, ill, poor, hounded by the FBI, and having turned to the bottle for solace.

By 1956, CPUSA membership had fallen to 17,000. Both McCarthyism and self-isolating practices were to blame. After the Smith Act verdicts, the Communist Party sent many leaders "underground," anticipating a fascist attempt to destroy it, but hiding out merely isolated the Party from what it called "mass work" and proved purposeless, given FBI ability to penetrate its apparatus. The Korean War's conclusion and McCarthy's disgrace seemed to mark a new period. After he was freed from prison in 1955, Eugene Dennis, the Party's general secretary, worked with *Daily Worker* editor John Gates, a veteran of the Spanish Civil War and Second World War, to urge a wide-ranging reexamination. Dennis and Gates were the party names of Francis Waldron and Solomon Regenstreif – an illustration not of Rankin's bigoted supposition that radicalism is un-American but of how the left in the twentieth century served as a road to Americanization for so many sons and daughters of immigrants, in this case German and Jewish. Together in January 1956, they proposed a path for the Communist Party back to the American "mainstream," meaning in their usage a turn toward organizations such as the NAACP and Democratic Party rather than tightly controlled Party satellite organizations.

Suddenly, a bombshell fell: Nikita Khrushchev addressed the Twentieth Congress of the Communist Party of the Soviet Union in closed session on February 25, 1956. Under Stalin, Khrushchev said, a "cult of the individual" had arisen placing "immense and limitless power in the hands of one person." Stalin's "grave abuse of power" included frame-ups against opponents in the 1936–1939 Moscow trials, purges of the Soviet officer corps before the Second World War, and a preference for "administrative violence, mass repressions and terror." As news of Khrushchev's address became public knowledge, it devastated many American Communists habituated to disregarding criticism of Stalin and the Soviet Union as falsehoods promoted by hostile forces. During the red scare, a dogged true-believer faith kept them going, but with Khrushchev's revelations, the entire scaffolding of belief in Stalin's infallibility and benevolence collapsed. As CPUSA members reacted with shame and anger at having been misled, Gates opened the pages of the *Daily Worker* to readers' perspectives, a startling process in which nothing was immune from reexamination. Reform was the spirit of the day, with most CPUSA members clearly seeking a new accountability to the American membership and a rootedness in American life.[22]

A massive exodus began of those who thought the Party was over. The stream of apostasy became a flood after November 1956, when Soviet tanks entered Hungary, subduing the reform Communist government of Imre Nagy and crushing the Hungarian workers' committees, which fought back in the streets. At the CPUSA's February 1957 convention, a broad-spectrum debate took place between three groupings: a reform bloc around Gates seeking a democratic and open party; a recalcitrant orthodox Soviet-devoted bloc around William Z. Foster; and a wavering band around Dennis looking for a middle ground. The Gates wing prevailed temporarily, passing a measure to relocate Party headquarters to Chicago to better implant it in the heart of the country, but the Foster group refused to acknowledge the convention's decisions once it was over. After Gates published a review in the *Daily Worker* critical of party historian Herbert Aptheker's defense of the Soviet invasion in the pamphlet *The Truth About Hungary*, the party simply shut down the paper. By 1958, Gates resigned from the party, declaring that the CPUSA was no longer an "effective force for democracy, peace and socialism in the United States." The withering away was so extensive that at the end of 1958 CPUSA membership was less than a quarter of what it had been at the start of 1956.[23]

Feelings of desolation and isolation were common among radicals in the fifties. "Radicalism in America is scattered, demoralized, and numerically insignificant," wrote Henry F. May in 1950. "Almost never have there been so few bold and vigorous critics of the social order." To Daniel Bell, socialism "as a social and political fact" was dead in America, "simply a notation in the archives of history." Nevertheless, the decade was not

[22] Nikita S. Khrushchev, *The Crimes of the Stalin Era* (New York: New Leader, n.d. [1956]), pp. 7, 12, 15. An example of refreshing iconoclasm during the post-1956 upheaval in the CPUSA is *Lifeitselfmanship* (1957), reproduced in Jessica Mitford, *A Fine Old Conflict* (New York: Vintage, 1978), pp. 323–333.

[23] Gates, quoted in Shannon, *Decline of American Communism*, p. 353.

simply a dark age in which the left was cowed but a transitional moment in which, despite the demolition of the Communist left, new radicalisms bubbled forth from beneath the surface and the language of organizing and protest mutated, with democratic values taking on new primacy as watchwords. The civil rights bus boycott that shook Montgomery, Alabama, in 1955–1956 signaled this new radicalism to the world, forged in a southern crucible.[24]

One trickle of the new southern radicalism came from military veterans from the Second World War and Korean War who had seen the outside world and resented serving in unequal rank, such as Aaron Henry and Medgar Evers in the Mississippi Delta and Robert F. Williams in North Carolina, who organized NAACP chapters. Another was found at Monteagle, Tennessee. There the Highlander Folk School was run for twenty years by the innovative educator Myles Horton, born into the poor white working class. Highlander trained labor organizers by a "percolator" system of pedagogy, with ideas coming "from the workers up," instead of a "drip" system transmitted downward. Horton saw "too much top down stuff" in the increasingly bureaucratic union movement, and when Highlander's formal affiliation to the CIO ended in 1953, the school announced it would prepare local activists throughout the South to promote desegregation in education and a wider democratization. Even before the Supreme Court's *Brown v. Board of Education* decision, Highlander's summer workshops in 1953 and 1954 brought together southern teachers, black and white, ready to promote school desegregation. Septima Clark, a teacher from Charleston, South Carolina, returned from Highlander "more vociferous" and "more democratic" to spearhead a neighbor-to-neighbor literacy program in the Sea Islands.[25]

Highlander's shift from labor to civil rights was underpinned by Horton's expectation that interracial teams of teachers and neighbors could, with sufficient inspiration and skill, push toward a speedy desegregation of local schools, but "massive resistance" by white racists throughout the South proved a tremendous obstacle. A few months after the Supreme Court's vague decree in 1955 that *Brown* be implemented with "all deliberate speed," a black 14-year-old from Chicago named Emmett

---

[24] Henry F. May, "The End of American Radicalism," *American Quarterly* 2 (winter 1950): 291; Daniel Bell, *Marxian Socialism in the United States* (Princeton, N.J.: Princeton University Press, 1967), p. 193 (originally published as part of Donald Drew Egbert and Stow Persons, eds., *Socialism and American Life*, 2 v. [1952]).

[25] John M. Glen, *Highlander: No Ordinary School 1932–1962* (Lexington: University Press of Kentucky, 1988), pp. 123–24, 127, 133.

Till, visiting relatives in Mississippi, was beaten and murdered by two white men, ostensibly for overfamiliarity in addressing a white woman. His mother, Mamie Till Bradley, insisted that the public see the bludgeoned face of her son at an open-casket funeral in Chicago attended by thousands. With the support of the Civil Rights Congress in one of its final campaigns, she powerfully denounced her son's murderers, who were acquitted by an all-white Mississippi jury.

When Rosa Parks – a long-time NAACP member who earlier that year had attended workshops at Highlander – was arrested in Montgomery, Alabama, in December 1955 for violating a bus-segregation ordinance, a left and labor heritage underlay the events that would soon capture the nation's attention. A seamstress by occupation, she had served as bookkeeper, record-keeper, and youth council advisor for her local NAACP chapter; her husband Raymond Parks was an NAACP activist who in the 1930s organized on behalf of the Scottsboro Boys; she had been recommended to Highlander by her employer Virginia Durr, a former Progressive Party candidate for the U.S. Senate and member of the Southern Conference for Human Welfare; and Parks was bailed out of jail by E. D. Nixon, long active in the NAACP and A. Philip Randolph's Brotherhood of Sleeping Car Porters. Jo Ann Gibson Robinson, a college English instructor who formed a Women's Political Council (WPC) in 1949, swung into action, printing and distributing thousands of flyers overnight that called for a one-day boycott of city buses. With success of that day's boycott and formation of a leadership body headed by the Rev. Martin Luther King, Jr., a mass meeting decided to extend the boycott indefinitely. If the Atlanta-born, 26-year-old King was new to Montgomery and protest leadership, he was not innocent of political ideas, having been exposed to the social gospel as a young seminarian in Boston some five years before. When Montgomery organizers initiated a mass boycott, they had prior examples not only in the "don't shop where you can't work" campaigns in northern black neighborhoods during the 1930s but in Gandhi's world-famous mass boycotts of British goods, well-known in African-American anticolonial consciousness.

A community-wide action of this sort required coordination to negotiate with city leaders, organize participants, communicate with supporters elsewhere, arrange substitute transportation for the black community, raise money, and defend the movement and its leaders from legal and physical attacks. At the same time, the boycott assumed a self-directed character, as if carrying out the Highlander critique of "too much top down stuff." Mass meetings in the overflowing sanctuaries of

Montgomery's black churches voted on whether to accept or reject compromises offered by the city's white officials. As the boycott held, with near-unanimous participation of the 50,000-strong black community, the goal shifted from making bus segregation more humane to abolishing it. Contrary to the longstanding assumption that integration was a characteristically "middle-class" goal, this was primarily a movement of working-class black Montgomerians, like Parks, who depended on buses to reach their workplaces. (King, a middle-class Baptist preacher, admitted he had never ridden one.) Those who owned cars donated them to create a shuttle system, following routes laid out by black mail carriers. Pick-ups were arranged by telephone, the fleet fueled and serviced by teams of volunteers. The few black attorneys in town worked to keep King and others out of jail and filed a lawsuit claiming the bus system violated the Constitution. When, after nearly thirteen months of boycott, the Supreme Court ruled in favor of the claimants, the campaign had obtained an outcome more successful than its initiators imagined possible. The Montgomery bus boycott had been, above all, a *mass direct action* that, for all its rootedness in religious moral tradition, pursued an ostensibly "liberal" goal of reform by means more radically democratic than many participants or observers then recognized.

Over the course of 1956, left-wing activists were prominent in building solidarity with the Montgomery boycott and helping to frame its strategy and tactics. In February, Ella Baker – a New York NAACP organizer and onetime follower of dissident Communist leader Jay Lovestone who knew Rosa Parks and E. D. Nixon from a regional NAACP meeting in Atlanta ten years earlier – pulled together a circle of social-democratic supporters of the Montgomery movement called In Friendship. One of her closest colleagues was Stanley Levison, an affluent attorney who once belonged to the Communist Party and was currently affiliated with the American Jewish Congress, then the more liberal of the two major American Jewish associations. The other was Bayard Rustin, the 1947 Journey of Reconciliation participant who had joined the War Resisters League staff after A. J. Muste compelled him to leave his Fellowship of Reconciliation position following a 1953 arrest for homosexual activity in a parked car in Pasadena, California. Also working with Baker were A. Philip Randolph, Socialist leader Norman Thomas, and Cleveland Robinson, a Jamaican-born leader of District 65, a left-wing New York retail workers' union. Rustin traveled to Montgomery in February to steep King in the tactics of Gandhian nonviolence, as did the FOR's

Glenn Smiley, another radical pacifist. A firebomb had been thrown into King's house and his associates had begun to stockpile weapons, which Rustin and Smiley urged King to remove from his house lest they be a pretext for further assaults and to safeguard the movement's moral claims about segregation's innate violence. From New York, In Friendship sponsored celebrity-studded fundraisers and encouraged King and other black ministers to form the Southern Christian Leadership Conference (SCLC) in 1957 as a vehicle for action across the South. Ella Baker became SCLC executive secretary, although traditional gender assumptions meant her years of organizing experience received less respect from King and the other ministers than Rustin's and Levison's enjoyed. She had, in any case, a well-developed skepticism of ministers and leader-focused campaigns, being more impressed by the "thousands of individuals, just black ordinary people" who had kept the boycott going, demonstrating "potential for wide-spread action throughout the South."[26]

Newly independent states shaking off colonial rule provided a further source of inspiration. In April 1955, an Afro-Asian Conference was convened in Bandung, Indonesia, whose independence leader Sukarno declared, "This is the first intercontinental conference of colored peoples in the history of mankind. . . . Let a new Asia and a new Africa be born." National liberation movements represented a new presence – a "third force" against the nuclear powers different from the one European leftists had earlier imagined. An American pacifist reported from the scene that "Bandung created a new bloc, a third camp" that would "help keep the peace the world so desperately desires": "Bandung may just be the hinge of history." When Kwame Nkrumah declared Ghana a state on March 6, 1957, in the first achievement of national independence in sub-Saharan Africa since the dawn of the colonial era, King was a guest of honor along with left-wing pan-Africanists including George Padmore and C. L. R. James.[27]

Such developments lent new life to black nationalism in major American cities, creating a multifaceted black radicalism even as the Montgomery developments seemed to herald integration as objective. Audley

[26] Baker, quoted in Barbara Ransby, *Ella Baker and the Black Freedom Movement: A Radical Democratic Vision* (Chapel Hill: University of North Carolina, 2003), p. 162.

[27] Sukarno, quoted in Anna Loewenhaupt Tsing, *Friction: The Ethnography of Global Connection* (Princeton, N.J.: Princeton University Press, 2005), pp. 81–85; Homer A. Jack, *Bandung: An On-the-Spot Description of the Asian-American Conference, Bandung, Indonesia* (Chicago, Ill.: Toward Freedom, 1955), pp. 34, 37.

FIGURE 2.2. Dr. Martin Luther King, flanked by Ralph Abernathy (l.) and Bayard Rustin (r.), leaves the Montgomery County Courthouse after they were arraigned with 87 others during the Montgomery Bus Boycott in 1956. © *GENE HERRICK/AP/Corbis.*

"Queen Mother" Moore, a Communist until she quit in 1950, was a well-known Harlem street speaker and early advocate of compensation (later called "reparations") to African Americans for centuries of slavery and oppression. The Nation of Islam, fostering black pride in a manner more geared to personal transformation than political action, grew in the mid-1950s. Other varieties of nationalism and pan-Africanism were taking new life in cities such as Detroit, Chicago, New York, and Philadelphia, especially after Nkrumah's triumph, which excited interest among people such as sociologist St. Clair Drake, a left-wing critic of the CPUSA who formed the Afro-World Fellowship as an alternative to the Council on African Affairs, which disbanded in 1955. Meanwhile, as black mobilization for civil rights picked up in the South, less prominent but nonetheless persistent campaigns in northern cities such as New York, Philadelphia, and Cincinnati sought throughout the 1950s to desegregate housing, jobs, theaters, and schools – and challenged suburban housing discrimination in Levittown, Pennsylvania.

A circuit of radicals, anticolonialists, pacifists, and socialists whose radicalism traced back a decade or two was playing a significant role in what seemed to be a new black freedom movement that sprang out of nowhere. Largely decoupled from the old modes of party and labor, they were still interlinked and highly attentive to popular potentialities. Drake had collaborated with Muste and Rustin in 1948 to promote black draft resistance. Rustin traveled to meet Nkrumah in 1952 and, after being fired by FOR, was hired by the War Resisters League, because David Dellinger insisted Rustin's sexuality was immaterial. In 1955, Rustin and Dorothy Day, the Catholic radical, arranged for 27 pacifists to remain outdoors when the federal government's first mass civil defense drill required citizens to clear the streets and "take cover." Soon Rustin was, along with Baker and Levison, advising King in Montgomery. Such were the associations that in the mid-1950s, with a red-scare fog still thick across the land, provided a mature strategic vision, allowing margin to approach mainstream through the medium of Montgomery.

In 1955 and 1956, Socialist Party leader Norman Thomas, assuming the role of venerable sage, addressed meetings in Terre Haute, Indiana, and Chicago, Illinois, on the centenary of the great Socialist tribune Eugene V. Debs's birth. At 70, Thomas was himself historic, and the Socialist Party long past its heyday, having dwindled only to less than a thousand members, although its tradition of honest municipal socialism was upheld in the three-term 1948–1960 mayoralty of Frank Zeidler in Milwaukee, Wisconsin. As he spoke, Norman Thomas was flanked by labor leaders and left-liberal mainstays such as Roger Baldwin, founder in 1920 of the American Civil Liberties Union. Under Thomas, the Socialist Party had a fairly strong record of opposing red-scare repression under the Smith and McCarran Acts, but his anti-Communism and

support for the Korean War lent him a sufficient respectability that the
Debs commemoration could be reported on politely by the *New York
Times*.

If a left revival was to emerge from the mid-1950s, youth would be
its creators, and despite talk of a "silent generation" pockets of discon-
tented young people did exist. Within the Socialist Party, young pacifist
dissenters, while immensely fond of Thomas, took the Debsian legacy seriously. They stood apart from – and against – the complacent Cold War
liberal celebration of "free enterprise." At the same time, they reflected
the Socialist Party's generalized hostility to totalitarianism, leading them
to define their socialism not only in democratic but libertarian terms. In
1952, the Young People's Socialist League even proposed that the Socialist Party go on record opposing laws against consensual homosexual
activity – on the grounds that it was a legitimate form of self-expression
and socialists opposed discrimination. This was an unusual position at
a time when many observers saw nothing but uniformity in "mass society" and described American life as a "lonely crowd." Instead, a self-
described "bohemian" spirit prevailed among young Socialists whose
political opposition accentuated their nonconformist identity. It stood to
reason that challenges to confining normality would emerge from those
attuned to political repression, since federal loyalty programs blended
"subversion" with "perversion" and deemed homosexuality a security
risk, forcing hundreds out of government jobs.

In 1948 in Los Angeles, Harry Hay, a member of the Communist Party,
contemplated a "Bachelors for Wallace" effort to advocate a Progressive
Party plank decriminalizing consensual sexuality. In 1950 Hay and a few
friends who had either left or were expelled from the Communist Party
as it imposed a strict injunction against homosexuality came together
in Edendale, an artistic enclave in Los Angeles, to form the first significant U.S. organization for gay freedom. The Mattachine Foundation was
named after a medieval French order of masked performers. In contrast to
the young Socialists' libertarian motif, Hay adapted the Communist theory of "oppressed nationalities," arguing that "androgynes" (gays and
lesbians) were an oppressed minority deserving of self-determination.
After police entrapped Mattachine cofounder Dale Jennings for violation
of antisodomy statutes, he boldly argued in court that his behavior was
not lewd and that he had been unfairly ensnared merely because he was
a homosexual. Impressed by his courtroom victory, hundreds sought to
join the group. A new layer of Mattachine leaders, worried about scrutiny
in the McCarthy era and opposed to the group's secretive, top-down,

CPUSA-modeled structure, would by 1953 steer the Mattachine Society toward a less political, more respectable model, although the magazine *One* (1953–1968), an outgrowth of the more radical origins of the Mattachine, would serve as an alternative pole of thought, emphasizing gay self-activity.

Coteries like those that created the Mattachine were bohemian pockets of a type tracing back to the early twentieth century, when a transgressive cultural left flourished in neighborhoods such as Greenwich Village in Manhattan, overlapping with political radicalism. Free-thinking rebels, romantic poets, and spirit-seekers at odds with paternal authority and sexual standards, they were refugees from the puritanism of "civilization." At the same time, the organized assertion at midcentury of legitimacy for those of "deviant" sexual orientation marked a significant departure from traditional radicalism. Whatever the association of the radical left with bohemianism since the early nineteenth century, labor and socialist movements had generally upheld a rather conservative cultural politics of respectability and conventional heterosexual masculinity. The charcoal drawings meant to represent the working class in the newspapers of the American left almost invariably used a brawny man in overalls to signify the proletariat. Some radicals scornful of homosexuality tried to give their prejudice a theoretical gloss, claiming that it was a dissolute behavior signaling capitalism's "decadence" – a view promulgated by Stalin as a means of reinforcing Soviet population objectives. The contradiction between movements advocating equality and an end to oppression in some spheres of social life, while replicating the dominant society's sexual repressions, now led some on the left to endorse libidinal freedom. With a cerebral justification in the émigré Marxist philosopher Herbert Marcuse's *Eros and Civilization* (1955), the new sentiment for sexual liberation given expression in Mattachine and among young Socialists would set in motion trends that would flourish in the sexual revolution of the 1960s associated with the counterculture and gay liberation movement.

As fledgling self-awareness arose among "homophiles" (a word meaning "lovers of the same" devised by Hay as an alternative to the largely pejorative "homosexual"), linked to like-minded efforts in Europe, especially Scandinavia, lesbians too began to explore their identity. By 1955, Del Martin and Phyllis Lyon, journalists and partners in San Francisco, established the Daughters of Bilitis (DOB), which, despite having little political motivation beyond associating freely, did attract a few adherents with left-wing pasts, such as the young black New York playwright

Lorraine Hansberry. A writer for Paul Robeson's Harlem newspaper *Freedom*, Hansberry in the DOB newsletter linked the cause of lesbian acceptance with women's equality in one of the few full-throttle feminist statements to appear in the era: "I think it is about time that equipped women began to take on some of the ethical questions which a male-dominated culture has produced and dissect and analyze them quite to pieces in a serious fashion.... Homosexual persecution and condemnation has at its roots not only social ignorance, but a philosophically active anti-feminist dogma."[28]

Despite its antecedents, such artistic–sexual bohemianism seemed fresh and daring in the 1950s and linked up with the idiosyncratic radicalisms coming out of the 1940s. In California, poet Kenneth Rexroth passed through Communist circles in the late 1930s, joined FOR in 1940, and adopted an anarchist opposition to the contemporary warfare state. Rexroth's political opposition was wedded to his search for transcendence of suffering, accomplished through union in sexual love and the artist's apprehension of wholeness in nature and cosmos. "Against the ruin of the world there is only one defense – the creative act," Rexroth declared, in a pithy summation of left-bohemian estrangement, while also insisting there was no escape from bearing personal responsibility for evil in the world. Eschewing formal refinement in poetry as an impediment to frank expression, his postwar Libertarian Circle of poets saw their purposes as "revolutionary" in building a new "social consciousness" apart from the bureaucratic and violent state. Rexroth helped kick off the San Francisco practice of frequent public poetry readings, understood as art conjoined to communal experience. Into this group came Robert Duncan, who had written on homosexuality for Dwight Macdonald's *politics* in 1944, briefly collaborated with the anarchists of Dellinger's *Direct Action*, and adopted the explicit term "bohemian" as a term unifying art and life amid free sociability. The creative individual experimenting with new forms was to Duncan the answer to the "permanent war state" and a conventional politics of coercive nationalism and "bankrupt authority."[29]

This left-bohemian milieu extended the suspicion of technological and economic rationality expressed by Macdonald in the 1940s. Its adherents saw alternatives to the straitjacket of "reason" in the passions and libido

---

[28] "Readers Respond," *Ladder* 1:11 (August 1957), p. 30.
[29] Richard Cándida Smith, *Utopia and Dissent: Art, Poetry, and Politics in California* (Berkeley: University of California, 1995), pp. 41–49, 408, 169, 414.

as well as in transcendent experience beyond empirical and everyday life. To Norman Mailer, writing in *Dissent* in 1957, a "ménage a trois" of bohemians, juvenile delinquents, and blacks bonded by marijuana and jazz had produced "the hipster," giving rise to a phenomenon he dubbed the "White Negro." For Rexroth and Duncan, however, who took "responsibility" as seriously as liberation, a release of desire and expression from restraints had to be matched by the cultivation of new disciplines that would check the danger of passion turning to violence. It was art, in collective settings, that helped confront such dilemmas – art, they maintained, that ought not be contained in exclusive museums shaped by the connoisseurship of the rich.

Through the 1950s, experimentation of this sort provided a meeting ground for cultural and political radicals in university towns such as Madison, Wisconsin, and urban neighborhoods where low rent could sustain communities of those uninterested in material acquisition. In 1957 in Greenwich Village, 23-year-old aspiring poet Hettie Cohen met a young black man with similar ambitions, LeRoi Jones of Newark, recently discharged from the Army for insubordinate behavior, which included subscribing to the *Daily Worker*. The two fell in love and lived together before marrying – an act so transgressive, because the love was interracial, that it broke Cohen's ties to her parents. Their household became a constant day-and-night traffic of friends, black and white, involved in a range of the arts – poetry, painting, theater, jazz – and scraping by on low-paid jobs as clerks or copyeditors. The "Beat" writers became familiars, notably including Allen Ginsberg, son of a socialist father and Communist mother, whose 1955 poem *Howl*, first performed aloud in the San Francisco scene generated by Rexroth, assailed a sexually repressed and militarized society for driving young people to madness. (The Beats and politics did not always mix: writers Jack Kerouac and William Burroughs were apolitical or hostile to the left.)

Quite a different instance of a marginal coterie fostering new experiments in dissent was that of radical pacifists. Garry Davis, who served on bombing flights over Germany in the Second World War, renounced his American citizenship in France in 1948 and declared himself a citizen of the world, opposing the nation-state as fomenter of war. In 1953, he founded the World Government of World Citizens, issuing passports recognized by some states, mostly in Africa. In 1957, on the August anniversary of the bombing of Hiroshima, eleven pacifists, including A. J. Muste and Jim Peck, were arrested for entering a restricted area of a military base in Nevada where test explosions of nuclear weapons were conducted. One was Albert Bigelow, a Harvard graduate and Navy captain in the Second World War who had concluded that modern war is immoral. In 1958, Bigelow set out from Hawaii in a thirty-foot sailboat named the *Golden Rule* (soon followed by another, the *Phoenix*), intending to trespass near the Marshall Islands to disrupt H-bomb testing. The boats were impounded by the Coast Guard. The group organizing these protests, the Committee for Non-Violent Action (CNVA), intended to win favorable publicity, and those arrested in Nevada and the Pacific did reach radio audiences with criticism of above-ground nuclear testing. However, a debate soon broke out between young pacifist militants who favored obstruction of nuclear base building – their first target was at Cheyenne, Wyoming – and those, like Bigelow, who favored symbolic actions on issues selected to resonate with a broader public. When Muste sided with the obstructionists, Bigelow quit the CNVA. Women played a significant role in radical pacifism, although gender played out complexly as male pacifists tried to combat images of pacifists as "sissies" by cultivating strongly masculine demeanors. Among those arrested with Muste for trespass at Strategic Air Command in Omaha, Nebraska, in protest of new intercontinental ballistic missiles (ICBMs) was Marjorie Swann, mother of four. Chastised as a "bad mother" by the judge who sentenced her to prison, Swann cast her action as maternal and responsible: "The children must know that we care enough."[30]

This newly energized direct-action pacifism often acted in concert with older pacifist organizations, including the American Friends Service Committee (AFSC) and the Women's International League for Peace and Freedom (WILPF), both dating back to the First World War, as well as new liberal counterparts, such as the Committee for a Sane Nuclear Policy (known simply as SANE), established in 1957. While some found the moral atmosphere in radical pacifist circles "too noble and pure and holy," as wrote the literary critic Maxwell Geismar, the new energy around issues of nuclear testing and disarmament would contribute strongly to left-revival sensibilities in the late 1950s.[31]

---

[30] James Tracy, *Direct Action: Radical Pacifism from the Union Eight to the Chicago Seven* (Chicago, Ill.: University of Chicago, 1996), p. 111; Marian Mollin, *Radical Pacifism in America: Egalitarianism and Protest* (Philadelphia, Pa.: University of Pennsylvania Press, 2006), pp. 91–92.

[31] Maxwell Geismar, *Reluctant Radical: A Memoir* (Nyack, New York: Circumstantial Productions, 2002), p. 140.

Liberation magazine, issued by Muste and Dellinger in 1956, was the most vibrant periodical of this milieu, taking up where Dwight Macdonald's *politics* had left off. *Liberation*'s opening editorial held that the two Cold War blocs represented "two sides of the same threat to the survival of civilization," their arms race being "a logical outgrowth of their basic economic and social orders." It recognized Marx's contributions but held that he underestimated the state's "emergence as an instrument of war and oppression." It rejected "faith in technology, industrialization and centralization" and sought "direct participation of all workers or citizens in determining the conditions of life and work," while calling for "action *now* – refusal to run away or to conform, concrete resistance in the communities in which we live to all the ways in which human beings are regimented and corrupted, dehumanized and deprived of their freedom."[32]

Beginning in 1956, a new left seemed possible, with prospects suddenly afoot from Bandung to Montgomery to Budapest. As the CPUSA entered its great crisis in early 1956, Muste hosted a public forum at Carnegie Hall on prospects for American radicalism featuring W. E. B. Du Bois and Norman Thomas as speakers and attended by two thousand people. The 71-year-old Muste – active since the mass strike of Lawrence, Massachusetts, millworkers in 1919, still imbued with pacifist and socialist aspirations, and not beholden to any particular group – was more than any other figure at that moment capable of exerting a moral authority respected across the left. The following year, he and Rustin were asked to be observers of the CPUSA's convention and he organized the American Forum on Socialist Education, a clearinghouse for the broad left, with Sidney Lens. Muste told his associates that "patterns that seemed fixed" in the world were dissolving: "Everywhere there is ferment and motion."[33]

Momentarily, "regroupment" became a precept on the left. But who should regroup – and in what manner? The shoals proved tricky to navigate as some radicals moved right, others left, not always in ways clear to themselves. David McReynolds of the Socialist Party's younger pacifist cohort suggested merger with Max Shachtman's Independent Socialist League, hoping it would strengthen the SP's left wing. Simultaneously,

---

[32] "Tract for the Times," *Liberation*, March 1956, pp. 3–6.
[33] Muste, quoted in John D'Emilio, *Lost Prophet: The Life and Times of Bayard Rustin* (Chicago, Ill.: University of Chicago, 2003), p. 251.

Norman Thomas engineered Socialist Party reunification with the Social
Democratic Federation (SDF), an aging Cold War group oriented toward
the Democratic Party. Unbeknownst to McReynolds, the merger with
SDF acted as a magnet on Shachtman, who for all his Bolshevik-sounding
verbiage and brilliant followers – Michael Harrington among them –
had grown weary of life on the margins. To Shachtman, the lesson of
1956 was not regroupment with disenchanted Communists, but resolute
anticommunism. Contrary to Muste and McReynolds's hopes, therefore,
a big-tent revitalized left-socialist "regroupment" did not materialize.
The Trotskyists took the 1956 watershed to validate their perspective,
although very few disillusioned Communists joined the long-stigmatized
SWP. The Young People's Socialist League (YPSL), the Socialist Party
youth group, joined Bayard Rustin in a Washington, D.C., march for
school desegregation by 10,000 high school and college students in fall
1958 addressed by Coretta Scott King, who hailed them for "proving the
so-called 'silent generation' is not so silent." Shachtman, however, soon
joined with the SP's old guard to support a Democratic Party "realignment" that his protégé Harrington articulated in a 1959 YPSL pamphlet,
The New Left: The Relevance of Democratic Socialism in America.[34]

Given the stirrings on the bohemian, youthful, and pacifist fringes and
the Montgomery victory, speculation percolated about "a new radicalism." Even a noted Democratic liberal remarked that in the aftermath of
McCarthyism the country stood at "a critical juncture" such as had typically marked the shift between "our periods of national apathy and inef-
fectiveness and the surges of political creativeness that followed them."
The New Left of the 1960s did not emerge from nowhere. Already in the
late 1950s, a loose assemblage of radical pacifists, anti-Stalinist socialists,
refugees from the Communist Party, and community organizers around
the country, encouraged by rising civil rights sentiment, perceived a coming breakthrough in left-wing activism they thought would be "new." It
would be new, first, in the sense of simply resuming protest for change –
and new because it would bear traits different from what had come
before. Racial equality and peace would be paramount issues, with a
defense of democracy and vigilance against totalitarian trends in the left
and modern society. Action from the bottom up rather than top down
would take precedence. Sympathy with the countries emerging from colonialism to independence constituted a basis of hope. And the new spirit
of radical protest, already heralded by independent radicals of the 1940s

[34] King, quoted in D'Emilio, *Lost Prophet*, p. 273.

and 1950s, had strong leanings toward nonviolence and decentralization. All this was accompanied by a cultural radicalism, moving from small-circle bohemianism to mass appeal. So it is that at the dawn of a new decade talk abounded on the left of new potentialities in which avant-garde ideas might become reality in short order, of new situations where margin might meet mainstream.[35]

[35] Chester Bowles, *The Coming Political Breakthrough* (New York: Ballantine, 1959), p. 7.

3

A New Left, 1960–1964

When the Movement came to town in 1961, Gloria Richardson was a 39-year-old single mother of two working in her family's pharmacy. Her 16-year-old daughter Donna was first to become involved when two young organizers for the Student Nonviolent Coordinating Committee (SNCC), one black, one white, first arrived in Cambridge, Maryland. SNCC – pronounced "Snick" – arose out of the sit-ins that swept the South after four black students requested a cup of coffee at a Woolworth lunch counter in Greensboro, North Carolina, on February 1, 1960. Its subsistence-pay field secretaries, fervent believers in "black and white together," were already at work in Mississippi, Alabama, and Georgia when Reginald Robinson, a Baltimore native, heard that Maryland's Eastern Shore was Dixie, psychologically speaking, despite its proximity to Washington, D.C. He and William Hansen arrived to find a white-dominated town of 12,000, with the 4,200 blacks packed into a ramshackle Second Ward demarcated from the white district by Race Street. "More hostile than Mississippi" is how the 22-year-old Hansen, son of an Ohio steelworker, who had spent 43 days in a Mississippi prison as a Congress of Racial Equality (CORE) Freedom Rider in 1961, described Cambridge after a mob beat him in the head during the first interracial attempt to enter a whites-only bar on January 14, 1962.[1]

As a lull set in while city officials promised progress, the SNCC-affiliated Cambridge Nonviolent Action Committee (CNAC, or

[1] "61 Seized in Race Demonstrations Freed on Bond," *Washington Post*, 15 January 1962, p. A19. The authors are grateful for e-mail correspondence from Bill Hansen, 28 and 29 July 2012.

"C-Nack") watched and waited under Gloria Richardson, its chair. In spring 1963, CNAC resumed direct action when the town's segregated movie theater announced it would confine blacks to a small area at the back of the balcony. High unemployment in the Second Ward aggravated by a packinghouse collapse in the 1950s led CNAC, which had a welfare recipient and factory worker on its executive committee, to believe economic justice as important as "integration," the goal most liberals took to be the movement's point. CNAC's demands included not only an end to school and public accommodations discrimination but low-cost public housing and hiring of blacks by all-white firms. As locals filled churches for mass meetings, dozens of college students, black and white, arrived each weekend from Washington, Baltimore, Philadelphia, and New York to fill the jails.

Gloria – as everyone in Cambridge called her – was rail-thin, with a silky voice and a tart tongue. She had a distinguished lineage: From 1912 to 1946, her grandfather, Herbert Maynadier St. Clair, represented the Second Ward on Cambridge's city council. It was a pride laced with indignity, for every year the annual council dinner found him at home, eating the meal sent there by segregationist custom. Born in Baltimore and raised in Cambridge, Gloria studied at Howard University in Washington, D.C., from 1938 to 1942, under E. Franklin Frazier – "as radical as they came during those days," she said – and obtained a degree in sociology. On returning to Cambridge, she was excluded from professional opportunities in social work or teaching, leaving her disinclined to seek accommodation. When a reporter told her in 1963 that Cambridge's mayor said that race relations were fine until recently, she replied, "That's true, because the Negro leaders never asked for anything before."[2]

Anger boiled over in Cambridge in June and July of 1963 after two 15-year-old black youths were incarcerated for picketing the Board of Education. "It is difficult enough to fight prejudice," Richardson said, "but when it is coupled with stupidity it becomes dangerous." SNCC organizer Reggie Robinson was devoted to nonviolence, as was CNAC, but the Second Ward was home to many hunters and veterans, armed and restive. One night in June, angry crowds gathered on opposite sides of Race Street, hurling bricks, throwing firebombs, and exchanging gunshots that left two white men wounded. The *Washington Post* designated

[2] John H. Britton, "Woman Behind Cambridge Revolt," *Jet*, 8 August 1963, p. 19; Robert E. Baker, "Negroes in Cambridge Tired of Waiting," *Washington Post*, 21 April 1963, p. B9.

Cambridge "a national symbol of racial suppression," and Maryland's governor sent in the National Guard in a move initially seen as protective of blacks. When the Guard left in July, violence again flared as carloads of whites careened through the Second Ward shooting, with blacks returning fire. The next day the Guard was redeployed, to remain a year.[3]

Attorney General Robert F. Kennedy, alarmed by these developments so close to the nation's capital, called Gloria Richardson to a Washington meeting with Cambridge's mayor and Maryland's governor. He brokered an accord granting school desegregation, new public housing, a black interviewer for public employment, and an amendment to the city charter desegregating public accommodations, in exchange for no more demonstrations. The victory made Gloria Richardson – "a radical, a revolutionary," in her own words – into what the *New York Times* called "a nationally acknowledged Negro leader." On August 28, 1963, she was invited to the steps of the Lincoln Memorial for the March on Washington for Jobs and Freedom, where 34-year-old Martin Luther King, Jr., gave his "I Have a Dream" speech. Organized by Bayard Rustin and presided over by A. Philip Randolph, his vision of a national march at last realized, the event saw 250,000 people, 70 percent black, gather in the largest protest demonstration yet in American history. The most radical speaker was SNCC's 23-year-old chairman John Lewis, who despite respecting Randolph's request to excise criticism of President John F. Kennedy's inaction in the South still proclaimed "a social revolution," used "black" rather than "Negro," and charged that American politics was allied with "open forms of political, economic, and social exploitation." No women were designated speakers in the three-hour lineup, but a "Tribute to Negro Women Fighters for Freedom" honored Mrs. Medgar Evers, Mrs. Herbert Lee, Rosa Parks, Diane Nash, Daisy Bates, Septima Clark – and Gloria Richardson, who exited the Memorial arm in arm with Lena Horne, the singer, who had shouted a single word into the microphone: "Freedom!"[4]

---

3 "Arrest of Negro Pickets is Called 'Unnecessary,'" *Washington Post*, 1 June 1963, p. C2; "Flames in the Night," *Washington Post*, 15 June 1963, p. A8.
4 "Militant Integrationist: 41-Year-Old Divorcee Leads Cambridge Fight," *Dallas Morning News*, 14 July 1963, p. 20; " 'Radical' Integrationist," *New York Times*, 13 July 1963; Taylor Branch, *Parting the Waters: America in the King Years, 1954–63* (New York: Simon and Schuster, 1988), p. 880; "200,000 Jam Mall in Mammoth Rally in Solemn, Orderly Plea for Equality," *Washington Post*, 29 August 1963, p. A1; "Capitol Wears a Drowsy, Holiday Look Through March," *Washington Post*, 29 August 1963, p. A26; "Warns of Civil War," *New York Times*, 22 July 1963.

No one that day would have predicted that Gloria Richardson would fall precipitously from grace in the following month, branded as irresponsible for boycotting a referendum on public accommodations forced by hostile whites. The October 1, 1963, referendum split the "white power structure," as the Movement called it. Moderate whites, including Cambridge's mayor and Chamber of Commerce, were responsive to the Kennedys' pressures and thought desegregation necessary to restore stability. Conservative businessmen, upholding "Americanism," defended the way "this country... has operated for the last 100 years." Working-class whites almost uniformly opposed desegregation, both out of racism and because they thought they, not elites, would bear any adverse material consequences from it. CNAC's boycott shocked the NAACP, liberals, and the press, but CNAC considered it unacceptable to subject human rights to an electorate in which whites outnumbered blacks by 3 to 1. "It is wrong to put our Constitutional rights to the vote of a white majority," said Richardson. In the end, all four white wards voted against the measure, and less than half of blacks voted.[5]

The press blamed Richardson for the defeat, but to others she was a hero of a no-compromise mood, North and South. She won praise from visitors including comedian Dick Gregory, Mississippi sharecropper Fannie Lou Hamer, and Harlem Rep. Adam Clayton Powell, Jr. In November 1963, Richardson attended the Northern Negro Grass Roots Leadership Conference in Detroit where she saw the Harlem radical Malcolm X mock "nonviolent revolution" as mythical. "I don't reject the Gandhian philosophy of nonviolence... and right now I'm using it as a tactical device," Richardson told the southern writer Robert Penn Warren, but she observed that whenever 500 marched in Cambridge, there were always "1,500, 1,600 Negroes that lined the streets ready to defend us." Despite it all, she hoped "underprivileged people" would unite "regardless of color": "Once they find that they have common problems, then the men that are getting all the money in this town, pocketing it, are going to be out of commission."[6]

---

[5] "2 Factions Clash in Cambridge, Md.," *New York Times*, 29 September 1963; "New Move Slated in Cambridge, Md., Race Strife," *New York Times*, 26 January 1964; "Vote Nears in Cambridge, Md., On Desegregating Restaurants," *New York Times*, 22 September 1963; "Cambridge Drive for Vote Spurned," *Washington Post*, 26 August 1963, p. B1.

[6] Gloria Richardson, interview by Robert Penn Warren, 2 March 1964, Vanderbilt University Library, available at http://whospeaks.library.vanderbilt.edu/interview/gloria-st-clair-hayes-richardson.

Gloria Richardson's last stand came in May 1964, when she led hundreds of demonstrators down Race Street to protest a speech by visiting Alabama Governor George Wallace, whose slogan was "segregation forever." Ordered by the National Guard to turn back, she pushed aside a bayonet, stepped forward, and was arrested; the Guard then sprayed clouds of tear gas over the hundreds of remaining protestors. The Civil Rights Act signed that summer by President Lyndon Baines Johnson ended the legal Jim Crow to which Cambridge had clung, if not its economic inequality and racial antagonisms. That September, Gloria Richardson remarried and moved to New York. In her absence, the new SNCC chairman and Black Power militant H. Rap Brown visited Cambridge three years later, in 1967, delivering a fiery speech widely blamed for arson that destroyed two square blocks of buildings in the Second Ward. After being arrested for incitement to riot, a defiant Brown called violence "as American as cherry pie." The Associated Press's account carried more than a hint of nostalgia: "The new rioting seemed to differ from the comparatively orderly demonstrations of the summer of 1963, when Gloria Richardson, a slender Negro woman, led Negroes. . . . " Once stigmatized, Gloria Richardson now looked reasonable.[7]

The Cambridge uprising from 1962 to 1964 manifested many key features of sixties radicalism: the moral power of the black freedom movement, the origins of dissent in social inequality, the importance of women despite their deprecation in popular culture, the capacity of sparkplug organizers to generate community mobilizations, the complex dynamic between liberalism and radicalism, the intergenerational links amidst a youth upsurge, the capacity of revolutionary consciousness to provide either tactical restraint or recklessness, the challenge of finding the right approach to check a bullheaded opposition, the coexistence of nonviolent strategy and armed self-defense, the many significant layers beneath charismatic figures such as Martin Luther King and Malcolm X, and the courage demanded to persevere. Just one upheaval in a decade of tumult, Cambridge was seared in the memories of its young campaigners, black and white, whose combined histories are a New Left mosaic. As Bernice Johnson Reagon – a SNCC Freedom Singer – stated, "The centering, borning essence of the '60s, of the New Left, is the civil rights movement."[8]

<hr />

[7] John Woodfield [AP], "National Guard in Cambridge to Halt Rioting," *State Times Advocate*, 25 July 1967, p. 5; "Brown Denounces LBJ, Moderation," *Dallas Morning News*, 28 July 1967, p. A5.

[8] "The Borning Struggle," in *They Should Have Served That Cup of Coffee*, ed. Dick Cluster (Boston: South End, 1979), p. 38.

The early sixties were a time of revitalization in which youth itself seemed to fuse with radical questioning to form a New Left. If one song captured the mood it was Bob Dylan's 1964 anthem "The Times They Are a-Changin'": "Your sons and your daughters are beyond your command, your old road is rapidly agin'." Dylan himself was new, having shed the chrysalis of Robert Zimmerman from Hibbing, Minnesota, to move to New York in 1961 at the age of 19, rename himself for the poet Dylan Thomas, and become a Greenwich Village singer-songwriter at the forefront of a folk music revival. The folk revival implied, as had the "people's songs" of the 1940s, that the best conveyor of political lyrics was the earnest acoustic balladeer. Pete Seeger, in his forties, preserved continuity, penning fresh songs such as the antiwar anthem "Where Have All the Flowers Gone?" (1961) – rapidly covered by Joan Baez, the Kingston Trio, and Peter, Paul, and Mary. The moral-aesthetic appeal of folk music owed much to the civil rights movement and its mass singing, with Odetta, Julius Lester, Guy Carawan, and others providing linkages. As hymns and ballads were refracted through Highlander Folk School and the Freedom Singers, picket lines and jailhouses resounded to "We Shall Overcome," "This Little Light of Mine," "Ain't Gonna Let Nobody Turn Me Round," and "I Woke Up This Morning With My Mind Set on Freedom."

The black freedom movement propelled the mass radicalization of the 1960s. In the decade's first half, the Movement – capitalized to convey its unity, like the Old Left's capitalization of the Party – focused eyes on the Deep South. As teens watched epic civil rights campaigns on television screens in their living rooms, identifying with the struggle of black Americans, the civil rights movement became a template for social action. The spillover effect was immediate as the sit-ins that began in February 1960 made dissent and protest legitimate again. In May 1960, hundreds of clean-cut students in San Francisco singing "The Star-Spangled Banner" in a civil-libertarian protest of a HUAC hearing were blasted with fire hoses and dragged by police down the City Hall steps, resulting in a HUAC propaganda film, *Operation Abolition* (1960), that painted the protest as Communist-instigated, a distortion that backfired, discrediting HUAC instead. In autumn, the Hollywood blacklist was broken for the first time as Dalton Trumbo received screen credit for *Spartacus,* a film about a Roman slave revolt leader. The upswing of mass democratic civil rights activity, in other words, helped to dispel the residual mists of McCarthyism by making political controversy and discussion legitimate again, an essential condition for the full flowering of a New Left. The Movement's triumph at the level of national law in the Civil Rights Act of 1964 and Voting Rights Act of 1965 was only a beginning as black action pushed forward toward a broader social and economic agenda across the nation of jobs, education, income, and schooling.

No single organization dominated radicalism in the 1960s, unlike the 1930s and 1940s. Students for a Democratic Society (SDS) is usually considered the premier organization of the New Left, but the black freedom organization SNCC was equally important as a New Left catalyst. California's Bay Area was a New Left greenhouse with very little SDS presence. The New Left's first campus showings were in specific initiatives such as the Harvard peace group Tocsin and student government slates such as VOICE at Michigan, ACTION at Columbia, and SLATE at Berkeley. Other focal points for student radicalism included the Liberal Study Group within the National Student Association, the YMCA and YWCA among young southern liberals, the Northern Student Movement and Southern Student Organizing Committee (both civil rights movement allies), and the Student Peace Union, which successfully campaigned against above-ground nuclear testing with the slogan "No Tests, East or West." In short, the New Left was not an organization but "the Movement": a congeries of committees, parties, magazines, groups, and unaffiliated independent radicals at work on a variety of issues, sometimes linked in common action but often shifting and recomposing.

When the sociologist and dissenter C. Wright Mills began to talk about a "New Left" in ways that would popularize the term among student radicals, his choice of words owed much to international developments, particularly in Britain and France. There the crisis of Communist credibility in 1956 as a result of the Khrushchev revelations and invasion of Hungary had a potent counterpart in the Suez Crisis. Egyptian President Gamal Abdel Nasser, a pan-Arab nationalist who led a revolution overthrowing dynastic rule in Egypt, moved to repatriate the Suez Canal in 1956, prompting Egypt's invasion by Britain, France, and Israel. Even as Communism entered a state of disgrace, so did the Western powers by blatantly exercising old colonial prerogatives along with those social democrats who had given blanket endorsement to "the West" in the Cold War. Consequently, radical pacifism gained momentum in Britain. The first march of the Campaign for Nuclear Disarmament (CND) – the group that invented the international peace symbol, combining semaphore signals for "N" and "D" within a circle representing world unity – was a march from London to the military base at Aldermaston on Easter Sunday 1958. Soon afterward, CND activists linked up with American expatriate Bill Sutherland in Ghana, joined by Bayard Rustin, in planning a West African direct-action protest against French plans to test its own bomb in the French Sahara, challenging both the nuclear arms race and French colonialism while showing solidarity with Algeria, whose independence movement the French were suppressing with torture.

These were the contexts in which erstwhile British Communist intellectuals E. P. Thompson and John Saville launched *The New Reasoner* to advocate "socialist humanism" in 1957, merging that periodical with the Oxford-homed *Universities and Left Review* in 1960, to create, significantly, *New Left Review*, which held that "the strength of the New Left will be tested by the strength of its ideas," and New Left Books, whose first book published was titled *Out of Apathy* (1960). Simultaneously, in Madison, Wisconsin, a group of graduate students, largely New York transplants once active in the Communist Party's defunct Labor Youth League and looking for what one of them, James Weinstein, called "a theoretical basis for a new socialist politics," commenced *Studies on the Left* in 1959. Mills's "Letter to the New Left," one of the most salient early expressions of the emergent spirit, first appeared in *New Left Review* and then, shortly afterward, *Studies on the Left*, giving transatlantic play to one of the first attempts to conjure a decisively "new" radicalism sufficiently vigorous to escape the tragedies besetting older lefts. All this expanded and developed the left revival program begun by *Liberation* and various discussants in the late 1950s.[9]

Mills was a Texas-born, motorcycle-riding, prolific Columbia University sociologist who wrote with punch and clarity and was the American New Left's foremost intellectual expositor before he died of a heart attack in 1962 at 45. His politics were congruent with the British New Left's in the drubbing he gave to "NATO intellectuals" – the Cold War liberals and social democrats such as Sidney Hook and Daniel Bell – or weary "ex-radicals," as Mills called them. Like the British New Left, Mills thought of the New Left as primarily a matter of ideas. There agreement ceased, however, and the New Left did not line up in a neat transatlantic queue, for Mills faulted the British New Left for clinging to the "labor metaphysic": a tendency to see "'the working class' of the advanced capitalist societies as the historic agency, or even as the most important agency, in the face of the really impressive historical evidence that now stands against this expectation." Students, the young, intellectuals: they, Mills posited, had driven events forward between 1956 and 1960 in Poland,

---

[9] "Editorial," *New Left Review* 1 (Jan.–Feb. 1960), p. 1; James Weinstein, "*Studies on the Left*," in *History and the New Left: Madison, Wisconsin, 1950–1970*, ed. Paul Buhle (Philadelphia: Temple University Press, 1990), p. 116.

Hungary, Turkey, South Korea, and Japan – and in the U.S. South. This analysis was refreshing insofar as it validated students as independent catalysts, a signal feature of sixties radicalism. However, Mills skipped over the sometimes decisive role of workers in the very same events he described, such as the Hungarian workers' councils of 1956, and did not acknowledge that to transform society students require alliances beyond the campuses, a fact that by decade's end would make many New Leftists look to the very working class whose existence Mills had cast in doubt by placing those words in quotation marks.[10]

The two signature organizations of the new radicalism in the United States certainly were comprised of students: Students for a Democratic Society (SDS) and the Student Nonviolent Coordinating Committee (SNCC). SDS and SNCC had many common features. Each came into being in 1960, drew upon and extended the nascent left revival of the late fifties, and yet provided a fresh vehicle in comparison to established organizations, seen as prone to excessive caution or exhaustion after the red scare. Each was devoted to a moral politics of bodies placed on the line, linked members together across a wide variety of locales, and held appeal for their sheer lack of fixity, their wide-open horizons of possibility shaped by anyone who joined and contributed to them. Each diverged from the earlier pattern of left-wing youth groups in that they were not directed by adult groups or beholden in any strict way to a line, but were independent and self-directing. Each held that power best flows from the bottom up, expressed in their mutual slogan, "Let the people decide."

SNCC – an interracial initiative that was nonetheless black-led, with a black-majority staff – influenced the predominantly white SDS far more than SDS influenced SNCC. SNCC's main focus of action until mid-decade was in rural communities of the South, whereas SDS was predominantly northern and campus-based, but SDS admired and emulated SNCC and extended solidarity to it. Both SDS and SNCC evinced a moral idealism that owed a great deal to the culture of the society they sought to transform. In SNCC, whose members more often came from modest working-class or rural upbringings, the teachings of the black church, such as redemptive love and moral courage, exerted an early hold. In SDS, whose members often came from middle-class or upper-middle-class homes, moralism derived more from the civic ideals of freedom, democracy, and "liberty and justice for all" instilled in primary school

---

[10] C. Wright Mills, "Letter to the New Left," *New Left Review* 5 (Sept.–Oct. 1960), p. 20–22.

and trumpeted by the Free World. The New Left was indignant at the distance between American ideals and American practice. In the name of Students for a Democratic Society, indeed, the most radical word was *for*, signifying that American society was not yet the democracy it claimed to be.

SDS began with a mere handful of members, most of them at the University of Michigan, where a student named Al Haber had in 1958 begun rebuilding his local chapter of the Student League for Industrial Democracy (SLID), a social-democratic educational society whose acronym had become painfully accurate as its chapters were reduced to only three universities, Yale and Columbia being the other two. Haber was the son of a New Deal economist who had helped draft the Social Security Act, and he recruited Sharon Jeffrey, daughter of United Automobile Workers (UAW) members in Detroit. In January 1960, Haber, by then working out of SLID's national office in New York City, renamed it Students for a Democratic Society and began to plan, serendipitously, for a conference on "Human Rights in the North." The following month, the Woolworth sit-in in Greensboro made national headlines. As the sit-in tactic, borrowed from CORE's work in Chicago in the 1940s, caught on, it sparked dozens of comparable actions throughout the South – soon echoed in the North, where national chain stores such as Woolworth also operated. Excitedly, Ella Baker, executive director of King's Southern Christian Leadership Conference (SCLC), convened a meeting of sit-in participants (attended by Haber as SDS's observer) in spring 1960. To give the Movement regional coordination in the loose fashion of a committee of equals letting local teams organize on the ground, SNCC was born, with the same philosophy of nonviolence and redemptive love as that of King and SCLC, although Baker urged the new group to retain its autonomy, spontaneity, and orientation toward direct action.

A layer of social-democratic advocates in the United States provided vital informal roles at this moment. Michael Harrington, who started out in the 1950s with Dorothy Day's *Catholic Worker* and Norman Thomas's Socialist Party before becoming a close strategic ally of Max Shachtman, paid attention to the northern students in SDS. Bayard Rustin – a radical pacifist associate of Baker and King also linked to Shachtman by this time – proved a magnetic presence among some of the earliest SNCC leaders, including the Trinidad-born New Yorker Stokely Carmichael. Rustin was preparing civil rights protests at the Republican and Democratic national conventions in summer 1960, including an appearance by King before the Democratic platform committee in Los Angeles. The

FIGURE 3.1. The Student Nonviolent Coordinating Committee carried out sit-ins against racial segregation throughout the South, including this one in Atlanta in 1963. © *Danny Lyon/Magnum Photos.*

sit-ins had given SDS its first major focus for action as northern students took part in protest pickets at chain stores. When Tom Hayden, raised in a lower-middle-class Irish Catholic household in Royal Oak, near Detroit, and editor of the University of Michigan's student paper, the *Michigan Daily*, went to California to cover the Democratic convention, the force of King's example persuaded him that a meaningful life required contributing to social justice, cementing his ties to Haber's SDS. On election day in November 1960, SNCC and SDS prepared a special joint supplementary issue of SNCC's *Student Voice* edited by Tom Kahn, a young associate of Rustin, Shachtman, and Harrington.

Within the civil rights movement, SNCC together with CORE – reviving at this time while still under James Farmer's leadership – would comprise a youthful direct-action left wing. They were radical in comparison to the legal gradualism of the NAACP and Urban League, with King's SCLC in an intermediate position. That said, NAACP chapters such as the one headed in Philadelphia by Cecil B. Moore could be radical, and King himself often tilted, given the quickening pulse of action, toward SNCC and CORE. In early 1961, responding to another Supreme Court ruling outlawing segregation in interstate travel, CORE launched a new

Freedom Ride modeled after its 1947 Journey of Reconciliation. Setting out for New Orleans from Washington, D.C., the Freedom Riders – parties of blacks and whites who rode together and broke the color line in bus-stop waiting rooms – confronted explosive violence. In Anniston, Alabama, the Ku Klux Klan firebombed one of the buses and beat Freedom Riders to bloody unconsciousness, including Jim Peck, a veteran of the 1947 ride and the only person to undertake both journeys. As CORE decided to halt its action, a contingent of SNCC activists in Nashville, Tennessee, led by Diane Nash, realized that if violence stopped the Freedom Rides it would embolden racists to simply annihilate the freedom movement everywhere. They therefore voluntarily undertook the next leg of the bus route from Birmingham to Montgomery, with white mobs threatening them at every turn. After further beatings, the Justice Department finally dispatched marshals to assure the riders' safety. SNCC recruited hundreds of volunteers to take buses from Montgomery into Jackson, Mississippi, where there was no violence but local authorities summarily arrested all comers and sentenced them to Parchman Penitentiary, an arrangement that left some Freedom Riders deeply dissatisfied in the Kennedy response since it was acceding in Mississippi's arrest of interstate travelers who were well within their Constitutional rights. In the process, SNCC, joined by CORE's James Farmer, reinvented the "fill the jails" tactic pioneered by the Industrial Workers of the World in its free-speech fights of the 1910s.

The Freedom Rides demonstrated SNCC's courageous dedication to struggle, while also galvanizing the Kennedy administration into a concerted attempt to convince SNCC to turn from desegregating public accommodations to registering black voters – presumably a tamer issue, although because denial of the right to vote was an equally important pillar of white supremacy, voting rights campaigns would prove equally dangerous. After a good deal of internal debate, SNCC agreed to refocus its energies away from direct action, commencing voter-registration efforts in small Mississippi towns during the summer of 1961, an initiative pioneered by the quiet, reflective Bob Moses, a Harvard philosophy graduate who admired Albert Camus's book *The Rebel* (1951) and whose adoption of white T-shirts and bib overalls from the southern rural population would typify an early SNCC style. To SNCC, the key to success lay in unlocking the capacity of local residents to organize their neighbors. Only local initiative, SNCC organizers believed, could stimulate the daring needed to confront the hammerlock that whites had on jobs, credit, and police power, an outlook of sustained "grass roots" empowerment

SNCC workers increasingly contrasted with King's charismatic style of leadership that always moved from one flashpoint to the next. When SDS's Tom Hayden joined the SNCC campaign of 1961 in McComb, Mississippi, and endured a severe beating from white supremacists, his own existential choice of working for change only deepened, and his pamphlet *Revolution in Mississippi* (1962), published by SDS, further popularized SNCC and the southern movement with northern students. A number of others – many of them white southerners – were active in both SNCC and SDS: Bob Zellner, Casey Hayden, Robb Burlage, Dorothy Dawson Burlage, Betty Garman, and Jim Monsonis. So it is that SNCC and SDS grew in symbiosis, along with CORE and more diffuse New Left sensibilities, to become the Movement.

What was the "New Left"? What, precisely, did "democracy" mean? By summer 1962, an energized SDS felt a need for clearer answers to these questions, so a few dozen members met for a five-day retreat at a camp-like conference center owned by the UAW at Port Huron, Michigan. *The Port Huron Statement*, drafted by Tom Hayden and reworked by the assemblage, was the most significant political document of the early New Left. After several years of activity, no group had so well described what a New Left should be. The frame of reference was the left-revival program of the late 1950s: racial equality, peace, "bottom-up" democracy, support for decolonizing nations, a direct-action spirit. As did *Liberation* in 1956 and Mills in his 1960 "Letter to the New Left," SDS emphasized its novelty – even if that obscured lineages evident on every side, including the Port Huron gathering's funding by the UAW, the Socialist Party, and the League for Industrial Democracy, SDS's social-democratic parent group. Nevertheless, the *Port Huron Statement* wove many strands together creatively into an eloquent, imaginative, highly effective statement of principles, making it the touchstone document of the early New Left.

"Participatory democracy," the central concept of the *Port Huron Statement*, called for a democracy in which the individual shared "in those social decisions determining the quality and direction of his life." This demanded that "power rooted in possession, privilege, or circumstance" be replaced with a "power and uniqueness rooted in love, reflectiveness, reason, and creativity," bringing people "out of isolation and into community" so that "private problems – from bad recreation facilities to personal alienation – are formulated as general issues." Since no complex modern society can avoid some manner of representation or delegation, and not all expertise is elitist, "participatory democracy" could strike conventional liberals as utopian or unrealistic, but the phrase had poetry and potency and the *Port Huron Statement* rang true in its assertion that too many institutions in American society had become bureaucratic, unresponsive, impersonal, closed, and – inverting Cold War assumptions about the Free World – virtually totalitarian.[11]

The structure of feeling that underlay the *Port Huron Statement* focused on the centrality of commitment in personal and public life. The new radicals drew on French existentialist philosophy, particularly Camus, to insist that individuals must take a stand; failure to make such choices was a sign of "apathy," a condition linked to powerlessness. The view that apathy or indifference could only be surmounted by movements that themselves embodied participatory democracy and by committed individuals who would exemplify moral acts of "choice" explained why the *Port Huron Statement* put the segment on "Values" in its forefront – a reordering made at the convention itself, rather than in Hayden's draft. Although SDSers looked more to the moral élan of the existentialists than to the Beats' ecstatic style, they made clear their affinity with the bohemians in their willingness to live and act outside the bounds of convention. Altogether, the document had a more overtly personal feel – expressive of yearnings for fulfillment and meaning – than typical left-wing manifestoes. At the same time its utopian and lyrical vision of participatory democracy was balanced out by long, humdrum segments more typical of a position paper on issues ranging from foreign policy to the economy, along with a social-democratic program to realign the Democratic Party toward a left-liberal agenda by expunging its segregationist wing. In those portions, the *Port Huron Statement* was more reformist, and less radical, than its 1940s and 1950s kin from Macdonald to the editors of *Liberation*, who opposed capitalism and clearly called for a libertarian socialism. The "Values" section, however, put visionary rather than practical qualities in the foreground, making a great impression on young readers. *The Port Huron Statement* captured the moral imagination of youth, giving voice to the radical democratic idealism so central to the social movements of the early 1960s.

A paradox of the New Left not fully appreciated at the time was that even as young people served as dynamos of a new radicalism, even as they saw

---

[11] *The Port Huron Statement*, reprinted in James Miller, *"Democracy Is in the Streets": From Port Huron to the Siege of Chicago* (New York: Simon and Schuster, 1987), p. 333.

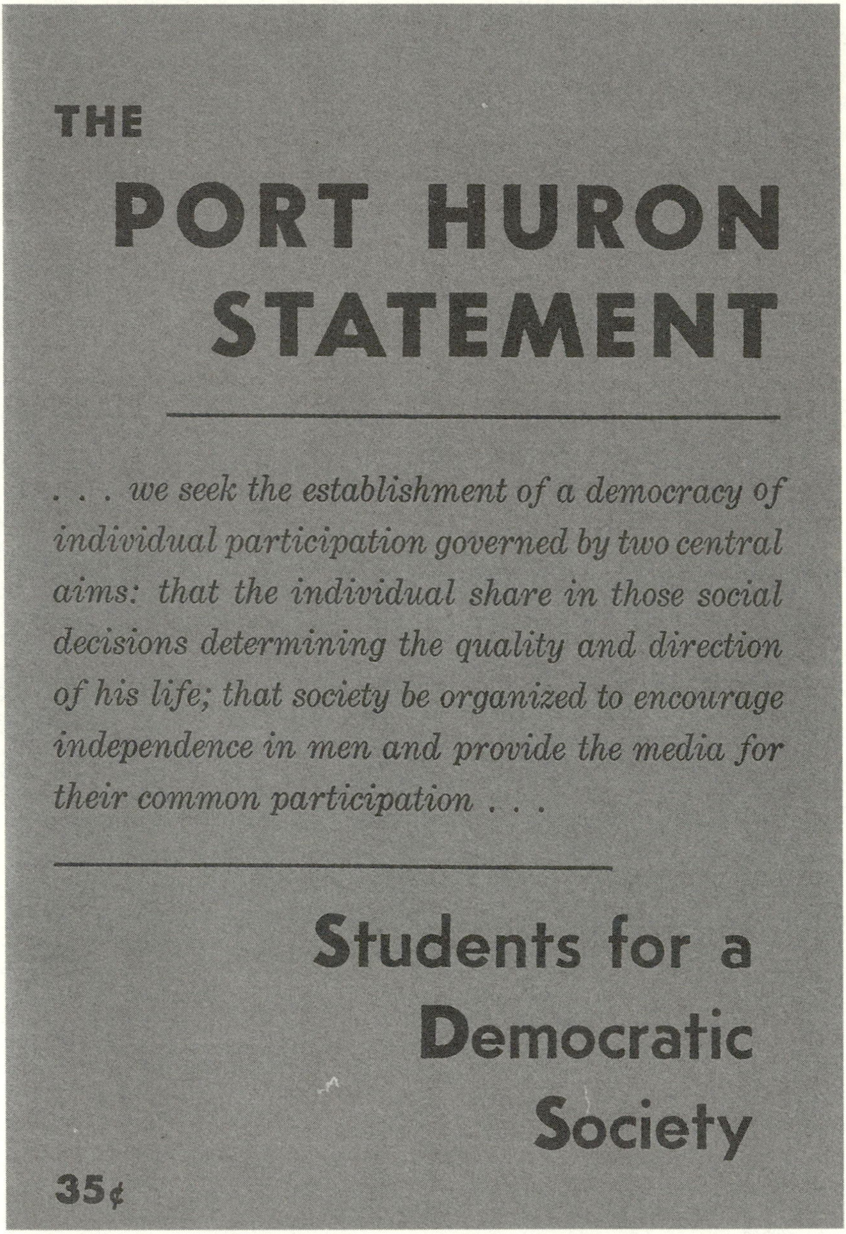

THE
PORT HURON
STATEMENT

. . . we seek the establishment of a democracy of individual participation governed by two central aims: that the individual share in those social decisions determining the quality and direction of his life; that society be organized to encourage independence in men and provide the media for their common participation . . .

Students for a
Democratic
Society

35¢

FIGURE 3.2. *The Port Huron Statement* issued in 1962 by Students for a Democratic Society, its first draft written by University of Michigan student Tom Hayden was a keynote declaration of the New Left. *Authors' collection.*

themselves breaking from the dreary fates of prior lefts, they were abetted and educated by middle-aged left-wing veterans. The Gloria Richardsons and Ella Bakers of the civil rights movement, the Pete Seegers of the folk scene, the many other intermediary figures with histories dating back to the thirties or forties, were everywhere. Anne and Carl Braden, Virginia and Clifford Durr, James Dombrowski, Stanley Levison, and Bayard Rustin played roles in the civil rights movement. Women Strike for Peace (WSP), formed in 1961, consisted mostly of young mothers, many of whom were "red-diaper babies" from Communist families, advocating disarmament in the name of their own children's lives. The best-seller lists of the early sixties were crowded with books by older radicals. Michael Harrington was a seasoned 34-year-old Socialist Party member when he published *The Other America* (1962), his influential book on poverty, itself popularized by a long article by none other than Dwight Macdonald in the *New Yorker*. Jessica Mitford, author of *The American Way of Death* (1963), an exposé of the funeral industry's exploitation of grief, had been a Civil Rights Congress organizer in the Bay Area. Betty Friedan, a former United Electrical Workers' staffer, wrote the pioneering women's rights work *The Feminine Mystique* (1963), which paradoxically challenged precisely the maternal identities that WSP mobilized for public protest by calling on women to enter public life as dynamic, achievement-oriented individuals. *Monthly Review, National Guardian, I. F. Stone's Weekly, Dissent, New Politics,* the *Militant,* and the *Nation* were all headed by older radicals, but read widely by – and often written for – new radicals. Even some intellectuals seen as quintessentially New Left, including Staughton Lynd, Howard Zinn, and Paul Goodman, had political histories tracing to the 1940s. New Left youth had many facets overlapping with the Old Left – both, after all, were *Left* – given the early SDS's weighting toward those raised in the major East Coast cities, with an élan of intellectual sophistication, often from Jewish households, and a motivating concern for unity of black and white.

What seemed to have changed across the span of generations was that the labor movement was replaced by the independent civil rights movement as the main oppositional force and source of energy for the country's social imagination. Unions, assumed by the left of the 1930s and 1940s to be an instrument for radical action, seemed by the 1950s to be sclerotic, bureaucratic, and tame. Some young sixties radicals, in tune with Mills's dismissal of the "labor metaphysic," would find appeals to working-class solidarity irrelevant, archaic, or unconvincing in light of racial divisions among workers. However, the labor movement was not

entirely absent from the mix of new protest. A four-month steel strike
in 1959 demonstrated the lasting power of the major industrial unions,
and an initiative that same year by an old left-led union of drugstore
employees known as Local 1199 to organize low-paid public hospital
workers in New York City turned a strike of black and Latino order-
lies into a Harlem community mobilization, hinting at a new unionism
to come that concerned race as much as class. The practice of "community organizing" owed much to Saul Alinsky's Chicago example of
the 1940s, and in Los Angeles one such effort led to the recruitment of
Cesar Chavez, who began an Oxnard, California, campaign in tandem
with an organizing drive by the Packinghouse Workers Union and led a
march of ten thousand unemployed farmworkers in 1959 to demand jobs
when the U.S. Secretary of Labor came to town. By 1962, Chavez and
Dolores Huerta would found the union that would come to be called the
United Farm Workers (UFW), fusing issues of racial equality and labor.
The UAW and the Packinghouse union both subsidized SDS and cospon-
sored the March on Washington for Jobs and Freedom, spearheaded by
A. Philip Randolph, the old lion of black labor. Unions were not, therefore, wholly quiescent in the early sixties, although most labor radicals would have concurred with the *Port Huron Statement*'s faulting of
unions for "accommodation and limited effectiveness" and its desire "for
a broader and more forceful unionism."[12]

How the New Left differed from the Old Left, then, was not as clear-
cut or straightforward a matter as it seemed. How would the New Left
position itself in a Cold War world? What analysis would it offer of the
Soviet Union? How would it handle the question of Communist participation in social causes? These were complex issues, not always answered
by the young in ways their elders approved. As an ideal, participatory
democracy seemed to characterize the New Left and distinguish it from
the Old Left. But by "Old Left," what precisely was meant? Was it Stalinism, a dictatorial, dogmatic system? Or Marxism tout court, with its
primary orientation toward the working class? Or was social democracy
included as well, since it was politically compromised by the Cold War
and subject to bureaucracy? In virtually every New Left self-definition,
the Old Left did include the Soviet Union, the Communist Party, and their
fellow travelers. However, New Leftists often criticized the old Popular
Front *from the left*. The trappings of Jefferson and Lincoln, the disguise
of "liberals in a hurry," meant Communists had not lived openly as

---

[12] Miller, *"Democracy Is in the Streets,"* 344.

radicals, had not exemplified their ideals in their lives, or so the New Left argued – a criticism that might apply, for example, to Friedan, who in promoting *The Feminine Mystique* presented herself as a middle-class suburban housewife and Smith College graduate rather than a former left-wing union staff member. At the same time, New Leftists were acutely aware that the right-wing stigmatization of dissent, including civil rights activism of any kind, as "Communist" had stifled democratic initiatives in the society. How would they eschew top-down models of the Old Left, but also set aside hysterical, prejudicial approaches to Communism that would replicate or validate the McCarthyist mentality?

Answering this would cause a good deal of strain between the New Left and left-wing social democrats such as Harrington, who was only a decade older than the young SDS core but far more shaped by the fierce anti-Stalinism of the 1950s democratic left. Harrington insisted, as the Young People's Socialist League (YPSL) representative at Port Huron, that SDS should take a position drawing absolute lines of exclusion against Communists within social movements, for fear of allowing the Communists renewed opportunities to camouflage themselves within new Popular Front maneuvers that would obscure their true aims of dominating social movements. Most on the New Left, by contrast, tended to believe the Communist Party had suffered so great a collapse, organizationally and morally, that it no longer posed a real threat. Exclusion therefore struck them as needless and unfair, partly since their own ranks included red-diaper babies such as Richard Flacks and Steve Max at Port Huron, or the editors of *Studies on the Left*. New Leftists were already predisposed to dismiss the more conservative Cold War social democrats who, having adjusted themselves to the existing system as a "democratic" alternative to Communism, were no longer in any real way oppositional. Harrington, by contrast, was still an energetic reformer, but his overbearing approach – at one point going so far as to collude in locking SDS out of its own office – made it seem that all social democrats were subject to irrational phobias about Communism.

Foreign policy was where such tensions became most frothy, particularly as the 1959 victory of Fidel Castro, Che Guevara, and their band of guerrilla rebels in Cuba, ninety miles off the coast of Florida, over a U.S.-backed dictator, proved attractive to the New Left. The new Cuba's populist social policies on literacy, health, and land reform led many in the United States – initially both liberals and radicals – to see it as a new style of revolution. In *Listen, Yankee* (1960), C. Wright Mills assumed the voice of a Cuban revolutionary to champion "the hungry-world bloc" over "the Communist bloc or the Capitalist bloc," and declare, still writing as if a ventriloquist of the Cubans, "We are new radicals. We really are, we think, a new left in the world." As tensions between Castro's government and the United States grew, many social democrats sided largely with American foreign policy – the Socialist Party's Max Shachtman, for example – while New Leftists tended to favor the approach of the Fair Play for Cuba Committee, formed in 1960 to encourage a more favorable public opinion of Cuba and organize tours of the island for sympathetic North Americans. Such a trip led the young jazz critic, poet, and playwright LeRoi Jones to publish "Cuba Libre" in the avant-garde *Evergreen Review* in 1960, an early indication of how black identification with revolution in Latin America, Asia, and Africa would grow.[13]

Other "hungry-world bloc" nations attracted the interest of American radicals in the early sixties: Algeria and its independence struggle from France, which produced ardent dissent among French radical intellectuals, including Jean-Paul Sartre, and inspired the Martinique-born psychologist Frantz Fanon's *The Wretched of the Earth* (1961), a book that would be especially affecting for young radicals of color in the United States; the Congo, which won independence from Belgium in 1960 only to see its new government under left-nationalist Patrice Lumumba fall victim to factional strife, stoked by residual Belgian interests and U.S. covert action; apartheid South Africa, where the Sharpeville massacre of black protesters in 1960 led to mass uprising and the banning of the African National Congress (ANC) and Pan-Africanist Congress (PAC); and Vietnam, a country in Southeast Asia where a guerrilla war had broken out in the south met by deepening U.S. counterinsurgency involvement. In *The Political Economy of Growth* (1957), Paul A. Baran – a Stanford University economist close to the magazine *Monthly Review* – denied that the world was divided between developed and "undeveloped" nations and instead posited a systematic *under*development of much of the world by leading nations that appropriated the surplus. By the early 1960s, it seemed that national liberation struggles were breaking out everywhere, their aim being to end not only direct colonial administrative rule but this kind of external economic domination, or what Ghana's Kwame Nkrumah called "neo-colonialism."

The Cuban Revolution, in particular, intersected with American radicalism in myriad ways. When Robert F. Williams, a militant NAACP chapter leader in Monroe, North Carolina, came under attack for

---

[13] C. Wright Mills, *Listen, Yankee* (New York: Ballantine, 1960), pp. 30, 43.

organizing armed self-defense against white-supremacist assaults in 1961, a small group of activists from the Socialist Workers Party (SWP) and the Fair Play for Cuba Committee spirited him out of the country, eventually to Cuba, as first of many radicals to take refuge there. Che Guevara was interviewed in the first issue of the New Left periodical *Root and Branch: A Radical Quarterly,* issued in Berkeley in 1962. An ill-fated CIA-backed coup attempt by right-wing Cubans who landed at the Bay of Pigs in 1961 and the Cuban missile crisis of October 1962 were signal events in the New Left's estrangement from conventional liberalism. These Cold War showdowns heightened fears that further escalation would lead to global nuclear holocaust, and made the charge that the Cuban government was drawing closer to the Soviet Union a self-fulfilling prophecy. William Appleman Williams, a historian with a major influence on *Studies on the Left,* argued in *The Tragedy of American Diplomacy* (1959) that U.S. foreign policy was characterized by a relentless expansionism often driven by liberals pushing the "open door" of markets and opposed to revolution, with the book's 1962 edition applying this same argument to explain U.S. policy toward revolutionary Cuba.

A tendency of youth to identify with the Cuban government even as it tipped toward the Soviet camp partly accounted for mild gains among the surviving remnants of the Old Left, derogated as the "Hereditary Left" or "The Leftovers" in contemporaneous books seeking to distinguish it from the actual New Left. Nonetheless, the Old Left managed to knit new outfits of its own. The Du Bois Clubs, widely recognized as the youth wing of the CPUSA despite disavowals, with red-diaper baby Bettina Aptheker a prominent member, were named after W. E. B. Du Bois, the black radical intellectual who joined the CPUSA symbolically before departing for Nkrumah's Ghana, where he died on the night before the March on Washington in 1963. The Young Socialist Alliance (formed in 1960) associated with the SWP, while orthodox in its Trotskyism, was highly active in Fair Play for Cuba and receptive to black nationalism. As "polycentrism" divided a global Communist world no longer centered on Moscow after the Sino-Soviet split of 1961–1962, vigorous partisans of Mao's ideas began to emerge as well, although in the early sixties such groupings were on the margins – even the margins of the left, where more amorphous, experimental, existentialist-inspired forms of New Left thought remained prevalent.

The undercurrents that would produce the shift from "Freedom Now" to "Black Power" in black radical thought and action equally arose

from world developments, in particular the independence achieved by
the new states of Sub-Saharan Africa – 17 in 1960 alone. The new black
internationalism and politics were manifest in black life in the early sixties, though largely out of sight of white society. *Liberator*, a magazine
launched in 1961 by the Liberation Committee for Africa, held a first public forum, "Nationalism, Colonialism, and the United States," featuring
James Baldwin, John O. Killens, and William Worthy. *Freedomways*, a
Harlem quarterly edited by Du Bois's wife Shirley Graham, linked Africa,
the Caribbean, and Latin America to the U.S. freedom struggle, with a
Popular Front sensibility. That project both contrasted and overlapped
with the thought of Harlem writer Harold Cruse, who considered the
Communists to have been manipulative in black life and espoused a revolutionary nationalism holding that black Americans suffered colonial
oppression within the United States. The Revolutionary Action Movement (RAM), formed in 1962 by Max Stanford, a Philadelphian student
at Central State in Wilberforce, Ohio, argued that the black rebellion
should orient toward revolutionary China and even, in a tremor of things
to come, that guerrilla tactics might be appropriate in the United States.
The young Bay area lawyer Donald Warden's Afro-American Association
condemned moderates and integration while advocating black-owned
businesses. All of these explorations reflected a desire to push beyond legal
rights toward power and equality, and were carried out in awareness of
the example of Robert F. Williams, who delivered "Radio Free Dixie"
broadcasts from Fidel Castro's Cuba before departing for Mao's China.
James Baldwin's *The Fire Next Time* (1963), originally printed in the
New Yorker, was a prescient, compelling expression of rising black anger.

By far the leading figure in this trend was Malcolm X. Born Malcolm
Little and raised in Nebraska and Michigan, he joined Elijah Muhammad's Nation of Islam while in prison for armed robbery committed in
Boston, adopted the Nation's practice of replacing the familial name with
an "X" signifying unknown African ancestry, and became head of the
Nation of Islam's Harlem mosque in the 1950s, espousing its principles of
black self-reliance, a puritanical-patriarchal moral code, and the right to
self-defense. Although often militant-sounding in its black pride, this orientation was politically quietist. By the early 1960s, Malcolm X wished
to interact with the rising black freedom movement, but Muhammad
was resistant. In 1963, when Malcolm X called Kennedy's assassination
"the chickens coming home to roost," alluding to white-supremacist and
U.S. government-sponsored violence at home and abroad, Muhammad
officially silenced him. Upon learning that Muhammad had impregnated

FIGURE 3.3. Harlem Trinidadian Claudia Jones (far left) and Eslanda Goode Robeson (at microphone), wife of the American singer Paul Robeson, at a meeting in England celebrate the life of Patrice Lumumba, the Congolese independent movement leader assassinated in 1961, linking women's and African interests. *Photographs and Prints Division, Schomburg Center for Research in Black Culture, The New York Public Library, Lenox and Tilden Foundations.*

several of his secretaries in contravention of Muslim morality, Malcolm X broke with the Nation of Islam but remained a Muslim. What followed was a period of reflection. When Malcolm X made the pilgrimage to Mecca required of every Muslim, he discovered Islam to be a religion of all of humankind, contrary to the Nation's black chauvinist interpretation of the faith, and as he traveled in Africa he was impressed by the socialism he found in the newly independent states.[14]

By autumn 1964, Malcolm X founded the Organization of Afro-American Unity (OAAU), modeled after the Organization of African Unity recently launched by African leaders. He continued to favor all-black organization as critical to acquisition of skills and power and advocated black community control of economic, educational, and social institutions. He saw racism as rooted in exploitation and was increasingly

[14] "Malcolm X Scores U.S. and Kennedy," *New York Times*, 2 December 1963, p. 21.

open to coalition with organizations of people of any complexion. Arguing that "America is a colonial power," he held that the 22 million "Afro-Americans" were "colonized," engaged in a fight that was joined to other national liberation struggles in what he called a global revolution. He was among the first to link the struggles of black Americans to the revolutionary independence war in Vietnam.[15]

Malcolm X was shot to death on February 21, 1965, at the age of 39, in the midst of a speech at the Audubon Ballroom in Harlem. Three black men, two of them members of the Nation of Islam, were convicted; one confessed but later pointed to two others as his real accomplices. Malcolm had believed he was under heavy surveillance and stated that forces in the power structure, not Black Muslims, might have been behind a recent firebombing of his home. His sister and other radicals later posited CIA and FBI involvement in his assassination, but no firm evidence exists of it. What is unmistakable is Malcolm X's radicalization. Just two days before his death he declared, "It is incorrect to classify the revolt of the Negro as simply a racial conflict of black against white, or as a purely American problem. Rather, we are today seeing a global rebellion of the oppressed against the oppressor, the exploited against the exploiter."[16]

Demonized in the news media as a hatemonger, Malcolm X in his lifetime found little support outside his own organizations apart from the Trotskyists in the SWP who published his speeches and hosted him at forums. Despite his isolation, he made a strong impression on young black radicals in SNCC, his thought would inspire the founders of the Black Panther Party, and by the end of the decade the linkage he made between racism and empire would be far more widely held. His path revealed that the issues at stake between the established civil rights model and emerging Black Power alternative did not hinge on "integration" and "separation" so much as the goal of self-determination and a willingness to *disaffiliate* from mainstream American society in order to achieve it, as well as the open advocacy of armed self-defense. Malcolm X rejected the idea – often too categorically – that the moral force of nonviolent protest and civil disobedience would reveal the better instincts of goodwill in white Americans. He asserted that African Americans had to act by "whatever means necessary," marshaling leverage to "get the man's foot off your neck," as another streetwise black American put it during the Watts uprising of 1965 in Los Angeles. The aim was to challenge and

---

[15] George Breitman, ed., *Malcolm X Speaks* (New York: Grove Press, 1965), p. 50.
[16] Breitman, *Malcolm X Speaks*, p. 217.

overthrow white supremacy, understood as intrinsic to the American way of life. Malcolm X espoused a radical perspective distinct from the interracial "beloved community" ideal of the early New Left, but envisioned a beloved community of another kind, helping to explain how SNCC later adopted his views. When he forswore trying to "change the white man's mind," he told black audiences, "We have to see each other with new eyes. We have to see each other as brothers and sisters. We have to come together with warmth so we can develop unity and harmony that's necessary to get this problem solved ourselves."[17]

Even in his own lifetime, Malcolm X's ideas had begun to influence other black radicals, from socialists James and Grace Lee Boggs in Detroit to the increasingly militant Brooklyn chapter of CORE. Similar moves appeared in other protest and organizing efforts. Around 1965, Mexican American organizers working alongside Cesar Chavez to unionize California's agricultural workers embraced the identity of "Chicano," formerly a term used pejoratively to identify the poorest, lowest, Spanish-speaking elements of the Mexican-American populace. That signaled an intention to disaffiliate with Anglo America. Yet Malcolm X's recognition that such struggles, rather than being identified with "minority" status, could be reconceived as part of a global independence-seeking majority served to keep a dialectic of margin and mainstream alive. To stand apart, if placed in such a worldwide field of vision, did not necessarily mean remaining a permanent exile or outsider.

As the pace of events accelerated in the early sixties sufficiently to induce vertigo, strains began to affect both liberals and radicals, sometimes pulling them apart. Even leaving aside the new urban currents of black liberation thought, the mainline civil rights movement when viewed from the perspective of white America in the early 1960s was a profound challenge to traditional power and prerogative. As it crescendoed, tensions grew between radical and liberal currents within it, and between it and self-described white "moderates" as well as white supremacists. King's "Letter from a Birmingham Jail" (1963) – its title evoking Alabaman fire hoses and police dogs, and signifying King's willingness to endure a criminal record in the name of a higher law – searchingly criticized moderates for their equivocation, calling for "creative extremists" to use

[17] Thomas Pynchon, "A Journey into the Mind of Watts," *New York Times Magazine*, 12 June 1966, pp. 34–35, 78, 80–82, 84; Malcolm X, in Breitman, *Malcolm X Speaks*, p. 40.

nonviolent direct action to "create such a crisis and foster such a tension that a community which has constantly refused to negotiate is forced to confront the issue." As conviction soared in black America of a coming transformation, reflected in soul singer Sam Cooke's "A Change is Gonna Come" (1964), the dominant impulse remained the approach of King and Bayard Rustin: demonstrations, direct action, and legal challenges to shame segregation while pushing the Democratic administration in Washington for national legislation. That approach was increasingly hard to sustain, however, pinioned between rising black militancy on one side and white intransigence on the other.[18]

For liberals who had invested hopes in the reformist potentialities of Camelot, tragedy struck with the assassination of John F. Kennedy on November 22, 1963, in Dallas, Texas, shortly after he advocated civil rights legislation. The apparent assassin, Lee Harvey Oswald, was brought up in fragmented familial conditions in New Orleans, joined the Marines, defected to the Soviet Union, returned with a Russian wife, posed for a photo while holding a rifle and copies of the *Militant* and the *Worker*, distributed Fair Play for Cuba Committee literature, and sent comradely letters to the national offices of both the SWP and CPUSA despite their bitter rivalry. The Warren Commission held that Oswald acted alone, but his political weirdness, his pronouncement that he was "a patsy," and his own murder by assailant Jack Ruby fueled theories of a larger conspiracy involving the CIA, FBI, military intelligence, the Mafia, or anti-Castro Cubans. Oswald was most likely a disturbed sympathizer of the Cuban Revolution out to avenge the Bay of Pigs, although his method was wholly at odds with the usual socialist objection to acts of individual terror as holding no solution to problems systemic in nature.[19]

Camelot had long lost its sheen among young civil rights workers disillusioned by the failure of Robert Kennedy's Justice Department,

[18] King, "Letter from a Birmingham Jail," reprinted in *The Radical Reader: A Documentary History of the American Radical Tradition*, ed. Timothy Patrick McCarthy and John McMillian (New York: New Press, 2003), pp. 365, 372.

[19] That Oswald was a sincere – if self-absorbed, ascetic, and pathological – sympathizer of the Cuban Revolution is suggested by Jean Davison, *Oswald's Game* (New York: W. W. Norton, 1983) and Norman Mailer, *Oswald's Tale: An American Mystery* (New York: Random House, 1995). Conspiracy theories are legion, often propounded by left-liberals or radicals, from Mark Lane in the 1960s to Oliver Stone in *JFK* (1991). The irony is that Oswald, most likely a radical seeking to leave his mark on history, is now doubted by most Americans to have acted alone, largely because of radicals suspecting intelligence agencies to be behind his actions. The controversy is unlikely to ever be resolved.

beginning with the Freedom Rides, to enforce rights recognized by the Supreme Court or to shield SNCC organizers from attack. White terror against the Movement remained fierce, with the successive murders of NAACP field secretary Medgar Evers in Jackson, Mississippi, in 1963; four young girls later that year in the bombing of a Birmingham church that had been a center of mass meetings; and young SNCC activists James Chaney, Michael Schwerner, and Andrew Goodman near Philadelphia, Mississippi, in 1964 at the beginning of Freedom Summer, an initiative that brought hundreds of northern students to the South to help register voters. SNCC's decisive alienation came when President Lyndon Johnson, seeking reelection, refused to supplant the white segregationist Mississippi delegates to the August 1964 Democratic national convention held in Atlantic City, New Jersey, with the Mississippi Freedom Democratic Party (MFDP), an integrated delegation fielded by SNCC-led voting rights activists who had faced violence and death in Mississippi all summer long. This estranged the New Left not only from the White House but from prominent liberals with whom they had worked loosely in a broad civil rights coalition, including Walter Reuther, Joseph Rauh, Bayard Rustin, and Martin Luther King, all of whom urged upon the MFDP an agreement that would allow two delegates to be seated while promising total remedy of delegate selection for the next convention in four years' time. What to liberals looked like a breakthrough was to SNCC and the MFDP far too little too late. "We didn't come all this way for no two seats when all of us is tired," said sharecropper Fannie Lou Hamer, who in her own statement to the credentials committee had said, "If the Freedom Democratic Party is not seated now, I question America."[20]

Similarly, the first great campus eruption of the decade, the Free Speech Movement (FSM) at Berkeley, saw the student New Left turn jaded about liberal administrators, contrary to the *Port Huron Statement*'s imagining of a coming together of campus liberals and socialists. The controversy began when the statewide University of California administration presided over by Clark Kerr, a reformer who had opposed McCarthyism on campus, felt pressure from conservatives to rein in student activists who had mounted vigorous civil rights protests assailing

---

[20] Hamer, quoted in Taylor Branch, *Pillar of Fire: America in the King Years, 1963–65* (New York: Simon & Schuster, 1999), p. 474; Hamer, "Testimony Before the Democratic National Convention," in *"Takin' It to the Streets": A Sixties Reader*, ed. Alexander Bloom and Wini Breines (Oxford: Oxford University Press, 1995), p. 42.

discrimination by San Francisco, Oakland, and Berkeley businesses. The Berkeley administration moved to enforce a longstanding rule restricting political petitioning, leafleting, and speechmaking on campus. When student Jack Weinberg was arrested at a civil rights table, the police car containing him was soon surrounded by students; in 32 hours of participatory democracy, the car's roof became a platform for anyone wishing to speak out on campus freedom. The FSM culminated in an occupation of Sproul Hall, the central administration building, followed by mass arrests. By early 1965 the FSM achieved decisive victory for freedom of speech on campus, but its larger effect was national news coverage of student protest. The FSM's eloquent spokesman Mario Savio, a philosophy student who had taken part in SNCC's Freedom Summer, held "well-meaning liberals" responsible for abrogation of freedom on campus and for insufficient action on desegregation in the Deep South. In criticizing the "knowledge factory," he, Weinberg, and other FSM leaders interacted with Hal Draper, a fiercely antibureaucratic veteran of the anti-Stalinist left who had become a professional librarian at UC Berkeley. An exponent of "socialism from below," as expressed in his much-reprinted essay "The Two Souls of Socialism," Draper organized an Independent Socialist Club. His writings, including *The Mind of Clark Kerr* (1964), influenced Savio, the much more public face of the FSM, who melded existentialism with a direct-action élan by declaring that "when the operation of the machine becomes so odious" it is time to "put your bodies upon the gears and upon the wheels, upon the levers, upon all the apparatus" to "make it stop" so that "unless you're free, the machine will be prevented from working at all!"[21]

The nation's universities in the 1960s saw massive growth, with student numbers more than doubling. Commentators often wondered how it could be that a generation so privileged, raised in the abundant society of the long postwar economic boom, could turn radical. That, however, was the point. Given robust employment markets, student protest took place in the knowledge that an arrest or controversial stance would not automatically thwart personal prospects. The experience of rising standards of living, moreover, bred confidence in the capacity of the future to deliver better social outcomes, emboldening dissent, while the discrepancies between the world's most abundant society and its inequities suggested that a far greater level of fairness and inclusiveness could be

---

[21]   David Lance Goines, *The Free Speech Movement: Coming of Age in the 1960s* (Berkeley, Calif.: Ten Speed Press, 1963), p. 361.

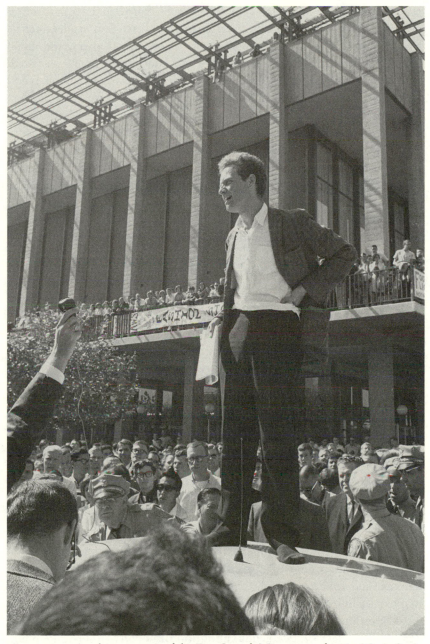

FIGURE 3.4. At a key moment of the Free Speech Movement of 1964, Mario Savio speaks from atop a police car containing his fellow student Jack Weinberg, who had been arrested for distributing political literature at Sproul Plaza, University of California, Berkeley. *Ronald L. Enfield.*

attained. Berkeley's example would soon be followed by many other protests as the youth radicalization deepened. New Left students challenged parietal rules, anticommunist restrictions on speakers, and racial segregation on campus – often with a charming irreverence, as when, at the University of Texas in 1964–65, the SDS chapter led a successful campaign to desegregate bathrooms under the inspired slogan "Let My People Go." As a national organization, however, SDS had largely directed its gaze off campus by 1964, emulating SNCC by seeking to stimulate "an interracial movement of the poor." Partly inspired by Harrington's *The Other America* (1962), this Economic Research and Action Project (ERAP) sponsored community organizing in the slums of northern cities such as Chicago, Cleveland, Newark, Baltimore, and Chester, Pennsylvania. There SDS radicalized further, once again testing the viability of a liberal–radical coalition. Work among the poor revealed the underdevelopment internal to the United States, exposing the paternalism, bureaucratic indifference, and sheer inadequacy of what liberals called the "welfare state." Social Security did not cover all workers, unemployment compensation was circumscribed, health care was often inaccessible, and inner-city schools were disastrous. "The welfare state is a myth," wrote Tom Hayden from Newark.[22]

In this, the New Left was engaging the very issues the black freedom movement was confronting as it moved from a primary concentration on legal rights to a more adamant pursuit of socioeconomic equality. After Kennedy's assassination, Johnson pushed through the Civil Rights Act in 1964 and the Voting Rights Act in 1965, but black ghetto uprisings simultaneously shook cities, beginning with Rochester, Harlem, and Philadelphia in 1964 and the Los Angeles district of Watts in 1965. The upheavals were a sharp reminder of what radicals had long said: that race was a national, not merely a southern, problem, and a matter of structural inequality, not attitude or law alone. In "From Protest to Politics," published in *Commentary* in 1965, Bayard Rustin held that "what began as a protest movement is being challenged to translate itself into a political movement" capable of addressing housing, employment, income, and education, and "concerned not merely with removing the barriers to full *opportunity* but with achieving the fact of *equality*." A "Freedom Budget" championed by Rustin the following year laid out a hearty social-democratic agenda: abolition of poverty, full employment,

---

[22] Tom Hayden, "The Politics of 'The Movement,'" in *The Radical Papers*, ed. Irving Howe (Garden City, New York: Anchor Books, 1966), p. 365.

universal health care. Rustin's view that protest was passé, however, implied that only within the Democratic Party could the coalition of unions, blacks, and liberals become a vehicle for an American social democracy. As two *Dissent* writers put it, "The main arena in which a radical coalition can work is the Democratic Party." In New Left circles, however, the MFDP's fate at Atlantic City had made "radical coalition" and "Democratic Party" a dubious pairing, implying radicalism's sacrifice to liberal *realpolitik*. To the young radicals, in contrast to Rustin, "protest" and "politics" were not antinomies; direct action, protest, and politics were complementary, as shown by northern school boycotts and rent strikes against slum conditions, black mobilizations for jobs and economic equality in places such as Cambridge, Maryland, and protests against police brutality by white officers patrolling black communities. Rustin's decision in 1964 to work for the AFL-CIO, a Cold War bastion under the hawkish George Meany, as director of a new A. Philip Randolph Institute appeared to young radicals increasingly suspicious of the "warfare-welfare state" likely to produce only cooption. Indeed, Randolph's long-held pacifism would be muffled at the height of the Vietnam War as he strove to sustain the Cold War liberal coalition, an irony given how unpopular the Vietnam War was compared to all the other wars Rustin had opposed. His "Freedom Budget" did not materialize as Vietnam dominated spending, crowding out programs aimed at meeting poor people's needs. Yet SDS's ERAP efforts proved no more successful and were abandoned as a method of compelling a redistribution of wealth as poor people proved hard to organize, white organizers were increasingly treated with skepticism in black neighborhoods, and New Left ambitions came to concentrate overwhelmingly on stopping the Vietnam War.[23]

Underlying the small chasm that had emerged between radicals and liberals by the mid-sixties was an array of generational differences in style and sensibility. By 1963 and 1964, observers recognized that cultural marginality was being embraced by numbers no longer quite so marginal. An ever-widening swathe of young people was attracted to avant-garde arts, free expression, easier sexual mores, and disaffection from the social and political mainstream – a "New Bohemia," as art journalist John Gruen called it, wider in scope than prior sheltered niches of aesthetes.

[23] Bayard Rustin, "From Protest to Politics," *Commentary*, February 1965; Emmanuel Geltman and Stanley R. Plastrik, "The Politics of Coalition," in *The Radical Papers*, ed. Irving Howe (Garden City, New York: Anchor, 1966), p. 387.

Something was happening out of the demographic bulge created by the postwar baby boom, consumer values of gratification disposing youth to experiment with illicit drugs and sexuality, the growth of student spaces around universities, and widening sentiment for civil rights and peace. Attendant to this was a romantic critique of profit, wealth accumulation, competition, and corporate power as inhibitive of self-fulfillment, free expression, intimacy, cooperation, and spiritual enlightenment.

One way culture, personal life, and political action were coming alive in this manner was in the first tremors of a new women's movement. The stirrings first emerged in the black freedom movement, where Rosa Parks, Ella Baker, Diane Nash, Gloria Richardson, and others impressed younger volunteer civil rights workers, suggesting assertive ways of being in the world very different from the passivity into which many postwar girls had been socialized. Young female civil rights workers read Simone de Beauvoir's *The Second Sex* (1953) and Betty Friedan's *The Feminine Mystique* (1963), which although it was later criticized for neglecting class and race was radical in objecting to the idea that women could be wholly satisfied by a life limited to domesticity and in arguing that no sphere of humanity should be closed off to their equal participation.[24] The National Organization for Women (NOW), soon to be founded by Friedan and others in 1966, would frame gender issues in civil rights terms, seeking to displace outmoded prejudices by education and legal reform – though it also included many seasoned activist women from the labor movement who vigorously promoted gender equality on the job. Young radical women took a more New Left approach in seeing biased gender norms as aspects of an overarching *system*. That view was first voiced within SNCC by two white southern-born women civil rights organizers, Mary King and Casey Hayden. In a 1964 SNCC position paper that they contributed anonymously for fear of ridicule, followed by "A Kind of Memo," a signed article in *Liberation* in 1965, King and Hayden identified a "sex-caste system" of male dominance within both society and radical movements, where leadership roles almost always went to men while secretarial and cooking chores corresponded to society's gendered division of labor. While the phrase "sex-caste" was clearly borrowed from the analytical prism of racial caste, the King–Hayden analysis also drew upon Port Huron in starting from the principle that private issues reflected public problems – "the personal is

---

[24] Simone de Beauvoir, *The Second Sex*, trans. H. M. Parshley (New York: Knopf, 1953), originally published as *Le deuxième sexe* (Paris, 1949).

political" – to challenge the male-dominated structures and ethos of the New Left.

Simultaneously, artistic currents were coming to assume more blatant political messages. *We Insist! Max Roach's Freedom Now Suite* (1960), a jazz album with a lunch counter sit-in depicted on its cover, had A-side songs on the Emancipation Proclamation's hundredth anniversary and the new protest movement, and B-side songs on African independence and apartheid. In "Alabama" (1963), saxophonist John Coltrane gave free-jazz expression to the freedom movement and rage at the Birmingham church bombing. Another indication of a trend toward a political arts, albeit in a more familiar folk form, was the young New Left singer-songwriter Phil Ochs, who took to the stage at rallies to sing the satirical "Draft Dodger's Rag" (1964) and "Love Me, I'm a Liberal" (1966), as well as his antiwar anthem "I Ain't Marching Anymore" (1965). In "Birmingham Sunday" (1964), Joan Baez memorialized bombing victims who died at the hands of white supremacists.

LeRoi Jones, meanwhile, cultivated an autonomous Black Arts movement, including poetry readings on the streets. The San Francisco Mime Troupe, a left-wing street theatre company with R. G. Davis as impresario, practiced what one of its creative lights, Peter Berg, in 1963 termed "guerrilla theater" – drama in public spaces to dislodge assumptions of the status quo. Mime Troupe actor Luis Valdez founded El Teatro Campesino in 1965 to support the UFW's Delano grape strike. Such efforts to take creative expression outdoors to provoke and inform pursued the avant-garde idea of breaking down distinctions between art and life. Street protest was ever more comfortable with theatrical expression, as giant effigies of warmongers and peace-lovers began to appear at rallies courtesy of German émigré Peter Schumann's Bread and Puppet Theater in the early 1960s.

By 1965, the young *Village Voice* editor Jack Newfield, writing in *The Nation*, pinpointed a "deep student alienation from the Great Society," with 1950s normality giving way to "underground movies, potsmoking, bohemian dress, idiosyncratic haircuts, and Bob Dylan" – and SDS and SNCC as "the political forms it takes." Here was a coming into plain view of an always-present but long-submerged element in the history of radicalism, namely the artistic criticism of bourgeois society. Both it and the left's more prominent pursuit, the social criticism of capitalist society for its inequalities and injustices, would flourish simultaneously, commingling and changing one another profoundly, in the sixties. The cultural left's bent toward transgression sharpened the strain between margin and mainstream for the radical left as a whole in the second half of the decade, and would present many issues. How was a political opposition in pursuit of a changed world to win influence among broad masses of people if the opposition flaunted its outsider status in esoteric cultural expression? Conversely, how could radicals striving to reach the mainstream expect to transform an oppressive society if they failed to shake free of the cultural and psychological costs of conformity? In the late 1960s, when interchange between margin and mainstream became not only conceivable but frequent, the interaction of artistic and social radicalism also became more fruitful, placing such questions in the forefront of the radical project.[25]

[25] Jack Newfield, "Idealism and Action," *The Nation*, 8 November 1965, p. 330.

4

The Revolution Will Be Live, 1965–1973

> The revolution will not be televised.
> The revolution will not be brought to you by Xerox
> in four parts without commercial interruptions...
> The revolution will be no re-run, brothers.
> The revolution will be live.
> – Gil Scott-Heron, "The Revolution Will Not Be
> Televised" (1970)

In spring 1968, the "Americong" – an inversion of Viet Cong, as Americans called the National Liberation Front in Vietnam – shocked the University of Pennsylvania by announcing a rally at which "home-made napalm" was to be applied "on the flesh of a dog." The Ivy League campus had already seen A. J. Muste address 1,200 at a 1965 teach-in, historian Gabriel Kolko lead a campaign of faculty and students that persuaded trustees to end secret chemical-biological weapons research in 1967, and protesters object to recruiting by Dow Chemical, napalm's manufacturer. Four years later, a photograph of nine-year-old Phan Thi Kim Phuc running naked down a road with burnt skin hanging from her back would epitomize the effects of the flammable jellied gasoline, but even in 1968, to napalm a dog was understood as appalling. At the appointed hour, two thousand people turned out to object – only to receive this message: "Congratulations, anti-napalm protest! You have saved the life of an innocent dog. Now your efforts should turn to protesting Dow Chemical and the U.S. government's continued use of this genocidal weapon against the civilian population of a tiny country 10,000 miles away."[1]

"The Americong" was 25-year-old Steven Kiyoshi Kuromiya, a member of Students for a Democratic Society (SDS) who early in the decade had taken part in Student Peace Union picketing against nuclear testing, a Congress of Racial Equality (CORE) sit-in on Maryland's highway, the 1963 March on Washington, and the 1965 Selma, Alabama, civil rights march. In 1966, Kuromiya started the Free University of Pennsylvania, making use of empty classrooms to offer radical classes. By 1968, he was growing his hair long and experimenting with psychedelics. Soon he would drop his first name and be known only by his Japanese names as his Asian American pride increased. His napalm dog fantasia showed a rare apprehension that consciousness is a matter of perspective, not just information, perhaps a function of his outsider status. Born in a relocation camp in Wyoming during the Second World War, he had known since he was nine, living in California, that he was attracted to other boys. When Kuromiya initiated the Gay Liberation Front (GLF) in Philadelphia in 1969, the name again was a play on National Liberation Front. "Do you think homosexuals are revolting?" read leaflets issued by New York's GLF. "You bet your sweet ass we are."[2]

It is safe to say that Che Guevara did not have gay liberation in mind when he called in 1967 for "two, three or many Vietnams" in his message to the Organization of the Solidarity of the Peoples of Africa, Asia, and Latin America, since revolutionary Cuba sent its known homosexuals to punitive labor camps. Gay liberation, however, was a product of the Vietnam radicalization. As draft resisters refused to serve in the military, Americans accused them of softness and weakness, prompting the New Left to greater militancy and masculinity. That, in turn, generated the eruption of both women's liberation and gay liberation, turning New Left analyses of oppression upon the New Left's own practices. The draft, meanwhile, compelled those attracted to others of the same sex to come to terms with their sexuality, since admission of homosexuality could disqualify one from service, sparing one from having to kill or die in Vietnam but eliciting ostracism from family, friends, and employers, accentuating a sense of injustice. "The army gave me a medal for killing

---

[1] "The Defiant Voices of S.D.S.," *Life*, 18 October 1968, pp. 80–96. The authors are indebted to the interview of Kuroshiya by Marc Stein, 17 June 1997, available at http://outhistory.org/exhibits/show/philadelphia-lgbt-interviews/interviews/kiyoshi-kuromiya.

[2] Donn Teal, *The Gay Militants* (New York: Stein and Day, 1971), p. 36.

a man," one bit of graffiti read, "and a dishonorable discharge for loving one."[3]

In 1969, as gays poured "out of the closets and into the streets" – a popular chant – Kuromiya was an eager participant. His first arrest had been in 1954 for having sex in a public park with another teenager; the judge warned him he was in danger of living a "lewd life." On the Fourth of July in 1965, Kuromiya took part in Philadelphia's first Independence Hall protest for homophile rights organized by Frank Kameny, a Washingtonian discharged from federal employment during the McCarthy era for homosexuality. The homophile milieu struck Kuromiya as courageous but staid, its male picketers wearing coats and ties, women dresses, to their protest. He preferred the late-decade eruption of gay liberation that identified with the hippie counterculture and the surging forces in the streets that the Rolling Stones's androgynous frontman Mick Jagger sang about in "Street Fighting Man" (1968) – the kaleidoscope of blacks, Puerto Ricans, Chicanos, American Indians, women, New Leftists, and antiwar demonstrators.

As a gay Third World militant, Kuromiya attended the Black Panther Party's Revolutionary People's Constitutional Convention at Temple University in September 1970. The Panthers inspired New Left awe, but Minister of Information Eldridge Cleaver had written in *Soul on Ice* (1968) that homosexuality is "a sickness, just as are baby-rape or wanting to become the head of General Motors." In August 1970, Panther founder Huey P. Newton overruled such prejudice, suggesting that homosexuals may be "the most oppressed people in the society" and stating that "a person should have the freedom to use his body in whatever way he wants." Gay men attending the Philadelphia Convention sought to push things further. In a statement read by Kuromiya to thousands of Panthers and their supporters, the gay male workshop argued for "all modes of human sexual self-expression" and "right of free physiological change," while opposing "false categories of homosexuality and heterosexuality." Kiyoshi Kuromiya thus personified the profusion of many radicalisms: Afro-Asian unity, racial equality, gay liberation, antiwar militancy, the counterculture. There were many revolutions within "The Revolution."[4]

---

[3] Kay Tobin and Randy Wicker, *The Gay Crusaders* (New York: Paperback Library, 1972), p. 10.

[4] Eldridge Cleaver, *Soul on Ice* (New York: McGraw-Hill, 1968), pp. 102, 109–110; Huey P. Newton, "The Women's Liberation and Gay Liberation Movements: August 15, 1970," in *To Die for the People: The Writings of Huey P. Newton* (New York: Random House, 1972), pp. 150–155; "Statement of Demands to the Revolutionary Peoples

The late 1960s and early 1970s saw what was, in range of constituencies tapped and scope of social, cultural, and political concerns addressed, the deepest, broadest radicalization of the twentieth century in the United States. The decisive year was 1968, a year of revolutionary aspiration akin to 1848 in European history, so climactic that a host of radicals would see themselves as "'68ers" for decades afterward. Between 1968 and 1973, both protesters and their established adversaries had the sense that the society as a whole was susceptible to a transformation that would make possible dramatically new ways of life. The Vietnam War – Vietnamese *Revolution* would better express its meaning for radicals – was revelatory for dissenters, showing all that was wrong with the old order and all the reasons for seeking a new one. Heightened contrast between old and new opened an exceptional historical moment. Suddenly, even in affluent societies believed to have achieved unprecedented stability, the range of social, cultural, and political criticism broadened, once far-out ideas gained wide audience, and provocative challenges to constituted authority and everyday assumptions not only took place but won the sympathy of many. The Vietnam-era radicalization called into doubt all established institutions (schools and universities; police, courts, and prisons; the press; conventional marriage) and authority in the workplace, military, professions, family, and culture. In the end, full-scale social reconstruction did not materialize, despite one outburst following another, with daring, sometimes foolhardy, moves. By 1970, the New Left rebellion was cresting with tremendous scope and force. It would remain dynamic until 1973 while undergoing a simultaneous fragmentation and experiencing repression that began to carry would-be revolutionaries, despite their convictions, back toward the margins.[5]

The year 1965 was a watershed for two reasons. First, passage of the Civil Rights and Voting Rights Acts meant federal action to eliminate legal racial segregation. With that success, the Southern freedom movement seemed to cede primacy to other causes; Malcolm X's assassination in February 1965 made him a martyr, and the burning of Watts in Los Angeles that summer by angry residents in response to police brutality indicated urban black America's profound restlessness in the face of deep-seated, ongoing structural inequities. The second event was

Constitutional Convention from the Male Representatives of National Gay Liberation," Temple University, Philadelphia, Sept. 5–7, 1970 [copy in authors' possession].

[5] According to one French '68er, the idea of Vietnam as a "revealing event" suffused the global radicalization: Michael Löwy, *The Marxism of Che Guevara*, 2nd ed. (Lanham, Md.: Rowman & Littlefield, 2007), p. 102.

President Lyndon Baines Johnson's massive escalation of the Vietnam War in February 1965, initiating the bombing of North Vietnam and deploying Marines to guard air bases in South Vietnam. Soon, Army soldiers were sent into jungles and rice paddies on routine search and destroy missions. With every subsequent year, the number of American troops in Vietnam increased, more bodies returned home in bags, and the antiwar movement multiplied in scale and feeling.

The result was a general radicalization of both the New Left and American society. The first half of the sixties had seen black momentum for freedom and the crystallization of a New Left embracing participatory democracy. The civil rights triumph demonstrated the capacity of movement-building and direct action to influence policy. That might have presaged the left-liberal alliance dreamt of in "realignment" scenarios, but because the Vietnam War was designed and escalated by liberals and endorsed by key liberal institutions, including most labor unions, New Leftists came to see liberalism as part of the problem. The black movement, now centered in the urban North, remained the central engine of American radicalism, but in the late 1960s Black Power became the keynote theme, new organizations such as the Black Panther Party took prominence, and even figures such as Martin Luther King sought to combine the dimensions of class and race in struggles for justice. Black militancy influenced related radicalisms among Chicanos, Asian Americans, Puerto Ricans, and others as the Vietnam War was borne disproportionately by draftees from poor communities of color. Neither of the New Left's two signature organizations – SDS and the Student Nonviolent Coordinating Committee (SNCC) – would outlast the decade of their birth, but the Vietnam-era radicalization was so deep, broad-based, and heterogeneous that it crested *after* their demise in 1969 and 1970. As the American armed forces in Vietnam destroyed villages to save them, revulsion at the "crackpot realism" of Establishment liberalism, as C. Wright Mills had put it, became widespread. Everything seemed worth reconsidering, including fixities in gender roles and human sexuality. Conversely, as peasant revolutionaries held out against the most powerful military on earth, anything seemed possible. The New Left expanded and morphed, its revolutionary imagination by turns visionary, innovative, and apocalyptic, with practical effects that were both liberating and self-marginalizing.

The Marines who splashed ashore at Da Nang in 1965 were told they were guarding a country from Communist invaders, but to the Vietnamese, the Americans were the invaders, following upon centuries of Chinese, French, and Japanese domination. U.S. intelligence officers entered Vietnam during the Second World War at the time of the alliance with the Soviet Union against the Axis Powers, in support of the Viet Minh, the Communist-led nationalist guerrillas then resisting Japanese occupation. Their leader, Ho Chi Minh, proclaimed Vietnam's independence in 1945, adapting Thomas Jefferson's Declaration of Independence, but the Truman administration opted to back France's postwar reassertion of colonial rule over Indochina – Cambodia, Laos, and Vietnam – in the belief that Ho was a Soviet proxy and that securing France's stability and cooperation was vital to the Cold War in Europe. France's attempt to subdue the Viet Minh, underwritten by the United States, ended in disastrous defeat at the mountain fortress of Dien Bien Phu in 1954. As France negotiated at Geneva its withdrawal from Vietnam, American radicals warned against picking up where it had left off. In *Monthly Review*, Leo Huberman and Paul Sweezy wrote, "Are we going to take the position that anti-Communism justifies anything, including colonialism, interference in the affairs of other countries, and aggression? That way, let us be perfectly clear about it, lies war and more war leading ultimately to full-scale national disaster."[6]

McCarthyism had purged the independent-minded "China hands" in the State Department who might have advised leaving Vietnam to the Vietnamese. The Geneva Accords partitioned the country into two zones in 1954: the north, controlled by Ho and the Communist-led Viet Minh, became the Democratic Republic of Vietnam, its capital in Hanoi; the south, its capital in Saigon, became the State (later, the Republic) of Vietnam. The Accords provided for Vietnam's reunification through elections in 1956, but American officials, fearing Communist victory, counseled South Vietnamese ruler Ngo Dinh Diem against allowing such elections. Among the architects of this approach were Cold War social democrats whose bitter experiences made them archcritics of "totalitarianism," willing to countenance almost anything to prevent a Communist advance. The Austrian émigré Gustav Richter, who took the name Joseph Buttinger, met Diem in Vietnam in the 1940s while serving as a CIA agent with the International Rescue Committee, provided half the funding to launch *Dissent* in 1954, then formed the American Friends of Vietnam in 1955. The *New Leader* praised Diem's "One-Man Democratic Rule," a

---

[6] Leo Huberman and Paul Sweezy, "What Every American Should Know About Indo-China," *Monthly Review* 6 (June 1954), pp. 70–71.

system the Vietnamese tended to see as dictatorship. By 1960 Viet Minh remnants responded to harsh repression emanating from Saigon by reconstituting themselves as the National Liberation Front (NLF) and initiating guerrilla war – characterized by quick strikes, after which fighters melt back into their native terrain – against the South Vietnamese government. The NLF in the South, though it included various nationalist elements, was Communist-led and underwritten and overseen by North Vietnam.[7]

At first Cold War conformity gave no hint that involvement in Vietnam would generate massive dissent. Neither the Second World War nor the Korean War had generated much protest outside radical pacifist circles, and the New Left took far more interest in Cuba. Kennedy, however, made Vietnam more noticeable as he increased the number of U.S. military "advisors" – often, in reality, combat soldiers – to 16,000. When Buddhist monks in South Vietnam began to immolate themselves against discrimination by the small Catholic elite that had collaborated with the French and continued to dominate the nation, the Kennedy administration and U.S. intelligence operatives in Vietnam countenanced a military coup that killed Diem and put an authoritarian junta in his place in 1963.

The radical left provided the earliest critics of the Vietnam intervention. The *National Guardian* reported on Indochina beginning in the 1950s and by 1962 was printing dispatches by Australian journalist Wilfred Burchett. At Easter 1963, members of the Student Peace Union (SPU) joined with the Young Socialist Alliance (YSA) to raise signs calling for withdrawal of U.S. military forces from Vietnam at a peace rally in New York City, but the liberal Committee for a Sane Nuclear Policy (SANE) complained, seeing the demand as one that would discredit the cause, and Bayard Rustin, War Resisters League (WRL) executive secretary, ordered the signs be taken down. In October 1963, the WRL, SPU, and SDS picketed in Washington and New York against visiting Madame Ngo Dinh Nhu, sister-in-law of Diem. Already in New Left circles, the premises of the looming war were viewed with skepticism. "How do the Negroes defending 'democracy' in Vietnam feel about the defense that democracy gets in Mississippi?" one Freedom Summer volunteer wondered in July 1964.[8]

One of the first organizations devoted exclusively to ending the Vietnam War was the May 2nd Movement (M2M), named for the date in

[7] Wesley R. Fishel, "Vietnam's One-Man Democratic Rule," *New Leader*, November 1959.
[8] Dave Dellinger, *From Yale to Jail: The Life Story of a Moral Dissenter* (1993), p. 189; Elizabeth Sutherland, ed., *Letters from Mississippi* (New York: Signet, 1966), p. 137.

1964 it set for protests against U.S. intervention in Vietnam. Controlled by the Progressive Labor Party (PLP), a radical group sympathetic to Mao's China, and calling openly for NLF victory against "imperialism," M2M's protests were small. The wider left became more active after August 1964, when Congress passed the Gulf of Tonkin Resolution, with only two Senators, both Democrats, opposed: Wayne Morse of Oregon and Ernest Gruening of Alaska. Passed at a moment when it seemed North Vietnam had fired on American ships (a claim later much disputed), the resolution authorized the President to use "all necessary steps" to repel aggression in Southeast Asia, giving Johnson a virtual blank check for war. Nevertheless, SDS endorsed Johnson in 1964's presidential election. SDS was still balancing a community-organizing, grass-roots radicalism with a "realignment" strategy of pushing the Democrats toward whole-hearted social reform. SDS went "Part of the Way with LBJ" – a modification of the Democrats' slogan "All the Way with LBJ" – in order to avert the threat posed by the extremely conservative Republican candidate Barry Goldwater, who opposed federal civil rights action and suggested he might use nuclear weapons in Vietnam. In *Liberation*, Sidney Lens objected that once-radical parties, from Socialist to Communist, had subordinated themselves thoroughly to the Democrats, making 1964 a low point for American radicalism. President Johnson, meanwhile, worried about a scenario of McCarthyism redux in which Republicans would blame him for losing Vietnam as they blamed Truman for losing China. During the campaign, he soft-pedaled Vietnam, vowing that he sought "no wider war" – while laying plans for escalation. Alongside a "War on Poverty" declaration intended to "out-liberal" the Kennedys at a time when most Americans still identified with liberalism, Johnson would use whatever force was necessary to prevail in Vietnam, short of replicating Korea by recklessly provoking China into the conflict.

Despite five years of the Movement, the New Left was still obscure to most Americans. The first *New York Times* profile of a "new student left" did not appear until 1965, and insofar as SDS was known, it was for civil rights, antipoverty organizing, and university reform, not foreign policy. On March 19, 1965, SDSers Todd Gitlin and Mike Davis organized a mass sit-in at Chase Manhattan Bank headquarters in New York City to object to loans to South Africa, in the first American civil disobedience against the apartheid regime. In that same spirit, SDS called the first national march and demonstration against the Vietnam War, setting a date of April 17, 1965, for Washington, D.C. The poster read, "Why are we burning, torturing, killing the people of Vietnam? . . . To prevent free elections." Because SDS – believing obsessive anti-Communism a hindrance – did not follow the standard Cold War liberal practice of excluding Communist front groups such as the Du Bois Clubs or M2M from the march's endorsers, Americans for Democratic Action urged liberals against attending, and the League for Industrial Democracy disassociated itself from SDS, which in the aftermath would relocate its national offices from New York to Chicago.

Coming after Johnson's escalation of the war by U.S. troop deployments and massive aerial bombing in February and March 1965, the planned demonstration swelled far beyond SDS's expectations. A crowd of 25,000 – then a stunning number for a protest against American foreign policy – arrived in Washington on April 17, picketed the White House for two hours, and gathered at the Washington Monument to hear speakers including I. F. Stone and Sen. Ernest Gruening, while President Johnson's Texas ranch was picketed by Austin SDSers. The most memorable address was by 25-year-old SDS president Paul Potter, who observed that the Vietnam War severed the "illusion that morality and democracy are the guiding principles of American foreign policy." The President's advisors were not "particularly evil men" – "if asked to throw napalm on the back of a 10-year-old child they would shrink in horror" – but their failure to abide by the Geneva Accords was resulting in destruction being "hurled indiscriminately on women and children, insurgent and neutral, upon the first suspicion of rebel activity." Potter concluded by posing an analytical problem:

What kind of system is it that justifies the United States or any country seizing the destinies of the Vietnamese people and using them callously for its own purpose? What kind of system is it that disenfranchises people in the South, leaves millions upon millions of people throughout the country impoverished and excluded from the mainstream and promise of American society, that creates faceless and terrible bureaucracies and makes those the place where people spend their lives and do their work, that consistently puts material values before human values – and still persists in calling itself free and still persists in finding itself fit to police the world? . . . We must name that system. We must name it, describe it, analyze it, understand it and change it.[9]

As Potter's speech illustrates, from the outset New Left radicals saw the war as a product of the same system that had generated racism, poverty, alienation, and bureaucracy. Potter left his audience searching

---

[9] *On April 17, 1965, 25,000 people participated in a March on Washington to End the War in Vietnam* (Chicago, Ill.: Students for a Democratic Society, 1965).

for the right words because he declined to use the words "capitalism" or "imperialism," to him the cant of the thirties. Carl Oglesby, Potter's successor as SDS president, would propose "corporate liberalism" as the system's name at a Washington demonstration half a year later – a phrase first suggested by William Appleman Williams and *Studies on the Left*. "The original commitment in Vietnam was made by President Truman, a mainstream liberal," Oglesby observed. "It was seconded by President Eisenhower, a moderate liberal. It was intensified by the late President Kennedy, a flaming liberal.... They are not moral monsters. They are all honorable men. They are all liberals." Not, however, liberals of the "authentically humanist" sort, like Thomas Jefferson and Thomas Paine, for corporate liberals sought to "safeguard ... American interests around the world against revolution or revolutionary change, which they always call Communism." In Iran and Guatemala, Oglesby noted, the United States intervened to overthrow elected governments; it supported white-supremacist regimes in Rhodesia and South Africa. It was an "illiberal liberalism" that believed in markets, little else. So eloquent was Oglesby in making a case that containment functioned to prevent democratic revolutions – elaborated in his book *Containment and Change* (1967) – that few then noticed that "corporate liberalism" better described an ideology or policy than the basic form of organization of the economy and society. By decade's end, indeed, many New Left radicals, including Oglesby, would name the system capitalism and imperialism.[10]

Radicals might aspire to transform the whole system so as to prevent a variety of interventions but the more immediate task was to educate a wider public about the Vietnam War. Among the first forms of anti-war organizing were "teach-ins." These marathon lecture and discussion sessions, begun at the University of Michigan, often included invitations to State Department officials or pro-war academics, but they tended to shy away from critical audiences, making the teach-ins forums for the war's opponents. The most controversial teach-in occurred at Rutgers in New Jersey in April 1965, where a 34-year-old Marxist historian of American slavery, Eugene Genovese, declared that he would welcome a Viet Cong victory. The largest was at Berkeley, where a Vietnam Day Committee (VDC) organized by Jerry Rubin and others drew tens of thousands to a 36-hour outdoor rally in May 1965, with speeches by New Left luminaries. Mario Savio connected the conditions that had

[10] Carl Oglesby, "Trapped in a System," in *The New Left: A Documentary History*, ed. Massimo Teodori (Indianapolis, Ind.: Bobbs-Merrill, 1969), pp. 182–188.

spawned the Free Speech Movement to the Vietnam War, holding that both revealed a bureaucratic liberal failure to allow ordinary people to make decisions. Hal Draper called for immediate, unconditional withdrawal from Vietnam, in contrast to negotiated or gradual withdrawal. Yale historian Staughton Lynd, who had organized freedom schools in Mississippi, stated that given the war's escalation, the "coalition" politics advised by Bayard Rustin and Michael Harrington would mean "coalition with the Marines." SNCC's best-known organizer, Robert Parris – the former Bob Moses, who had adopted his middle name as surname so as not to be cast as Moses and left Mississippi so that his new media renown not inhibit participatory democracy – connected American attitudes toward the Vietnamese and black Americans. When Parris looked at a photo taken in Vietnam he said he saw "a little colored boy standing against a wire fence with a big huge white Marine with a gun in his back.... But what I knew was that the people in this country saw a Communist rebel. And that we travel in different realities. And that the problem in working for peace in Vietnam is how to change the isolated sense of reality this country has."[11]

By autumn 1965, the VDC was making plans to block trains carrying draftees to leave for Vietnam. Tactics would not have progressed so quickly against the war – from education to civil disobedience – without a ten-year backdrop of action stretching back to Montgomery. In fact, as Berkeley's teach-in showed, the civil rights, radical pacifist, and student movements were retooling themselves to form a new mass antiwar movement. In August 1965, veterans of Mississippi Freedom Summer and the Freedom Democratic Party convened an Assembly of Unrepresented People in Washington to challenge the major parties' consensus, ending with a march on the Capitol against the Vietnam War. Hundreds were arrested. When New York City's Fifth Avenue Peace Parade Committee was established in September 1965, its leaders included WRL chair Norma Becker and Cora Weiss, a Women Strike for Peace (WSP) activist who had led a recall effort in Madison, Wisconsin, in 1953 aimed at Sen. Joseph McCarthy (the "Joe Must Go" campaign). In March, Alice Herz, an 82-year old German-Jewish émigré and WSP member in Detroit, immolated herself in protest, emulating Vietnam's Buddhist monks, to be followed in November by the self-immolation of Baltimore Quaker Norman Morrison outside the Pentagon. Both acts prompted debate

[11] *We Accuse* (Berkeley, Calif., and San Francisco, Calif.: Diablo Press, 1965), pp. 150, 156.

among radical pacifists between those who saw it as a powerful form of witness and those for whom suicide was itself violence. In January 1966, SNCC became the first civil rights organization to go on record against the war and for draft resistance. "We maintain," SNCC stated, "that our country's cry of 'preserve freedom in the world' is a hypocritical mask behind which it squashes liberation movements which are not bound and refuse to be bound by expediency of U.S. Cold War policy."[12]

"Dancing in the Street," a 1964 hit for Motown group Martha and the Vandellas, celebrated urban summers, but the song provided another backbeat as "long hot summers" took on new meaning. The Watts uprising, when young blacks trashed white-owned businesses and were suppressed by the National Guard, established a pattern in which real or rumored white police brutality against black people led to upheavals lacking a clear direction or voice. "The masses were fighting *against* something," wrote two black radicals after Watts, "but it was not a rebellion *for* something." That did not prevent governmental authorities, the news media, or much of the white public from linking these upheavals to "Black Power," a slogan raised by SNCC field secretary Willie Ricks on a march through Mississippi in June 1966 to protest the shooting of James Meredith who had been on his own solo march for civil rights. In SNCC's new chairman Stokely Carmichael, Black Power found a brilliant exponent as SNCC organized the Lowndes County Freedom Organization in an Alabama county where a black majority was deprived of voting rights and political representation. Here Black Power was merely an extension of "Let the People Decide." The slogan arose at a time when all the nation's major city mayors were white, and in 1966, when the Georgia state legislature refused to seat duly elected Julian Bond, a 25-year-old SNCC officer, on the pretext of his opposition to the Vietnam War. Not until 1967 would Carl Stokes in Cleveland, Ohio, become the first elected black mayor of a major American city.[13]

Black Power both had a basic democratic meaning and reflected the alienation felt by many young black radicals. Sometimes the move toward disaffiliation was total. When Robert Parris, traveling in Africa late in 1965, noticed State Department publications using his story to claim vitality for American democracy, he broke off all ties with white friends

---

[12] SNCC, "Statement on Vietnam War," in *The New Left*, ed. Teodori, p. 252.
[13] Richard Price and Bob Stewart, "Watts, L.A.: A First Hand Report – Rebellion without Ideology," *Liberator*, September 1965, p. 6.

and relocated to Africa. To government officials and the press, however, Black Power suggested an ominous turn toward inverse racism and violence. When a riot broke out in Atlanta in 1966, its police chief blamed SNCC, arrested Carmichael, and called SNCC "The Non-Student Violent Committee." Later that year, SNCC's efforts to implant itself in Philadelphia, Mississippi, were damaged when police raids yielded two sticks of dynamite, which SNCC's James Forman said were planted by an informant. Insofar as Black Power did mean a shift away from nonviolence, it was at least initially toward armed self-defense as advocated by Malcolm X and practiced by the Deacons for Defense and Justice, a group that by 1966 was countering the Klan with several hundred members in Louisiana and Mississippi. For Carmichael and others, the freedom movement had always been more about self-determination than integration.[14]

Radical initiatives increasingly took place on parallel white and black tracks. The Southern Student Organizing Committee (SSOC), a white analogue to SNCC founded in 1964, aimed to organize poor white southerners against racism, even as SNCC underwent a wrenching transformation. To remain at the center of black radicalism after 1965 would require SNCC to shift from South to North, from rural to urban, and from a staff organization to a mass membership base. After Atlantic City in 1964, with black skepticism of white liberal paternalism mounting, something on the order of one hundred white students chose to remain on SNCC staff rather than return from Mississippi Freedom Summer to their studies. Although the presence of whites in certain southern localities merely provoked segregationist ire, and although black fieldworkers were better at encouraging local people to organize, whites from northern middle-class backgrounds often had a verbosity that caused them to take over decision making, and SNCC's black members perceived them to be more self-involved than altruistic. Tensions lingered over interracial sexuality between black men and white women during Freedom Summer. SNCC had traditionally been majority-black, and some black field staff sought an all-black organization. Under the strong influence of *The Autobiography of Malcolm X,* published posthumously in 1965, and the new currents of black liberation swirling, they despaired at the seeming implacability of white society and the hypocrisy of law enforcement, as when a verdict of innocent was returned for the killer of Sammy Younge, Jr., a black SNCC worker shot in January 1966 for trying to use a whites-only

[14] "Atlanta's Image Tarnished as 1,000 Negroes Riot," *Seattle Daily Times,* 7 September 1966, p. 2.

rest room while registering voters in Macon County, Georgia. Longtime white SNCC staff understood the logic of self-determination behind their being asked to leave in December 1966, but still felt profoundly the loss of black and white togetherness. Texas-born Casey Hayden, active in SNCC since 1960, found herself "conflicted and depressed," both "empathizing with the feelings expressed and sure that the public implications were tragic." As other organizations, including CORE, underwent similar transformations, financial support from northern white liberals plummeted as a result of hostile press about Black Power, SNCC's "human rights" positions in regard to Vietnam and Palestine after the 1967 Arab-Israeli War, and Carmichael's journeys to Hanoi and Havana in 1967.[15]

To the press, Black Power seemed a broadside against all whites, but that was not the point as far as black radicals were concerned: it was the absence of power for blacks in American society that produced their anger. Their quest to refashion America was often drowned out by media hyping the most reckless proclamations, including those by Carmichael's successor as head of SNCC, H. Rap Brown, who encouraged urban destruction with the slogan, "Burn, Baby, Burn!" The tempo of black rage climaxed in the summer of 1967 in 59 cities, including Newark and Detroit, where trigger-happy police and National Guardsmen killed many in crowds looting and torching mainly white-owned ghetto stores, followed by federal troop deployment and arrests of 7,200. LeRoi Jones (soon to change his name to Amiri Baraka), arrested in the Newark upheaval for possession of illegal handguns, organized a Black Power conference that attracted 700 nationally visible black militants to Newark, including Carmichael and Brown. For white radicals, the 1967 eruptions made a profound impression. Tom Hayden, writing from Newark, where he had organized for four years, termed them "rebellions," protests against injustice. While warning that "stagnancy and conservatism are essential facts of ghetto life," he suggested "conditions slowly are being created for an American form of guerrilla warfare based in the slums." In Detroit, where high winds spread fires, block after block of businesses and homes were ruined, the damage totaling $40 million. Longtime Detroit radicals James and Grace Lee Boggs were moved to distinguish rebellion from revolution – the former, they implied, inchoate, the latter tied to communal responsibility. Before long, the Dodge Revolutionary Union Movement (DRUM) emerged from a May 1968 wildcat

---

[15] Casey Hayden, "Fields of Blue," in *Deep in Our Hearts: Nine White Women in the Freedom Movement* (Athens: University of Georgia Press, 2000), p. 368.

strike at a Chrysler plant in Detroit as a challenge to both management and union, from which the League of Revolutionary Black Workers would emerge in 1969, fusing race and class politics.[16]

On a national level, the breakthrough organization of 1967 was the Black Panther Party for Self-Defense, which provided a new, transfixing model for the left, at first primarily in the Bay Area. It had been founded in October 1966 in Oakland, California, by Merritt College students Huey P. Newton, born in Louisiana, and Bobby Seale, born in Texas, who had taken part in a Soul Students Advisory Council influenced by Max Stanford's Revolutionary Action Movement. As an animal ferocious only if attacked, the panther was first used as a symbol by the Lowndes County Freedom Organization. Oakland's Black Panthers gave armed self-defense new meaning as they shadowed white police officers through the night in black neighborhoods, bearing rifles and law books as they monitored police conduct. Their 10-point program called for "power to determine the destiny of our black community"; a United Nations plebiscite to determine whether black-majority communities should remain politically part of the United States; housing, jobs, and education; exemption of black men from military service; and freedom for all black inmates given their conviction and sentencing by white-dominated courts. This heady mix of black-nationalist disaffiliation from white America, a socialist vision of an economy run for public benefit, and an ethos of community service offered to finesse the conflict between black identity and interracial leftism. The Panthers pursued their agenda with publicity-seeking brio. In May 1967, when California legislators and Governor Ronald Reagan threatened a bill forbidding loaded weapons from being carried in public in order to halt Panther patrols, thirty Panthers clad in leather jackets, berets, and dark sunglasses entered the State Capitol building in Sacramento carrying loaded rifles and shotguns, making international news. Their tough, even menacing, talk against authorities was a bravura combination of publicity and performance. The 25-year-old Newton – arrested after a 1967 shootout left a white police officer dead – compared black American urban areas with Third World colonies, stating from jail that black people were "brutalized" and "treated very much as the Vietnamese people." Since the Panthers' revolutionary black nationalism was set against narrow "cultural nationalism" and open to alliance with radical whites, "Power to the People" soon gave a Panther inflection to New

[16] Tom Hayden, *Rebellion in Newark: Official Violence and Ghetto Response* (New York: Vintage, 1967), pp. 68–69.

FIGURE 4.1. The Black Panther Party, founded late in 1966, made "armed self-defense" a major priority and heightened black militancy. Lt. Elmer Dixon leads a 1969 Panther protest on the steps of Washington state capitol, Olympia, Washington, to protest a bill that would make it a crime to display firearms in a manner meant to intimidate others. *State Governors' Negative Collection, 1949–1975, Washington State Archives. Original images held at the Washington State Archives, Olympia, WA.*

Left aspirations for democracy from below. Given the deradicalization of Bayard Rustin, black pacifism seemed in eclipse; SNCC's last act before vanishing in 1969 after a brief, ill-fated alliance with the Panthers was to strike "Nonviolent" from its name.[17]

Mounting black militancy from 1965 to 1967 reverberated throughout the New Left just as the Vietnam War became a hot-button issue. Criticism of the war gained steam by early 1966 in elite circles as televised hearings were convened by J. William Fulbright of Arkansas, chair of the Senate Foreign Relations Committee. Later that year, antiwar insurgent Robert Scheer achieved 45 percent of the Democratic primary vote

[17]   Newton quotations from the film *Off the Pig* (Newsreel, 1968).

in California's Oakland-Berkeley U.S. House district, nearly defeating a war-supporting incumbent. By 1970, the same district would elect black antiwar social democrat Ron Dellums. Such developments gave rise to talk of "New Politics" – a bloc against war and racism within the Democrats – but such work "inside the system" had limitations, given that Democratic leaders were the architects of the Vietnam War and that youth in a number of states could not vote, despite being subject to the draft. Not until 1971, after massive campus revolts, would a Constitutional amendment fix the voting age at 18, one of many democratizing achievements provoked by New Left activism.

Opposition to the war mainly registered in mass protest. As SDS did not wish to be defined by a single issue or devote all its resources to national antiwar demonstrations, that crucial task fell to an ad hoc coalition that operated across the late sixties under a series of names, usually with Mobilization in the title. Known colloquially as "the Mobe," this included pacifist organizations such as the WRL and Committee for Non-Violent Action (which merged into the WRL in 1968), as well as the Socialist Workers Party (SWP) and Communist Party USA (CPUSA), which set aside their many differences to build massive protests in Washington, New York, and the Bay Area in 1966 and 1967. Here again Old Left mingled with New. *Viet-Report*, launched in 1965 by 25-year-old editor Carol Brightman, carried one article in its first issue by graduate student Martin Nicolaus, 24, and two by Yale historian Staughton Lynd, 35.

A major uptick in campus dissent came after February 1966, when the Selective Service announced that university students, formerly given automatic deferments, would be subject to conscription if their academic performance was weak. To SDS this made the war no longer *an* issue but *the* paramount issue – an assessment made more out of moral objection rather than personal worry, since studies consistently showed that New Left students had higher-than-average grade points, making them the least likely to be drafted. What drove student dissent was perceived university complicity in the apparatus of war. At the University of Chicago, SDS led an occupation of the administration building in objection to "transformation of this University into a coding and classifying machine for the Selective Service." While the class-rank schema was modified within a year, the draft continued to be a focal point of student unrest – and not only among men targeted by the draft. In October 1966, ten SDS women of the Austin, Texas, chapter sat in for a day at the Selective Service office to show that conscription did not affect men alone. Soon radicals were targeting universities for complicity in the war via military recruitment, Reserve Officer Training Corps (ROTC) programs, and military-funded research. Students carried out "power structure" research to reveal the compromising links of their institutions to the central decision makers of "the system." At Harvard in late 1966, Secretary of Defense Robert McNamara arrived to speak to a select handful of students but found his car surrounded by a thousand rowdy SDS-led protesters.[18]

Countless new constituencies entered into opposition against the war, well beyond the campuses. A Lawyers Committee on American Policy Toward Vietnam, formed in 1965, argued that the war was unconstitutional and violated international law. Within the military, dissent materialized: James Johnson, Dennis Mora, and David Samos, Army privates at Fort Hood in Texas, refused assignment to Vietnam in 1966; Special Forces sergeant Donald Duncan wrote an antiwar article that same year for *Ramparts*; and Captain Howard Levy, a Fort Jackson, South Carolina, doctor, was court-martialed in 1967 for refusing to train Green Berets leaving for Vietnam. The rapid expansion of opposition to the war was nowhere more clear than on April 4, 1967, when Martin Luther King, Jr., delivered an address at Riverside Church in Manhattan linking the war to racism and misguided social priorities while condemning "the greatest purveyor of violence in the world today – my own government." The *New York Times* and *Washington Post* condemned the speech as too radical, as did NAACP and Urban League leaders. Speaking to a large audience of Clergy and Laity Concerned About Vietnam, King joined not only longtime religious opponents of war, such as the Quakers, but also Protestants such as Yale's chaplain William Sloane Coffin, rabbis such as Abraham Joshua Heschel, and Catholics such as the brother priests Daniel and Philip Berrigan, who often engaged in civil disobedience, as when Philip Berrigan was arrested with three others in 1967 for pouring blood over Selective Service records in Baltimore. In 1967, Muhammad Ali, the 25-year-old black Muslim heavyweight boxing champion of the world, refused to be drafted, declaring, "Man, I ain't got no quarrel with them Viet Cong." Soon protest signs appeared stating, "No Viet Cong Ever Called Me Nigger."[19]

To radicals, the Vietnam War was not merely a "mistake" but the consequence and crowning symbol of empire, a social system. Yet in seeing the war as immoral they shared a great deal with those Oglesby had called "humanist liberals." The technologies used in Vietnam, including fragmentation bombs, napalm, and the defoliant Agent Orange; the

---

[18]   Kirkpatrick Sale, *SDS* (New York: Vintage, 1974), p. 256.
[19]   Mike Marqusee, *Redemption Song: Muhammad Ali and the Spirit of the Sixties* (New York: Verso, 1999), p. 162.

Pentagon's measurement of success by body counts; the declaration of "free-fire zones"; and the routine burning of villages led critics of the war to see American strategy as directed against civilians. Opponents thought the war presented Americans with a moral responsibility akin to that faced by ordinary Germans under the Nazis. For this reason the movement was disposed to put bodies upon the levers, in Savio's phrasing, rather than replicate German obedience and acquiescence in the destruction of European Jewry. The postwar sense of the Second World War as a "good war" in this way cut against preservation of consent during the Vietnam War. Early in 1967, when former Stanford University student president David Harris and others in California urged young men to openly defy Selective Service in a "fill the jails" campaign modeled on the civil rights movement, they called their effort The Resistance, borrowing the name of French opposition to collaboration with Nazism.

Despite the admonitions of the Johnson administration that criticism of the war emboldened the Communist enemy, organizers often sought internationalist solidarity with the people of Vietnam. In late December 1965, Lynd and Hayden traveled together with Communist historian Herbert Aptheker to North Vietnam to meet NLF representatives. A few hundred more American visitors would follow suit in coming years – including Muste, who turned 82 in Hanoi on his final birthday in 1967. While often denounced as traitors or naïve, some of the travelers returned with released U.S. prisoners of war or messages home to their families. American radicals connected with Vietnamese delegates at meetings in other locations as well, from Stockholm to Bratislava, and a reciprocal internationalism arose in the spread of protests around the world against the U.S. war. From France to Japan, Vietnam propelled a global surge of youth radicalism that was opposed not only to conservatism but also to social-democratic labor parties subordinate to American foreign policy and to stodgy Communist states – or what Trotsky's biographer Isaac Deutscher at Berkeley's Vietnam Day called "capitalist oligarchies here, bureaucratic oligarchies there." When Che Guevara spoke of "two, three, or many Vietnams" in 1967, radical leftists took his call as ennobling Vietnam, Cuba, and Che himself, the Argentinian doctor who risked all for the Cuban Revolution and was killed that year in the Bolivia highlands. "Let me say," he wrote in "Socialism and the New Man" (1967), "with the risk of appearing ridiculous, that the true revolutionary is guided by strong feelings of love."[20]

---

[20] Isaac Deutscher in *We Accuse*, p. 51; *Venceremos! The Speeches and Writings of Ernesto Che Guevara* (London: Weidenfeld and Nicolson, 1968), p. 398.

Amidst this broadening circle of internationalist solidarity and revolutionary enthusiasm were numerous fissures in the worldwide left and antiwar movement. In the United States, the "democratic left," or social democracy, was so wedded to anti-Communism that it tread warily, not wanting to give comfort to a North Vietnam in the Soviet camp. Many liberals and social democrats endorsed the Johnson administration and Cold War, while others, such as Arthur Schlesinger, called for cease fire and negotiations. Radicals considered such calls for negotiation merely a pretext for the United States to prolong its hold in Vietnam, insisting instead on unconditional, immediate withdrawal. Bayard Rustin, in a move at odds with his long record of radical pacifism but in keeping with his new "coalition" politics, called for negotiation, as did Max Shachtman. The Socialist Party, dominated by such moderate and right-wing social democrats, declined to oppose the Vietnam War categorically in the 1960s, which rendered it mostly irrelevant to young sixties radicals. Irving Howe, likewise, penned "New Styles in 'Leftism'" in the summer 1965 *Dissent*, rapping young radicals for indifference to Communist dictatorship in the Third World, irresponsibility in their bohemian style, and moralism in place of strategy. New radical styles nevertheless kept unfurling, sometimes with both theatricality and efficacy, as when the VDC's Jerry Rubin, subpoenaed by HUAC in 1966, appeared in an antiquarian Revolutionary War costume to protest aspersions against dissent as "un-American."

To Hal Draper and the Independent Socialist Clubs, who sought a third camp independent of Washington and Hanoi, a slender reed of hope in Vietnam existed in the Buddhist movement. *New Politics* offered the case for a socialist-Buddhist "third way" in an article by Tran Van Dinh in 1966. It had to be acknowledged, however, that the NLF would prevail in event of American withdrawal, given its popularity in comparison to the U.S.-subsidized Saigon regime. This gave rise to heated debates in *Liberation* in 1965–66 over whether radical pacifists could keep their principles while entering into the antiwar cause with those favoring NLF victory. Would that simply invert the mistake of those who chose the United States? Would it be tantamount to condoning NLF violence? Or should social revolutions for national self-determination be supported even if the oppressed chose means pacifists would not prefer? When Bradford Lyttle, a veteran of Muste's Committee for Non-Violent Action (CNVA) who helped create *Liberation* and participated in 1950s antibomb protests, argued that Vietnamese opponents of the Saigon dictatorship should mobilize "massive and imaginative non-violent resistance" rather than guerrilla warfare, Staughton Lynd responded that devastating levels of bombing by the United States and terror by the South Vietnamese regime meant American pacifists should emphasize withdrawal of U.S. forces, not second-guess tactics chosen by the Vietnamese resistance. In his search for a middle way between absolutist pacifism and unrestrained revolutionary violence, Lynd argued against torture by any party and criticized the International War Crimes Tribunal – convened in Europe by Bertrand Russell and Jean-Paul Sartre in 1967 with several Americans taking part, including Carl Oglesby – for investigating only U.S. and South Vietnamese government atrocities, not ones committed by Communists.[21]

Most demonstrators and marchers did not worry over fine points of strategy; they were simply "against the war." Key organizers, however, disagreed over many aspects: whether mounting large demonstrations or civil disobedience was best; whether the movement should openly support the NLF and North Vietnam or not; whether to engage in electoral politics and, if so, through independent campaigns or with peace-minded Democrats; and whether to limit demands at mass rallies to ending the war, or add other left-wing demands. In such debates, certain groups held firm positions. The SWP and its YSA affiliate were workhorses in the Mobe and Student Mobilization Committee (SMC), carrying out essential but thankless tasks. As revolutionary socialists, they were often programmatically radical – insisting on "Out Now" – but tactically moderate, seeking to attract as many Americans as possible to antiwar demonstrations. Civil disobedience they saw as costly in bail, court fees, and time. Their single-issue, safe-and-legal, mass-action approach bothered New Left radicals who saw it as inhibiting or resented "the Trots" for caucusing and pressing their line, although their view wasn't so far from that of the Beat poet Allen Ginsberg when he wrote, "Announce it is a safe march, bring your grandmother and babies, bring your family and friends." Even The Resistance came in for criticism by other New Left radicals who instead of openly defying conscription favored its evasion: failing the draft physical, admitting drug use, declaring psychological troubles, or fleeing to Canada. Revolutionary socialist groups, in yet a third approach to conscription, tended to advise members to accept being drafted and organize within the military, as the Bolsheviks had done fifty years earlier during the Russian Revolution of 1917.[22]

---

[21] Bradford Lyttle, "Nonviolence in Vietnam," *Liberation*, September 1965, p. 18; Staughton Lynd, "Comment," *Liberation*, September 1965, p. 19.
[22] Allen Ginsberg, "Berkeley Vietnam Days," *Liberation*, January 1966, p. 42.

As SDS grew from 3,000 members in 1965 to 15,000 in 1966 and 30,000 by 1967, it coursed with debates over strategy and theory. A generational shift meant that the Port Huron cohort, by 1966 called the "Old Guard," had ceded control to newcomers who began to inject new perspectives in the pamphlets issued by the SDS-affiliated Radical Education Project and *New Left Notes*, a newsletter launched in 1966. The Old Guard established the Movement for a Democratic Society (MDS) and the New University Conference (NUC), adult counterparts to SDS and clearinghouses for radicals in the professions. With their exit, SDS lost most of its social-democratic "realignment" bloc while retaining commitment to participatory democracy and grassroots organizing, now grafted onto a new "prairie populism" arising from public universities such as Nebraska (Carl Davidson), Iowa State (Gregory Calvert and Jane Adams), and Texas (Jeff Shero and Robert Pardun). This leadership, largely male, had a more homespun, action-oriented style than SDS's early, largely Eastern-bred intellectual leadership. Reflecting the rising oppositional mood on campus, skeptical of liberalism and the state, and inclined toward decentralism, it favored a move away from the Economic Research and Action Project (ERAP) and back to the campuses, a return inspired by the Free Speech Movement, with a bent toward what Davidson called "student syndicalism." In affinity for the new youth culture, most "prairie power" men sported droopy mustaches.

Simultaneously, Progressive Labor (PL) dissolved its May 2nd Movement and entered SDS in 1966. Although SDS was disinclined to bar anyone from joining and thought of itself as too amorphous to be capturable, PL's entry would prove fateful, ultimately transforming SDS. Created in 1962 by Milton Rosen, a one-time William Z. Foster supporter suspended from the Communist Party for criticism of Khrushchev's Soviet Union, PL had a cadre disciplined in promoting "Marxism-Leninism" and loyal to a leadership outside SDS. Initially PL had a bohemian air but by 1966 its male members were cropping their hair short and wearing work shirts in assumed proletarian style despite their strength on elite campuses such as Harvard, Columbia, and Yale. PL claimed to possess the one true position, and its line could pivot sharply. Its members would argue repetitiously, tying up conversations once full of mutual give-and-take. Furthermore, PL's Maoism gave it some advantage as China's "Great Proletarian Cultural Revolution" unfolded between 1966 and 1968, with throngs of Chinese students marching in Red Guards, waving little red books, and backing Chairman Mao against his opponents, perceived or real, in the Communist party-state. These developments in a faraway, largely quarantined country were hard to parse. Some on the left, such as PL, valued Mao for upholding the legacy of Stalin, to which they remained loyal against Khrushchev's "revisionism"; others, paradoxically, were drawn to the Cultural Revolution as *anti*authoritarian and *anti*bureaucratic. Mao's admirers among American radicals in the 1960s were grouped around *Monthly Review* and the *Guardian* (*National* was dropped from the title as its founders were pushed out and it came under New Left control in 1967). They felt substantiated by *Fanshen* (1966), a book by William Hinton, an American eyewitness to the early Chinese Revolution from 1945 to 1953, as well as reports from the few Americans living in China, such as longtime Communist advocate Anna Louise Strong, black radical Vicki Garvin (who polished translations for *Peking Review*), and David and Nancy Milton, whose son Chris, upon returning to the United States, gave an interview about what he had seen to the Bay Area newspaper *The Movement*, reprinted as an SDS pamphlet. That developments in China gave off every semblance of a mass purge accompanied by inculcation of a cult of personality under Mao was maintained by many Trotskyists, social democrats, and independent radicals, but many on the New Left – even those who disdained PL – were attracted to Mao's Cultural Revolution by 1968 because it seemed consonant with the worldwide youth rebellion, the Black Panthers espoused it, and it looked like a dynamic alternative to dreary Soviet-style statism.

Until 1968, PL was kept at bay by the New Left's strong sense that students could play catalytic roles and that the industrial working class was absorbed within the system and far from revolutionary in advanced capitalism. The latter theme, suggested by Mills, was also associated with Herbert Marcuse, a German émigré philosopher, in *One-Dimensional Man* (1964). Among SDS regulars – particularly in New York – a parallel eclectic social theory was developing that saw a "new working class" as central in technological society, making possible a "post-scarcity" economy. As a term, "new working class" was drawn from French New Leftists André Gorz and Serge Mallet, who described those who did not own capital but were highly educated, including technical, clerical, professional, and white-collar workers motivated by a search for expanded control, meaning, and creativity in work rather than material demands. This helped explain both the massive postwar expansion of "the multiversity" and why a radical movement had arisen of students demanding greater democratic control over their lives.

Two of the national SDS leaders most identified with the new working class perspective had, in fact, been raised in old working-class households, Carl Davidson in Pennsylvania and Greg Calvert in Washington state. Calvert, son of a logger, was raised by Finnish grandparents who belonged to the Industrial Workers of the World. In a widely reproduced speech given at Princeton, he cited Guatemalan guerrillas who, upon entering a village, did not talk about the "anti-imperialist struggle" or pass out Mao's *On Contradiction* but asked villagers to speak about their individual lives so they would recognize their problems were shared. Radicals, Calvert argued, see society as oppressive and seek to free *themselves*, whereas liberals see *others* as oppressed and wish to "uplift" them. If, as new working-class theory indicated, white students were part of an exploited work force rather than "middle class," they would have an interest in uniting with others. Calvert was the first SDS leader to speak of SDS as "revolutionary" and himself as a "revolutionary socialist." Those were ambiguous terms given his evocation of Third World guerrillas, but his own intention was to signal the revolutionary pacifism of *Liberation* magazine, which had become an open forum for New Left radicalism.

In 1967, in a phrase Calvert coined, SDS began to move "from protest to resistance": from objecting to the war to halting it. Simultaneously, mass protest reached new dimensions. Half a million people turned out in San Francisco and New York for the April 15 Spring Mobilization, with 170 young men, including a Green Beret reservist, burning their draft cards in the Sheep Meadow in Central Park. Vietnam Veterans Against the War (VVAW) formed soon afterward, to be swollen in the following years by ranks of returning American combat soldiers embittered at a government that, as one put it, was "mainly interested in protecting American business interests around the world by using us as cannon fodder for their war." VVAW would march together with Veterans for Peace at the head of many parades with banners stating, "Support our GIs . . . Bring them home, now!" Vietnam Summer, the brainchild of scholar–activist Gar Alperovitz, repurposing a concept first tried in Freedom Summer, sent three thousand young canvassers door to door around the country in 1967 to spark local organizing and pressure legislators. In August, longhair radicals Abbie Hoffman and Jerry Rubin threw fistfuls of dollars from the observer platform at the New York Stock Exchange and watched traders scurry after the bills, with Hoffman setting fire to a few dollars on Wall Street afterward, stating it was "more important to burn dollar bills than draft cards" since dollars symbolized the system.[23]

---

[23] VVAW organizer Mark Hartford quoted in Lauren Kessler, *After All These Years: Sixties Ideals in a Different World* (New York: Thunder's Mouth, 1990), p. 41; Hoffman quoted

Militancy heightened in autumn 1967. New Left radicals began experimenting with tactics under the influence of the summer's ghetto explosions, the Black Panthers, and the Zengakuren (Japanese students who wore helmets and carried thick poles for battling police), as well as the "foco" theory of Fidel Castro and Che Guevara, which suggested that small bands of revolutionaries in "a mobile strategic force" could spark socialist revolution, as popularized by French writer Régis Debray in *Revolution in the Revolution?* (1967). Although Guevara was killed in Bolivia as he tried to enact foco theory, his death enhanced his romantic allure, and Debray's book, published by Monthly Review Press, was read avidly by SDSers seeking an alternative to PL. Others too sought bolder resistance, but within a nonviolent framework. The first day of Berkeley's "Stop the Draft Week" in mid-October saw Joan Baez and dozens more arrested in civil disobedience at the Oakland draft induction center, followed in successive days by more combative attempts of students to shut it down by clashing with baton-wielding police in the streets – and succeeding in doing so on one day. In Madison, a Dow recruitment sit-in ended in a mêlée as police used brute force to clear a university building. That month in Washington, D.C., the largest Mobe demonstration to date featured a speech by Dr. Benjamin Spock, whose baby-care book was a perennial bestseller, and a march on the Pentagon, where youths sat down before Army soldiers and placed flowers in their gun barrels while Abbie Hoffman and Allen Ginsberg tried to "levitate" the building in a new hallucinogenic style some found ridiculous, others bemusing.

Even as the antiwar movement increasingly united in seeing itself as up against a military-industrial *Pax Americana*, internal divisions widened. Some radicals advocated outreach, organizing, and demonstration to further the erosion of support for the war in public opinion. Others, frustrated by horrific death and destruction in Vietnam despite years of demonstrations, were increasingly in favor of confrontation, no matter how alienating to the American public, so as to raise the cost of the war by making the country ungovernable. "One of the great political fallacies of the movement is to make a direct association between the choice of tactics and the degree of radical commitment to end the war and change the system," warned 31-year-old Mobe co-chair Sidney Peck at the end of 1967. To reach beyond the movement's "very limited social base" of students, he observed, would require "profound confidence in the wisdom

in Jonah Raskin, *For the Hell of It: The Life and Times of Abbie Hoffman* (Berkeley: University of California Press, 1996): 112.

of the people to recognize that a war of this kind, by whatever name, is harmful to their genuine interests."[24]

The year 1968 was one of global rebellion, crystallizing a worldwide New Left turn toward revolution East and West, North and South. In January and February in Vietnam, as U.S. troop levels peaked at more than 500,000, the NLF carried out the Tet Offensive, a coordinated assault against military targets in more than 100 locations. Within weeks, U.S. and South Vietnamese forces beat back and decimated the NLF, but the rebels' prowess – penetrating even the U.S. embassy compound in Saigon – made a mockery of U.S. claims of progress toward victory. By March, polls showed a steep decline in the percentage of Americans who believed the Vietnam War winnable or worthwhile. In May in France, *gauchiste* student strikes sparked factory occupations by workers. Millions teemed through the streets of Paris, their slogans including "All Power to the Imagination" and "Be Realistic, Demand the Impossible." As youthful *enragés* tore up cobblestones to erect barricades, France made it seem possible that revolution might materialize even in advanced capitalist countries built around ostensibly benevolent welfare states – at least until conservative President Charles de Gaulle regained the upper hand. In Czechoslovakia, the Prague Spring, a reform Communism permitting greater freedom of expression under head of state Alexander Dubček, was crushed in August by the tanks of the Soviet Union, now led by Leonid Brezhnev, who had deposed Khrushchev and reverted toward neo-Stalinist bureaucratic rule. In Mexico, untold numbers of student protesters were shot and killed in Tlatelolco Plaza in October, and later that month at the Olympics in Mexico City, sprinters Tommie Smith and John Carlos, American gold and bronze medal winners in the 200-meter dash, bowed their heads and raised black-gloved fists in a Black Power salute while "The Star-Spangled Banner" played, later to be stripped of their medals for the protest.

Even in the United States, revolution began to gain appeal, especially as violence seemed to shut down all openings for reform. Senator Eugene McCarthy, an opponent of the Vietnam War, scored a surprise near-win in New Hampshire's Democratic primary in March 1968, prompting the still more popular liberal Senator Robert F. Kennedy to enter the presidential race. On March 31, President Johnson, reeling from Tet and the

---

[24] Sidney M. Peck, "Notes on Strategies and Tactics: The Movement Against the War," *New Politics*, Fall 1967, pp. 42–55.

electoral challenge, announced he would not stand for reelection. The New Left was elated at having deposed a war-making president, but the exuberance was cut short on April 4, when Martin Luther King, who had told advisors he considered himself a democratic socialist and was organizing a Poor People's Campaign, was killed while visiting Memphis in support of a black garbage workers' strike. For many radicals, black and white, King's assassination spelled the end to nonviolence. Riots broke out in 125 American cities, compelling federal troops to set up machine guns on the steps of the nation's Capitol. A few weeks later, at Columbia University in New York City, the Students' Afro-American Society and campus SDS chapter led students in occupying five buildings and held a dean hostage to object to university war complicity in the Institute for Defense Analysis and plans to build a gym encroaching on Harlem. Faculty liberals were appalled, but student leftists found support from other New York intellectuals, including a white-haired Dwight Macdonald returning to the radical fray. Before the action Columbia SDS was divided between an analysis-oriented "praxis axis" and confrontational "action faction," but all were radicalized after police bloodied and arrested many hundreds of students and faculty. The Columbia takeover brought national visibility to SDS. Tom Hayden – who took part in the occupation of Mathematics Hall – called for "Two, Three, Many Columbias" in *Ramparts*. By autumn, SDS had some 80,000 members.[25]

In June, Bobby Kennedy, who had just won California's primary, was assassinated, all but guaranteeing the Democratic nomination would go to Vice President Hubert Humphrey, a Cold War liberal and Vietnam War supporter. That August at the Democratic National Convention in Chicago, peaceful protests called by the Mobilization – with Hayden and Rennie Davis, old SDS hands, as organizers alongside Dellinger – included a speech by Black Panther Bobby Seale and facetious nomination of a pig for President by Abbie Hoffman and Jerry Rubin, now calling themselves "Yippies." As the police force of Mayor Richard J. Daley's Democratic machine meted out brutal beatings to delegates and demonstrators alike while television cameras rolled, protestors chanted, "The whole world is watching!" Polls showed the American public endorsed the police, appalling radicals who increasingly spoke of a "fascist" danger even as they discerned a need for revolution. That November, Republican Richard Nixon's presidential victory seemed to signal even greater likelihood of repression. A New Left protest vehicle, the Peace and Freedom

[25] Tom Hayden, "Two, Three, Many Columbias," *Ramparts*, 15 June 1968, p. 40.

Party, mounted a presidential campaign in thirteen states, including California and New York, but even with two recognized figures at the top of its ticket, Black Panther Chairman Eldridge Cleaver or the black comedian Dick Gregory, depending on the state, Peace and Freedom trailed that year's actual third party, George Wallace's American Independent Party, a white backlash campaign that endorsed the war and opposed the civil rights revolution.

Everywhere, a youth "counterculture" – new styles of living extrapolated from the small bohemian pockets cultivated by earlier cultural radicalisms – expanded exponentially after the so-called Summer of Love of 1967 in San Francisco's Haight-Ashbury neighborhood. Hippies were often apolitical, seeking to free body and mind through a Dionysian revelry of drugs, sexual freedom, dance, and mysticism. Some, as Hunter S. Thompson wrote, saw politics as "just another game," being "content to lie back in their pads and smile at the world through a fog of marijuana smoke." But the hippies did share values with New Left "politicos" – community, freedom, honesty, love, indifference to possessions – and left–counterculture syntheses found expression in the Yippies and the underground press. With forerunners in *The Village Voice* and satirist Paul Krassner's *The Realist* (created in 1955 and 1958, respectively), underground papers began to sprout up after the onetime Trotskyist Art Kunkin launched the *Los Angeles Free Press* in 1964. The *Berkeley Barb*, *East Village Other* (New York), *Fifth Estate* (Detroit), *Rag* (Austin, Texas), *Chicago Seed*, *Great Speckled Bird* (Atlanta), *Old Mole* (Boston), *Rat* (New York), and *San Francisco Express Times* followed suit. Often published by collectives, they printed news copy distributed by Liberation News Service (LNS), founded in 1967 by Raymond Mungo and Marshall Bloom. A glossier variant was *Ramparts*, which broke some major investigative stories, as when, in 1966, it exposed Michigan State University linkages to South Vietnam. In 1967, *Ramparts* showed that the CIA had for many years funded the National Student Association; later it proved the CIA had subsidized other key Cold War liberal institutions, including the Congress for Cultural Freedom, *Encounter,* and the *New Leader*. The counterculture and New Left commingled in other "freak" settings: food co-ops, "free universities," G.I. coffeehouses, bookstores, communes, radio stations. Rock 'n' roll eclipsed folk music – which John Lennon of the Beatles called "people with fruity voices trying to keep alive something old and dead" – as the center of left-wing musical expression. Many rock bands mocked the war. The Fugs, founded by Ed Sanders and Tuli Kupferberg, sang "Kill for Peace" as early as 1965. Country Joe and the Fish, fronted by red-diaper babies who came together for Berkeley's 1965 teach-in, wrote "The 'Fish' Cheer/I-Feel-Like-I'm-Fixin'-to-Die Rag" (1967) and played Woodstock in 1969. This was the politicized edge of the counterculture, which John Sinclair, manager of the Detroit band the MC-5, called a "revolutionary culture" created by a "youth colony" up against the "death machine." Small clusters of anarchists, owing something to the Dutch Provos and French Situationists, began to mix surrealist art with radical politics. The anarchist collective Black Mask changed Wall Street signs to "War Street" in 1967; the Diggers, inspired by seventeenth-century English radicals, distributed free food and clothes in the Bay Area; and Up Against the Wall Motherfuckers, a Lower East Side group named for a line in a LeRoi Jones poem, spread humorous chaos wherever they went.[26]

Also blending cultural and political revolution were revolutionary black nationalism and Marxism, paradigms far more influential in the zeitgeist of 1968 than anarchism. Among black radicals revolutionary nationalism was ascendant, although differences existed over what form it should take. The Republic of New Afrika, formed at a Detroit meeting in 1968 by attorney Milton Henry and others, advocated a new and separate black nation of five southern states and reparations for slavery, while James Boggs, in a 1966 essay included in his brisk-selling collection *Racism and the Class Struggle* (1970), declared, "The City is the Black Man's Land," arguing that blacks should seek power in urban America. Maoism's appeal was rising, synchronously, as a revolutionary alternative to conventional Communism on a global scale. Jean-Paul Sartre and other French intellectuals embraced Mao's criticism of Soviet "revisionism," which seemed to explain Soviet suppression of dissent in Czechoslovakia as well as French Communist Party (PCF) attempts to blunt student–worker militancy during May 1968. Aphorisms from *Quotations from Chairman Mao* – "Let a hundred flowers bloom," "A revolution is not a dinner party," "Political power grows out of the barrel of a gun" – appeared with increasing regularity on the American left. In "Revolution" (1968), the Beatles sang, "if you go carrying pictures of Chairman Mao, you're not going to make it with anyone anyhow," but the song's blaring chords conveyed a revolutionary élan, and John Lennon

[26] Hunter S. Thompson, "The 'Hashbury' Is the Capital of the Hippies," *New York Times*, 14 May 1967, p. 124; John Lennon and John Sinclair in *Counterculture and Revolution*, ed. David Horowitz, Michael P. Lerner, and Craig Pyes (New York: Random House, 1972), pp. 70–85, 197.

would soon wear a Mao cap. The vogue of Maoism made the CPUSA, if still perceived as "subversive" by many Americans, seem relatively conservative for giving tacit support to the Democratic Party against the Goldwater–Nixon–Bircher right and holding to a pro-Soviet allegiance. It did, however, find a hip new face in Angela Davis, a Marcuse protégé resplendent in her Afro, although her status as an icon of militancy was always at variance with her organizational affiliation, considered stodgy by most of the New Left.

Tet, Paris, Prague, Mexico: the system-shaking revolts of 1968, East and West, North and South, also gave new influence to Trotskyism, a revolutionary Marxism opposed to capitalism and bureaucratic Communism alike. In France, Alain Krivine and others in La Jeunesse Communiste Revolutionnaire (JCR) were prominent in the May upheaval. In Britain, many in the *New Left Review* circle were drawn to Trotskyism, including prominent antiwar leader Tariq Ali, a young Pakistani Oxford graduate. Isaac Deutscher and the Marxist economist Ernest Mandel lent Trotskyism intellectual gravitas, criticizing the Eastern European states and Western "neo-capitalism" while applying Trotsky's theory of permanent revolution to underdeveloped countries such as Cuba and Vietnam – although differences among Trotskyists soon erupted over whether, in underdeveloped nations, guerrilla struggles waged from the countryside could substitute for mass labor organizing in the cities.

Revolutionary socialism's attractiveness owed much to the deep impression made by the Black Panther Party. Before 1968 the Panthers had fewer than one hundred members, but in the aftermath of King's assassination, as black anger fueled desire for organization, chapters shot up in dozens of cities including Milwaukee, Indianapolis, Winston-Salem, Baltimore, Seattle, and New Orleans. Membership peaked at around five thousand in 1969, with a fame reaching far beyond. By demanding black community control, toting arms, and building alliances with the Peace and Freedom Party and other chiefly white organizations, the Panthers hit upon a potent formula that spoke to black militancy while offering a focal point for the whole left. Their magnetism was enhanced by riveting iconography, from stylized dress to Emory Douglas's brilliant artwork in the party newspaper, and by Eldridge Cleaver's sly cleverness as a speaker. So impressive was the Panther example that many kindred groups sprang up between 1967 and 1970: the Young Lords Party among Puerto Ricans, the Brown Berets among Chicanos, the Red Guards and I Wor Kuen among Asian Americans, the Young Patriot Party among Appalachian migrants to Chicago, and the White Panther Party of John Sinclair in Michigan. New Left radicals read *Soul on Ice*, raised the clenched fist, and wore Panther buttons proclaiming "Free Huey!"

Despite their electrifying effect on the whole radical movement, the Black Panthers had many contradictions. They were at one and the same time inspirational and unstable, brilliant and reckless, eloquent and crude, idealistic and corrupt, formidable and vulnerable. The Panthers reclaimed a "black is beautiful" dignity in the face of official brutality, challenging white-dominated law enforcement, but armed self-defense always competed in their thought and practice with schemes to drive "pigs" from the black community in a hail of bullets. A few days after King's death in 1968, teenage Panther Bobby Hutton died unarmed with hands raised in an Oakland gunfight the Panthers blamed on police but which Cleaver later stated was motivated by his desire to avenge King and elevate his moxie to a plane coequal with Huey Newton's. Charged with the attempted murder of two police officers, Cleaver fled to Cuba late in 1968 and from there to Algeria, unwilling to return to incarceration since prior marijuana and rape convictions had once confined him to Soledad and Folsom prisons. Although polls showed a broad radicalization among black Americans, few older black working people joined the Panthers, seeing them as an invitation to trouble. Young white and black radicals, however, were dazzled by the Panthers' audacity and chants:

> The revolution has come!
> Off the pig.
> Time to pick up the gun.
> Off the pig.

Despite the Panthers' courage and boldness, two major problems hamstrung them. The first was the aspect of chaos swirling beneath the surface even as media images of tight Panther formations imparted an aura of discipline. The Panthers held that the poorest and most downtrodden were the optimal revolutionary subjects. Many of their members were former gang members or convicts, which added to the Panther view of violence as a legitimate means of freeing colonial subjects from oppression and resulted in physical intimidation within their ranks and against rivals. Police provocateurs bore probable responsibility for a shootout with Ron Karenga's nationalist U.S. Organization on the University of California, Los Angeles, campus in 1969 that left two Panthers dead: Bunchy Carter, who had once headed the feared Slausons gang, and John Huggins, former college student. In many other instances, however, the Panthers themselves were initiators of bloodshed. In 1969 in

New Haven, Connecticut, the Panthers brutally tortured and executed Alex Rackley, a 19-year-old Panther from Florida wrongly accused of being a police informant. Despite Panther efforts to draw lines between revolutionary discipline and what they called "jackanape" behavior – robbery and other criminality – they directly organized some underworld activity themselves, and in predicating themselves on a volatile demographic of street toughs distanced themselves from other segments of the black community in whose interest, as a whole, they sought to speak.

By 1969, the Panthers sought to soften their image and build a better base in the community, initiating a Free Breakfast for Children program to "serve the people" and put "politics in command" above military strategy, the phrases being Mao's. The first Panthers had all been men, but women were crucial to these community programs, and after SNCC member Kathleen Neal married Cleaver in 1967, becoming Kathleen Cleaver, she was the first woman to join the Panther central committee. At the same time Panther warrior culture entailed a machismo typified by Eldridge Cleaver's talk of "pussy power," the notion that women should withhold sexual pleasure from men who were not committed Panthers. When the 100-strong chapter in Des Moines, Iowa, founded by Mary Rem and linked to chapters in Omaha and Kansas City, was told by Oakland leaders to make Cleaver's book *Soul on Ice* mandatory reading, Iowan Panthers were shocked by his confessions of rape as an insurrectionary act. "Why would you do women like this?" one of them, Charles Knox, remembers asking. The Des Moines chapter adhered to party policy against drugs and alcohol, but when its members visited Oakland they discovered Panther leaders condoning usage "in moderation." As incarceration and exile left leadership vacuums, women such as Elaine Brown and Ericka Huggins assumed leadership positions and argued against misogyny within the movement. When Huey Newton was released on a technicality in August 1970 he issued a strong Panther endorsement of the women's and gay liberation movements, but he turned out to be a poor speaker and insecure leader who resided in a luxury penthouse while indulging heavily in cognac and cocaine. Some black-owned stores in Oakland that donated food to the breakfast program accused the Panthers of extortion.[27]

<hr />

[27] Reynaldo Anderson, "Practical Internationalists: The Story of the Des Moines, Iowa, Black Panther Party," in *Groundwork: Local Black Freedom Movements in America*, ed. Komozi Woodard et al. (New York: New York University Press, 2005), p. 294.

A second critical problem for the Black Panther Party was the tremendous ferocity of state repression visited upon it, magnified by ambiguity within Panther ranks as to whether taking up arms implied self-defense or guerrilla action. Taunting police forces for their blatant racism showed extraordinary courage, propelling the Panthers' rise, but calling them "pigs" destined to become "bacon" while openly displaying firearms was a magnet for harassment. Hundreds of Panthers were arrested between 1968 and 1970, tying up their time and resources. In Houston, Lee Otis Johnson, chairman of the local SNCC chapter and a Black Panther member, was sentenced to 30 years in jail in 1968 for passing a single marijuana joint to an undercover officer. Chicago police killed Fred Hampton, Illinois's highest-ranked Panther, and Peoria chapter leader Mark Clark in a 1969 raid while Hampton was asleep in bed. Panther Chairman Bobby Seale was charged with "conspiracy" in the Chicago protests of 1968, bound and gagged for outspokenness in court, and then charged separately with ordering the Rackley murder; he was found not guilty but imprisoned anyway for contempt of court. The New York leadership was arrested in 1969 and accused of a massive bombing plot, becoming the "Panther 21" until fully acquitted in 1971. While all of this repression was real, in a painstakingly methodical 1971 *New Yorker* article the investigative journalist Edward Jay Epstein found the oft-repeated claim that police had outright murdered twenty-eight Panthers to be without basis. Additional factors weakened the Panthers, including political differences, personal tensions, and rapid growth. Panther leaders who had never worked closely together, separated by great distances, had little basis for trust. In 1971, Newton purged Cleaver's more insurrectionist followers and directed all Panthers to move to Oakland, where for several years they acquired some local influence under Elaine Brown, despite Newton fleeing to Cuba to avoid prosecution on charges of killing a prostitute. By the late 1970s, the party, despite running a respected school, had withered even in Oakland.

The Black Panther Party had a galvanizing symbolic effect comparable to James Brown's "Say it Loud, I'm Black and I'm Proud" (1968). It also, for all its contradictions, left a material legacy. The Panthers' free-breakfast programs fed many needy children at a rate that the War on Poverty, initially, found hard to match. When a U.S. Senator asked the federal school lunch program coordinator if it was true that the Black Panthers fed more poor children than the state of California, the official was forced to admit it was "probably true." As Congress, embarrassed at being outdone by black militants, mandated free lunches for all children below poverty level, school breakfast funding quintupled from $3.5 million in 1969 to $18 million in 1973. In Pennsylvania alone, the number of free meals rocketed from 25,000 to 2.8 million within a year.[28]

The end of the 1960s saw a duality of crescendo and fragmentation in radicalism. A crescendo came as more Americans than ever before saw the Vietnam War as unjust, as white and black youth identified with black liberation, and as the radicalization achieved a vastness of scale and forms. After a decade of political and cultural metamorphosis, many anticipated a consummate social transformation lying ahead. Revolution was a live option, the exhilaration well captured by San Francisco rock band Jefferson Airplane in "Volunteers of America" (1969), a song that made revolution a verb: "Look what's happening out in the street / Got a revolution, got to revolution." This revolutionary hopefulness produced many searching and creative innovations that would reshape American culture, although in some insurrectionary fantasies or apocalyptic visions it took on surreal qualities. The Movement, once expressed with a capital letter, began to fragment and divide so that it became difficult to imagine it singularly. One radical in 1969 perceived it as "a time when most movement meetings look like something from *Marat/Sade*," alluding to a play set in a lunatic asylum.[29]

The left's disintegration was actively sought by the Federal Bureau of Investigation and its director J. Edgar Hoover, who considered radical dissent of all types to be subversion, rather than an exercise of rights to association and speech. Hoover's first COINTELPRO – or Counterintelligence Program, aimed at disruption of radicalism, not mere surveillance – targeted the Communist Party in 1956; a second such program, in 1962, the Socialist Workers Party. Under Hoover, the Bureau's special agents were virtually all white and all male. In 1967, the FBI launched a COINTELPRO against SNCC, the Black Panther Party, and other black radical groups, intending to "disrupt, misdirect, discredit, or otherwise neutralize the activities of black nationalist" organizations so as to prevent "the rise of a 'messiah' who could unify, and electrify, the militant black nationalist movement." A COINTELPRO against the broad New Left was launched in 1968, supplemented by Army Intelligence, the MHCHAOS program of the CIA, and local red squads. These surreptitious efforts, unknown to

---

[28] Susan Levine, *School Lunch Politics: The Surprising History of America's Favorite Welfare Program* (Princeton, N.J.: Princeton University Press, 2008), pp. 139, 141.
[29] Steve Halliwell, "The Liberation Conference," *Liberation*, November 1969, p. 40.

the public, continued until 1971, just before Hoover's death. They flourished as older and more open methods, such as HUAC, were blunted by court rulings or lost cultural power. In addition to the FBI's illicit break-ins and thousands of paid informants, COINTELPRO techniques included spreading false derogatory information known as "bad jacketing" against honest radicals. Operatives spread rumors, for instance, that Stokely Carmichael was a CIA agent.

Given the shadowy nature of the FBI's role and the incompleteness of documentary releases, its precise place in the shattering of the New Left is impossible to gauge with precision. When Marshall Bloom, Liberation News Service's founder, committed suicide in 1969, it may have been due to inner conflicts about his homosexuality – or to a poison-pen letter the FBI circulated about him. Richard Aoki, a Japanese American, had long been a paid FBI informant when he provided the Black Panthers with their first guns in 1967. The Panthers' security captain in Chicago was a paid informer who supplied the FBI with the map police used in the raid that killed Fred Hampton. In Washington, D.C., police paid for the creation of an entire radical bookstore and meeting space, the Red House Collective, to gather intelligence on leftists. Provocateurs sought to discredit radicals, as when an Army intelligence sergeant posing as a New Leftist threw a chair at right-wing San Francisco State president S. I. Hayakawa during a speech of his in Colorado. In other instances, law enforcement agencies encouraged moderation, as the FBI did in pseudounderground newspapers it created and published in Texas and Indiana. The New Left's increasing need to devote time and resources to legal defense surely hampered its growth, but repression did not always succeed. A barrage of "conspiracy" charges was countered, often effectively, by radical lawyers William Kunstler, Charles Garry, Leonard Weinglass, and others. Economic repression could be effective, as when the FBI persuaded major record companies to cease advertising in underground newspapers, drying up a major source of income, or when employers discharged radicals from employment, as when New Left historians Staughton Lynd and Jesse Lemisch lost their positions at Yale and the University of Chicago, respectively. The FBI sought to disorient and demoralize radical leaders, sending Martin Luther King a transcript of his sexual dalliances along with a suggestion he commit suicide, for example, and strove to foment division and dissension within radical organizations, already alive with internal controversies over strategic dilemmas.

As factionalism, paranoia, and violence rose, nowhere did they prove more destructive than in SDS. By 1968 and 1969, SDS's national council meetings and conventions, dominated by youth in their twenties, were an ongoing battle. SDS regulars, led by a "national office collective" in Chicago that was impressed by black radicalism, warred with PL, which posited itself as the champion of the industrial working class. Most SDSers resented PL's obstructionism as it condemned the Black Panthers, SNCC, and DRUM on the grounds that "all nationalism is reactionary" and called the Vietnamese NLF "sell-outs" for negotiating with the United States and taking "revisionist" Soviet aid. All the same, Marxism was gaining among young radicals whose opposition to the war had led them to object to capitalism and imperialism, lending plausibility to PL's idea of building a Worker-Student Alliance. To meet this challenge, SDS regulars called for a Revolutionary Youth Movement (RYM) favoring solidarity with the Panthers and outreach to white working-class youth. To them the struggle was not merely between themselves and PL but between PL and the Movement. In countering PL, however, they became more like it: more dogmatic, more given to citations of Lenin and Mao, more enthralled by centralized power, less likely to listen to idiosyncratic perspectives. Lost were quieter voices. Disturbed by armed-struggle language he considered unsuited to the United States, Greg Calvert thought both PL and RYM posed as auxiliaries to someone else's revolution, whether blacks or workers, thus succumbing to white guilt and upper-middle-class self-hatred. When SDS issued a James Forman pamphlet, *Liberation Will Come from a Black Thing*, whose title Calvert felt slighted the many other constituencies whose contributions would be needed to carry out revolution, he left for Texas. In a similar vein, the lesbian pacifist Barbara Deming published "On Revolution and Equilibrium," a call for more reflective radical approaches, in *Liberation* in 1968.

Out of the debate in SDS came Weatherman, soon to test new extremities in radical marginality. Its name derived from a line in a Bob Dylan song that supplied a catchy title for an otherwise ponderous document, "You Don't Need a Weatherman to Know Which Way the Wind Blows." The paper, which I. F. Stone called a "mishmash of ill-digested pseudo-Marxist rubbish" and which Carl Oglesby said if read closely would cause one to go blind, held that the main clash in world politics was between national liberation movements and imperialism, so that the real revolution lay in the Third World and black ghettos, not U.S. factories or campuses. The document title's reference was a jab at PL as a pseudovanguard, but Weatherman was equally cocksure, an attitude that may have arisen out of the clash with PL or because Weatherman (a particular faction within RYM) was comprised disproportionately of the offspring of wealthy families. Weatherman saw no promise in organizing American workers around their material interests, which it thought would merely cement privileged workers' loyalty to imperialism and white workers' "white skin privilege." For perhaps the first time in American history, a band of radicals vowed to take *from* the working class: "All of the United Airlines Astrojets, all of the Holiday Inns, all of Hertz's automobiles, your television, car and wardrobe already belong to a large degree to the people of the rest of the world." Most in SDS, even in RYM, did not believe that this was an effective way to persuade Americans to forsake empire. Mike Klonsky, Carl Davidson, Noel Ignatin, and others constituted RYM II, an alternative faction in favor of working-class organizing. Soon, however, RYM II itself splintered into dozens of would-be vanguards each with its own Mao-derived rigidity. One, the Bay Area Revolutionary Union led by Leibel Bergman and Bob Avakian, openly sought to revive Stalin, putting his picture on the cover of its *Red Papers* in 1969. RYM II and Weatherman had sufficient short-run unity on Vietnam and the Panthers to coalesce at a raucous SDS national convention in June 1969 in Chicago, expel PL from SDS, and elevate three Weathermen (Jeff Jones, Bill Ayers, and Mark Rudd) to SDS's top national offices. At the base of the organization, many ordinary SDS members, aligned with none of the small self-declared revolutionary leaderships, were appalled. "We feel that the people who will make a revolution do not need a vanguard to tell them how to run either that revolution or the society which will emerge," came a missive from the Fayetteville, Arkansas, SDS chapter in 1969. "All Power to the People!!! NO POWER TO THE STALINISTS."[30]

What would have happened had SDS, with its many tens of thousands of members, kept intact and organized against war and racism, no one can say. Having gained control of SDS, Weatherman, drawing on foco theory and the film *The Battle of Algiers* (1966), believed violent confrontation could compel a choosing of sides or provoke repression, leading in turn to radicalization. Calling for a National Action in Chicago in October 1969 to attack "pig city," and predicting a turnout of many thousands, the Weathermen called on "mother country" radicals to rile up outcasts – gangs and street toughs, akin to the Panthers' lumpen – as a "white fighting force" to "Bring the War Home." That summer, they organized collectives, sought to "combat liberalism" in withering "criticism/self-criticism" sessions, worked to "smash monogamy" by requiring couples

[30] *Weatherman*, ed. Harold Jacobs (Ramparts, 1970), pp. 52, 492; Sale, *SDS*, pp. 615–616.

to break up or rotate partners, held in contempt "bourgeois" concerns such as cleanliness, and practiced invasive discipline down to whether one could read a book or leave the house. On the theory that beating up poor whites would win their respect, thirty Weathermen marched up a Detroit beach chanting "Ho, Ho, Ho Chi Minh, the Viet Cong is Gonna Win" and punching those who objected. Nine Weatherwomen – the nomenclature was mutating to deflect sexist implications – burst in upon a Macomb Community College sociology exam, barricaded the door, delivered a harangue against imperialism, and used karate on those who tried to leave. In Pittsburgh, seventy-five Weatherwomen ran through a high school shouting and punching teachers. At the Harvard Center for International Affairs, twenty Weatherpeople ripped out phones and dragged secretaries down the stairs.

Almost all other radicals, from the *Guardian* to Liberation News Service, denounced these acts as senseless and self-defeating. Carol McEldowney – a Port Huron SDSer active for years in Cleveland's ERAP who traveled to North Vietnam in 1967 – saw in Weatherman "totally antagonistic politics which don't provide alternatives, which don't speak to people's needs and what makes them act and take risks, which are based on hate that has slightly fascist overtones." To Boston's *Old Mole*, Weatherman reflected "the needs not of oppressed peoples – American or Vietnamese – but of frustrated people in the radical movement." Weatherman Bill Ayers, 25-year-old son of the president of Commonwealth Edison, answered such critics by claiming, "Nothing we could do in the mother country could be adventurist." He added, "When a pig gets iced that's a good thing," and offered the slogan, "Fight the people" (an inversion of Mao's "serve the people"). In Madison, Wisconsin – where SDS meetings still drew hundreds – Weatherman Jeff Jones stormed a stage in September 1969, flanked by a few others he called "stone communist revolutionaries," not "motherfucking students." The hundreds of Madison SDSers simply turned their chairs around and resumed meeting as if he were not there. "You don't need a rectal thermometer to know who the assholes are," SDSers in Madison took to saying.[31]

Chicago Panther leader Fred Hampton called Weatherman "anarchistic" and "Custeristic in that its leaders take people into situations

---

[31] Carol McEldowney, "Communications: Weathermen," *Liberation* (Nov. 1969), p. 39; "Don't Mourn – Organize," *Old Mole*, 14–23 October 1969, p. 15; *Weatherman*, pp. 184, 191–193, 202; Thai Jones, *A Radical Line: From the Labor Movement to the Weather Underground, One Family's Century of Conscience* (New York: Simon and Schuster, 2004, pp. 175–176.

where the people can be massacred, and they call that revolution." But Weatherman refused to heed Black Panther criticism of the planned National Action, despite routinely calling the Panthers the vanguard and making ritualistic denunciations of "white skin privilege." In the end, only a few hundred elite Weather cadre – absent the promised army of working-class white toughs – showed up for the October 1969 National Action. The Weatherpeople ran through downtown Chicago, breaking store windows and trashing cars. "I don't know what your cause is," said one passerby, "but you have just set it back a hundred years." Seeking money to pay the resultant fines from the National Action, which they renamed the "Days of Rage," Ayers and other Weathermen entered the Vietnam Moratorium offices in Washington that November, allegedly demanding $20,000 to abstain from violence at the Moratorium's upcoming national demonstration. Moratorium leaders condemned the "shakedown."[32]

Thoroughly alienated from "pig Amerika," Weatherman began to celebrate barbarism and cast themselves as Vandals and Visigoths. Gathering at Flint, Michigan, on December 27–30, 1969, they plastered the hall with a "Piece Now" banner bearing an image of a gun as well as pictures of their heroes, including RFK assassin Sirhan Sirhan and hippie cult leader Charles Manson, whose followers murdered a pregnant Hollywood actress and several others. "Dig it!" declared Weatherleader Bernardine Dohrn in reference to the Manson murders. "First they killed those pigs, then they ate dinner in the same room with them, then they even shoved a fork into a victim's stomach! Wild!" For the remainder of the Flint gathering, Weatherpeople flashed "fork" greetings at one another: four fingers upraised and spread slightly apart. Having steeled themselves for mayhem, Weatherman demolished SDS, disbanding its national and regional offices and throwing away the mail lists so no other faction could reconstruct the organization. Just as the group divided into clandestine cells, an immense explosion in March 1970 destroyed a Greenwich Village townhouse owned by the father of Weatherwoman Cathy Wilkerson, a wealthy radio station investor, killing three Weatherpeople: Diana Oughton, 28; Ted Gold, 22; and Terry Robbins, 22. The collective had blown itself to pieces while making dynamite pipe bombs crammed with nails, intended for detonation at a dance for Army officers and their civilian girlfriends at Fort Dix, New Jersey. They had brought the

---

[32] Jones, *A Radical Line*, p. 204; "Weathermen Accused of 'Shakedown,'" *The Washington Post*, 18 November 1969, p. A1.

war home, literally. Only Cathy Wilkerson and Kathy Boudin, daughter of the prominent left-wing lawyer Leonard Boudin, escaped, running naked to a neighbor's house and then into hiding. To Tom Hayden, the Weatherpeople were "not the conscience of their generation, but more like its id."[33]

Even radicals who rebuked Weatherman saw its violence as a product of the movement's soaring frustration at seeing millions of Southeast Asians die. U.S. government violence was vastly greater than that of American radicals in the 1960s, epitomized by the massacre of hundreds of Vietnamese women and babies by U.S. troops in the hamlet of My Lai. Nor was Weatherman alone in adopting insurrectionary tactics of street violence, bombing, and property destruction as new waves of youth reared on sensational notions of "radicalism" in the mass media entered the campuses, seeking to live the projected image. Venceremos, a Bay Area organization headed by Stanford literature professor Bruce Franklin, called for imminent armed struggle. *Scanlan's* – launched by former *Ramparts* editor Warren Hinckle – spoke of "Guerrilla War in the USA," documenting 503 acts of sabotage and terrorism in the United States in 1969 and 546 in 1970, the year when students in Santa Barbara burned a Bank of America branch to the ground. The results could be tragic. When four radicals detonated a van full of explosives in an attempt to destroy the Army Mathematics Research Center at the University of Wisconsin in 1970, they killed Robert Fassnacht, 33, physics graduate student and father of three, while the military research unit continued its work unimpeded. When two ex-convicts joined Brandeis radicals Susan Saxe and Katherine Anne Power and robbed a Boston bank, police officer Walter Schroeder, 41, father of nine, died in the gunfire. In 1971, a bomb set in a federal building in Los Angeles killed janitor Thomas Ortiz, 18. The FBI's Ten Most Wanted list soon had leftists in its majority, and alarmism became commonplace among radicals. From exile in Algeria in 1970, Eldridge Cleaver predicted that within two years "we will have a military coup in the United States and a military dictatorship, because by that time there will be a full-scale war going on.... Election for the presidency will be out of the question."[34]

---

[33] Tom Hayden, *Trial* (New York: Holt Rinehart Winston, 1970), p. 94; *Weatherman,* pp. 299, 347.

[34] Lee Lockwood, *Conversation with Eldridge Cleaver: Algiers* (New York: Dell, 1970), p. 118.

The late New Left's trashings and firebombings did come in for criticism from other radicals who saw them as strategically unwise. Peter Camejo, much admired for a stirring antiwar speech he had given on the Boston Commons to 100,000, distinguished "mass action" or movement-building from both "ultra-leftism" (over-the-top rhetoric and hyper-militant tactics) and "reformism" (conventional politics that water down radical objectives). William Appleman Williams advised the Movement to "start dealing with large numbers of Americans, however misled or mistaken we may consider them, as human beings rather than as racists and stupids to be jammed up against the wall." SNCC veteran Julius Lester observed that one could support the Black Panthers' right to be free from attack *despite* their destructive politics, bemoaning "militancy for the sake of militancy": "In the act of building, life is generated and regenerated within us." The main antiwar coalitions continued to organize large, vibrant demonstrations, honoring the Vietnamese, who consistently urged sympathetic Americans to organize a unified, massive, and effective antiwar movement, although they were weakened by a 1970 split of the New Mobilization Committee into two: the SWP-dominated National Peace Action Coalition hewing to the singular demand "Out Now," and the People's Coalition for Peace and Justice, which included radical pacifists and Communists and was open to inclusion of other radical political objectives.[35]

Increasingly, radical dispositions were resonating in American popular culture, tacking between margin and mainstream in ways often more effective than the hypermilitancy that captured most news coverage. Garry Trudeau's *Doonesbury*, a cartoon strip begun at Yale, was syndicated in 1970, putting a New Left viewpoint on the funny pages – or editorial pages – of hundreds of papers nationwide. Actors Jane Fonda and Donald Sutherland embarked on an "FTA" ("Fuck the Army") tour for troops in Southeast Asia. Jon Voigt starred in *The Revolutionary* (1970), and producer Bert Schneider and actor Marlon Brando gave money to the Panthers – notwithstanding writer Tom Wolfe's mockery of such largesse as "radical chic" (referring to a Black Panther soirée at composer Leonard Bernstein's apartment in 1970). Francis Ford Coppola made organized crime a metaphor for capitalist venality in *The Godfather* (1972), with

[35] Peter Camejo, *Liberalism, Ultraleftism, or Mass Action* (New York: Pathfinder, 1970); William Appleman Williams, "An American Socialist Community?" *Liberation*, June 1969, p. 11; Julius Lester, "Aquarian Notebook," *Liberation*, June 1970, p. 41.

Brando as Don Vito Corleone. "If Cosa Nostra had been black or socialist, Corleone would have been dead or in jail," Brando told *Life*.[36]

One powerful change of consciousness attendant with the late New
Left was "Third World" identification among people of color. Sometimes this Third World sensibility was literal, as when Stokely Carmichael
moved to Guinea and took the name Kwame Ture, but in countless realms
within American life as well people of color saw themselves as throwing
off shackles of colonial dependency. The American Indian Movement
(AIM), created in Minnesota in 1968, campaigned against police harassment, powerlessness, and the despair of high suicide rates and alcoholism.
On South Dakota's Rosebud Sioux reservation, Mary Ellen Moore issued
Red Panther; in California, "Indians of All Tribes," including Mohawks,
Cherokees, Eskimoes, Ojibwe, and others, occupied Alcatraz Island from
1969 to 1971; on Thanksgiving 1970, AIM seized a *Mayflower* replica at
Plymouth, Massachusetts; in 1971 Indian occupiers renamed Mt. Rush-
more "Mount Crazy Horse"; and a "Trail of Broken Treaties" caravan to
Washington, D.C., in 1972, saw 700 Indians from 200 tribes occupy the
Bureau of Indian Affairs (BIA). Among Mexican Americans, a walkout
took place in Los Angeles high schools in 1968 to protest Anglo bias,
and the following year they founded MEChA – El Movimiento Estudi-
antil Chicano de Aztlán – to promote Chicano Studies in universities.
Aztlán being Aztec for far north, adoption of the name implied that what
Anglos called the "Southwest" was actually an occupied territory won
by force in 1848. An independent Chicano party, El Partido de la Raza,
was organized in Texas in 1970. Among Puerto Ricans in Chicago and
New York, a Panther-style Young Lords Party challenged police brutality
and job discrimination and supported self-determination for Puerto Rico.
The "yellow peril" of racist lore was upended by Asian Americans calling
for "Yellow Power!" In many cases, such Third World "nationalism"
was metaphorical: AIM was pan-Indian; the Asian-American movement
was comprised of youth of Chinese, Japanese, Filipino, Korean, and other
heritages; and there were broader Third World umbrellas, as with the San
Francisco State strike of 1968–69 that united black, Asian, and Latino
students in a Third World Liberation Front and a similar 1969 Third
World strike at Berkeley. Above all, Third World identification meant a
new assertiveness and pride against racial denigration.

Consequences of the New Left were also felt in the challenges to
authoritarianism that arose in the family, various occupations, schools,

36 Peter Manso, *Brando* (London: Weidenfield and Nicolson, 1994), p. 752.

prisons, asylums, the military – and to the rule of private property. Calls for "GI rights," or freedom of political expression in the ranks, undermined obedience so powerfully that rank-and-file military resistance prompted Nixon's "Vietnamization," a draw-down of U.S. forces on the ground in Southeast Asia. New forms of schooling to encourage creativity rather than rote learning reached a peak around 1970 with the proliferation of "free" schools in the United States. Radical prisoners and lawyers sought to limit the arbitrary power and violence of prison guards and wardens while promoting prisoner access to education and the arts. Psychological and psychiatric authoritarianism were assailed by an Insane Liberation Front formed in Oregon in 1970 and a Mental Patients' Liberation Front formed in Boston in 1971, opposed to widespread use of electroshock therapy and other abusive treatments. In the mid-1960s mothers receiving welfare benefits protested in Los Angeles, New York, Boston, Columbus, and Cleveland, demanding greater dignity in provision including coverage of children's school clothing, access to job training usually limited to men, and an end to degrading surveillance to ferret out a "man in the house." In 1966, these efforts came together in a National Welfare Rights Organization (NWRO) launched by George Wiley, a former university chemistry teacher and CORE worker. In 1968, a thousand "welfare mothers" descended on Washington to testify before Congress on the shortcomings of Aid to Families with Dependent Children (AFDC), enduring verbal abuse from southern Senators. NWRO contested fixed ideas of self-reliance and stigmas about the undeserving poor laced with racial stereotypes, advocating a guaranteed annual income.

A challenge to property came in April and May 1969 with People's Park, an effort by Berkeley radicals to convert unused land of the University of California into a communal garden. Frank Bardacke – a radical prominent as a result of Oakland's Stop the Draft Week – defended People's Park by evoking the Costanoan Indians who once inhabited northern California, who "had no concept of land ownership," instead believing "the land was under the care and guardianship of the people who used it and lived on it." This Native American anticipation of countercultural, New Left, and Third World sensibilities, Bardacke observed, had been lost to a "piece of paper saying who owned the land . . . passed around among rich white men," a deed "covered in blood." When the university administration fenced off People's Park, several thousand marched to reclaim it and clashed with police, who fired buckshot, killing one bystander, James Rector, blinding another, and injuring dozens. A few days later, National Guard helicopters sprayed tear gas on the campus to punish a silent march to protest the authorities' use of deadly force. For many this crackdown marked the end of a decade of Bay Area protest, but when Mario Savio returned to the steps of Sproul Hall that June he called People's Park a challenge to "the property relations of this society." Communal dispositions toward property and interest in decentralist socialism were flourishing as the New Left entered the 1970s.[37]

Of all the breakthrough movements of 1968–69, women's liberation had perhaps the deepest, most lasting effect on American life. Women's liberation groups – autonomous vehicles for radical women to meet and act in self-organized spaces, as distinct from the early-decade stirrings of criticism of "caste" made within the organizations of the New Left – first emerged in 1967, the year of Black Power, urban rebellion, and more militant antiwar resistance. Young radical women sought an implicit alternative to the Movement's increasingly aggressive macho style even as the very name "women's liberation" implied an analogy to national liberation and black liberation. In 1967 and 1968, radical women's groups began to flourish and to develop a theory of how the oppression of women pervaded everything from advertising to schooling. Their numbers included New York Radical Women, Chicago Women's Liberation, DC Women's Liberation, Redstockings, The Feminists, Bread and Roses, and Cell 16. Some of these women had SDS backgrounds, such as Heather Booth and Marge Piercy. Others were intellectuals, such as University of Chicago psychologist Naomi Weisstein. Ti-Grace Atkinson and Florynce "Flo" Kennedy emerged from the relatively militant New York City chapter of the National Organization for Women (and in Kennedy's case, from decades of familiarity with leftwing parties as well as a leaning toward Black Power even as she collaborated with white women). Still others had varied backgrounds in antiracist and antiwar radicalism, including Robin Morgan, Jo Freeman, Elizabeth Martinez, Shulamith Firestone, and Roxanne Dunbar. Together, these young radicals discerned an inequitable order of power deployed by men to derive benefits from the services of women – economic, domestic, emotional, and sexual – requiring not just a change in attitudes but an overturning of the system of power relations that sustained those inequities. They resurrected the term "feminism" for their independent movement, distinguishing it from the suffrage campaign of the early twentieth century by making clear this was to be a radical

---

[37] Frank Bardacke, "Who Owns the Park?" in *Counterculture and Revolution*, p. 49; Savio, quoted in Seth Rosenfeld, *Subversives: The FBI's War on Student Radicals, and Reagan's Rise to Power* (New York: Farrar Strauss Giroux, 2012), pp. 472–473.

or revolutionary feminism dedicated to overthrowing male supremacy and create a wholly new society of thoroughgoing gender equality. From the beginning the movement had internal critics, such as Flo Kennedy and Pamela Parker Allen, who argued that women's liberation needed to address issues of class and race so as not to become a vehicle only for white middle-class women's advancement.

Some other women chose to pursue women's equality through and within the New Left. For many women in SDS, including the group's first female national secretary, Bernardine Dohrn, the model was the Vietnamese woman guerrilla with rifle in hand who disproved sexist stereotypes by taking part as a combatant in the common struggle for socialism and national liberation. The Jeanette Rankin Brigade, named for the nation's first Congresswoman who after being elected to represent Montana had cast votes against war in 1917 and 1941, was arranged by Women Strike for Peace, comprising a 3,000-strong women's contingent in a 1968 antiwar demonstration. More militant women's liberationists, however, rejected both WSP maternalism and what they saw as the SDS-style pressing of radical women into the service of movements that were not primarily about women's objectives. Instead they sought independent organization, in mirror image of Black Power, on the grounds that "sisterhood is powerful." That feminist sensibility gained strength as advocates for women's equality were dismissed and belittled by New Left men who claimed that the war and racism were more pressing issues.

In 1968, the women's liberation movement won national media coverage at protests in Atlantic City against the Miss America pageant, which radical women faulted for portraying women as mindless sex symbols, ties to corporate advertisers that foisted superfluous commodities on women, and racist exclusion of women of color from its finalists. These themes gave signs of a New Left worldview, but when *Ramparts* first covered the new feminist radicalism in 1968, its cover photograph featured a woman's cleavage, her head cropped above the neck. Even more flagrantly, New Left men sometimes shouted down women challenging male supremacy, as occurred most notoriously in a shower of vulgarities at the 1969 "counterinaugural" against Nixon organized by the Mobe in Washington, D.C. The spirit of women's liberation nevertheless owed much to the New Left from which it had emerged. At Grinnell College in Iowa in 1970, ten women appeared completely naked before a *Playboy* model recruiter, with one speaking extemporaneously: "Pretending to appreciate and respect the beauty of the naked human form, *Playboy* is actually stereotyping the body and commercializes it.

Playboy substitutes fetishism for honest appreciation of the endless variety of human forms." The Chicago Women's Liberation Rock Band (1969–1973) recorded "Papa Don't Lay That Shit on Me," "Abortion Song," "Secretary," "Ain't Gonna Marry," and other original songs. Rapidly the new feminist radicalism articulated a series of objectives, including legalized abortion, access to birth control, equal pay for comparable work, an end to rape and domestic abuse, shared housework, and social forms beyond the traditional male-headed "bourgeois family," namely through equal participation of men in childrearing and communal child care centers. The women's movement would achieve substantial policy victories, including Title IX in 1972, which compelled educational gender equality and had a major impact on college sports. The movement also created the context for the Supreme Court's landmark *Roe v. Wade* decision in 1973, which classed abortion as part of the right to privacy, in effect legalizing it nationwide. Feminism would continue to burgeon in the 1970s, proliferating in forms but carrying its momentum forward long after the wider New Left had receded.[38]

Gay liberation, similarly, seemed to burst upon the scene when it materialized in summer 1969 after a police raid on the Stonewall Inn, a Greenwich Village gay bar, when young gay men, particularly androgynous "flame queens," fought back with rocks and bottles in four days of riots. Gay liberation had precursors in the homophile organizations such as the Mattachine Society, which by the mid-sixties were showing a new assertiveness, especially on the East Coast, in adopting protest strategies inspired by the black freedom movement, but its esprit was far more countercultural, and it owed much to the radical antiwar, women's, and Black Power movements, inspiring the slogan, "Gay Power!" It had begun earlier in 1969, with organizations such as the Committee for Homosexual Freedom in San Francisco and Fight Repression of Erotic Expression (FREE) at the University of Minnesota. Stonewall was not new even in the fighting, for victims of raids had fought back against police before, if not with such ferocity and endurance. However, the post-Stonewall formation in 1969 of the Gay Liberation Front (GLF), built by New Left gays and lesbians who seized on the moment to identify sexual freedom as part of the same struggle that opposed the Vietnam War, racism, imperialism, and capitalism, made a major difference in the nation's media capital and the traditional center of radicalism. As other GLFs sprang up around the country, a new movement surged. From San Francisco, the New Leftist

[38] Anonymous Grinnell protester quoted in Ruth Rosen, *The World Split Open: How the Modern Women's Movement Changed America* (New York: Penguin, 2000), p. 163.

FIGURE 4.2. An openly gay contingent marches against the Vietnam War in 1971, just two years after the Stonewall Rebellion, indicating the profusion and interplay of radical movements at the height of the Vietnam-era radicalization. *Photo by Diana Davis, Manuscripts and Archives Division, The New York Public Library.*

Carl Wittman – who as a Swarthmore student had participated in the Cambridge, Maryland, civil rights campaign, and then in SDS's Newark ERAP – penned "Refugees from Amerika: A Gay Manifesto" (1969), articulating a program and philosophy of sexual liberation.

In that early moment "gay" was not associated with men alone but was a term embraced by many women as well, including GLF members Karla Jay and Martha Shelley, and the concerns of gay liberation dovetailed with feminist criticisms of the authoritarian patriarchal family and sexual satisfaction geared largely to heterosexual male pleasure. One explicit connection between gay and women's liberationists lay in the insight that antigay stigmatization of gay men as "effeminate" or "sissies" only held power if women were devalued. The gay liberation movement shared much with the New Left, down to manifesting the very same features of crescendo and fragmentation in 1969–70. GLF split before its first year was out, with some of its founders, including Marty Robinson and Arthur Evans, peeling off to form the Gay Activists Alliance (GAA), which focused on specific legal protections of rights for gays and lesbians through militant direct action. GAA "zaps," undertaken with sixties theatricality, interrupted public appearances by politicians to challenge them to endorse repeal of antisodomy laws. GLF, for its part,

sought alliances with the wider revolutionary New Left, including the
Black Panther Party; explored communal living; published a newspaper
called *Come Out!*; and practiced "consciousness raising" in a manner
akin to women's liberation organizations. By 1973, virtually all of the
dozens of GLFs that had sprung up nationwide were extinct, but they
had shot forth multiple other shards, including the Lavender Menace, a
lesbian organization that compelled Friedan's NOW to remove its restrictions against lesbian participation in 1971. A newly open and celebratory
gay life began to flourish, epitomized by the scene created by the migration
of tens of thousands of gay men to San Francisco in the 1970s.

Early on, both feminist and gay voices could be heard among people
of color. In 1970, SNCC veteran Frances Beal published an essay entitled
"Double Jeopardy: To Be Black and Female" telling of black women's
struggles against male domination, in implicit rebuttal to revolutionary
black nationalist groups who resisted the women's movement as divisive
to race unity, while also making it clear to white feminists that gender
equality could not be separated from a race-conscious fight against white
supremacy, especially on issues such as forced sterilization. In the same
year, two transgender GLFers, Sylvia Rivera, who was Puerto Rican, and
her friend Marsha Johnson, who was black, formed Street Transvestite
Action Revolutionaries (STAR). Third World Gay Liberation, which
also emerged from GLF, challenged the "triple oppression" of capitalism, racism, and sexism and issued a sharp critique of "the bourgeois
nuclear family" and "all institutional religions" for nurturing oppressive
sex roles and homophobia, while advocating a "revolutionary socialist
society . . . where the needs of the people come first." In 1971, more than
600 Chicanas met in Houston, Texas, dubbing themselves *mujeres de La
Raza*, challenging machismo in the barrio, raising demands for 24-hour
daycare and free, legal abortion, in direct criticism of the conservatism
of the Catholic Church. Each of these pioneering efforts at articulating
what later feminists would call "intersectionality" often battled to be
heard amidst traditional preoccupations of the left, but they also helped
to deepen appreciation of difference and an understanding that, as the
poet Audre Lorde wrote, "Revolution is not a one-time event."[39]

---

[39] Third World Gay Liberation, "What We Want, What We Believe" (1971), in *The Radical
Reader*, eds. Timothy Patrick McCarthy and John McMillian (New York: The New
Press, 2003), pp. 589–592; Mirta Vidal, *Chicanas Speak Out* (New York: Pathfinder,
1971); Audre Lorde, *Sister Outsider: Essays and Speeches* (Berkeley, Calif.: Crossing
Press, 2007): 140.

To see 1965–73 as an exceptional historical moment of radicalization, with countless creative bursts of dissent, is not to say there existed a "revolutionary situation" but rather a situation in which a revolutionary imagination flourished. Although radical prospects were set back by the dissolution of SNCC and SDS, the battering of the Black Panther Party, and other turn-of-decade fragmentations, much of what is thought of as "the sixties" extended well into the early 1970s. At a moment when Marvin Gaye's *What's Going On* (1971) was taking soul music to a new political level, protest continued on a scale larger than ever. In May 1970, the largest student strike in American history shut down more than four hundred campuses in protest of Nixon's expansion of the Vietnam War into neighboring Cambodia and against National Guard and police killings of students at Kent State in Ohio and Jackson State in Mississippi. On April 24, 1971, the biggest national demonstration to end the Vietnam War occurred, with approximately three quarters of a million people filling Washington, D.C., including Vietnam Veterans Against the War, who stood on the Capitol steps and cast away their medals. The militant 1971 "Mayday" (signaling both emergency and the radical holiday) that followed a week later, seeking to use mass civil disobedience to shut down the capitol, resulted in 13,000 arrests. Meanwhile, a move "from protest to politics" took place in a manner very different from what Bayard Rustin had intended by that phrase as openly radical candidates began to win local political elections. Justin Ravitz, a Marxist elected in 1972 to a ten-year criminal court judgeship in Detroit, wore jeans and cowboy boots beneath his judicial robes during his swearing-in ceremony, stated that most of those arraigned should be released without bond, and conjectured that in the event of severe government repression, "I will be with the people and would voluntarily leave the bench." That same year, a Human Rights Party in Ann Arbor, Michigan, won two seats while running against the Democratic and Republican parties on a socialist platform of rent control, workers' control, and legalized marijuana. In 1973, Paul Soglin, a Vietnam War protestor arrested for civil disobedience and known for his participation in the University of Wisconsin's Dow Chemical protests, was elected mayor of Madison, Wisconsin.[40]

All the same, the radicalization faced headwinds in the new strength of conservatism. The Nixon victory in 1968 on a slogan of "law and order" indicated that despite the left's excitement, the year had brought a

---

[40] "Marxist Judge-Elect Plans 'Improvement' for Court," *Omaha World-Herald*, 22 December 1972, p. 44.

gathering of "counterrevolution," as Herbert Marcuse called it, including white southerners and working-class ethnics resentful of the civil rights revolution and campus radicalism. Authorities were increasingly inclined to answer social disruption through reprisals rather than concessions, with the brunt born by the black liberation movement, which experienced a decapitation as Medgar Evers, Malcolm X, Martin Luther King, Jr., and Fred Hampton were killed within a seven-year span. The jailing or exile of hundreds of black militants between 1969 and 1973 halted the advance of a black freedom dynamo that had propelled American radicalism for two decades. In May 1970, the killings of student demonstrators at Kent State and Jackson State – both working-class campuses, one white, the other black, showing how deeply antiwar sentiment coursed among youth – made clear that student demonstrators were fair game as well, with the subsequent pall of mourning and vulnerability conveyed intimately by Crosby, Stills, Nash, and Young in "Ohio" (1970).

If there was a single standout incident of ferocious repression against radicalism, it was Attica, site of a massive prison rebellion in upstate New York. Attica had an almost all-white guard corps presiding over over-crowded facilities bursting with inmates, most of them black and Puerto Rican. In September 1971 a revolt broke out when guards attempted a disciplinary action at a time when feelings were raw because of recently arrived news of the killing of prisoner George Jackson – a Black Panther, lover of Angela Davis, and author of letters collected in *Soledad Brother* (1970) – in a California breakout attempt. One thousand Attica inmates seized two cell blocks and held thirty guards hostage, clubbing an officer, who later died, while seizing the control room. The prisoners demanded improved living conditions, including more than one shower a week; relief from racist abuse; and amnesty for the rebels. Although there were four revenge killings among inmates during the occupation, none of the hostages were harmed. After four days, the state prison chief and liberal Republican Gov. Nelson Rockefeller declared amnesty nonnegotiable. In the end, an armed assault to retake the prison by state troopers resulted in the deaths of twenty-eight inmates and nine hostages, making Attica the bloodiest prison revolt in American history.

Another charged standoff took place in South Dakota in February 1973 when Lakota Sioux elders invited AIM youth to occupy Wounded Knee, infamous site of an 1890 U.S. Cavalry massacre of some 290 Sioux men, women, and children. The Pine Ridge Indian Reservation was home to 12,000 destitute Oglala Lakota, their traditionalist full-bloods deeply at odds with the U.S.-backed tribal council led by mixed-blood president

Dick Wilson. AIM's young, braided-haired leaders had just led a protest in nearby Custer, South Dakota, against authorities' failure to charge a white man with first-degree murder for an Indian's death, ending in the torching of the courthouse and Chamber of Commerce. Lakota elders beckoned AIM to come to Pine Ridge and stand up to Wilson, seen as a corrupt "Uncle Tomahawk" collaborator of the federal BIA. Proud of the warrior heritage of Sitting Bull and Geronimo, several hundred AIM members seized Wounded Knee, brandishing a few dozen rifles, demanding Wilson's removal and the BIA's dissolution, and declaring an independent Oglala Nation. With national news cameras filming, federal forces laid siege. Wishing to avoid a second Wounded Knee massacre, they did not mount a full-scale attack, but gunfire was frequent. Radical opponents of the Vietnam War acted in solidarity with the occupiers, providing two aerial drops of supplies – but most food and electricity were cut off. In May, after 71 days, Oglala elders stood down in exchange for promised investigation of Wilson's abuses and of unmet treaty obligations. The half-starved AIM holdouts accepted the judgment, surrendering their guns. Hundreds of arrests and indictments of the occupiers followed, with allegations swirling that a black radical's disappearance during the occupation was because he had been killed by AIM as a suspected spy. Virtually all those indicted, including AIM leaders Dennis Banks and Russell Means, were acquitted or saw charges dismissed, but the legal snarl, combined with ongoing reprisals against AIM supporters on Pine Ridge by Wilson's forces, caused militant Indian organization to dissipate even though national polls showed a good deal of public support for the protestors and Indian treaty rights, and although the protest sparked a rebirth of Indian traditional ways on American reservations.

Already in late 1972 one radical had written, "The radicalization seems to have come to a complete halt." That perception would be almost universally held by 1973. Despite the end-points signified by Kent State, Attica, and Wounded Knee, the 1968 generation would be forever shaped by its experience of mass outpourings and imagining of wholesale social transformation. A remarkable crescendo had widened and diversified the radical agenda, resulting in much richer radical visions of freedom, equality, and community. No single thread of theoretical or ideological argument, no single concise platform, could represent all the dimensions of that radical moment, from gays and lesbians to Chicanos, from opponents of war and empire to opponents of male chauvinism and sexual repression. In this sense, the Vietnam radicalization stood beyond the "Old Left," which in its day claimed to stand upon a monolith of socialism,

Communism, or labor. That self-image of coherence was always illusory. Radicalism's history was always an ensemble of causes, partly in concert and partly straining against each other. Nonetheless, during the first half of the twentieth century, the left had put paramount emphasis on the pursuit of economic equality in a society where class conflict was hard to ignore. Themes of class and equality would continue to exert a power in the imagination of the left, but the story of the radical left since 1973 has inescapably been one of diffusion of the common thread or common platform.[41]

---

[41] Ron Young to Allen Young, 20 Sept. 1972 (Allen Young Papers, University of Wisconsin, Box 2, Folder 6).

5

Anticipation, 1973–1980

First in her family to attend college, Julia Reichart was raised in a blue-collar Republican household in a small New Jersey town, her mother a nurse and her father a grocery store meat cutter. At orientation at Antioch College in Yellow Springs, Ohio, in 1964, she listened as others introduced themselves by their parents' occupations: "engineer," "professor" – and, flushed with shame, she lied about her own. She wrote a first-year essay defending conservative Barry Goldwater but was impressed by the thoughtfulness of her roommate Amy's parents, who she learned had once been Communists. Feeling out of place at college, Reichart dropped out, only to return two years later. An interest in photography led her to attend the march on the Pentagon in 1967, but as she took pictures of antiwar protesters putting flowers in soldiers' guns and saw a friend's head bloodied, she suddenly felt more a participant than an observer. Back in Yellow Springs, she joined the packed meetings of the Radical Studies Institute (RSI), where Marxist readings were discussed, excitedly making connections between empire, race, and capitalism. "We working-class people can be agents in history," she realized. "We don't need to be embarrassed about the fact that we don't know Sartre or what a metaphor is." The question was, "How do we overthrow capitalism?"[1]

At the RSI men did almost all the talking, with women struggling to be heard, so after a friend returned from a women's "consciousness-raising" session in Gainesville, Florida, in 1968, Reichert helped her start

[1] Victor Cohen, "Interview with Julia Reichert," *Works and Days* 55/56 (2010), p. 198. This invaluable interview is the source for much of the biographical information in this passage.

an Antioch women's center and began a campus radio show called "Sisters, Brothers, Lovers: Listen." For her senior project Reichert decided to make a film on women with her boyfriend Jim Klein, whose interest in audio complemented hers in visuals. *Growing Up Female* (1970) was the first film to reflect the values of the new women's movement, examining the lives of six ordinary women and girls, ages four to thirty-five. After a year abroad in Europe, Reichert and Klein returned to the United States in 1971 to find the left hardening and dispersing. Many of her radical friends had joined Marxist-Leninist groups, while her feminist friends were forming lesbian communes. Reichert sought a distributor for *Growing Up Female*, but Newsreel, a New Left collective, declined to distribute it, instead issuing *The Woman's Film* (1971), which concluded with a call for revolution. So Reichert toured the country, showing her film in living rooms, high schools, universities, anywhere – an experience that led her and Klein to organize New Day Films and write a do-it-yourself guide on film distribution.

Soon Reichart was living in a collective household in Dayton, Ohio, and taking part in the New American Movement (NAM), which sought "a humane and radical socialist democracy in the United States" when more than 400 people, most of them sixties veterans in their twenties, created it on Thanksgiving weekend 1971. NAM was wary of models amounting to a "vanguard without a rearguard," as one of its leaders, Dorothy Healey, a former Communist, put it. It chose the small city of Davenport, Iowa, as its founding location to signal a desire to find a way back to the American mainstream. Within a few years NAM would have more than forty chapters, some comprised entirely of women, such as one in Durham, North Carolina, named for the early feminist Charlotte Perkins Gilman, or Blazing Star, a Chicago lesbian group that joined NAM en masse. By this time, the feminist field had become highly variegated. New Left women's liberationists had, in the upsurge of 1969–1970, challenged "patriarchy" or domination by men in pursuit of a new society based on thorough gender-neutral equality. As this kind of revolutionary feminism faded along with the wider New Left movement, a considerable segment of feminists had turned by the mid-1970s toward a politics that, while equally opposed to patriarchy, focused on nurturing distinctive women's values and separate women-only counterinstitutions. NAM's "socialist feminist" politics, by contrast, viewed male domination as interrelated with class exploitation as targets to be overcome in the movement toward a more egalitarian and democratic society. Open to both collaborations with men and women-only caucuses, socialist feminism was distinct, as well, from liberal feminism – which sought to remove legal–attitudinal barriers to opportunity, not to overturn a whole social system. NAM's commitment to feminism marked it off from those segments of the organized left, including Communists and Maoists, who considered feminism "petty bourgeois" (a stance estranging those currents, as NAM leader Barbara Ehrenreich pointed out, from the many "women working in alternative health centers or crisis centers, setting up day care services, organizing women workers, starting consciousness raising groups, etc."). In an era when no president – Kennedy, Johnson, or Nixon – had appointed a single woman to his cabinet, NAM required leadership bodies to be 50 percent women and organized a National Conference on Socialist Feminism in 1975 at Antioch attended by more than 1,500. Its feminism was always conveyed with a sense of humor. "I'm much less competitive than you will ever be," two men said to one another in a NAM cartoon.[2]

NAM's conception of the working class included public, white-collar, and service workers, not only the factory proletariat. Influenced by French philosopher André Gorz, it sought to promote "structural reforms" requiring systemic transformation; based on the Italian Marxist Antonio Gramsci's concept of "hegemony" it interpreted the 1970s not as a "war of maneuver" warranting armed insurrection but a "war of position," a contestation over popular consciousness. This contestation could include, for example, protest of the type Reichart organized in 1973 when the American Film Institute (AFI) declared that its inaugural film series at the Kennedy Center in Washington, D.C., would not include the previously accepted *State of Siege* (1972) by the French director Costa-Gavras. Based on Uruguayan guerrillas' 1970 kidnapping and execution of a United States Agency for International Development (USAID) advisor who oversaw the torture of leftists, *State of Siege* "rationalized political assassination," held the AFI, making it inappropriate for a center named for John F. Kennedy. Suspecting the real problem was its depiction of U.S. foreign aid as a prop for corrupt elites, Reichert organized a festival boycott. French New Wave director François Truffaut pulled his film, Paul Robeson withdrew from a planned tribute, and altogether a third

[2] Barbara Ehrenreich, "Left-wing Anti-feminism: A Response," NAM *Discussion Bulletin*, no. 14 (May 1976): 38; cartoon, unattributed, *New American Movement*, January 1976, p. 16.

of the films were withdrawn. *State of Siege* opened in New York a few weeks later, to rave reviews.[3]

How might her own radical filmmaking, Reichert wondered, reach mass audiences? Through NAM, she had met Alice and Staughton Lynd, who had relocated to Youngstown, Ohio, to practice labor and public interest law. The Lynds had just published an oral history, *Rank and File* (1973), and Reichert became entranced by the three women included among the book's two dozen personal working-class histories. She and Klein set out to interview them – Kate Hyndman, Stella Nowicki, and Sylvia Woods – in Chicago in 1974. With sparkle and candor, the women told of their victories and setbacks, bringing pearls of Old Left wisdom to a new generation. As Reichert and her colleagues worked to edit the interviews into a film that would combine women's history with labor history, they struggled to find good historical footage. When they searched the National Archives card catalogue, the very class and gender biases they opposed proved obstacles. Under "women strikers" or "women workers" they found nothing – until they looked under "girls." Under "strikes" they found little – until they looked under "riot." *Union Maids,* the resulting movie, premiered in San Francisco on May Day 1976, after a Dayton screening the night before attended by the Lynds, Hyndman, Nowicki, and Woods. The *New York Times* called the film a work of "grace and nobility" and, in a rare honor, *Union Maids* was nominated for an Academy Award. A sortie had been won in the war of position.[4]

As the sixties wave washed out, radicals continued to remain active and look forward, inspired by hope of contributing to the germination of a new society. Orienting themselves for the long duration, radicals in the 1970s anticipated that new revolutionary opportunities might very well present themselves again and that the left might better take advantage of them if radicals built upon the New Left's wide-ranging criticism of race, bureaucracy, and empire but overcame its mistakes, in particular by folding in new insights of gender, sexuality, and ecology. This project was accompanied by a recuperation of historical lessons from the

[3] Nick Rabkin and Jim Weinstein, "NAM Conference: Notes from Davenport," *New American Movement*, January 1972, p. 1; Roberta Lynch and Judy MacLean, "NAM's 3rd Convention: Growth and optimism vs. left's isolation," *New American Movement*, September 1974, p. 10; "Capital Film Festival Opens to Dispute; Called a Protest," *New York Times*, 4 April 1973, p. 34.

[4] Vincent Canby, "Film: 3 Women Who Didn't Wait for Lefty," *New York Times*, 4 February 1977, p. 48.

labor-focused and party-oriented midcentury left, its veterans now valued for their perseverance and endurance. The direction of national politics in the 1970s was uncertain as a sharper contest with the right was felt, but as economic crisis brought class politics into more definite focus, radicals sought to go well beyond the campuses and ghettoes that were at the center of sixties militancy to reach new swathes of Americans and forge a new egalitarian majority.

Three crucial factors mark 1973–1974 as a dividing line separating "the sixties" of 1956–1973 from what followed: American withdrawal from Vietnam, economic recession, and the Watergate scandal that brought down President Richard M. Nixon. These affected radicalism's prospects in complex ways. Beginning in 1969, Nixon and his Secretary of State Henry Kissinger began shifting from ground troops to air power in Vietnam while pursuing détente toward Mao's China and Brezhnev's Soviet Union. The war's "Vietnamization" was a direct response to New Left disruption at home and GI rebelliousness in the field. Its result was more bomb tonnage dropped across more national boundaries, devastating Laos and Cambodia, but since far fewer Americans were drafted or stationed in Southeast Asia it succeeded in reducing the incentive for radical student dissent at home, especially after withdrawal of U.S. forces from South Vietnam and the end of the draft in 1973. The mid-decade economic downturn, with unemployment peaking at nearly ten percent and remaining high throughout the decade even as inflation rose, meant the end of capitalism's long postwar boom. As corporations faced declining profitability, American radicals were presented with both new pitfalls and new possibilities. The recession, while it created new popular discontents, also displaced easy assumptions of perpetually rising standards of living and available work – favorable underlying conditions for sixties radicalism. Simultaneously, the recession broke the confidence of liberal policymakers to fine-tune the economy by alternating between deficit spending to stimulate growth and taxation to countermand inflation, at the very point when elite confidence was strained by the Watergate crisis. As a result, issues of political economy, class, and labor were put front and center in a way never quite true in the prior decade, dominated as it had been by war and race.

Among radicals the dissipation of sixties dreams was a common sensation. Gil Scott-Heron's "Winter in America" (1974) marked the receding of the black liberation movement; Bob Dylan's "Tangled Up in Blue" (1975) seemed wistful as it recalled a time when "there was music in the cafes at night and revolution in the air." Folksinger Phil Ochs's suicide in

1976 seemed an epitaph for the New Left, and the news media dubbed the 1970s the "Me Decade," profiling inward-turning stories such as that of Rennie Davis, a dedicated antiwar organizer who turned to proselytizing for a 15-year-old Indian guru. Most radicals, however, did not spend their days looking backward at the glory days of the sixties but forward, in pursuit of changes yet to come. In their way of looking at contemporary history, 1968 was but a dress rehearsal for a more effective social revolution. This time around, the left would connect with a wider segment of the American populace, tap older traditions of the left rooted in labor and economic justice, overturn the existing order, and replace it with a new society more fair, tolerant, democratic, and egalitarian. This anticipation was fed by a sense that opposition to "the system" was in many ways more plausible than ever in the 1970s, given the crisis of government authority associated with the Watergate scandal and the recession's shakeup of the longtime supposition that modern capitalism produced greater stability and equality.

Watergate was a direct outgrowth of the political repression visited upon sixties radicals. Starting in 1969, the Nixon White House had carried out secret illegal wiretaps and break-ins against antiwar radicals and reporters. After publication in 1971 of the Pentagon Papers, classified U.S. documents on the war's origins, the White House authorized a secret team known as "the Plumbers" charged with plugging news leaks. Made up of former CIA agents and right-wing Cuban exiles from the failed Bay of Pigs operation, the Plumbers carried out illegal wiretaps on reporters; burglarized the office of the psychiatrist of Daniel Ellsberg, the defense analyst who had leaked the Pentagon Papers; and undertook other improper operations. By 1972, the campaign against Nixon's "enemies" paid for by the Committee to Re-elect the President (CRP) included forging documents to sabotage Democratic primary candidate Edmund Muskie's primary campaign, planting provocateurs in Vietnam Veterans Against the War, spying on radicals in 38 states, and a break-in and attempted illegal wiretap of the Democratic National Committee's offices at the Watergate, an office–residential complex in Washington, D.C. As *Washington Post* reporters probed and as Congress convened hearings, it became clear that the covert activities reached all the way to the White House, which paid hush money to cover them up. In an astonishing development, Nixon, facing impeachment, resigned in 1974. Subsequent Congressional inquiries, such as those led by Idaho Senator Frank Church in 1975, exposed the extent of the FBI's COINTELPRO – first revealed when Philadelphia antiwar activists broke into a Media, Pennsylvania, FBI office – and the

National Security Administration's Project MINARET, a watch list for-
malized in 1969 after the CIA requested monitoring of "U.S. individuals
involved in either civil disorders, radical student or youth activities, racial
militant activities, radical antiwar activities, draft evasion/deserter support activities, or in radical related media activities."[5]

Such exposures of government intrusion in the democratic process
could have radicalizing effects, including on guilt-ridden personnel in
the responsible agencies. Former CIA agent Philip Agee, in *Inside the
Company* (1975), described the agency's role in propping up dictatorships in the interest of U.S. multinational corporations. *Covert Action
Information Bulletin*, established by Agee and veteran New Left radicals in 1978, exposed American undercover agents and "assets" until a
new law forbade them from doing so. At the same time, the effects of
Watergate and related disclosures could tend in the opposite direction,
against a renewal of radicalism. They deepened popular cynicism, creating a mood of resignation, withdrawal, and disengagement very different
from the political culture of democratic idealism that produced the early
New Left. The economic recession, furthermore, sounded a death knell
for many underground newspapers, communes, and other weakly capitalized counterinstitutions. Opposition to "the state," as radicals called
it, after Watergate could just as easily take the right-wing form of railing
against "big government" and "limousine liberals," the language of a
rising New Right that fomented anger at taxes, welfare, and bureaucratic
red tape in Washington.

Nonetheless, radicals at first saw many new opportunities even in
talk of the "end of an era" and "limits." Some radicals active in the
environmental cause – one of the vast social movements to grow out
of the sixties – used the new mood to emphasize the wisdom of constraints on headlong growth. Conservative talk of a "crisis of the welfare
state," implying that regulatory interference and social spending should
be curtailed to return to the verities of free-market economics, was turned
around by radicals to suggest that postwar liberal claims to a humanized
capitalism were illusory and that more far-reaching social transformation
was warranted to replace class society. James O'Connor argued in *The
Fiscal Crisis of the State* (1973) that the contradiction between the state's
need to pacify popular discontent (by means of social-welfare expenditures) and its support of corporate profits (by limiting tax demands

5 Senate Select Committee to Study Government Operations, *Final Report*, Book III (Washington, D.C.: Government Printing Office, 1976), p. 751.

on businesses) would challenge the stability of capitalism itself. Those grouped around Irving Howe's *Dissent* advocated going *"beyond* the welfare state" – pursuing new forms of economic democracy by stronger wealth redistribution and more extensive planning for industrial policy and public welfare, rather than assuming that the arc of growth would float all boats. Veterans of the New Left hoped that as these crises sank in, popular discontent in the 1970s would no longer be understood by other Americans as a concern only of aggrieved minorities, whether defined racially, generationally, or politically, but of a social majority, permitting another foundation for an American left. If days when "revolution was in the air" seemed distinctly part of the past, renewed mass mobilizations from below could be imagined without great difficulty once the "new social movements" of black, brown, red, yellow, women, gay, student, environmental, and countercultural constituencies were merged with a broader working-class constituency – joining, in essence, the free spirit of the 1960s to the mass-production insurgency of the 1930s and 1940s – to make once-marginal ideas enter a mainstream of common sense once again.

Within the academic disciplines, the transition of student radicals to young professionals had produced caucuses from the Union for Radical Political Economics (URPE) to the Committee of Concerned Asian Scholars, organizations such as Science for the People, and journals ranging from *The Black Scholar* and *Critical Sociology* to *Radical History Review*. These provided centers for the cultivation of critical perspectives, often with links to activist nodes outside the universities, such as the North American Congress on Latin America. In such incubators of dissenting thought, radicals sought to integrate the "new social movements" with revived working-class themes. The word "new" was a misnomer in that radical concern for issues of race, gender, sexuality, and culture had a long history, but it spoke to heightened awareness of such issues wrought by independent movements in the 1960s. These concerns coexisted in the 1970s with a reinvigoration of labor-based socialist visions, community organizing, and campaigns for economic justice, all overlapping in various ways. The challenge was to forge a coherent left out of these diverse elements. Many radicals hoped the next American left, while showing continuities with the New Left, would be more deeply resonant with the American scene, more committed to empowering ordinary people and more focused in its pursuit of a program of transformation associated with socialism or some other sort of "economic democracy."

Certainly by the mid-1970s Americans talked more openly than they had in decades about "class" as a dividing line and "the working class" as comprising the great bulk of Americans, terms that Cold War culture had banished from discourse, but even as criticism of the overweening power of big business found resonance, conservatives and corporate interests recognized the threat and mobilized to counteract it. The decade would end in what writer Kevin Phillips had called the "emerging Republican majority," bankrolled by corporate dollars, producing Ronald Reagan's 1980 election as president. If this outcome suggests that left-wing hopes of regeneration were delusional, the defeat was far from foreordained. For radicals the 1970s were a time of peril and promise alike. Having experienced a caesura, a break in momentum, they could easily imagine renewed radical ascension. The turn away from the late New Left's tactical excess and confrontational actions meant radicalism was less frequently found on the front pages, but it also meant a return to more serious forms of below-the-radar organizing. Across the 1970s, some protest movements actually increased in visibility and mass popularity, while the left as a whole retained enough vigor and hope to take part in real contests over American life and politics.

As the Vietnam War induced employment, growth, and inflation, a new strike wave emerged in the United States in the late 1960s and early 1970s coinciding with comparable upsurges in France, Italy, and West Germany. Wildcats – spontaneous strikes not authorized by union leaders – increased as management pressure for speed and output intensified. The new worker unrest, which extended to public employees, manufacturing workers, and miners, was shot through with influences of the Vietnam radicalization. Black radicals in Detroit's auto plants, for example, argued that the United Automobile Workers (UAW) officialdom for all its liberalism had not achieved racial equality in job classifications and pay. The nation's work stoppages climaxed in 1970, when days lost to strike action hit a point higher than any other postwar year excepting 1946 and 1959, with General Motors and General Electric among the major companies hit. In a massive postal wildcat, workers struck in 200 cities in March 1970, winning a 14 percent wage increase and an improved promotion system.

This labor upsurge captured the imagination of a New Left that recognized, increasingly, a need to win over working-class Americans. After May 1968, when millions of workers struck in France, revolutionary class action in the advanced capitalist countries was once again imaginable,

while the dangers of working-class conservatism were brought home
when hard-hat construction workers beat up antiwar demonstrators on
Wall Street in 1970 and Alabama's racist Governor George Wallace made
inroads into the ranks of white working-class voters as a presidential
candidate in 1968 and 1972. In *An Essay on Liberation* (1969), Herbert Marcuse called the working class a "counterrevolutionary force" in
relation to New Left student and black demands, but stated that "the
transformation of a social system" would still depend on it. In *New Left
Review*, Ernest Mandel asserted that mere "trade-union consciousness,"
the pursuit of simple bread-and-butter demands, might soon come to have
"a major revolutionary potential . . . under the impact of the international
competition of capital."[6]

Perhaps no strike symbolized the times more than the three-week 1972
strike in Lordstown, Ohio, at a state-of-the-art General Motors Chevrolet plant staffed by a largely young and white workforce. Lordstown's
8,100 workers appeared to herald a new breed – long-haired, marijuana-
smoking, fed up with authoritarian bosses and sped-up production, and
contemptuous of the old bargain of good money for degrading labor. The
strike seemed to manifest an instinctive drive for greater meaning in work
and workers' control of production. Lordstown workers won reinstate-
ment of some workers laid off in management's drive toward speed and
disciplinary control, demonstrating shopfloor power.

To many radicals, the wildcats showed the need for a "rank and file"
labor orientation: opposition to corrupt, authoritarian union bureaucrats;
advocacy of direct election of union officers and votes on contract ratification; more inclusive forms of organizing and union representation; rejection of weak contracts; and more militant job actions. That agenda often
pitted far-left radicals against social-democratic union leaderships. Such
had been the case in the 1968 Brooklyn strike of the United Federation of
Teachers led by Al Shanker in Ocean Hill-Brownsville, in which a union of
mostly Jewish teachers struck against a new school board trying to intro-
duce new curricula and more teachers of color into a white-dominated system in a black community. Similarly resistant to black militant demands
and lulled by a cooperative postwar bargaining relationship, UAW leaders
in 1973 urged strikers back to work when Chrysler was hit by a nationwide string of walkouts and sit-downs over speed-up, racist foremen, and
maiming accidents. Elsewhere radicals faced more blatantly corrupt union

---

[6] Herbert Marcuse, *An Essay on Liberation* (Boston: Beacon, 1969), pp. 16, 53; Ernest
Mandel, "Where Is America Going?" *New Left Review* no. 54 (March–April 1969): 15.

FIGURE 5.1. A surge of strike action in the early 1970s gave rise to hopes of a militant rank-and-file labor movement, but economic recession blunted labor's revitalization. Here a striker with the United Farm Workers carries a flag stating "Huelga" ("Strike") at San Luis, Arizona, in 1974. *Ben Garza / Walter P. Reuther Library, Archives of Labor and Urban Affairs, Wayne State University.*

bureaucracies. In the United Mine Workers (UMW), a typically rigged election in 1969 saw union dissident Jock Yablonski win a stunning third of the votes against strongman Tony Boyle, who couldn't countenance even that. His enforcers murdered Yablonski and his wife and daughter in their home on New Year's Eve 1969. Outraged, the opposition organized Miners for Democracy and won control of the union in 1972, a success that inspired other rank-and-file union democracy campaigns.

These stirrings coincided with the turn of significant numbers of New Left radicals toward the working class. One group to send its members into industry was the International Socialists (IS), formed out of the Independent Socialist Clubs, with many former Berkeley student radicals among them, including Free Speech Movement activist Jack Weinberg, who took a job in steel. IS members concentrated in the auto, trucking, and telephone sectors just as the economic recession hit hard. In 1975, the IS helped a variety of rank-and-file caucuses unify to form Teamsters for a Democratic Union (TDU), a caucus within the most notoriously autocratic, corrupt union in the country, dominated by nepotistic cabals often aligned with the mafia, who cut sweetheart deals with the trucking companies for kickbacks. TDU raised the slogan, "Ready to Strike." In the United Steelworkers union, which agreed in 1973 to give up strikes in exchange for regular cost-of-living raises, a dissenting caucus called Steelworkers Fight Back organized in 1975 with a platform rejecting that concession, objecting to intensified shopfloor discipline, and calling for ratification of contracts by the whole membership.

Steelworkers Fight Back gained national publicity with a union presidential campaign by Chicago-Gary dissident Ed Sadlowski, but when Sadlowski lost in 1977, the organization faded. The democracy movement in the coalfields also faded as its leaders, elected to UMW leadership, proved ineffectual in tough economic times and a hard-fought strike. Significant rank-and-file democracy initiatives continued into the 1980s, including a New Directions movement in the UAW spearheaded by St. Louis auto activist Jerry Tucker with support from Walter Reuther's socialist brother Victor Reuther, but TDU alone had a major impact and survived in the long run owing to the perseverance of its IS core, who in 1979 also created *Labor Notes* to enable communication between fightback-inclined rank-and-file unionists in different workplaces and economic sectors.

The traditionally white, male, industrial concentration of union membership began to shift by the 1960s and 1970s, since in government offices and hospitals – growth sectors for union representation – women and people of color figured prominently. In 1973, a group of Harvard University secretaries schooled in the women's movement began a campaign to organize clerical workers through a new organization, 9to5, with special emphasis on workplace sexual harassment and other gender issues. By decade's end, twelve such local groups combined into a 10,000-member National Association of Working Women. Before long, the group's efforts merged together with the Service Employees International Union (SEIU), a janitors union reorganized in 1968. Its greatest organizing success was among clerical staff at the University of Washington in SEIU Local 925, but all such campaigns were uphill battles as the administration of labor law proved less and less hospitable to unions. The Coalition of Labor Union Women (CLUW) drew 3,300 to its founding convention in Chicago in 1974 and promoted women's interests within the traditionally masculine AFL-CIO. Even popular culture registered the new women's labor activism in the aftermath of two successful independent documentaries, Reichert and Klein's *Union Maids* and Barbara

Kopple's *Harlan County, USA* (1976). Three Hollywood movies featured women workers and organizers: *Norma Rae* (1979), based on a true story of a mother who spearheaded successful unionization of her J. P. Stevens North Carolina textile plant in 1974, starring Sally Field and directed by former blacklistee Martin Ritt; *Nine to Five* (1980), starring Jane Fonda, country singer Dolly Parton, and comedian Lily Tomlin, inspired by the clerical workers' campaign; and *Silkwood* (1983), starring Meryl Streep, concerning the mysterious 1974 death of Karen Silkwood, a rank-and-file Oil, Chemical, and Atomic Workers (OCAW) activist who with the support of radical union staffer Tony Mazzocchi agitated for plant safety in the manufacture of nuclear fuel rods, in an early instance of what would later be called labor environmentalism.

Complementing the rank-and-file labor upsurge was a general turn of the New Left toward socialist ideals. The circle associated with *Studies on the Left*, including historians James Weinstein and Martin J. Sklar, as well as Stanley Aronowitz, a former union staffer with the clothing and oil workers' unions, argued that socialism was the best way to reach an American popular mainstream, far preferable to self-isolating militancy. As they revived the idea of a heterogeneous mass socialist party, Martin Luther King, Jr., had begun to call for the "restructuring of the architecture of American society," saying that "something is wrong with capitalism" and "America must move toward a democratic socialism." Even in urbane liberal circles, John Kenneth Galbraith, Harvard voice of Keynesianism, declared, "The Democratic Party must henceforth use the word socialism." Hunter S. Thompson saw no prospect of the Democrats doing any such thing (he called the Democrats a "gang of senile leeches," specifically naming Cold War labor head George Meany, Philadelphia's bigoted mayor Frank Rizzo, and Chicago mayor Richard J. Daley) but the *Rolling Stone* writer too was speaking in strikingly redistributive terms by 1972, casting the country as "ready for a presidential candidate who is genuinely radical, someone who might campaign for the confiscation of all inherited wealth, for instance."[7]

Equally leftward-tending in the general radicalization was Michael Harrington, bestselling author of *The Other America*, who saw a new

---

[7] David Garrow, *Bearing the Cross: Martin Luther King, Jr., and the Southern Christian Leadership Conference* (New York: Vintage, 1988), pp. 537, 540; John Kenneth Galbraith, *The American Left and Some British Comparisons* (London: Fabian Society, 1971), p. 24; Thompson, *Fear and Loathing on the Campaign Trail '72* (New York: Popular Library, 1973), p. 488.

"democratic left" in the offing, committed to socialism as a distant goal while urging strong reforms in the here and now aimed at economic planning for the public good. A three-way factional breach had opened in the Socialist Party of America at the dawn of the seventies. On the right was Max Shachtman's circle of archly anticommunist Cold Warriors supportive of the Vietnam War, hostile to the New Left, and aligned with Meany's AFL-CIO. Rechristened Social Democrats, USA (SDUSA), this faction's few hundred graying members, which included Bayard Rustin, had a hawkish liberal politics akin to those of Democratic Senator Henry "Scoop" Jackson, with some of its members taking on hues of neoconservatism in sync with the journal *Commentary*. Diametrically opposed to them was the left wing of the Socialist Party, organized in a Debs Caucus led by David McReynolds, which was largely pacifist (or at the very least opposed to the Vietnam War) and became the Socialist Party USA (SPUSA), preserving the traditional socialist strategy of electoral campaigns. The SPUSA, which rarely rose above a thousand members in following decades, would barely make a dent politically despite having former Milwaukee Mayor Frank Zeidler as its chair, except to make a showing in liberal university districts in eastern Iowa, electing a mayor in University Heights from 1976 to 1987 and a member to the Iowa City council from 1989 to 2000.

Harrington's circle, the final cluster in this three-way Socialist Party split, formed the Democratic Socialist Organizing Committee (DSOC). Of the three, it was destined to have the greatest influence, largely because of Harrington's vigor and recognition as an intellectual. The social movements of the sixties had given rise to a middle-class left-liberal "New Politics" expressed in Arnold Kaufman's *The Radical Liberal* (1970). Such reformers, seeking to end the Vietnam War, opened up the Democratic Party's delegate nominating process, diminishing the power of party bosses. Buoyed by this development, DSOC endorsed South Dakota liberal George McGovern's Democratic candidacy of 1972, which SDUSA opposed from the right and SPUSA from the left. DSOC hewed to the "realignment" logic of orienting toward reform Democrats (or what Harrington called "the left wing of the possible") while looking to Sweden and other Scandinavian democracies as models of the good society. This aim of influencing policy from within appealed to a layer of union officials, social service providers, teachers, civil servants, and political staffers, intersecting with the readership of *Dissent*. DSOC, although never larger than a few hundred members, attracted some prominent left-liberal voices in the AFL-CIO leadership, including William Winpisinger, president of the International Association of Machinists. Harrington played a prominent part across the decade as an intellectual trying to bring socialism to popular attention, pushing hard for a program funneling the resources of affluent America to meet human needs that markets did not recognize. He was full of conflicting sentiments in the 1970s, sometimes convinced a new opening for democratic socialism had arrived, at other times worried about radicalism's fragmentation and the threat of a growing right wing. He envisioned a society in which "invidious competition is no longer programmed into life," "cooperation, fraternity and equality become natural," and "social productivity will reach such heights that compulsory work will no longer be necessary" – making socialism "more relevant to the humane construction of the twenty-first century than any other idea."[8]

Many veteran radicals shared those ideals but looked instead to workplace and community struggles instead of conventional politics to realize them. James Weinstein and Martin Sklar in the inaugural editorial of their journal *Socialist Revolution* in 1970 held that the "basic economic contradictions of capitalism" – between economic growth and unmet needs, between abundance and alienation – were "once again reappearing at the point of direct production." To cultivate the new discontent and shape it into a socialist consciousness, they wrote, would require a redefinition of "abundance and the good life" to include "decentralization, public transportation, the merging together of work, recreation, and residence, etc." This echoed Marx's theory that capitalist development made collective control of production and consumption possible, with an emphasis on workers' subjectivity, the ability to reclaim selfhood by choosing aims in work as well as leisure. *Socialist Revolution* predicted that the modern liberal program of state-sponsored social relief would not be able to stave off class conflict forever and that a new popular left-wing politics would grow.[9]

Similar principles inspired the New American Movement, which regarded any angling for influence in the Democratic Party as futile but unlike the SPUSA did not engage in symbolic bids for federal office, although some members took part in local races or in ballot measure politics. Lacking substantial links to the labor movement – despite some members in public-sector unions and the involvement of Aronowitz,

---

[8] Michael Harrington, *Socialism* (New York: Saturday Review Press, 1972), pp. 3, 344.

[9] "Editorial Statement: The Making of Socialist Consciousness: Part I," *Socialist Revolution* 1 (January–February 1970), pp. 9–11.

whose book *False Promises: The Shaping of American Working Class Consciousness* (1974) was widely read – NAM put its energies into community organizing for adequate public services and into establishing socialist adult education schools in cities such as Los Angeles and Portland, Oregon. Some of its members emphasized participatory democracy in opposition to capitalism in classic New Left fashion, while others looked to the new "Eurocommunism" in Italy, Spain, and France as suggesting possible grounds for convergence of the socialist and communist traditions, even as socialist feminism predominated as NAM's guiding ethos and practice.

The theme of "economic justice" was gaining a much wider audience. In calling for a Poor People's March in 1968, Martin Luther King had held that only a multiracial campaign against economic inequality and poverty could subdue white resentment of black advancement. Similarly, in 1970, National Welfare Rights Organization (NWRO) founder George Wiley sent the young white organizer Wade Rathke to Little Rock, Arkansas, to build grassroots campaigns among whites and blacks, welfare recipients, and workers for improved public services and a voice in public affairs. With a close collaborator in young black organizer Gary Delgado, Rathke founded the Arkansas Community Organizations for Reform Now (ACORN), bringing a popular antipoverty campaign to the South and rallying various groups effectively to win a furniture allowance for welfare recipients, school lunches for black students in working-class areas, lower electric utility bills for the poor, medical care for poor whites at the University of Arkansas Medical Center, and a stop to construction of a large coal-fired power plant that would have contaminated the land and crops of nearby farmers. Meanwhile, Wiley encountered mounting conflicts with welfare mothers on NWRO's national board who felt his national staff usurped too much decision-making power from actual welfare recipients. Soon after resigning from NWRO at the start of 1973, Wiley set up a new organization, the Movement for Economic Justice (MEJ), which he imagined as a "majority movement" rooted in local organizing all over the country that would tackle income, taxes, housing, and health insurance. Wiley toured the country to visit a community union of white welfare recipients in West Virginia and an interracial housing action group in Chicago fighting redlining (the denial of housing loans to certain neighborhoods based on race or class) and tax inequities favoring the wealthy. Indeed, before "tax reform" became a conservative rallying cry for upper middle-class homeowners, Wiley helped build campaigns, most notably in the white working-class Boston neighborhood of Chelsea, for tax fairness to close loopholes enjoyed by the rich and relieve burdens on the poorest earners.

Although Wiley died in 1973 and MEJ never really got off the ground, some of his collaborators built effective citizen-action groups for tax equity and national health care. By the mid-1970s, ACORN became the *Association* of Community Organizations for Reform Now. In 1977, it mobilized hundreds of unemployed black teenagers to demand jobs from local authorities in Memphis, New Orleans, and Philadelphia. Aiming at establishing offices in twenty states by 1980, ACORN also promoted a guaranteed annual income and began agitating against the nuclear arms race. Leaders of ACORN believed these campaigns raised elementary, and piercing, questions of who has social power. Nonetheless, ACORN ran into some of the same difficulties as Wiley's NWRO, with complaints growing against the leadership's attempt to build a national staff apparatus that acted too unilaterally, choosing which campaigns to pursue and defining the strategies of protest. Harry Boyte, a white southern civil rights movement veteran and NAM member, later criticized ACORN for a top-down "mobilizing" strategy, rather than a bottom-up organizing strategy. ACORN's methods, he said, were less effective than some other community action campaigns that collaborated with labor unions and local churches to sink deep roots in local neighborhoods. Nonetheless, ACORN had some 60,000 active members nationwide by the 1980s, mostly poor, black, and Latino, and it was daring enough to commence a squatting campaign to reclaim abandoned buildings in government hands to house low-income families on the principle that human rights should trump property rights.

The socialist revival took other forms as radicals further to the left sought tighter and more coherent forms of revolutionary organization in the 1970s. Trotskyist organizations, for example, experienced growth, energy, and hardening. American Trotskyism's flagship remained the Socialist Workers Party (SWP), which built on its position in national antiwar coalitions to rebound from a small membership of a few hundred in the mid-1960s to a membership of several thousand by 1976, with more than 30,000 paid subscribers to the *Militant*. The IS had initially propounded a "socialism from below" politics in many respects closer to NAM and the New Left, but in the process of "industrializing" had by the mid-1970s adopted a stricter Leninism. These groups were rivals with one another and various tiny Trotskyist groupuscules on their periphery, but they shared three positions in common: criticism of

Communist states for bureaucratic rule rather than workers' power, advocacy of a labor party over left-wing strategies within the Democratic Party, and valuation of revolutionary socialist organization.

In the 1970s, such views were sufficiently commonplace among radicals that DSOC leader Harrington agreed to debate SWP presidential candidate Peter Camejo one day before the national election in 1976, when President Gerald Ford, a moderate Republican who inherited the Oval Office from the disgraced Nixon, was running against the centrist Georgia Democratic nominee Jimmy Carter. Harrington took the position that corporate elites preferred Ford, whereas organized labor, blacks, and women preferred Carter; that Carter had committed himself to full-employment legislation; and that the Democratic Party, while a mass of contradictions, needed the left in its midst advocating a bolder program. Camejo held that the key question about the Democratic Party was not its constituencies but who controlled it, namely its corporate backers; that change comes from independent mass political movements such as the civil rights and antiwar movements; that the left should work toward a mass labor party free of capitalist assumptions; that the 1964 election, when many on the left voted for Johnson in fear that Goldwater would escalate the war in Vietnam, proved outcomes are determined by the underlying social system that both parties serve; and that New York City's budget cuts under Democrats in the 1970s illustrated that a Carter presidency would offer no alternative to austerity. Where Harrington and Camejo agreed was in rejecting the suggestion that the worse things got, the more people would radicalize. "What makes people radical," said Harrington, "is the feeling that they can win something."[10]

Of the revolutionary party-building impulses of the 1970s, the most sizeable cohort was not Trotskyism but what the *Guardian* in 1972 termed a "new communist movement" initially inspired by ideological affinity with Maoist China's Cultural Revolution. Looking across the Pacific for guidance rather than the Atlantic as so many prior American radicals had, this Maoist current emerged out of the late New Left and Third World liberation movements. That it embraced the word "communist" reflected a widespread sense that older party-centered, labor-oriented forms of radicalism deserved reconsideration; that it nevertheless called itself "new" reflected a characteristic New Left desire to transcend

---

[10] Michael Harrington, Peter Camejo, et al., *The Lesser Evil? The Left Debates the Democratic Party and Social Change* (New York: Pathfinder, 1977), p. 34.

the mistakes of the Old Left. A strong complement came out of SDS's RYM II faction, opposed to both Weatherman's adventurism and Progressive Labor's disparagement of the Black Panthers and Vietnamese National Liberation Front (NLF). Also critical to the new communist movement were formations of people of color including the Puerto Rican Socialist Party, the Black Workers Congress, the Third World Women's Alliance founded by SNCC feminist Frances Beal, the Communist League, and a variety of groups of Asian Americans and Pacific Islanders such as Wei Min She, I Wor Kuen (IWK), the Union of Democratic Filipinos (KDP), the Japan Town Collective, and the East Wind Collective (whose leader Shin'ya Ono, brother of John Lennon's partner Yoko Ono, had been a *Studies on the Left* editor, then a Weatherman at the Days of Rage, but came to regret the late New Left's indiscriminate tactics and pursued Japanese-American community organizing).

The themes of this "Marxist-Leninist" (or "M-L") left were a Third World Marxism emphasizing the centrality of opposing racial oppression in the United States, admiration for various guerrilla struggles abroad, a "proletarian" orientation, and identification as "antirevisionist" to contrast its communism with that of the Soviet Union and CPUSA, both criticized for revising, or watering down, Marxism. Study groups read the Marxist classics and Mao's writings (too often taken as a finished body of truths) as well as articles from the *Guardian* and Paul Sweezy and Harry Magdoff's *Monthly Review*, at a peak circulation of 11,500 in 1977. Their ranks were initially large and their activism had moments of great efficacy. Between 1972 and 1974, the Revolutionary Union (RU), initially the largest of the trend's formations, spearheaded strike support committees around the country for 4,000 Farah pants manufacturing workers, mostly Chicana women, who won a recognition strike in Texas and New Mexico. In 1972, members of the October League (OL), RU's main rival, led a strike at the mostly black 1,100-worker Mead Packaging plant in Atlanta, portrayed in the documentary film *Wildcat at Mead* (1972). In 1974, when construction began in New York's Chinatown on Confucius Plaza, a 764-unit federal housing complex, Jerry Tung's Asian Study Group launched Asian Americans for Equal Employment, whose protests won a few dozen construction jobs for Chinese Americans with the slogan, "The Asians built the railroad: Why not Confucius Plaza?" In 1976, the Puerto Rican Socialist Party led 40,000 marchers in Philadelphia calling for a "Bicentennial Without Colonies," contrasting the original American Revolution against colonial rule to the country's present-day position of domination over Puerto Rico. Such radicals also staved off destruction of the International Hotel (or "I-Hotel") on Kearny Street in San Francisco, home to many elderly low-income Filipino and Chinese residents, between 1969 and 1977. Taken together, this new communist movement was the largest current on the far left, but not necessarily its most promising, since developments abroad and infighting would keep it from coalescing.[11]

Trotskyism and Maoism were separated by many shades of sensibility – and not just on the merits or liabilities of particular Communist states. Trotskyist groups were more open to women's caucuses and the gay movement, Maoists to "cross-class" alliances. The two did, however, share some things in common, even if they were loath to admit it. Each was based on the doctrines of a chosen master thinker, emphasized correctness of line (Maoism) or program (Trotskyism), and saw Soviet Communism as insufficiently revolutionary. Above all, Maoist and Trotskyist currents shared admiration for Lenin's theory of a vanguard party, holding that overly inclusive, loose formations – the Mensheviks in early Russian Marxist debates or NAM and DSOC at present – would result in ineffectuality and reformism, whereas a tight socialist organization would prove most effective in holding out against social pressures and a formidable capitalist state.

The revival of Leninism in these various forms struck some American radicals as a terrible mistake, a retreat into sterile formulae of a discredited Old Left. The journal *Root and Branch* in Boston, Fredy Perlman's situationist-syndicalist Black & Red Press in Detroit, and many writers for *Radical America* argued in the 1970s that Leninism was elitist and authoritarian. By and large, Maoism or Trotskyism proved so attractive, however, that they even permeated the socialist–feminist NAM. The argot of the broad left was dotted with philosophical terms such as "contradiction," a favorite of Mao's, and "criticism/self-criticism." The idea of a revolutionary party that would hone and project the will of its cadres held appeal because of recent political experience, both globally and domestically. The CIA-backed military coup in Chile that overthrew Salvador Allende in 1973 seemed to prove moderate electoral strategies incapable of dislodging implacable ruling classes unwilling to accept democratic inroads on their privilege. Many New Leftists, meanwhile, had tired of a "participatory democracy" that in practice benefited informal, unaccountable, often media-selected leaderships – or what women's liberation activist Jo Freeman had termed "the tyranny of structurelessness." One

---

[11] William Wei, *The Asian American Movement* (Philadelphia: Temple, 1993), p. 220.

Texas radical remembers an SDS comrade bursting into her bedroom early one morning, waving Lenin's *What is to be Done?* and shouting, "You've got to read this! It has all the answers!"[12]

If being possessed of "all the answers" was dangerously illusory, Leninism did attract a surprising range of sixties-era participatory democrats. The hope was that a selective "party of a new type" would draw together the most combative, advanced workers, allow for variety in thought while securing unity in action, and use members' skills around the clock rather than rely on a paper membership. Orientation toward working-class organizing – and Lenin's criticisms of left-wing terrorism as an alternative strategy – seemed more rational than the "armed struggle" fantasies that still cropped up elsewhere. An inchoate post-Panther offshoot, the Black Liberation Army, attacked police until 1973, and the Weather Underground Organization set off its last bombs in 1974 with the winding down of the Vietnam War, but from the Red Army Faction in Germany to the Red Brigades in Italy, others persisted. In the United States, the Symbionese Liberation Army (SLA), a small cell, made headlines from 1973 to 1975 by murdering a black school superintendent in Oakland, issuing bizarre slogans ("Death to the fascist insect that preys upon the mind of the people"), kidnapping newspaper heiress Patty Hearst, and robbing banks until most of its core members were annihilated in a firefight with Los Angeles police, reflecting the ultra-left hallucination that tiny clusters of people can compel revolution at random.

By comparison the new communist party-building strategy looked to be more grounded in sober working-class reality, but "Marxism-Leninism-Mao Zedong Thought," as adherents called it, was otherworldly and esoteric in an American context. Each of the M-L groups claimed to uphold the one true correct line, leading to bitter rivalries among them and an inflated sense of self-importance across the board. When some took over important broad-based organizations, including Vietnam Veterans Against the War (captured by the Revolutionary Union) and the Southern Conference Educational Fund (captured by the October League), the style of rule-or-ruin domination killed off the prized conquest. Sects sparred over whether or not the old Communist theory of the South as a Black Belt nation held value, whether the Soviet Union was a "social-imperialist superpower" or part of a "socialist camp," and

---

[12] "From the desk of the Field Secretary, Minnesota Fabian-Leninists," *New American Movement*, April 1974, p. 12; Susan Torian Olan, "Blood Debts," in *No Apologies: Texas Radicals Celebrate the'60s* (Austin, Tex.: Eakin Press, 1992), p. 30.

whether, in 1974, Boston's school busing plan represented a challenge to racism that should be defended (as OL and most other groups thought) or a ruling-class plot to stoke divisions among working people (as RU held, damaging its reputation among people of color). Because of "two-line struggle," the Maoist concept that every revolutionary party has bourgeois and proletarian tendencies, political differences could be construed as irreconcilable class differences, mandating splits. "When I look back on all the fighting we did against each other," said Pat Sumi, a Japanese American communist, "I realize that we cared about being right more than we cared about each other."[13]

The search for revolutionary rectitude produced a host of antagonistic groups outdoing one another in dogma and rhetoric, each claiming to be the vanguard. RU morphed into the Revolutionary Communist Party (RCP), with Berkeley radical Bob Avakian as its Chairman, while the OL, headed by former SDS leader Mike Klonsky, became the Communist Party (Marxist-Leninist). Neither of these parties nor their many smaller rivals attracted many ordinary workers, since the boldest refusers of managerial authority on the shopfloor were usually uninterested in subordinating themselves to the direction of a central committee. Another striking failure of Marxism-Leninism in the 1970s was that it permanently estranged many lesbians and women from the left, because Mao-inspired groups typically disparaged homosexuality and feminism. Marxist-Leninist dogmatism could have comical effects, as when the May Day Singers struggled to find lyrics rhyming with "Soviet social-imperialism." More often than not, the consequences were tragic. Marlene Dixon, a professor discharged in 1969 from the University of Chicago for support of radical student protests, came by the mid-1970s to lead a Bay Area organization, the Democratic Workers Party, which had an atypically heavy lesbian composition for a Marxist-Leninist group, feminist politics, and an unusual cachet among intellectuals, but capricious purges propelled by its leader's substance abuse left its members reeling as the group turned cultish. By decade's end, virtually all of the "Marxist-Leninist" vanguard parties – which might better be called neo-Stalinist – saw their members drained, demoralized, and distrustful. Many members quit, concluding that the Leninist notion of "democratic centralism" in

---

[13] Ryan Msaaki Yokota, "Interview with Pat Sumi," in *Asian Americans: The Movement and the Moment,* ed. Steve Louie and Glenn K. Omatsu (Los Angeles, Calif.: UCLA Asian American Center Press, 2006), p. 30.

party organization meant, in practice, nothing but top-down autocratic rule by a central committee and maximal leader.[14]

Anticipation of new degrees of influence in touching the mainstream, that signal ambition of American radicals in the 1970s, was equally typical of radical black nationalism. Amiri Baraka played a leading role, aiming early in the decade to overcome the 1960s breach between "revolutionary nationalists" (such as the Black Panthers) and "cultural nationalists" (such as Ron Karenga's US Organization). Initially aligned with Karenga's call for a reawakening of black identity built on a separate culture rooted in African heritage, Baraka wanted to end the violence within the movement and focus on founding a broad-based but distinctly black political party to challenge white supremacy. In this lay the origin of campaigns that would last decades under the rubric of a "Black United Front." The first step in this campaign was a large convention on Labor Day 1970 in Atlanta establishing a Congress of African People (CAP), which promoted the political unity of blacks in the United States. Black nationalism for Baraka and his allies meant, in a Third World vein, identifying as "African" and pushing for independence for black communities to undertake their own plans of development as well as solidarity with liberation movements in Africa. One major event was African Liberation Day on May 27, 1972, when up to 60,000 people rallied around the country to protest U.S. support for white-supremacist South Africa and Rhodesia as well as Portuguese colonial power in Angola, Mozambique, and Guinea-Bissau – a renewal on a mass scale of the sort of anticolonialism voiced in the 1940s by the Council on African Affairs.

Above all, Baraka pushed for a National Black Political Convention, which met in March 1972 in Gary, Indiana. An ecumenical forum bringing together civil rights leaders, new black officeholders such as Gary's mayor Richard Hatcher, and radical black nationalists, the convention arose from assemblies that first convened at city and state levels to fashion proposals that would lead to a National Black Agenda for social and economic reconstruction. Over ten thousand people, including 1,800 black elected officials, convened in Gary, seeming to occupy common ground in calling for autonomous black political mobilization. Although

[14] Chris Kando Ijima, "'Make It Snappy!' What Rhymes with 'Soviet Social-Imperialism'?" in *Legacy to Liberation: Politics and Culture of Revolutionary Asian Pacific America*, ed. Fred Ho (San Francisco, Calif.: Big Red Media and AK Press, 2000), pp. 243–253.

independent politics had considerable black support, including from Chicago's Rev. Jesse Jackson (at that time the advocate of a Liberation Party that he suggested could run Michigan Rep. John Conyers for U.S. president), it was unlikely that representatives of the Congressional Black Caucus (CBC) were really prepared to break from the Democratic Party. Baraka, for his part, imagined that a militant platform stemming from the grassroots assemblies, if pushed by black politicians in Democratic Party circles, would quickly hit a brick wall within the two-party system, leading to an independent black party by 1976.

The Gary Agenda called for black control of new land in the rural South and housing in urban centers, offered one of the first attacks on environmental racism ("the powerful pollute, while the powerless suffer the atrocities of the pollution"), and encouraged "exploration of alternative forms of economic organization and development of a system that promotes self-reliance, cooperative economics, and people ownership and control of means of production and distribution of goods." From Gary, Baraka returned to Newark's ghetto to continue a model project of black-implemented reconstruction on a 100-acre "liberated zone," a large complex that was to include low-income housing, a medical center and home for seniors, space for cooperative businesses, community meeting halls, and black-run radio and television. The ambitious plan was doomed by the racial polarization of Newark politics, despite the election of a black mayor, Kenneth Gibson. White politicians and neighbors assailed the "racial" idea of public aid for a Black Power initiative, overlooking the historic and overtly white bias of urban political and economic development. The city council, ultimately with Gibson's consent, denied the expected tax abatements for Baraka's center. The project collapsed. On the national level, a related split had emerged after the Gary meeting over whether to support Israel and school integration busing, which black elected officials in the CBC proposed to do, or carry forward Gary resolutions in support of Palestinian self-determination and opposition to compulsory racial integration of schools. Baraka saw all of this as a rapid reversal of the hopes aroused by the Gary convention and by 1975 remade himself, joining the new communist movement as a Marxist-Leninist distrustful of a purely racial solidarity and critical of the black bourgeoisie.[15]

---

[15] Gary Agenda quoted in Komozi Woodard, *A Nation within a Nation: Amiri Baraka (LeRoi Jones) and Black Power Politics* (Chapel Hill: University of North Carolina Press, 1999), p. 213.

As many black militants turned to socialist politics in the 1970s, even Ron Karenga was skeptical of "black capitalism." Some, like Baraka, joined multiracial formations, others all-black organizations. Kwame Ture (the former Stokely Carmichael) organized U.S. branches of his All-African People's Revolutionary Party. The successors to the 1960s League of Revolutionary Black Workers fragmented by 1975, but movement veteran Ken Cockrel, a young lawyer, was elected to the Detroit city council as an avowed socialist in 1977, advocating city-owned utilities and opposing auto company tax breaks. Coleman Young, whose roots were in Detroit's Communist-centered Old Left, had become the city's first black mayor in 1973, but the city's black elected officials faced a declining tax base brought on by white flight and loss of manufacturing, making them more managers of urban crisis than architects of social reconstruction.

Meanwhile, black women began to raise more vocal criticisms of patriarchal and masculine assumptions within nationalist movements of people of color – a line of criticism that also found expression among Asian American and Latina women. In the early 1970s, pride in black womanhood was amplified by widely supported "Free Angela" campaigns for Angela Davis (although she herself was at the time a critic of feminism, maintaining the old Communist line that politics of class unity would end women's oppression). A Black Women's United Front (BWUF), which spoke largely in a black nationalist framework, called for "abolition of every possibility of oppression and exploitation" and declared the "right of a woman to self-defense," rallying support for black women inmates who had killed prison guards who assaulted them, most notably Joan Little, acquitted of murder in North Carolina in 1975 after a national campaign to free her. Yet other black women, including those in a National Black Feminist Organization founded in 1973, adopted an explicitly feminist rhetoric, at first primarily among educated professionals but soon spreading to more diverse elements of the black community.[16]

In 1974, a small group of mostly lesbian black feminists in Boston formed the Combahee River Collective, adopting the name of the spot in South Carolina where Harriet Tubman freed 750 slaves in 1863. They released a statement in 1977 that would be much reproduced in following decades and drew attention to "our specific oppression" and "the concept of identity politics." Born here, the phrase "identity politics" would in years to come be a target of criticism made by liberals and radicals

[16] Woodard, *A Nation within a Nation*, pp. 180–184.

who saw such assertions of particularity as fracturing the unity of broad
constituencies for change, but that was hardly the impulse behind the
Combahee formulation. The few dozen women who comprised the collective asserted they could neither find a place in black nationalist circles
that assumed women's submission nor accept the kind of feminism that
assumed a uniformity of women's interest without forthrightly examining the differences generated by racial oppression. They would not identify with middle-class women's groups indifferent to working women.
While drawing attention to their "own specific oppression," Combahee
members held that "the major systems of oppression are interlocking"
and called for "coalition with other progressive organizations and movements," making them ready, they said, to "become involved in workplace
organizing at a factory that employs Third-World women or picket a hospital that is cutting back on already inadequate health care to a Third
World community, or set up a rape crisis center in a black neighborhood." As this suggests, the meaning of "identity politics" in this document was precisely the opposite of what left-liberal critics later made
of the term, since its emphasis was on coalition-building rather than a
rampant particularism.[17]

Self-identification as "Third World" continued to be broadly common
among 1970s radical activists of color. Given the revolutionary models
offered by Cuba, China, and Vietnam, as well as influential works such
as Guyanese historian Walter Rodney's *How Europe Underdeveloped
Africa* (1972), the sense was strong that people of color worldwide were
in motion, freeing themselves from centuries of slavery, genocide, and
imperialism – and that America's inner cities suffered Third World underdevelopment within the First World. Asian Americans identified with
the Vietnamese Revolution and Mao's China; Puerto Rican and Filipino
radicals were buoyed by connections with their homelands' struggles;
and black radicals gazed upon African liberation struggles with pride.
This Third Worldism intersected, to a great extent, with Marxist-Leninist
currents.

Radicals of color also operated, however, within other frameworks
apart from the M-L milieu. The indigenous radical project spearheaded
by the American Indian Movement (AIM) emphasized sovereignty, spirituality, revival of ancestral folkways, respect for elders, and harmony

---

[17] Combahee River Collective, "A Black Feminist Statement," in *This Bridge Called My
Back: Writings by Radical Women of Color* (New York: Kitchen Table Press, 1983),
pp. 210, 212, 217.

FIGURE 5.2. Following the occupation of Wounded Knee, South Dakota, in 1973, the American Indian Movement continued to lead a traditionalist indigenous revival against both corrupt tribal administrations and racism in communities surrounding Indian reservations but was weakened by reprisals from officials and its own paranoia. © *AP/Corbis.*

with the earth. An elaboration of that indigenous agenda came when Women of All Red Nations, created by AIM women in 1974, sought to address involuntary sterilization, domestic violence, child malnutrition, and adoption of Indians by non-Indians, but in general AIM found the 1970s tough going. Organizing proved hard to sustain at AIM's Pine Ridge stronghold after Wounded Knee given the brutality of the Guardians of the Oglala Nation ("GOONs," as tribal boss Dick Wilson openly boasted) and scores of unsolved murders of AIM supporters. In 1975, AIM reeled with the discovery that its director of security, Douglass Durham, was a paid FBI operative. When two FBI agents pursuing a suspected thief drove onto a Pine Ridge radical encampment tense from prior shootouts with the GOONs, gunfire erupted, the FBI agents were killed at close range, and one militant died. Of three Indians charged in the agents' deaths, one was found guilty: Leonard Peltier, sentenced to two consecutive life sentences. Critics faulted the evidence and the all-white judge and jury, calling for his release. In 1976, the body of 30-year-old Annie Mae Aquash, AIM's foremost female leader, was discovered frozen below a remote Pine Ridge bluff, shot in the head. AIM blamed the FBI but decades later two low-level AIM members were convicted for executing her, with others testifying she had been under suspicion of being an informant. Much murkiness hangs over the period. In 1979, AIM chairman John Trudell – a half-Sioux, half-Mexican Vietnam veteran who led the Alcatraz occupation of 1969 – burnt an American flag at FBI headquarters in Washington, D.C. Hours later, his pregnant wife, their three children, and his wife's mother died in a fire at their home on the Duck Valley Indian Reservation on the Nevada-Idaho border. The cause of the fire was never determined, although Trudell suspected retribution for his radicalism. Trudell soon left the AIM leadership to pursue music, writing, and film acting.

Third Worldism as a whole reached an impasse in the 1970s, in large part owing to its tendency to cast certain states and struggles as the repository of political virtue, just as an older generation of Communists had done with the Soviet Union. Those who identified with Mao's China in the 1970s, for example, experienced a crisis over Portuguese Africa, where revolutionary movements, particularly one led by Amilcar Cabral in Guinea-Bissau, had exerted a hold on the black radical imagination. When a coup by left-leaning generals toppled António Salazar's dictatorship in Portugal in 1974, setting in motion independence for the regime's African colonies, a crisis resulted, paradoxically. Seizures of state power by the Front for the Liberation of Mozambique (FRELIMO) and the Popular Movement for the Liberation of Angola (MPLA) in 1975 were followed by an armed rebellion in Angola by a smaller group, the National Union for the Total Liberation of Angola (UNITA), initially funded by China and later backed by the United States and apartheid South Africa. American Maoists were at a loss to explain why China, the supposed revolutionary lodestar, was suddenly in league with the country they considered most imperialist (the United States) and the country they considered most racist (South Africa) to defeat a newly freed African state.

This pointed to developments in the People's Republic of China itself. Nixon's diplomatic overture to Mao in 1972 was part of a reshaping of Chinese foreign policy in which it began to join with the United States to support rearguard guerrilla resistance to more prominent anticolonial forces that had Soviet backing, such as the MPLA. After Mao's death in 1976, Deng Xiaoping steered the Chinese state toward market reforms, prompting the ultimate shattering crisis for the whole of the China-oriented left. American Maoists could either continue to support China and thereby effectively give support to U.S. foreign policy, against which Vietnam-era radicals defined themselves; embrace the Soviet Union, long seen as "revisionist"; conclude that no existing Communist state was worthy of support, placing them in approximation to their scorned Trotskyist rivals; or champion Enver Hoxha's Albania, which upheld Maoist ideology after China abandoned it but was a dictatorial autarky of distinctly limited appeal. None of these choices being very attractive, the movement began to disintegrate.

The withdrawal of U.S. troops from South Vietnam and the fall of Saigon in 1975 to combined NLF and North Vietnamese forces posed different conundrums. In one sense, the outcome was a triumph for all who had sought Vietnamese self-determination. Vietnamese Communists inherited a much-ravaged land, however, and although the Communist bloodbath long predicted by U.S. war supporters did not ensue, they did establish a single-party, top-down state that carried out political reprisals, population relocations, and use of "reeducation" camps, resulting in many hundreds of thousands of "boat people" fleeing Vietnam. Even more disturbingly, news began to trickle out of neighboring Cambodia after the Khmer Rouge took power and renamed the country Democratic Kampuchea in 1975. Pol Pot, the Khmer Rouge leader, took the Maoist precept of the radical peasant countryside encircling the bourgeois city to the utmost, presiding over mass executions of all suspected intellectuals and urban elites while claiming to construct an egalitarian peasant paradise freed of capitalist practices and modern degeneracy. The piles of skulls and bones found in the killing fields of Cambodia after 1979, when neighboring Vietnam invaded and overthrew the Khmer Rouge, were a chilling reprise of Stalinism – carried out, if anything, more ruthlessly. Noam Chomsky, a prominent American critic of the Vietnam War, suggested that the Cambodian bloodbath was a result of mass psychosis induced by years of U.S. carpet-bombing. The strand of American Maoists who had supported the Khmer Rouge spun into crisis, in a cautionary tale about the credulous tendency of certain radicals to assume that all forces opposed to U.S. empire deserve blanket support.

Trotskyists observed that classical Marxism had been rooted in the urban working class and sought to fulfill rather than destroy modernity, culture, and civilization, but the Cambodian bloodbath forever cast doubt on naïve, uncomplicated formulations of Third World liberation. The grim pall over Third World enthusiasms deepened when Jim Jones and his hundreds of followers in the Peoples Temple – a multiracial congregation prominent in San Francisco, which had relocated to Guyana to create a communal paradise in Jonestown – had committed mass suicide, apparently triggered by an investigation headed by Congressman Leo J. Ryan. Although the decade ended in 1979 with revolutions against the Shah's dictatorship in Iran and Anastasio Somoza's dictatorship in Nicaragua, both of them authoritarian regimes that had been armed and supported by the United States, the idea that revolutionary Third World social transformation was the road to a new world was in grave doubt. "A committed, resilient radicalism," wrote Adam Hochschild in *Mother Jones*, "must look at *all* countries – East, West, Third World, socialist – with no blinders on."[18]

The emergence of mass radical environmental politics in the 1970s presents another image altogether, that of the archetypal "new social movement" eluding the categories of an older socialist left. The new environmentalism extended beyond older traditions of wilderness conservation to focus on industrially generated toxins and destruction of whole ecosystems. Here too the takeoff point was in the 1960s, when Rachel Carson's bestseller *Silent Spring* (1962) exposed the deadly effects of the pesticide DDT on species and people. The possibility of environmental political action was demonstrated by the Wilderness Society's promotion of the Wilderness Act passed by Congress in 1964 and the successful

[18] Adam Hochschild, "Examining the Left's Myopia," *Mother Jones*, April 1980, p. 5.

Sierra Club campaign, led by David Brower, to scotch federal plans for two Grand Canyon mega-dams in the mid-1960s. Two events in 1969 provided further spurs to action: a massive oil spill from an offshore rig near Santa Barbara, California, and the catching fire of the chemically polluted surface of the Cuyahoga River in Cleveland, Ohio. A mass movement emerged with the first Earth Day on April 22, 1970, estimated to have had 20 million participants. Just as early twentieth-century campaigns for conservation and wilderness preservation were often apolitical, romantic protests of culturally conservative reformers against modernity, the renascent environmentalism had a mixed character. Earth Day was spearheaded by liberal Wisconsin politician Gaylord Nelson and acquired a countercultural feel with the participation of Abbie Hoffman but the day was also endorsed by Nixon and celebrated in the media as an occasion for unanimity, a relief from the yawning divides in American society. Many radicals regarded Earth Day as a phony, establishment-fostered diversion from inescapable conflicts of race and war, their cynicism reinforced when Nixon launched his invasion of Cambodia four days later. Yet from the beginning – even back in 1935, at the time of the founding of the Wilderness Society, one of whose founders, Bob Marshall, was a socialist – there were significant links between radicalism and ecology.

An early advocate of synthesizing radical criticism and environmental causes was Murray Bookchin, a Communist, then Trotskyist, and then anarchist writer. While still a Marxist writing under the pseudonym Lewis Herber, Bookchin penned an article on "The Problem of Chemicals in Food" in 1952 in the left-libertarian *Contemporary Issues* as well as a book, *Our Synthetic Environment* (1962), that clearly located environmental degradation in capitalist production. The biologist Barry Commoner began raising the issue of radioactive isotopes entering food and water supplies from nuclear fallout in the late fifties, and in *Science and Survival* (1966) called for science to be guided by social responsibility instead of profit or military uses. In 1969, the radical folksinger Pete Seeger launched his sloop *Clearwater* on the Hudson River to dramatize toxic pollution. That same year, Sierra Club director David Brower, dismayed by his board's willingness to temporize on nuclear power plant construction, left to form a more uncompromising group, Friends of the Earth. The most dynamic protest group to emerge after Earth Day was Greenpeace, founded in 1971 in Vancouver, British Columbia, its very name linking ecology with internationalism. Greenpeace revived Committee on Non-Violent Action (CNVA) tactics from the 1950s, sailing a boat near the underground U.S. nuclear testing zone off the coast of

Alaska. It continued to challenge both the arms race and environmental destruction, particularly in regard to whale populations, through the 1970s and 1980s in daring direct actions. To protest France's atmospheric nuclear testing in the South Pacific, Greenpeace sent boats into the test zone; France retaliated with a "black-ops" reprisal in 1985, sinking a Greenpeace ship moored in a New Zealand harbor and killing one of its crew.

As oil prices spiked in 1973–1974 as a result of an Arab oil producers' embargo following the 1973 Arab-Israeli war, and again in 1979–1980 as a result of the Iranian Revolution, energy issues took prominence. The radical left generally preferred conservation or renewable sources such as wind and solar to nuclear power. Apprehension about nuclear plants – particularly the dangers posed by the possible meltdown of reactors and the difficulty of discarding radioactive waste safely – had been voiced since the 1960s, when the well-known anthropologist Margaret Mead took up the issue in her popular *Redbook* magazine columns. During the early 1970s, local gadflies in the Northeast began to turn up at hearings convened by public utility regulators to oppose granting construction permits and the commissioning of nuclear power plants. When a group of antiwar activists living on a collective farm in northern Massachusetts sensed local residents' antipathy to nuclear power, they saw the issue as an extension of their peace activism that would ground it in community organizing and help the locals' cause by bringing protest tactics to bear on it.

The Massachusetts collectivists combined direct action with loosely defined principles of decentralism, emphasizing self-determination of small groups coming together in mass action. One of them, Sam Lovejoy, practiced what anarchists had long termed "propaganda of the deed" in 1974, using a crowbar to knock down a utility tower for a coming nuclear power project in Montague. In 1975, nearly 30,000 protesters in West Germany occupied a site to block plans by the government to build a new reactor, spurring Lovejoy and his colleagues in the following year to organize the Clamshell Alliance to oppose activation of a nuclear plant at Seabrook, New Hampshire. Seabrook residents had long opposed the plant, warning that its thermal pollution would kill coastal clambeds, since the design relied on recycling seawater to cool the nuclear core. When over 2,000 people rallied at Seabrook in April and May 1977, 1,400 willingly surrendered to arrest for trespassing, a mass environmental civil disobedience beyond the small, intrepid bands of Greenpeace voyagers. The Seabrook action was planned with help from the Movement for a New Society, a Philadelphia-based, Quaker-influenced radical pacifist action group whose first action had been to block shipments from the port of Philadelphia to Pakistan's military dictatorship in 1971.

The most significant Clamshell emulator on the West Coast was the Abalone Alliance, mobilized to oppose licensing of Pacific Gas & Electric's Diablo Canyon nuclear plant near San Luis Obispo, California. As in the case of the Clamshell Alliance, that campaign had its origins in a group of peace agitators (the city's Mothers for Peace, formed during the Vietnam War) and took the name Abalone in behalf of creatures shown to have been harmed by test runs of the plant's cooling system on the coast. Abalone's first large protest took place in August 1977, and rallies – usually accompanied by the arrest of a select number of protesters who trespassed on the construction site – continued to mount in the next few years. In this case, the plant's proximity to an earthquake fault enhanced fears of a catastrophic accident if the plant went into operation. The demonstrations reached a climax in 1981, when a last-ditch effort at a mass blockade of the construction site led to 1,900 arrests. Engineers discovered serious design errors that put off operation of the plant for safety reasons, and although the plant ultimately started up, the combination of public opposition and a partial reactor meltdown at Three Mile Island, Pennsylvania, in April 1979 suspended new nuclear power plant construction around the country and ushered in a long moratorium for the industry's growth.

At the height of this movement, other Alliances arose around the country, typically choosing as a name an endangered element of the local environment. Motivated by a mix of ecological and peace concerns, they were directed at corporate greed and tapped a radical sense of the capacity of ordinary citizens to make decisions about their surroundings. This ethos gave new life to "consensus" decision making, which in its ideal form called for open collective discussion, respect for individual disagreement, and action undertaken only if all could abide it. This procedure was believed to avoid the division and domination of standard voting and majority rule, although advocates of majority-vote procedures offered counterarguments premised on the right to dissent without feeling pressure to bend. In action, the Alliances popularized the model of small "affinity groups," a term that traced back to the Spanish Civil War's anarchist *grupos de afinidad* and resurfaced in the United States in the movement against the Vietnam War. In the antinuclear movement, such circles of one or two dozen activists – subsets of a larger group such as the Clamshell Alliance – underwent nonviolence training, planned actions by consensus, and sent delegates to a coordinating body known as a "spokescouncil," whose role was not to "steer" the large group hierarchically but maintain communication along the multiple spokes of a wheel, back and forth, with the action groups on the rim and the council at the hub. These procedures did not always work well when serious differences over tactics and strategy arose. If the centralism of the new communist movement was brittle and constraining, seeking consensus could be equally frustrating. The Clamshell Alliance itself broke up over disagreements over matters of tactics and strategy, namely whether to hold peaceful rallies arranged with official permits or carry out civil disobedience with mass arrests, and whether to undertake aggressive actions often advocated by anarchists scornful of private property, such as cutting company fences to occupy construction sites, or keep illegality to obstruction alone.

As Ernest Callenbach's novel *Ecotopia* (1975) illustrated, environmentalism at this stage was not just about halting objectionable developments; it offered comprehensive visions of a preferable future. And at its best, the "no nukes" movement – in the 1970s focused mainly on power plants, with nuclear weaponry reviving as a major concern only at the decade's end – was able to cross a number of dividing lines in left-wing politics. Advocates of civil disobedience and mass demonstrations generally found ways of framing jointly acceptable actions. Often this new environmental mass movement succeeded beyond expectation in surmounting the breach between the more countercultural radicals and mainstream locals in a bridge between margin and mainstream. One who showed this was the sixties radical Abbie Hoffman, who under the name "Barry Freed" became a widely respected grassroots activist fighting nuclear waste shipments on the St. Lawrence River in New York, even as he lived incognito to evade federal prosecution on a drugs charge. The link between nuclear danger and profit-driven corporations suggested a link between ecology and socialism, or at the very least a vigorously regulatory left-liberalism, as shown when consumer advocate Ralph Nader hosted a Critical Mass conference on energy concerns in 1974 that brought many of the local initiatives into dialogue, giving self-definition to the movement and alerting it to dimensions of national policy. Given synergies of left and labor in the 1970s, it stood to reason that some participants would seek to overcome the apparent breach between environmentalists and labor unionists stirred by the strain between "antigrowth" sentiments and workers' needs for jobs and rising wages. Some began to argue that "nuclear safety is a labor issue," pointing to a common interest in healthy, safe workplaces and communities. At least a few unions made themselves allies of antinuclear forces, including the United Mine Workers (out of self-interest in coal-fired generators) and the Oil, Chemical, and Atomic Workers (which represented nuclear-plant employees).

In 1978, the working-class suburban neighborhood of Love Canal in Niagara Falls, New York, was shaken by environmental crisis. The Hooker Chemical Company discarded waste chemicals there for decades prior to construction of tract housing on the site. Buried toxins leached into backyards and basements, burning the skin of children and apparently causing higher rates of miscarriage and birth defects. A noisy picketing campaign arose among Love Canal's working-class mothers against corporate malfeasance and government cover-up. The most dynamic of them, Lois Gibbs, went on in the 1980s to become a national leader of grassroots organizing against toxic chemical dumps. "Women who at one time looked down on people picketing, being arrested and acting somewhat radical are now doing those very things," she said. Gibbs lent her support to women's protests against the arms race in the early 1980s and urged communities beset by toxins to ally with unions that represented people like her own husband, a Goodyear Chemical plant worker. Gibbs did not have to be a highly ideological leftist to represent precisely the kind of congruence that radicals always imagined could bring margin and mainstream together.[19]

Despite hopes for forging a wider left after the sixties, the new movements of the 1970s faced a growing counterforce as the decade proceeded. The opposition to radical dissent took two decisive forms: the rise of a mostly white conservatism with a cultural and religious objection to women's equality and gay rights, and an increasingly hostile turn by business against unions and government. The pushback began at the very moment the women's and gay movements appeared, particularly after an Equal Rights Amendment to ban all discrimination on grounds of sex – originally the aim of suffragist Alice Paul in the 1920s – passed the House of Representatives in 1972 and was headed, many presumed, for ratification in the states. Republican right-wing activist Phyllis Schlafly founded her STOP ERA campaign that year, arguing that ERA's backers were determined to shatter the integrity of the American family, a replay of the argument raised against suffrage that held that women's engagement in

[19] Gibbs in Robert Gottlieb, *Forcing the Spring: The Transformation of the American Environmental Movement* (Washington, D.C.: Island Press, 2005), pp. 303–304.

politics would foment "a civil war in every household." Raising anti-ERA objections on the basis of the then-unthinkable specter of women partic- ipating in military combat, or unisex bathrooms, Schlafly and her allies held feminism – and its arguments for women's autonomy – responsible for rising divorce rates. Feminists, they claimed, disdained housewives. By 1977, 35 states had approved the ERA, requiring only three more to ratify it, but anti-ERA organizing effectively stalled the momentum – even in the Illinois legislature, where the required supermajorities did not materialize. The 1973 Supreme Court decision legalizing abortions in the first two trimesters of pregnancy, *Roe v. Wade*, likewise, spurred a countermobilization of antiabortion forces whose first major victory was the Hyde Amendment in 1976, which forbade use of Medicaid funds in abortions. Conservatives similarly objected to measures to prevent discrimination on the basis of sexual orientation, notably in a 1977 cam- paign by citrus-industry spokeswoman Anita Bryant that painted all gay men as child molesters, resulting in repeal of a gay rights ordinance in Miami-Dade County, Florida.

This right-wing backlash was met by a swelling of the women's and gay rights movements. The decade began with often sharp philosophi- cal conflicts between different currents in feminism, especially its liberal, radical, and socialist variants. Some sought gender-neutral egalitarianism, while others fostered a separate feminist space premised on distinct and presumedly superior women's values. Such debates never abated entirely, and were aggravated by sometimes bitter personal antagonisms and divi- sions of race, class, and sexuality across the 1970s. At the same time, however, feminists were coalescing broadly around a general set of aims, particularly as liberal feminists moved leftward, feeling the pressure of their critics among lesbians, women of color, labor union women, and those with a sixties background. The result was a widening and deep- ening of the feminist agenda to include, at its core, ratification of the ERA, defense of reproductive rights including legal abortion and an end to sterilization without consent, pressure on the legal system to take rape and domestic violence seriously, expansion of daycare facilities and other critical social services for women, and embrace of equal rights without regard to sexual orientation.

Feminism in the 1970s was without question a *movement*, its propul- sion generated by a tremendous range of self-activity. Flo Kennedy – a black lawyer called by *People* magazine in 1975 "the biggest, loudest and, indisputably, the rudest mouth on the battleground where feminist- activists and radical politics join in mostly common cause" – was insistent that women get active to avoid "loserism": "Loserism is when oppressed people sit around and think up reasons why they can't do something. Thinking up reasons why you can't is the Establishment's job." As mainline women's organizations moved toward greater inclusivity, and as many New Left women opened up to the idea of self-organization, feminism and lesbianism inspired the creation of innumerable women-centered counterinstitutions, including rape crisis lines, battered women's shelters, health clinics, community bookstores, women's studies programs, coffee houses, musical groups, publishing houses, and newspapers. Feminist writers continued to dissect and ridicule sexism, as when Gloria Steinem wrote "If Men Could Menstruate: A Political Fantasy" for *Ms.* in 1978, which projected how positively men would view menstruation if they were the ones getting their periods every month.[20]

In response to the United Nations declaration of 1975 as International Women's Year, left-liberal Congresswoman Bella Abzug won federal funding for a National Women's Conference to be held over four days in Houston in November 1977. Convened with 2,000 official delegates sent from local and state assemblies and a total of 20,000 in attendance, including large numbers of women of color, the conference marked a high point of popular feminism. A small contingent of antifeminist delegates attended, while Schlafly rallied 15,000 conservative women at a counter-convention across town. The main conference was so mainstream that it featured three First Ladies (Lady Bird Johnson, Betty Ford, and Rosalynn Carter) as honored guests. Nonetheless, the convention's National Plan of Action urged bold policy initiatives on Congress and the President and showed the vitality of forces in American life still urging the expansion of a more egalitarian welfare state rather than its destruction in favor of free-market economics. The Plan of Action emphasized federally funded child-care accessible regardless of income; federally funded community centers to shelter battered women and combat child abuse; expansion of Medicare and Medicaid to cover all needed women's health services, including abortion; new educational curricula inclusive of study of women's roles in history and society; affirmative action for women in the major political parties and all state boards and commissions; not only an end to employment discrimination but full employment for all women desiring it, paid maternity leave, labor organizing rights for women, and application of

[20] Patricia Burstein, "Lawyer Flo Kennedy Enjoys Her Reputation as Radicalism's Rudest Mouth," *People* 3:14 (14 April 1975), http://www.people.com/people/archive/article/0,,20065145,00.html.

FIGURE 5.3. With the feminist movement broadening and deepening, a National Women's Conference was held in Houston, Texas, in 1977. Here Billy Jean King, Susan B. Anthony II, Bella Abzug, Sylvia Ortiz, Peggy Kokernot, Michele Cearcy, and Betty Friedan march to its opening session. *Copyright © 1977 Diana Mara Henry / www.dianamarahenry.com.*

fair labor standards to household workers; recognition of housework as a basis for calculating Social Security benefits; state and federal civil rights laws banning discrimination on grounds of sexual orientation; enhancement of benefits to the poor understood as "wages for housework" rather than "welfare"; and reduced military expenditures to make possible the additional social spending required for all these measures.

As mainstream as it was to advocate such things at the time, most of the aims articulated in Houston would never get governmental attention, aside from Congressional action to extend the deadline for state ratification of the Equal Rights Amendment. Abzug, the chair of President Jimmy Carter's National Advisory Council for Women established after the conference, was dismissed in January 1979 after she assailed Carter's hike in military spending and inaction on full employment. Mainstream politicians were responsive to feminist individual rights claims but not to substantial outlays or shifts in the allocation of resources, reconfigurations of power, or transformations of roles within the family.

For the gay movement, the 1970s were simultaneously a time of modification as the radical phase of gay liberation faded along with the New
Left, duress as it came under attack from the right, and vitality as it fought
back. The vernacular was increasingly that of civil rights rather than that
of the revolutionary vision of a world of sexual freedom beyond capitalism that the Gay Liberation Front of the early 1970s had advocated,
but the movement built effective new coalitions in a profound challenge
to avowedly "traditional" morality. When conservative California state
legislator John Briggs sought to copy Bryant's Florida campaign with a
ballot referendum banning gays and lesbians from teaching in the state's
public schools, Harvey Milk spearheaded the opposition. A photography
shop owner in the largely gay Castro district of San Francisco, Milk won
election as an openly gay man to the San Francisco Board of Supervisors in
1977 in a historic campaign, with union labor backing him because of his
work in urging gay bars to respect the Teamsters' union boycott of Coors
beer. In answer to the charge that gay teachers would "recruit" children
to a "gay lifestyle," Milk would tell crowds, "My name is Harvey Milk –
and I want to recruit you. I want to recruit you for the fight to preserve
democracy from the John Briggs and Anita Bryants who are trying to
constitutionalize bigotry." The defeat of California's Briggs initiative by
more than one million votes – reinforced by Seattle's simultaneous repudiation of an attempt to repeal its gay rights law – marked a significant
advancement in the struggle for gay equal citizenship. The sweet taste of
victory was still fresh when Milk and George Moscone, the liberal San
Francisco mayor allied with him in the fight for gay rights, were assassinated by a disturbed former conservative supervisor, prompting a mass
candlelit march that filled all of Market Street.[21]

Given both mounting right-wing opposition and resilient left-wing
social movements, it was unclear in the late 1970s which way political affairs would swing in the United States. Certainly the decade had
begun with widespread social criticism of the political and economic status quo. Opinion surveys had shown widespread distrust of corporations
and businessmen, suggesting a reservoir of potential support for a left
that would challenge the powers that be and the norms of economic life.
In 1971, fifteen percent of college students in one poll called their own

---

[21] Milk quoted in Dudley Clendinen and Adam Nagourney, *Out for Good: The Struggle
to Build a Gay Rights Movement in America* (New York: Simon and Schuster, 1999),
pp. 381–382.

viewpoint "revolutionary." Another poll two years later found that a third of freshmen and a half of seniors called themselves leftists, while nearly half of college students supported nationalizing the oil industry, widely suspected of price gouging and taking advantage of the oil crisis to reap giant profits. Watergate revelations of under-the-table funding for Richard Nixon's reelection campaign and corporate roles in promoting the 1973 military coup in Chile helped tarnish corporate America's image. By the mid-1970s only about 20 percent of respondents in one poll had confidence in the CEOs of major corporations, compared to more than half of respondents on the same question ten years before. The most admired figure among students was the corporate critic Ralph Nader, a crusading attorney who burst on the scene in 1965 as a muckraking researcher whose criticism of the auto industry resulted in federal legislation mandating that auto manufacturers include seat belts for every passenger, padded dashboards and steering wheels, shatter-resistant windshields, and other safety engineering features. His co-authored book *Taming the Giant Corporation* (1976) proposed citizen representation in major managerial decisions, a form of economic democracy. Tom Hayden's Campaign for Economic Democracy, based in California, explored the same kind of idea while simultaneously encouraging public policy that would foster conversion to solar power. So widespread was the sense that corporate priorities were at odds with democratic ones that in 1975 the archconservative columnist James J. Kilpatrick was compelled to write an article in *Nation's Business* entitled "Why Students are Hostile to Free Enterprise."

Indeed the persistence of criticism of American economic and political life on campus made higher education seemingly a bastion, as the "neoconservative" writer Irving Kristol would have it, of an "adversary culture" dangerous to capitalism. Already in 1971, Lewis Powell, then general counsel for the U.S. Chamber of Commerce and soon to be appointed to the Supreme Court, had warned of an attack on "the American free enterprise system" that demanded a concerted counterinitiative by business to finance the gestation and propagation of antiregulatory, probusiness ideas on campus and in think tanks. His message reached corporate executives facing declining rates of profit. Perceiving taxes, regulation, and high wages as burdens, and fearing that a left turn in public sentiment in the wake of the Vietnam radicalization posed a threat of further public interest legislation and labor gains, business groups geared up for a pushback. They sponsored free-market educational programs at small conservative Christian colleges through the Southwest, created new centers such as the Business Roundtable (1972) and Heritage Foundation (1973), gave lavishly to established right-wing public policy think tanks such as the American Enterprise Institute, and endowed new business schools and chairs at universities, all matched by a much more ideological cast to the *Wall Street Journal*'s editorial page. The sum total was a self-conscious right-wing "counterestablishment" dedicated to annulling liberal social and economic policy.

Late into the 1970s public sentiment remained nebulous. Left-leaning and right-leaning notions could be uttered in the same breath as Americans confronted high unemployment, hyperinflation, long lines at the gas pump, and the Carter administration's humiliation due to the seizure of American hostages by Iranian militants in Tehran after the deposing of the long-ruling U.S.-backed dictator, the Shah. Pollsters in the late 1970s found a rise in the proportion of Americans willing to voice profound disenchantment with national institutions to an extent greater even than Vietnam-era dissent. While inchoate and sometimes contradictory, such sentiment was not at the outset a knee-jerk anti-Washington sentiment opposed to government in itself. It reflected a skepticism that in many ways was the result of the spadework performed by left-of-center radical dissent. Majorities agreed that economic and political affairs were run for the benefit of the few, not the many; that the tax system was unfair in making employees pay too much compared to the rich; and that politicians couldn't be trusted for intellectual, moral, or administrative excellence. While pundits would subsequently boil this down to an "antigovernment" sentiment that cleared the way for Ronald Reagan's conservative laissez-faire policies, it initially had a strong anticorporate streak. When Carter gave his notorious "crisis of confidence" speech in July 1979, he wasn't wrong to sense a malaise in the national mood – even if he mistook the problem for the cynical self-interest of consumers no longer imbued with self-sacrifice in the national interest. Just how strained the labor-liberal consensus had become, and how much frustration there was over Carter's own concessions to business, was demonstrated when UAW President Douglas Fraser resigned from Carter's Labor-Management Group in 1978, charging that corporate America was waging a "one-sided class war."[22]

As economic crisis disciplined workers and dissipated the rank-and-file upsurge, however, a drift toward moderation began to take hold on the

[22] "Auto Union Head Protests Role of Business, Quits Carter Panel," *New York Times*, 20 July 1978, p. B4.

left. The New Left *Ramparts* disappeared in 1975, its place taken by the liberal *Mother Jones*. *Socialist Revolution* was renamed *Socialist Review* in 1978. In Chicago, James Weinstein launched a new weekly newspaper, *In These Times*, which by placing Congressman Ron Dellums on the cover page in its inaugural issue in 1976 gave indication of Weinstein's increasing focus on working through the Democratic Party even as he remained committed to building an openly left-wing presence in American life. Similarly radical in tone and moderate in tactics was Tom Hayden's 1976 U.S. Senate Democratic primary candidacy in California. Drawing on the vast financial resources of his wife, the actress Jane Fonda, Hayden ran a surprisingly competitive race on a platform holding big government and big corporations to be one and the same, charged his opponent with putting popular needs below those of oil companies and the Pentagon, called for "economic democracy" through boldly progressive taxation, and stated that "if you want to bring down interest rates, put some consumers on the Federal Reserve."[23]

David Dellinger, perhaps the most famous remaining radical pacifist, argued against this turn toward putting resources and energy into electoral activity, holding that "the changes of structure and of spirit this country needs so badly will not be initiated in any of the three branches of government," but from "alternate centers of power outside the formal Government." Nevertheless, many on the left perceived a transformed Democratic Party more open to women, blacks, and youth, given the incursions of "New Politics" and the precedent set by the presidential primary campaign of black Congresswoman Shirley Chisholm in 1972. They hoped the Democratic Party could be made susceptible to left-wing influence, even if Carter and the Democratic-controlled House and Senate – their majorities strengthened after Watergate – were adopting an economic agenda of deregulation and austerity much more conservative than the policies of Nixon, who had toyed with the idea of a guaranteed annual income. In 1978, Michael Harrington's Democratic Socialist Organizing Committee, always oriented toward the labor union wing of the Democratic Party, decided to make a serious bid to have its members shape the Democratic platform by writing planks for full employment, a more progressive tax system, and national health insurance. DSOC wanted to challenge Carter's right turn, as the president withheld support for the Humphrey-Hawkins full-employment bill before Congress, expanded the

---

[23] Quoted in Tom Wicker, "Unradical, Unoriginal, Untried," *The New York Times*, 17 February 1976, p. 29.

Pentagon budget, and talked of cuts in social service programs. Through a vehicle known as Democratic Agenda, DSOC and its supporters among labor leaders went into an unusual midterm 1978 convention of the Democratic Party aiming to reassert the most liberal elements of the 1976 party platform and chastise the president for backing away from them. DSOC failed to outvote Carter's loyalists but made a showing strong enough for reporters at *Business Week* to note its influence: "Socialism is no longer a dirty word to labor."[24]

Even at the end of the decade, the left was still animated by a great sense of practical possibilities rooted in on-the-ground mobilization. When a major Youngstown, Ohio, steel plant faced closure as a result of mismanagement and insufficient reinvestment, a community coalition of church, labor, and radical activists strove to save hundreds of threatened jobs by reopening the plant under self-management in an employee–community ownership structure suggested by Staughton Lynd along with Gar Alperovitz of the National Center for Economic Alternatives. Such initiatives coincided with a vibrant, diverse range of radical intellectual and cultural life. Works of fiction inspired by both feminism and New Left radicalism reached popular audiences, including Ursula K. LeGuin's *The Dispossessed* (1974) and Marge Piercy's *Woman on the Edge of Time* (1976). Five Marxist-Feminist Groups ("MF1," "MF2," etc.) met regularly in Boston and New York, their participants including economist Heidi Hartmann, political scientist Rosalind Petchesky, historians Rosalyn Baxandall and Linda Gordon, and lawyer Kristin Glen, later a New York state family court judge. Psychological therapies popular in the 1970s were not wholly indulgent and narcissistic, despite their disparaging critics; many located causes of depression in experience of social oppression. In social theory, radicalism achieved new levels of sophistication and force, ranging from dense and eclectic work in journals such as *Telos* to the more readable journal presided over by the historian Eugene Genovese, *Marxist Perspectives* (1978–1980). A lighter touch in the left's engagements with popular culture was felt when philosopher Bertell Ollman, author of *Alienation: Marx's Conception of Man in Capitalist Society* (1971), created and marketed the board game *Class Struggle* (1978), a variation on *Monopoly*.

---

[24] David Dellinger, "Radicals, It Is Argued, Are Alive and Well...," *New York Times*, 9 Oct. 1976, p. 19; *Business Week*, quoted in Timothy Stanley, *Kennedy vs. Carter: The 1980 Battle for the Democratic Party's Soul* (Lawrence: University Press of Kansas, 2010), p. 77.

Despite such signs of creative energy through the end of the 1970s, left-wing fortunes deteriorated rapidly as the decade turned. The November 1980 presidential election saw conservative Republican Ronald Reagan defeat the unpopular centrist Democratic incumbent Carter. This was a watershed in American politics even if it was, at the time, more the result of reaction to a poorly performing economy and the Iran hostage crisis than a conscious validation of Reagan's philosophy. Even in that election, radicals were still striving to avoid the imposition of a right-wing solution on the crisis. At the outset of 1980, DSOC backed Senator Edward Kennedy's spirited liberal primary challenge to President Carter's perceived conservatism. Despite an enthusiastic early rush, Kennedy's bid faltered as the party chiefs rallied, in a typical pattern of presidential bids for a second term, around the president. Harrington's socialism, in any event, played hardly any role at all in Kennedy's campaign. In health care policy, Kennedy, long a proponent of universal coverage, moved away from advocating an extension of Medicare to all, instead advocating mandatory private coverage by employers and individuals that would leave the corporate insurance industry intact. In the general campaign, Harrington threw his support to Carter, though some DSOC members supported an upstart organization, the Citizens Party, headed by scientist and activist Barry Commoner, who combined environmentalism with economic justice. Commoner won the support of NAM and the IS as well, but independent politics had only peripheral appeal given Reagan's surge, which pushed most left-inclined voters back to Carter as a lesser evil. The best-performing independent candidate of 1980 (in large part because he, unlike Commoner, was allowed to take part in the televised presidential debates) was a moderate breakaway Republican, Illinois Rep. John Anderson, whose clean-government, pro-choice, and pro-ERA politics appealed to affluent professionals disconcerted by Reagan's hard-right politics and Carter's own conservatism. Anderson's 7 percent tally bested the pitiful 0.3 percent for the more radical Commoner. In the end, Ronald Reagan defeated Jimmy Carter, carrying 44 states in 1980. A number of liberals in the Senate fell as well, the loss of twelve Democrats giving the Senate to the Republicans and signaling victory for the laissez-faire American right on the heels of Margaret Thatcher's similar 1979 Conservative trouncing of the Labour Party in Britain.

The 1970s had been a decade of considerable anticipation and activity in radical circles. Even in the second half of the decade, the balance of forces still seemed sufficiently fluid as to leave things up for grabs. A return to left-wing themes of economic inequality, working-class life and struggle, capitalist instability, and democratic planning during the 1970s coexisted with the growing "new" movements of women, gays and lesbians, and environmentalists. Efforts to combine all these in a broad new left-wing program persisted in anticipation of a "next left," as some would take to calling it. With a strong public presence and some popular appeal, a melding of the best of the Old Left and the New Left could amount, radicals hoped, to more than the sum of its parts. Syntheses were underway of the red and the black, the red and the green, and socialism and feminism, each in its own way creative and fertile.

These efforts to build a next left in the 1970s were, however, ultimately unavailing, whether envisaged in revolutionary, radical populist, or social-democratic terms. Even at a time when confidence in capitalist normality seemed to crack in a period of crisis, a reinvigorated and ascendant political New Right surged ahead, entering the 1980s able to enact significant elements of a free-market, antiwelfare state program that had enjoyed no success in American politics since before the Depression. Despite the McCarthyite red scare, there had been something of a long-term upward trend to left-wing activism ever since the Second World War, persisting despite setbacks and misfires, and most evident from 1956 through the mid-1970s. Only afterward would the long recessional of the left begin to sink in, anticipations of radical renewal giving way to a greatly reduced sense of future possibilities. Perhaps nothing signified the changed mood better than the final scene of John Sayles's film *Return of the Secaucus 7* (1979), in which a sixties radical, his personal and political dreams having curdled into sourness, was left standing alone to chop wood angrily, splitting one log after another in half.

6

Over the Rainbow, 1980–1989

When Benjamin Linder graduated in mechanical engineering from the University of Washington in 1983, he had no intention of becoming a "yuppie," the popular eighties term for a young urban professional pursuing consumer gratification, so he declined opportunities to work for Boeing or any other military contractor. As revolution swept the Central American isthmus, Linder admired the Sandinista National Liberation Front (FSLN), which in 1979 overthrew a Nicaraguan dictatorship supported for decades by the United States. Nicaragua seemed to be forging a revolution of a new type: pluralistic, democratic, favoring neither total state control nor free market, and led collectively rather than by a strongman *caudillo*. "We have not reproduced the sociopolitical mechanisms of the United States *or* the Soviet Union," a Sandinista leader told *Playboy* in 1983. "We're not following *any* form. What we are doing is seeking a profound solution. To what? To the poverty of this country."[1]

Linder moved to Managua, Nicaragua's capital city, as one of the first of tens of thousands of American *internacionalistas* – analogous to the *brigadistas* of 1930s Spain, although in developmental rather than combat roles. North American visitors were sponsored by groups in the United States such as the Nicaragua Network, whose volunteers joined in coffee harvests; TecNica, which sent welders, lathe operators, and computer programmers; and the Quixote Center, a Roman Catholic relief

---

[1] "Friends of Slain American Say He was There for Humanitarian Reasons," The Associated Press, 29 April 1987; "Playboy Interview: The Sandinistas," *Playboy*, September 1983, p. 64 (emphasis in original).

organization. Thousands of *co-operantes*, most in their twenties, had long-term stays as teachers, doctors, nurses, veterinarians, and architects. American conservatives labeled them traitors, but the United States was not officially at war with Nicaragua even if Reagan accused the Sandinistas of trying to establish a "Soviet beachhead" while the CIA covertly armed the *contras*, the bands of counterrevolutionaries whose core came from the former dictatorship's National Guard.[2]

Ben Linder was more radical geek than radical chic. Short, skinny, his beard a scraggly red, and never without a pen in his pocket, he did not fit reporters' image of the "Sandalista," a frivolous, Birkenstock-wearing revolutionary tourist. One friend described Linder as "wry about the country's problems and the revolution's shortcomings, unlike other starry-eyed, dogmatic internationalists." Unable at first to find work as an engineer, he juggled, clowned, and acted the part of Uncle Sam in street theatre. "I go to some godforsaken country to save the world with my newly acquired skills," he wrote his parents. "And what happens? The only work I can do is clowning around. I guess there is some justice somewhere." On his hundredth day in Managua, his application for employment in the national energy utility was approved. In contrast to *internacionalistas* who socialized mostly with each other, Linder lived with a Nicaraguan family. "When you talk to any of the Nicaraguan people," he said, "it's clear that their fear is not the Soviet Union, their fear is not communism, their fear is the constant attacks on the people of Nicaragua being supported by the U.S. government."[3]

In 1985, Linder moved to El Cuá in the remote mountainous north, assuming responsibility for a small-scale hydroelectric project. The town was accessible only by narrow roads that wound past fields of corn and beans tended by *campesinos*, or peasants. Its two thousand inhabitants lived in wooden shacks with tin roofs, lacking sewerage. The main road became a muddy pit in the rainy season. Almost everyone, whether in camouflaged army uniforms or not, carried AK-47 rifles. Linder lived with 70-year-old Don Cosme Castro, who had fought with Augusto Sandino, the rebel leader of the 1920s and 1930s whose name the Sandinistas honored. The hut's corrugated tin roof was painted red and black after the Sandinista flag.

[2] Reagan quotations in *American/Sandinista*, dir. Jason Blalock (2008; IndiePix Films), DVD.
[3] Joan Kruckewitt, *The Death of Ben Linder* (New York: Seven Stories, 1999), pp. 32, 46, 62, 73, 82; *American/Sandinista*.

Linder worried he wasn't knowledgeable enough but was excited by the project's challenges. He and the two other *internacionalistas* present, one American, one Canadian, were equally committed to alternative energy and appropriate technology. They sought the community's involvement in decisions. Hoping to shatter the underdevelopment mentalities of lax discipline and deference to authority, they trained four locals as electricians, which required teaching them math. At last, on May 1, 1986, the hydrogenerator was switched on and electricity arrived in El Cuá. Medicine could now be refrigerated, literacy classes taught at night, beer kept cold. Jubilantly, Linder pedaled around town on his unicycle, wearing his red clown nose, celebrating with El Cuá's children.

From that moment on, the humming turbine was a target. Contra policy was to attack infrastructure – bridges, farm cooperatives, health clinics – so as to frustrate Sandinista social objectives and destabilize the economy. "The contras generally don't attack against the army," said Linder in a radio interview. "They attack against campesinos. We're expecting them, although hoping that they don't attack our project." A CIA-distributed manual, *Psychological Operations in Guerrilla Warfare*, told contras to "neutralize carefully selected and planned targets, such as court judges." The contras killed seven European aid workers (including a West German waving his passport) and more than 40,000 Nicaraguans. In March 1987, when they finally attacked El Cuá one night, the hydroplant's Nicaraguan operator, Oscar Blandón, cut the generator, shrewdly darkening it and saving it from damage. "I'd be lying if I said that there isn't anything to worry about," Linder admitted to his parents. As millions of dollars poured to the contras, he weighed whether to carry a gun. He had been a pacifist on arriving in Nicaragua and still doubted he could ever pull a trigger. In the end he accepted a rifle. Its sight was badly misaligned but he hoped that its mere presence would be a deterrent and diminish the need for Sandinista militia to endanger their lives protecting him.[4]

Early one morning – April 28, 1987 – Linder was constructing a weir in a stream near San José del Bocay, even further north than El Cuá, hoping to determine whether it was a suitable spot for another hydroelectric plant. The week before, he wrote his sister that he found "peace at certain times," as when "I'm walking along a stream, looking at the stream for its own sheer beauty, looking at it for generating electricity,

4   "Friends of Slain American," Associated Press, 29 April 1987; "Excerpts from Primer for Insurgents," *New York Times*, 17 October 1984; Kruckewitt, p. 96.

or just... scrambling over rocks, taking a quick bath in a little pool formed in the rock." As Linder set down his rifle and crouched to take notes, a grenade exploded. The contras had lain in wait; they finished him off with a bullet to his temple. Two Nicaraguans accompanying him also died, neither having managed to return fire. As the first American to perish in the Nicaraguan conflict, the 27-year-old's death led network news broadcasts in the United States. "Who killed Ben?" his father asked. "Someone who paid someone who paid someone who paid someone and so on down the line to the president of the United States."[5]

When President Ronald Reagan took office in 1981, his supporters heralded a "Reagan Revolution." On the left, however, Reagan's ascendancy was seen as a reactionary attempt to turn the clock back. Reagan-era conservatism inveighed against liberalism, state power, and bureaucracy, as had the New Left, but rather than see the welfare state as inadequate, conservatives saw it as excessive. Reagan constituencies included a Christian right that rejected feminism, abortion rights, and homosexuality in favor of "traditional family values" as well as a racial conservatism that Reagan courted by beginning his 1980 campaign by speaking of "states' rights," the old slogan of secessionists and segregationists, near the location in Philadelphia, Mississippi, where three civil rights activists were murdered in 1964. Reagan may have begun as a New Deal Democrat and had a brief postwar flirtation with the Popular Front, but he was shaped by informing for the FBI as president of the Screen Actors Guild during the Hollywood blacklist and becoming a spokesman in the 1950s for General Electric. As a telegenic actor cast as the very personification of America, Reagan reshaped the country's political culture in the 1980s. The Reagan ascendancy threw the left on the defensive and dislodged an old welfare-state liberalism. Nevertheless, radicalism continued to innovate and even to win some victories during his time in office.

"This country is more dissident now than at any time I can remember," Noam Chomsky said in 1988, "more so than during the Vietnam War." Indeed, some of the largest social mobilizations in American history occurred in the 1980s. Feminists, gays and lesbians, civil libertarians, and religious progressives contested the evangelical right's agenda. Labor activists and farmers pushed back against economic retrenchment. Radical ecology spawned new tactics and philosophies. Themes of solidarity

---

[5] Kruckewitt, p. 308; "Nicaraguan President Appeals for Peace at Slain American's Funeral," Associated Press, 1 May 1987.

and survival were voiced by those opposed to the nuclear arms race, U.S. intervention in Central America, and South African apartheid. Because the country was dotted by New Left veterans, now in their thirties or forties, joined at marches by chartreuse-haired young punks and white-haired leftists, the sixties' legacy sustained radical hopes that resistance to the right might prove effective.[6]

Reagan won two elections, the second more decisive than the first, but the House remained in Democratic hands during his tenure. In polls, even those who voted for Reagan did not support many of his most conservative policies, and at end of decade fissures were evident in the Reagan juggernaut. The stock market crashed in 1987, while junk-bond king Michael Milken and arbitrageur Ivan Boesky – whose "greed is all right" remark typified Wall Street's new smugness – were jailed for fraud and insider trading. Meanwhile, Reagan's National Security Council, working out of the White House, was revealed to have sold arms to America's ostensible archenemy Iran in exchange for release of American hostages in Lebanon, diverting the proceeds to the Nicaraguan contras, which had been denied funding by Congress. If all of this took much of the shine off Reaganism, it produced no real gains for the left. The stunning transformation of Eastern Europe in 1989 as popular movements toppled Communist dictatorships ended up restoring capitalism rather than yielding the democratic socialist outcome radicals had long sought – a result that proved the coup de grace that would leave the radical left reeling.

The 1980s saw a rapprochement of radicalism with liberalism, more in sync than ever since their antagonism of the 1960s. This confluence arose partly because of radicals' self-awareness of the sectarian errors of the intervening decade, and partly because the program of the left largely became defensive – compelled to defend the New Deal state as it once existed and seeking to prevent the destruction of past social gains rather than secure new ones. Working with humility and outside the limelight, radicals sought to build multi-issue coalitions, work with others of different dispositions, and think strategically for the long run in a rainbow of social movements. Many sought to enter the Democratic Party and transform it through the Rainbow Coalition fashioned by civil rights leader Jesse Jackson. Even if organizers on the left were convinced that on many issues they, not Reagan, represented American majorities, and even if their organizing produced both strong coalition efforts and

[6] Jay Parini, "Noam is an Island," *Mother Jones*, October 1988, p. 38.

new creative fields of action at the margins, particularly in radical ecology and activism to address acquired immune deficiency syndrome (AIDS), the radical vision of a society transformed at its roots would prove more elusive and remote than ever – somewhere over the rainbow.

Shortly after Reagan took office in 1981, he fired 11,000 striking federal air traffic controllers. That signal of free reign to the antilabor agenda of corporate America was accompanied by Reagan's appointment of business loyalists to the National Labor Relations Board. As the Federal Reserve imposed high interest rates, inflation subsided but unemployment spiked to 10 percent between 1981 and 1983. Reagan cut funding for Medicaid, welfare, food stamps, child nutrition, and mental health, resulting in skyrocketing homelessness, including whole families living on the streets. His budgets stripped out money for art and theatre, social work, and community organizing – vital material bases of the American left. Attacking regulation as "red tape," Reagan shrank the Occupational Safety and Health Administration (OSHA) and continued the process begun under Jimmy Carter of deregulating federally insured savings and loan (S&L) associations, ultimately costing taxpayers $341 billion after many S&Ls capsized in the late 1980s and early 1990s because they made speculative investments or engaged in outright fraud.

Liberals could and did object to these fiscal and economic priorities. "From auto safety to antitrust to banking to food safety," Ralph Nader wrote Reagan in 1982, "your administration has joined with reckless business powers to strip away safeguards vital to consumers." But liberalism was largely powerless against a right-wing juggernaut cast as necessary "reform" (a word that before then had almost always signaled progressive measures to ameliorate burdens or countermand business power). The marginal tax rate for the wealthy fell from 70 to 28 percent under Reagan, justified by "supply-side" theories that claimed investment would correspondingly increase and regenerate the economy. The result was the most significant income redistribution in American history, from poor to rich. As a mid-decade bull market in stocks and bonds reaped outsized returns for Wall Street and the wealthy, the share of the nation's wealth held by the top 1 percent of Americans rose from 22 percent in 1979 to 39 percent in 1989. Because of his adminstration's tax cuts and military spending increases, Reagan never submitted a balanced budget to Congress. The national debt ballooned to $2.8 trillion, transforming the United States into the world's largest debtor nation. Reagan's boyish budget director David Stockman – a fiscal conservative ideologue despite having belonged to SDS at Michigan State University in the 1960s – was disillusioned when he found Reagan unwilling to take essential deficit-reducing measures to close corporate tax loopholes; cut loan subsidies to corporations such as Westinghouse, General Electric, and Lockheed; or confront waste and mismanagement in Pentagon contracting. "Supply-side," Stockman admitted, "is 'trickle-down' theory."[7]

Farmers were among the first to erupt in protest as small and mid-sized farms cascaded into bankruptcy in the 1981–1983 recession. The farm protest had begun in late-1970s drive-on-Washington "tractor-cades" organized by the American Agriculture Movement against Carter's human-rights embargo of grain sales to the Soviet Union. Under Reagan, the outcry grew. The North American Farm Alliance (headed by Merle Hansen, a white-haired Nebraskan whose father had been a socialist), Prairiefire Rural Action, the Wisconsin Farm Unity Coalition, and like-minded groups objected to the coziness that wedded agricultural lobbies such as the Farm Bureau and Cattlemen's Association with the U.S. Department of Agriculture and multinational food companies such as Cargill. Jim Hightower's election as Texas State Commissioner of Agriculture in 1982 elevated an outspoken left-populist voice advocating moratoria on bank foreclosures of small farms, production controls to preserve crop prices, elimination of farm subsidies for giant farms, debt restructuring, conversion of erosion-prone farmland into nature preserves, and legislation to prevent land concentration in corporate hands. In 1985, 15,000 participants from 18 states filled a coliseum in Ames, Iowa, hanging budget director Stockman in effigy. T-shirts reading "Farms, Not Arms" linked disarmament to agriculture, and at the United Farmer and Rancher Congress in St. Louis in 1986, 1,500 delegates were addressed by a representative of the Nicaraguan Farmers' and Ranchers' Union. Farm activists were unable to prevent 263,000 farms from going out of business from 1981 to 1985, but they provided a strong counterweight to far-right anti-Semites who blamed the farm crisis on Jewish financiers or a "Zionist Occupation Government."

Labor unions too were battered from every side. Even as Reagan hailed the Solidarność trade union movement that seized the Lenin Shipyards in Communist Poland in 1980, his domestic policies combined with

---

[7] Justin Martin, *Nader: Crusader, Spoiler, Icon* (New York: Basic Books, 2002), p. 207; William Greider, "The Education of David Stockman," *Atlantic*, December 1981, http://www.theatlantic.com/magazine/archive/1981/12/the-education-of-david-stockman/305760/.

corporate plant relocations to devastate American unions. The shift from manufacturing to finance well under way in the prior decade became more painfully evident in the 1980s than ever before. Across the manufacturing sector the numbers of production workers declined sharply between 1978 and 1984: 25 percent in steel, 20 percent in auto, 15 percent in machine tools, 10 percent each in aircraft and meatpacking. The unionized portion of the private sector plunged from about 20 percent in 1980 to 12.5 percent a decade later.

Labor radicals striving to preserve mid-twentieth-century gains in collective bargaining, pensions, and grievance handling criticized AFL-CIO leaders who proposed an orderly retreat through "concessionary bargaining," or acceptance of corporations' wage and benefit cuts in order to save jobs. In Pennsylvania's Monongahela Valley hundreds of unemployed steelworkers formed the Mon Valley Unemployed Committee, hired a director from the historically left-wing United Electrical Workers (UE), set up a food bank, and campaigned in noisy street rallies for extended unemployment benefits, rent freezes, and moratoria on utility cut-offs, all while demanding that "the government and the companies . . . get this economy that they control back in shape." In California, auto companies closed five of six assembly plants from 1980 to 1982, but an alliance of five thousand autoworkers and the surrounding black and Chicano communities fought to keep the last one, a General Motors plant, open in the Van Nuys district of the San Fernando Valley in Los Angeles. Activists there threatened a national GM boycott and argued the company owed something to its employees and the community given that the plant, which assembled popular Chevrolet Camaros and Pontiac Firebirds, was profitable. The UAW local regularly reelected a combative leadership opposed to concessions, including radicals such as Eric Mann, a sixties activist who entered industrial work in the 1970s. GM never formally conceded, but the plant did operate for ten more years until 1992. Mann and others would found the Labor/Community Strategy Center in Los Angeles in 1989 to organize for economic and social justice primarily within working-class communities of color.[8]

These uphill struggles never coalesced into a nationwide labor upsurge despite the stagnation of wages even as employment returned to normal. Critics pointed out that economic growth under Reagan owed much to

[8] Mon Valley Unemployed Committee, quoted in Dale Hathaway, *Can Workers Have a Voice? The Politics of Deindustrialization in Pittsburgh* (University Park: Pennsylvania State University Press, 1993), p. 146.

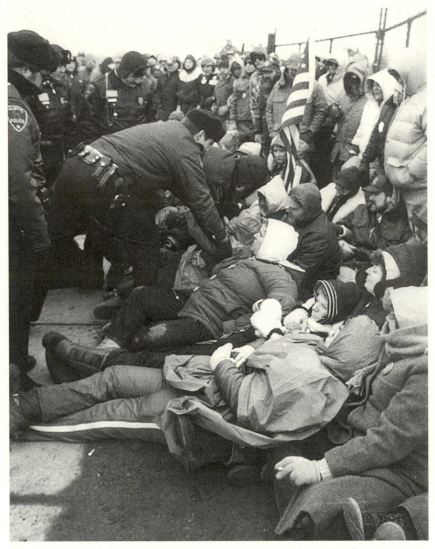

FIGURE 6.1. In mass civil disobedience meant to evoke the civil rights movement, striking workers and their families blocked the gates of the Hormel meatpacking plant in Austin, Minnesota, during the winter of 1985–1986, raising the slogan "No Retreat, No Surrender" in resistance to corporate attacks on wage rates and unions. *Austin Daily Herald*.

falling global oil prices and his "military Keynesianism," high spending on arms and technology outlays rather than New Deal-style public works. As the AFL-CIO, still locked in a Cold War liberal framework, looked to congressional Democrats, not rank-and-file mobilization, to turn things around, radicals faulted labor leaders' lack of imagination and complacent business unionism. In Austin, Minnesota, rebel Local P-9 of the United Food and Commercial Workers (UFCW)—led by homegrown militant Jim Guyette, who carried forward the old Packinghouse workers' tradition of left-wing unionism—struck against the Hormel meatpacking company for ten months in 1985–1986 to halt industry-wide wage cuts, taking the motto "No Retreat, No Surrender" from a recent Bruce Springsteen song. Local P-9 engaged in plant-gate civil disobedience and a "corporate campaign" to embarrass those doing business with Hormel, but went down to defeat at the hands of the UFCW's own national leadership, which put P-9 in receivership and bowed to Hormel's demands.

Labor's battles in the 1980s mostly ended in defeat, but there were some draws and a few victories. Effective organizing drew on community involvement, networks of solidarity spanning the country, and confrontational protest tactics. From 1985 to 1987, one thousand strikers at a frozen-food packing plant in Watsonville, California – almost all Chicana women – held out for eighteen months to win a new Teamsters contract and preserve health benefits. In 1989–1990, coal miners fought Pittston Coal Company in Virginia to save retiree health benefits, sitting down before coal trucks and picketing the company's bank in far-off Boston. Justice for Janitors, launched in 1985 by a former United Farm Workers organizer in the Service Employees International Union, confronted real estate management by way of raucous demonstrations mounted by workers of color inside office buildings, culminating in a 1990 Los Angeles strike. At the national level, however, no way forward presented itself. Europe, for so long the American left's model of labor's potentiality, provided no solace. In Britain, the government of conservative Prime Minister Margaret Thatcher vanquished a militant national miners' strike in 1984–1985, in a complete debacle for the cause of labor in the world's oldest industrial society.

Some American veterans of the New Left had taken up positions as union staffers, trying to apply all they had learned in past movements to regenerating the labor movement. Other radicals concluded that unions themselves were the problem. The Chinese Staff and Workers' Association, founded by former union organizer Wing Lam in 1980 in New York's Chinatown, called itself a "workers' center" (a device that other

radicals would pick up as labor law offered fewer advantages to formal unionism), organized a Chinatown Labor Fair, taught English to
immigrants, and in 1988 won a $760,000 lawsuit for nonpayment of
wages to restaurant workers. Staughton Lynd and *Workers' Democracy*,
a newsletter by labor radicals in St. Louis, called for shopfloor committees to organize slowdowns on the job and refusal to sign contracts,
suggesting that collective bargaining as such was the source of conventional unionism's failings. *Labor Notes* hewed to a vision of rank-and-file
caucuses taking union office to compel reform. Despite their fine points
of difference, these varied radical efforts shared the view that the soul of
the labor movement rested with ordinary workers' activity. Watsonville
strike supporter and sixties veteran Frank Bardacke argued that "radical
mass democracy is not just one ideal among others, but is crucial to the
strategic breakthroughs that reorder the political world."[9]

On June 12, 1982, one million people marched through the streets of
Manhattan, converging in Central Park for a giant rally in favor of a
Nuclear Freeze. Amid rising Cold War tensions begun in the late 1970s,
an eruption of European peace protest had rekindled American activism,
making this the most massive peace action in American history, far larger
than any Vietnam-era demonstration. The Freeze was a modest demand,
so modest that it called for no disarming at all, only that the United
States and the Soviet Union "freeze" their arsenals without adding to
the numbers or virtuosity of their nuclear weapons. Nonetheless, the
rally indicated deep opposition to Reagan's military buildup and to his
moving ahead with plans begun under Carter to deploy a new generation of intermediate-range nuclear missiles in Western Europe aimed at
the Soviet Union. Here was the unmistakable sign of a new movement,
just a few years in the making, broadening "No Nukes" from opposition to nuclear power plants toward the more threatening danger of the
arms race in a stunning display of mass opposition to Reagan's military
buildup.

For organizers, the campaign held the urgency of a "politics of survival": the prevention of a nuclear war that would threaten human existence itself, leaving merely "a republic of insects and grass," as Jonathan
Schell put it in *The Fate of the Earth* (1982). The theme of survival dovetailed with economic concerns bred by Reaganomics. Herbert Daughtry,

---

[9] Frank Bardacke, "Watsonville: A Mexican Community on Strike," in *Reshaping the US Left*, eds. Mike Davis and Michael Sprinker (New York: Verso, 1988), p. 181.

head of the National Black United Front, told the great Freeze rally that Reagan's military expansion was being paid for with deep cuts to programs for the poor. A heightened sense of militaristic danger was palpable since the brief interlude of détente in the 1970s had ceded to what radicals termed a "second Cold War," severe superpower tensions like those that characterized the immediate postwar years. The reversion had begun under Jimmy Carter, who appointed as his National Security Adviser the hardline anti-Soviet intellectual Zbigniew Brzezinski and boosted military spending starting in 1978. In answer to Soviet deployments of SS-20 missiles in Eastern Europe, Carter sought to develop and deploy two new systems: an updated intermediate-range ballistic missile called the Pershing II and low-flying guided cruise missiles, whose precision critics said would give the United States a "first-strike" capacity that would destabilize the ever-fragile balance of nuclear terror.

An even more apocalyptic lexicon arrived with Reagan, who in 1983 dubbed the Soviet Union "an evil empire" and the following year used a microphone check to joke, "We begin bombing in five minutes." In Europe, concern rose that Reagan's cowboy attitudes might lead the United States, the only country to have dropped nuclear bombs, to again put humankind in the crosshairs. West Germany, slated to be a prime base of the new Pershings, saw some 300,000 people demonstrate in 1982 at a NATO summit meeting in Bonn. The tenor of protest was expressed by Germany's new Green Party, founded in 1979, which brought together feminists and Marxists, longhairs and punks, gays and environmentalists in a second New Left against the second Cold War. After calling for removal of all nuclear weapons from Europe, the Greens won 5.6 percent of the parliamentary vote in 1983, qualifying them for 27 seats in the 498-seat Bundestag. On the Greens' executive sat an East German dissident Marxist, Rudolf Bahro. Their 35-year-old leader, Petra Kelly, had studied in the United States in the late 1960s and drew inspiration from Martin Luther King, Jr. "My analysis," she said, "is that Europeans probably feel closer to the Soviet Union in a strange way because the Soviet Union has lost 20 million people in the war. Young people, my generation, are saying, 'Who dropped the bomb, really?' There are a lot of dead people in the cellar of the West and a lot of dead people in the cellar of the East. We are trying to figure out if there is a time you don't have to live with an enemy."[10]

[10] James M. Markham, "Germany's Volatile Greens," *New York Times*, 13 February 1983.

In the United States, concerted opposition to nuclear weaponry emerged in the late 1970s. Mobilization for Survival (MfS) was founded in 1977 by longtime independent radical Sidney Lens, who published *The Day Before Doomsday: An Anatomy of the Nuclear Arms Race* that year, and by other seasoned antiwarriors, including Norma Becker of the War Resisters League. The Freeze campaign came about when a Boston disarmament activist named Randall Forsberg was alarmed by Carter's nuclear rearmament policy following the Soviets' 1979 invasion of Afghanistan. Forsberg proposed a mutual, verifiable U.S.–Soviet freeze on testing, production, and deployment of new nuclear weapons. Through 1980 and 1981, the antinuclear movement accelerated, both in the United States and Europe. In western states, activists opposed a new MX missile system that would mar mountains with massive concrete loops for a "racetrack" to move mobile missiles from silo to silo. Reagan tried to co-opt the Freeze with a "zero option": if the Soviets withdrew all their intermediate-range weapons from Europe and Asia, the United States would forgo its new cruise and Pershing deployment, a proposal he fully expected the Soviets to refuse. Protest continued to mount, with 2,300,000 petition signatures delivered to the United Nations during the great 1982 Freeze march. That fall, Freeze ballot measures passed in eight states and several dozen cities, from Rhode Island to North Dakota, in what the *New York Times* called "the largest referendum on a single issue in the nation's history."[11]

Amid rising fears of nuclear holocaust, Reagan began to talk of a laser shield in space, the Strategic Defense Initiative, although critics mocked the plan as the "Star Wars" initiative and warned it would further unsettle U.S.–Soviet relations by suggesting the United States was prepared to launch a nuclear first strike. Antinuclear groups and efforts multiplied, from the Union of Concerned Scientists (founded in 1969 to uphold science against its misuse in war and in regard to the environment) to the Lawyers Committee on Nuclear Policy (founded 1981) to *Nuclear Times* magazine (1982–1986). In this mix, MfS was the movement's left wing, advocating unilateral disarmament and total abolition of nuclear weapons. Since 1978, it had grown to have 150 local affiliates, with a direct-action bent, by 1983. In New York, MfS sought a ban on ships carrying nuclear weapons from Staten Island's naval base. In Cambridge, Massachusetts, home to Harvard, the Massachusetts Institute of

11 John Herbers, "Widespread Vote Urges Nuclear Freeze," *New York Times*, 4 November 1982.

Technology, and many defense-contracting scientific firms, it proposed a ban on all nuclear weapons-related research. MfS held that "deadly connections" linked the nuclear arms race and Cold War to U.S. interventions in Central America – and the Middle East, following Israel's invasion of Lebanon in 1982. On June 20, 1983, an MfS-sponsored International Day of Nuclear Disarmament featured fifty demonstrations around the country at Pentagon-contracting corporations.

The heart of antinuclear activism was mass civil disobedience of the kind pioneered in the 1970s against nuclear power plants – complete with affinity groups, spokescouncils, and consensus method. Plowshares, initiated by Vietnam War activists Daniel and Philip Berrigan, entered missile sites and poured blood on them in fulfillment of the Biblical injunction to beat swords into plowshares. In California, the Livermore Action Group (LAG), an offshoot of the Abalone Alliance, was devoted to closing the nuclear weapons program at the Lawrence Livermore National Laboratory east of San Francisco Bay. In June 1983, a thousand LAG members blocked the road leading to it and were arrested. About 500 women, jailed for eleven days in a Santa Rita tent camp, successfully resisted the judge's intent to impose a two-year probation on all offenders to inhibit further civil disobedience. In the camp they created what one of them, Barbara Epstein, called "anarcha-feminism," with the view that women's communitarian bonds fostered radically egalitarian social relations devoted to ecological ways of life. They drew on the example of women "waging peace" near the Royal Air Force base at Greenham Common in Britain the year before. Another Women's Peace Camp commenced in late May 1983 at the Seneca Army Depot in upstate New York, near the historic home of suffragist Elizabeth Cady Stanton. About 15,000 activists that summer took part in several actions yielding mass arrests. These all-women ventures indicated a grafting of a cultural feminism, promoting what these activists regarded as women's distinctive mores, onto geopolitics.

In the social movements of the 1980s, *survival* and *solidarity* became entwined themes. The antinuclear movement was international, bringing Eastern European dissidents, German Greens, and Japanese atomic survivors together in common cause with American opponents of nuclear weapons. At the great Freeze march, signs borrowed the Biblical injunction, "Choose life, so that you and your children may live." The English socialist historian and campaigner E. P. Thompson defined the way of life of both the Cold War antagonists as "exterminism." Survival was manifest as a keynote in numerous other radical campaigns of the 1980s, from family-farm advocacy to "biocentric" environmentalism to action against silence over AIDS. Solidarity, for its part, was not only the very name of Solidarność in Poland and the clarion call of the beleaguered Local P-9 in Austin, Minnesota, but would animate American activists protesting against U.S. intervention in Central America and U.S. complicity in South African apartheid.

Central America, a cauldron of hot wars in the new Cold War and one of the few spots worldwide where a revolutionary left seemed ascendant in the 1980s, was the greatest focus of U.S. solidarity activism. When the Nicaraguan Revolution erupted, the Carter administration, plagued by other crises, hesitated to intervene except to permit the ousted dictator Anastasio Somoza to flee to Miami. The Reagan administration, by contrast, moved quickly to arm the contras and right-wing authoritarian regimes in neighboring countries. In El Salvador, government soldiers and far-right paramilitary death squads killed labor organizers, intellectuals, priests, and other "subversives" in order to defeat the left-wing guerrillas in the Farabundo Martí National Liberation Front (FMLN). Archbishop Oscar Romero, a Catholic critic of the Salvadoran regime, was killed while saying mass in 1980; that same year four American Catholic church-women, three of them nuns, were raped and murdered. In Guatemala, a military dictatorship carried out a bloodbath against Mayan Indians. The numbers of dead were staggering: 70,000 in the Nicaraguan insurrection leading up to 1979; 45,000 in the contra war that followed; 75,000 in El Salvador; 200,000 in Guatemala. Many of "the disappeared" were never found. Hundreds of thousands became refugees. The left argued that attributing such instability to the Soviets obfuscated the real cause of discontent, social injustice, and that encouraging military solutions to social and political problems would only guarantee human rights violations. Radicals, largely inspired by the Nicaraguan Revolution, pointed to independent human rights reports finding that despite missteps the Nicaraguan government was not as repressive as many states armed by the United States, including Argentina, Chile, Saudi Arabia, Iraq, South Korea, and the Philippines.

Numerous solidarity organizations sprang up in the United States, the largest and most vibrant being the Committee in Solidarity with the People of El Salvador (CISPES), founded in 1980. One early CISPES paper identified three overlapping forms of North American consciousness regarding Central America conflicts: *anti-interventionist* (an objection to military action that could take isolationist form); *solidarity* (an internationalism supportive of national liberation movements that seeks to "educate the

U.S. people as to the justness and inevitability of the revolutionary cause in Latin America"); and *anti-imperialist* ("in favor of the abolition of the economic system that produces foreign domination and aggression"). CISPES was perfectly willing to make use of plain anti-interventionism – "El Salvador is Spanish for Vietnam," read one pin – but its objective was solidarity, with many on its staff committed to ending empire as well.[12]

In the Boland Amendment of 1982, won by the Central America solidarity movement's lobbying, Congress prohibited use of U.S. funds to overthrow the government of Nicaragua. The movement also took to the streets in an insurgent spirit – marching, demonstrating, and sitting-in to challenge the revived big-power heavy-handedness typified by Britain's Falklands War against Argentina in 1982 and the U.S. invasion of the tiny Caribbean island of Grenada in 1983. In 1984, the CIA was revealed to have mined Nicaragua's harbors, an act the World Court declared a violation of international law. In response, a Pledge of Resistance was signed by 80,000 Americans who committed themselves to civil disobedience and draft resistance in the event of a U.S. invasion of Central America. Another direct-action technique was developed by the Sanctuary movement of hundreds of churches and synagogues begun in Tucson, Arizona, in 1982, which harbored refugees from El Salvador and Guatemala who were denied political asylum by the Reagan administration. Veterans for Peace (established 1985) demanded closure of the Army's School of the Americas at Fort Benning, Georgia, which trained Central American military personnel, while Witness for Peace (formed 1983) invented a potent tactic for pacifism by sending four thousand "human shields" into Nicaraguan combat zones to deter or monitor atrocities, a process it called "ordinary people doing a radical thing."[13] As part of a Veterans Peace Action Team at the Concord Naval Weapons Station in California in 1987, Vietnam veteran Brian Willson lost both legs when he was run over by a train he was seeking to prevent from carrying weapons bound for Central America.

Based on spurious claims that CISPES was arming El Salvadoran revolutionary "terrorists," the FBI infiltrated and burgled 180 of the group's chapters around the country between 1983 and 1985 at a cost of nearly

---

[12] "Solidarity Movement and Anti-Intervention Movement Defined" (1983), quoted in Nicholas David Witham, "After the New Left: US Cultural Radicalism and the Central America Solidarity Movement, 1979–1982" (PhD diss., University of Nottingham, 2011), pp. 9–10.

[13] Christian Smith, *Resisting Reagan: The U.S. Central America Peace Movement* (Chicago, Ill.: University of Chicago, 1996), p. 77.

$1 million. CISPES did supply humanitarian aid to rebel-controlled areas of El Salvador, but even a Justice Department lawyer held that it had engaged solely in "First Amendment activities." In contrast, Americans who supplied lethal aid to the contras were not investigated by the FBI, despite evidence of contra attacks on civilians. Reagan's National Security Council drafted a plan called Rex 84 for a "State of Domestic Emergency" that would impose martial law and detain people deemed national security threats in the event of U.S. troop deployment in Central America. Nevertheless, in May 1985, demonstrations assailing the trade embargo the United States clamped on Nicaragua took place in eighty cities; on one day alone, 900 were arrested in civil disobedience. Such opposition stiffened the spine of the Democratic-controlled House in refusing to authorize contra military aid, rendered "low-intensity warfare" in Central America unpopular in polls, and may well have prevented a full-scale U.S. invasion of Nicaragua.[14]

A solidarity movement with South Africa grew coextensively as the whites-only regime there faced a serious challenge from a triple alliance of the African National Congress (ANC), the Congress of South African Trade Unions (COSATU), and the South African Communist Party (SACP). Nelson Mandela, imprisoned since 1962, was the black-led movement's inspiration, with Bishop Desmond Tutu, winner of the 1984 Nobel Peace Prize, its voice. Uprisings in the impoverished township of Soweto in 1984 prompted creation of a Free South Africa Movement in the United States by Randall Robinson, director of TransAfrica (formed 1977), U.S. Civil Rights Commissioner Mary Frances Berry, and Rep. Walter Fauntroy, all of whom were arrested in November 1984 at the South African embassy in Washington, D.C., as they protested Pretoria's jailing of 13 black labor leaders. Because the ANC and COSATU called for economic and political isolation of the hated regime, TransAfrica launched a divestment campaign targeting U.S. companies and investors. On hundreds of campuses between 1985 and 1987, students demanded that university endowments divest shares of companies doing business in South Africa. Tactics included constructing mock shantytowns dramatizing those of black South Africans living under apartheid as well as petitioning and occupying administration buildings. In 1985, after a massive three-week student sit-in, Columbia University announced it would shed itself of $39 million in South Africa-tied investments, making

---

[14] Senate Select Committee on Intelligence, *Hearings on the FBI Investigation of the Committee in Solidarity with the People of El Salvador (CISPES)* 100th Cong., 2nd Sess. (Washington, 1988), 85–86.

FIGURE 6.2. Students in solidarity with Central America occupy a building in 1986 to protest Central Intelligence Agency recruitment on campus at the University of Massachusetts Amherst, denouncing "Covert Inhumane Atrocities" following revelations that the CIA had mined the harbors of revolutionary Nicaragua. *Department of Special Collections and University Archives, W.E.B. Du Bois Library, University of Massachusetts Amherst.*

it one of more than one hundred institutions to divest. While some administrations disciplined student radicals harshly, including expelling them for sit-ins, the divestment drive was highly effective. Goodyear, Mobil, and Hewlett-Packard were among the many companies that withdrew from doing business in South Africa. In 1986, Congress passed the Comprehensive Anti-Apartheid Act over Reagan's veto, banning new investment and trade with South Africa.

Anti-apartheid action coincided with revived activism on campus intended to challenge racist behavior by white students, promote ethnic studies programs and other curricular changes, and defend affirmative action in student admissions. Due to the creation, as a result, of new required courses concerning the dimensions of race, class, and gender in society and culture, conservatives held the curriculum was being "politicized" at the expense of the traditional canon focused on Western civilization. Liberals and radicals, however, argued that a wider range of differing voices – in the makeup of the student body and faculty as well as in the content of courses – enhanced intellectual life. As such works as bell hooks's *Ain't I a Woman?* (1981), Angela Davis's *Women, Race, and Class* (1982), and Alice Walker's *The Color Purple* (1982) became classroom staples, more American university students in the 1980s and 1990s were exposed to black women's perspectives and radical viewpoints than at any prior time.

A confluence of issues, international and domestic, was evident by mid-decade. A Minneapolis activist told the Mobilization for Survival annual conference in 1984 that most members "have the consciousness that the roots of war come from racism, sexism and the capitalist system." On the MfS staff was Leslie Cagan – a red-diaper baby who once traveled to Cuba on a Venceremos Brigade – and she organized demonstrations in April 1985 against four trends: U.S. intervention in Central America, the arms race, growing poverty and inequality at home, and South African apartheid. A Washington, D.C., march against Central American intervention and apartheid in April 1987 saw fully a third of placards bear union insignias, including the Communication Workers of America and National Education Association, over the objection of AFL-CIO leader Lane Kirkland who claimed the march condoned Communism. On October 11, 1987, Cagan, who by this time was also on the staff of Jesse Jackson's Rainbow Coalition, served as key organizer of yet another March on Washington, this time of half a million calling for lesbian and gay rights. So it was that even in the Reagan years radicals were able to play significant roles in linking movements, fostering perceptions of systemic problems, and building coalitions of solidarity beyond the limited domains of single-issue considerations.[15]

One pronounced feature of the 1980s left was a flourishing of grassroots religious participation. Press coverage dwelt on the Christian evangelical New Right, including Jerry Falwell's Moral Majority and Pat Robertson's Christian Broadcasting Network, but the antinuclear and Central

---

[15] Minneapolis quotation from Harvey Klehr, *Far Left of Center* (New Brunswick, NJ: Transaction, 1988), p. 149.

American solidarity movements were alive with a vibrant religious left. Radical spirituality in the 1980s took an immense variety of forms, from feminist practitioners of Wicca (or witchcraft, reconceived as a life-giving pagan tradition of nature-worship) to black liberation theology, from Buddhism to conventional Protestant denominations. Periodicals of the faith-based left included *Sojourners* (founded 1971 by evangelical Jim Wallis), *Commonweal* (a Catholic liberal magazine founded 1924), and *Tikkun* (founded 1986 by New Left veteran Michael Lerner as a Jewish counterweight to Norman Podhoretz's neoconservative *Commentary*). The most energizing inspiration was Catholic liberation theology, which emerged in Latin America in the 1960s and 1970s, positing that oppressive social structures are sinful and the Church must practice love through action to transform this world, and whose advocates included Sandinista Minister of Culture Ernesto Cardenal, a poet and Jesuit priest who studied at Thomas Merton's Trappist monastery in Kentucky. Although the North American religious left, tending toward pacifism, was never fully at ease with left-wing armed struggle in Central America, Sanctuary sponsors, willing to risk jail, included Lutherans, Presbyterians, Baptists, and Mennonites. In 1982, Levon Hucks, a United Methodist minister in South Carolina who had voted for Reagan, read a criticism of "nuclear idolatry" that caused him to read Thoreau, watch the film *Gandhi* (1982), and march for the Freeze. In Ohio, congregants of one church in a middle-class Republican town showed their solidarity with the Salvadoran poor by hoisting a white sheet in their chapel marked by two red handprints – the warning that El Salvador's right-wing death squads placed on doors of prospective victims as part of their terror campaign against the left.

Not all solidarity efforts managed to transcend parochialism. Irish-American Catholics in Boston and New York who sympathized with oppressed Catholics of Northern Ireland organized material aid for the Provisional Irish Republican Army – especially as British recalcitrance led to the death of Bobby Sands and other Irish republican hunger strikers in an Ulster prison. Bernadette Devlin McAliskey and other Irish nationalists were often socialists, and Irish Americans on the left such as Tom Hayden identified with their struggle, but the republican cause never fully coalesced with the broader American left. Irish Americans who identified with the cause of the rights of Catholics in Northern Ireland were not immune from racism – evident as Boston's white working-class neighborhoods rose up against school desegregation in the 1970s – and they were often indifferent to solidarity with resistance movements in Central America or South Africa. At the same time, the crisis of the labor movement in the 1980s diminished one of the means that had linked many working-class Irish Americans with a wider American left-leaning milieu.

Different frictions of religion and solidarity emerged in regard to the Middle East. Most leftists in the United States, including Persian students, welcomed the Iranian Revolution in 1979, but enthusiasm cooled as power concentrated under Ayatollah Khomeini, a Muslim cleric with theocratic aims. Soon Iran's Marxist left, including the Tudeh Party once significant among oilfield workers and university students, was suppressed by club-wielding Islamists who saw historical materialism as atheistic blasphemy. As hundreds of pro-Khomeini students seized the American Embassy in Tehran and took its personnel hostage, humiliating the Carter administration, U.S. press accounts began to refer to "radical Islam" and "Islamist radicalism" – misnomers to left-wing radicals who thought Islamic fundamentalism gained popularity as a tormented kind of anti-imperialism only because Cold War policy had already helped suppress left-nationalist and socialist alternatives. That perspective was espoused by the Middle East Research and Information Project (MERIP), which had issued *MERIP Reports* since 1971, and in the revolutionary socialist journal *Khamsin* (1978–1989), whose main initial support was from Matzpen, an Israeli leftist organization comprised of Arabs and Jews.

During the Iran hostage crisis, random acts of bigotry against Arab Americans (notwithstanding the fact that Iranians are Persians, not Arabs) prompted formation of the Arab-American Anti-Discrimination Committee in 1980. The Palestinian-American scholar Edward Said plumbed anti-Arab bigotry in his books, *Orientalism* (1978) and *Covering Islam* (1981). Against ultraconservative decrees by Khomeini and other Islamists that women's bodies be covered and veiled, Middle Eastern radicals held out for secular, tolerant, democratic outcomes – even socialist ones – but their arguments were hardly ever heard in the United States. In the bloody Iran–Iraq War of 1980–1988, in which Iraqi dictator Saddam Hussein was supported by the Reagan administration even as he used chemical weapons against his own country's Kurds, neither clashing power elicited left-wing sympathies. The Soviet invasion of Afghanistan to prop up a failing Communist state in 1979, likewise, found few defenders on the American left. As Reagan's CIA and Saudi Arabia's ruling family armed the *mujahedeen* against the Soviets in Afghanistan, however, leftist critics perceived U.S. policy as one of First World reactionaries underwriting those of the Third.

Israel made for a uniquely vexing case. Most leftists – from social democrats to Communists – had supported the State of Israel's creation in 1948, appalled by the Nazi genocide and charmed by the *kibbutzim*, the collective farms of socialist Zionism. A turning point came with the six-day Arab–Israeli War of 1967, when Israel's preemptive smashing of Egypt's air force shamed the "Arab revolution" of Gamal Abdel Nasser, whose left-wing nationalism proposed to supplant "feudal" Arab states. As Israel occupied the West Bank, Gaza, and East Jerusalem, many radicals – black militants in particular – objected to Israel's dispossession of Palestinian Arabs and described Israel as a "settler-colonialist" state in a U.S.-dominated imperialist world system. Conversely, many American Jews saw Israel's vulnerability as the war's main lesson, leading to stronger identification with Israel by Irving Howe's *Dissent*, Norman Podhoretz's *Commentary,* and, later, Martin Peretz's *New Republic.* As the Palestinian Liberation Organization (PLO) and related groups targeted civilians in events such as the massacre of Israeli athletes at the Munich Olympics in 1972, "Palestinian" and "terrorist" became coextensive for many Americans. Mainline Jewish groups such as the American Jewish Congress, American Jewish Committee, and the Anti-Defamation League typically labeled American Jews who criticized Israel's suppression of Palestinian rights as "self-hating" and other critics simply as anti-Semitic. Nevertheless, left-wing unease with Israel grew with the rise of the right-wing Likud party in 1977, the 1982 invasion of Lebanon, Israeli arms sales to apartheid South Africa, and the *intifada*, a desperate Palestinian youth uprising that began in 1987 in the Jabalia refugee camp involving strikes, boycotts, and stone-throwing against occupying Israeli forces. Pained to see their David becoming a Goliath, dissenting American Jews launched organizations such as New Jewish Agenda (1980–1992) and Americans for Peace Now (created 1981).

The 1980s left – Arab and Jewish – typically supported a two-state solution to allow independent Palestinian self-government in the West Bank and Gaza, while denying that criticism of Zionism (the credo of Jewish statehood) or Israeli policy was tantamount to anti-Semitism (the racist disparagement of Jews). Some doves held that Israel's oppressive policies threatened its security, while others held the very idea of a Jewish state to be exclusionary. Edward Said, who served on the Palestinian National Council from 1977 to 1993, became the most visible Arab-American intellectual, while Noam Chomsky in *Peace in the Middle East?* (1974) and *The Fateful Triangle* (1983) advocated a binational Arab-Jewish state as part of a secular, democratic Middle East. A complex question that could excite vehemence, Israel-Palestine divided American radicalism.

In 1981, a botched $1.6 million Brinks armored car heist at Nyack, New York, left a security guard and two police dead, including the only black officer on the local force. Captured at the scene were Kathy Boudin and her lover David Gilbert, sixties radicals and former Weather Underground members who had commanded a getaway vehicle for black radicals they construed as anti-imperialist but who in fact sought the money to support cocaine habits. Portrayed in the news media as proof that radicalism was unsuited to the times, the Brinks robbery certainly did underscore that the 1980s were not the 1960s. Its solidarity movements were equally large in numbers, but middle-aged in composition, making them generally far less volatile. Clusters of youth radicalized but were outliers as young voters went for Reagan in 1980 and 1984. Popular culture moved rightward as *The Big Chill* (1983) and other films reduced the sixties to nostalgia and portrayed protest as outmoded, along with bellbottomed jeans and the word "groovy." Bobby Seale published a book on barbeque. Jerry Rubin became a Wall Street investment counselor. "This is the 1980s," Rubin said. "A lot of former radicals are like me. They're out there making money, and they might feel better about investing with me."[16]

As neoconservative intellectuals asserted that a radical "new class" of professionals had assumed a posture hostile to the lower middle class and working class, some New Leftists turned conservative. David Horowitz and Peter Collier, onetime *Ramparts* editors, published "Lefties for Reagan" in the *Washington Post* in 1985, declaring "goodbye to all that – to the self-aggrandizing romance with a corrupt Third Worldism; to the casual indulgence of Soviet totalitarianism; to the hypocritical and self-dramatizing anti-Americanism which is the New Left's bequest to mainstream politics." Philosopher Michael Novak, former Clergy and Laity Concerned leader Richard Neuhaus, and black writer Julius Lester all foreswore their radical youths, as did the essayist Joseph Epstein, who once considered radical "an honorific term" since it meant "going to the root causes" but now thought "there was something terribly self-congratulatory about thinking oneself a deep thinker."[17]

Never keen on radicalism, the news media now routinely framed it as passé. When sixties prankster Abbie Hoffman was arrested protesting

---

[16] Maryln Schwartz, "Jerry Rubin: From the Chicago 7 to the Wall Street 9-to-5," *Dallas Morning News*, 11 August 1980, p. 30.

[17] Joseph Epstein, "A Virtucrat Remembers," in *Political Passages: Journeys of Change Through Two Decades, 1968–1988*, ed. John H. Bunzel (New York: The Free Press, 1988), pp. 37–38; Peter Collier and David Horowitz, "Lefties for Reagan," *Washington Post*, 17 March 1985, p. 8.

CIA recruitment at the University of Massachusetts in 1986 with Amy Carter, daughter of the former president, news reports framed him as a throwback. After Hoffman committed suicide in 1988, *People* magazine ran a "Death of a Radical" story, saying, "He was the madcap firebrand of sixties protest, but when times changed, he didn't." Whether because of increasingly consolidated corporate ownership, or because tactics once novel and ideas once dangerous now seemed stale, the media treated radicalism as history. Pervasive claims that radicals were dinosaurs, sellouts, or burnouts, however, overlooked three salient aspects of the 1980s: the permanent leftward shift of many localities, the creativity and perseverance of many sixties radicals, and the recalibrations of radical organizations and theory in changed circumstances.[18]

Local political cultures stretching from New England to the "Left Coast" showed the lasting imprint of radical social movements. In Vermont, Bernie Sanders, a Jewish native of Brooklyn who moved there with many other New Left and back-to-the-land communalists in the 1970s, was elected mayor of Burlington in 1981 after an old-fashioned, shoe-leather, knock-on-doors campaign. A socialist who ran as an independent and spoke to bread-and-butter concerns, Sanders was supported by a majority on the city council who organized themselves as the Vermont Progressive Party and undertook, in what was jokingly referred to as a "People's Republic of Burlington," environmental cleanups and opposition to corporate cable television monopoly. After four consecutive mayoral terms, Sanders was elected to the House of Representatives in 1990. In California, Tom Hayden was elected to the state assembly from Santa Monica in 1982. Berkeley Citizens Action (BCA) helped elect Gus Newport mayor from 1979 to 1986 on a program of rent control. Promoting the slogan "Think Globally, Act Locally," the BCA used Berkeley's city government to promote an alternative foreign policy through sister-city projects with Nicaragua and a South Africa township.

As sixties radicals matured, many sought to sustain their youthful ideals of social responsibility, personal autonomy, cooperation, and equality. Typically, radicals sought meaning and purpose more than money or status in callings that allowed them to align vocation with social vision: teaching, social work, psychology, religion, law, or medicine. Appreciation that social change can come slowly could, to be sure, reflect faltering confidence. "The revolutionary, youthful me of twenty years ago is not there anymore," one New Leftist admitted, putting her shift down to

---

[18] *People*, 1 May 1989, cover.

"eight years of Ronald Reagan": "I mean there is no longer that sense of possibilities. . . . I just want to keep disaster at bay." Some sixties radicals persevered, such as Lowell Bergman, who drew on his underground newspaper days to conceive of hard-hitting investigative journalism as a producer for the television show *60 Minutes*, but Reagan-era popular culture, with its open celebration of possession, could be disorienting. Dire Straits' "Money for Nothing" (1985), Randy Newman's "It's Money that Matters" (1988), and Oliver Stone's film *Wall Street* (1987) all pilloried the money culture but were taken to celebrate it, just as Springsteen's "Born in the U.S.A." (1984), a song about a disaffected Vietnam veteran, was greeted by many as a patriotic anthem. "Today the conservative culture is dominant," said Stew Albert, a Yippie who tried to hold onto his sixties' ideals. "Everything around you is saying you're a sap for holding on to these values; you know, just get it for yourself, get it for your family."[19]

All the same, the left imagination remained vital through the 1980s. The *Nation* featured dueling British columnists Alexander Cockburn and Christopher Hitchens, the punk scene spawned sardonic artists from the Dead Kennedys to Michelle Shocked, a revived *New Politics* journal was lively with left-wing debate, and lecture halls filled for Noam Chomsky's barbed criticisms of American foreign policy. The film *Reds* (1981), with Warren Beatty as the early Communist John Reed, was Hollywood at its most generous in evoking American radicalism, a nostalgia made possible amid the new Cold War perhaps only because the actually existing organized revolutionary left was in crisis. One small party after another succumbed to cultish weirdness. The Socialist Workers Party (SWP) traded Trotskyism for Castroism and purged most of its longtime members. The Revolutionary Communist Party embarked on a campaign resulting in a Supreme Court ruling, *Texas v. Johnson* (1989) that held flag desecration protected by the First Amendment, while publishing books with such titles as *Democracy: Can't We Do Better Than That?* The Communist Workers Party proclaimed, fancifully, that the "80's Economic Crisis Will Make the 30's Depression Look Like a Picnic." *Workers Vanguard*, paper of the minuscule Spartacist League, heaped vituperation on all others as petty-bourgeois backsliders. In rejection of all such small-group capers, other radicals joked, "Don't practice unsafe sects."

Among more moderate socialist organizations, the 1980s had a dual effect, promoting humility and realism while also pulling their politics

---

[19] Lauren Kessler, *After All These Years: Sixties Ideals in a Different World* (New York: Thunder's Mouth, 1990), pp. 36, 54, 200, 202.

rightward. The New American Movement (NAM) combined in 1982 with the Democratic Socialist Organizing Committee (DSOC) to form the Democratic Socialists of America (DSA). A significant percentage of NAM members criticized the merger as a "shift to the 'center,'" refusing to accept Michael Harrington's Fabian-like strategy of "permeating" the Democratic Party; to others, however, affiliation with the Socialist International headed by former West German chancellor Willy Brandt offered radical promise, given Socialist François Mitterand's ascension to power in 1981 on a promise of a "rupture with capitalism." Although Mitterand effected an "austerity turn" within only two years, social democracy's appeal continued to rise in the 1980s among intellectuals of New Left vintage as they sought to protect the welfare state against the Reagan onslaught. DSA became the largest American socialist group on paper, with some 6,000 members including co-chair Barbara Ehrenreich, a wry socialist–feminist. DSA helped revive the Socialist Scholars Conference in 1983, an annual gathering of thousands in New York. *Dissent* and *In These Times* were the right and left poles, relatively speaking, in this milieu. Irving Howe welcomed refugees from the New Left while saying he now thought the Popular Front was correct, after all – except for its Stalinism – as it subordinated socialism in favor of liberal alliances. Many Communists who had resigned in 1956 or 1968 had arrived at precisely the same conclusion, having in essence become social democrats, although they were less inclined than Howe toward sharp criticism of the Soviet bloc. Yet many social democrats ceased to identify with radicalism at all. Writing in *Dissent*, Theda Skocpol slighted the New Deal for "halfway victories," advocated "social-democratic restructurings," faulted twentieth-century liberalism for its fixation on growth, and argued for redistribution of wealth and income, all positions that would once have been telltale signs of radicalism, but she declined that label: "'Radical' connotes for all too many Americans mindless, even violent, militancy. It brings to mind images of bra-burners, street-demonstrators, and bomb-throwers."[20]

For much of the revolutionary left, too, the eighties were a time of modesty and reconsideration after the sectarian dead ends of the 1970s. "Any small disciplined group claiming to be, or pushing to build, *The Party*," one new communist movement veteran wrote, "makes it *more*

---

[20] "Why It Matters Now," Philadelphia chapter's statement on leaving the New American Movement, 15 November 1980, mimeograph; Theda Skocpol, "Legacies of New Deal Liberalism," *Dissent*, Winter 1983, p. 42.

difficult to win leadership and unite with other honest revolutionaries."
The *Guardian* opened its pages to a variety of voices, making it broadly
read on the far left in the 1980s, while several surviving small far-left
groups sought recombinations. League of Revolutionary Struggle, formed
in 1978 from unity of two formations, one Chicano, the other Asian,
and later joined by Amiri Baraka's black-led organization, supported
Deng Xiaoping's China despite its openings to the market, while another
Marxist–Leninist unity project, Line of March, oriented toward the Soviet
bloc. Two other Maoist-derived groups fused to form Freedom Road
Socialist Organization (FRSO) in 1985, while the Trotskyist-originating
revolutionary left also saw "regroupment" become a watchword. Solidarity, created in 1986 from a merger of the International Socialists and
two smaller groups, published *Against the Current*, espoused workers'
democracy, permitted pluralism on how to interpret the Soviet Union
and Cuba, and declared itself for socialist feminism. Certain orthodoxies
lingered in these projects, but they mounted plausible efforts to uphold
revolutionary vision and politics during times of profound rightward
drift. The road forward was, nonetheless, far from clear, and a number
of other far-left groups simply dissolved.[21]

One strength of the radical theory that remained in the 1980s was
a keen, sincere interest in international experience quite different from
past inclinations of some leftists simply to mimic foreign "models" such
as Russia or China. *Fire in the Americas* (1987) by Roger Burbach
and Orlando Nuñéz, written jointly by a Nicaraguan and an American, emphasized the diversity of particular national contexts, the centrality of democracy in the revolutionary process, and multiclass civic
alliances, not state power alone, as a way of contesting and constraining
the market. On the whole, however, the trend was toward intellectual
disintegration on the left. The crisis of worldwide labor and changes in
world capitalism that brought an end to what theorists called "Fordism"
(mass-consumption, mass-production smokestack economies dense with
unionism and high wages) led many intellectuals to doubt the relevance
of historic radicalisms predicated on working-class action. Increasingly,
self-defined "postmodern" theories displaced Marxism as a pole of attraction for avant-garde academics. Here, too, international influences were
strong. The French writer Jean-François Lyotard defined postmodernism

---

[21] *The New Communist Movement: An Obituary* (Eugene, Ore.: The Movement for a
Revolutionary Left, 1981), p. 5. The author was Al Szymanski, a former SDS member
and sociologist, who would commit suicide in 1985.

as "incredulity" toward any "metanarrative implying a philosophy of history" such as "progress" in either its liberal or socialist guises. Michel Foucault's writings about the effects of "power/knowledge" – the ways social domination worked more potently through the norms of everyday life and ordinary institutions such as family, school, and hospital rather than by overt coercion by states – gained enormous influence in American universities. In all, "postmodern" dispositions suggested that perspectives highlighting the fragmentary, dispersed, or unstable ("decentered") nature of things were most apt in the contemporary world. These were theories, not coincidentally, that had emerged after the defeat of the 1968 hopefulness in France and out of widespread dissatisfaction with what another French theorist, Gilles Deleuze, called the "micro-fascism" of the 1970s Marxist–Leninist left.[22]

Postmodernism's leading American interpreter, paradoxically, was a Marxist: Fredric Jameson, who published his signal essay on the subject in *New Left Review*. For Jameson, postmodernism was "a cultural dominant," the sensibility of "late capitalism" manifest in all aspects of the imagination from styles of art and architecture to the meaning of history itself. He understood the playful architectural style (a mixing and matching, or "bricolage," of odd and diverse elements) evident in new corporate headquarters and grand hotels as a sign of the ways contemporary multinational capitalism disordered everyday experience. Operating across the whole surface of the world, late capitalism made it ever more difficult for people to grasp the continuity of history or the basic mechanisms of the system, whose scope and span exceeded common modes of perception. The paradox, then, was this: capitalism was firmly in the saddle, but critics had lost the ability to "map" its dimensions and hence construct a coherent opposition to it; thus, Jameson suggested, Marx's historical materialism remained essential to critical analysis but stood, for the moment, apparently helpless.[23]

One early, acute critic of all such lines of inquiry was Russell Jacoby in *The Last Intellectuals* (1987). Earlier in the twentieth century, radicals were "public intellectuals," Jacoby held. They aspired to reach broad readerships by writing with elegance. As gentrification and high rents crowded out bohemia, and the university experienced postwar expansion,

[22] Jean-François Lyotard, *The Postmodern Condition: A Report on Knowledge* (Minneapolis: University of Minnesota Press, 1984), p. xxiv; Deleuze quoted in James Miller, *The Passion of Michel Foucault* (New York: Simon and Schuster, 1993), p. 239.

[23] Fredric Jameson, "Postmodernism, or The Cultural Logic of Late Capitalism," *New Left Review* 146 (July–August 1984), pp. 53–92.

the basis of intellectual life altered. The sixties generation entered the academic disciplines seeking to change them, but the academic profession had instead changed the radicals. Unlike C. Wright Mills, who wrote with clarity and brio, radical academics in the 1980s, according to Jacoby, wrote in a technical, obscure, recondite style – with Jameson his Exhibit A – that bore all the earmarks of tenure, promotion, and peer review. "Academic freedom meant nothing more than the freedom to be academic," Jacoby concluded. As higher education subsumed radical intellectual life, right-wing handwringing over "tenured radicals," Jacoby suggested, was much ado about nothing. What is telling, in retrospect, is the degree to which, for all their many differences, Jacoby and Jameson converged in the mutual perception that radicalism's prospects had contracted, and in thinking that the main agenda for historical materialist analysis was to explain its own eclipse. The forward-looking anticipation of the 1970s was most definitely no longer the radical temper.[24]

One area where everything – theory, tactics, ends – remained indubitably radical was ecoradicalism. The movement accelerated in the 1980s, particularly in the West, where mounting pressures on wilderness threatened "biodiversity," a newly coined word. Major environmental groups such as the Sierra Club, Audubon Society, and Friends of the Earth by the 1970s had settled into a liberal interest-group pattern, obtaining money from donors to pay staff and researchers and adopting legislative strategies predicated on trade-offs to avoid defeat so as not to be branded a "loser" in the never-ending fight against industry lobbyists. This pragmatism was typified by the Sierra Club's appointment of a Republican as executive director after Reagan's election. In 1980, the Wilderness Society's third-ranking officer, Dave Foreman, decided he would not "put my heart in a safe deposit box and replace my brain with a pocket calculator," returned to the Southwest of his youth, and formed Earth First!, vowing "No Compromise in Defense of Mother Earth."[25]

Foreman had grown up in a right-wing household, his first political activity being for Barry Goldwater. As a student in the 1960s he led New Mexico's Young Americans for Freedom and joined the Marine Corps but lasted only a month because he loathed military authoritarianism, sending

[24] Russell Jacoby, *The Last Intellectuals: American Culture in the Age of Academe* (New York: Basic Books, 1987), p. 119.
[25] Dave Foreman, *Confessions of an Eco-Warrior* (New York: Harmony Books, 1991), p. 4.

him ricocheting toward the counterculture as a beer-loving hippie redneck with an affinity for the magnificent sunset palettes of the Southwest. While living in the Jemez Mountains outside Santa Fe, he came into contact with the Black Mesa Defense Fund, a group formed in 1970 against the strip-mining of Hopi and Navajo desert highland which employed tactics ranging from lawsuits to vandalism of heavy equipment. He read Edward Abbey's *Desert Solitaire* (1968), a polemic against developmental, industrial, and tourist encroachments on the Southwest, and Aldo Leopold's *Sand County Almanac* (1949), an ode to land as "biotic community," not commodity. Louisa Willcox, another early Earth First! member, said the group's founders felt, "There needs to be a benchmark on the left. There needs to be a voice which speaks for the rights of wild country."[26]

Reagan's first Secretary of the Interior, James Watt, provided Earth First! with a perfect foil from 1981 to 1983. Watt gave companies bargain-basement lease rights to oil, gas, coal, and mineral wealth in federal lands and committed countless gaffes (viz., in reference to his coal study commission: "I've got a black, a woman, two Jews, and a cripple"). Earth First! dogged Watts as he traveled the West, demanding that cattle overgrazing be curtailed and millions of new acres returned to wilderness to restore every regional ecosystem. Earth First! had no office, no leaders, no tax status; its approach was in-your-face and do-it-yourself. "It's time to have the courage of the civil rights workers who went to jail," wrote Foreman in the *Earth First! Journal*. In 1981, Earth First!ers dropped a 300-foot sheet of black plastic down the Glen Canyon Dam on the Colorado River, creating a symbolic crack on its face, and at Yellowstone they donned giant bear suits to publicize the plight of the grizzlies. The wolf howls and clenched fists of Earth First! put the wild back in environmentalism.[27]

Soon Earth First! spread to Oregon's firs and northern California's redwoods, where the last of the country's centuries-old rainforests and their attendant species, including the Northern spotted owl, were in jeopardy as billions of board feet were logged annually in the 1980s. As Earth First! found itself at the center of a rising Pacific Northwest movement, it spawned a rebirth of anarchist direct-action culture. To Foreman, wilderness defense entailed no politics, left or right; in any case, Edward Abbey had the greatest influence on him. Born in Pennsylvania

[26] Susan Zakin, *Coyotes and Town Dogs: Earth First! and the Environmental Movement* (1993; New York: Penguin, 1995), p. 138.
[27] Zakin, *Coyotes and Town Dogs*, pp. 142, 145, 211.

in 1927 to an Industrial Workers of the World member, Abbey had moved to the Southwest after a Second World War stint in the Army and completed a University of New Mexico philosophy master's thesis in 1956 entitled "Anarchism and the Morality of Violence." His novel *The Monkey Wrench Gang* (1975) was a romantic tale based on actual early-seventies Arizona teenagers who called themselves the Tucson Eco-Raiders and opposed development by cutting down billboards, pulling up survey stakes, and pouring sand down bulldozer gas tanks. Earth First! coyly claimed not to advocate this sort of monkeywrenching but defended it as a last resort after legal processes and protest were exhausted. In *Ecodefense: A Field Guide to Monkeywrenching* (1985), Foreman justified "ecotage" as self-defense against rape of the planet. Abbey's "Forward!" to the book advised, "Spike a few trees now and then when you enter an area condemned to chainsaw massacre by Louisiana Pacific and its affiliated subsidiary the U.S. Forest Service. You won't hurt the trees; they'll be grateful for the protection; and you may save the forest."[28]

Some liberal environmentalists appreciated Earth First! for making them look reasonable; others thought the ecoradicals were discrediting the cause. Earth First! invented tree-sitting, in which activists took to platforms atop eighty-foot-high trees to ensure they weren't felled, but no tactic linked "radical" to "environmentalism" in the public mind more than tree-spiking, the sinking of metal nails into tree trunks to make them hazardous to harvest. Resentment of the practice in forestry-dependent rural working-class communities was stoked by an industry-funded Yellow Ribbon Coalition. Earth First! informed federal agencies whenever trees were spiked to scuttle timber sales, and Foreman argued that it was companies' responsibility to provide expensive metal detection equipment he hoped would diminish the profitability of forest destruction. In 1987, however, a 27-year-old worker at a Louisiana-Pacific mill in California was badly hurt when a spike shattered his helmet visor after hitting a sawblade. No evidence linked Earth First! to the spiking but the group was classed as "ecoterrorist" and federal infiltration grew more intensive, leading to Foreman's arrest in Tucson by the FBI in 1989 for alleged involvement in a power-line monkeywrenching.

By then, ecoradicalism had spun other variants. In 1982, the Animal Liberation Front took its first action in the United States, removing cats

---

[28] Edward Abbey, "Forward!" in *Ecodefense: A Field Guide to Monkeywrenching*, 2nd. ed., eds. Dave Foreman and Bill Haywood (Tucson, Ariz.: Ned Ludd Books, 1987), p. 9.

from a scientific research lab in Washington, D.C. In 1986, the Sea Shepherd Conservation Society – based in Washington state – sank half of Iceland's whaling fleet, two 430-ton vessels, by pulling their bottom valves, then destroyed its only whaling processing station after Iceland disregarded an International Whaling Commission call for a halt to commercial whaling. These actions reflected the philosophy of "deep ecology," which sought to replace Western civilization's assumption of dominance over other species with the view that all nature has intrinsic worth. As Foreman put it, "Grizzly bears and mosquitoes and redwoods and algae have value in and of themselves and are important just like we are."[29]

On one level deep ecology bore comparison to American Indian radicalism, for both inverted assumptions of "advanced" and "primitive" cultures, valorized a hunter-gatherer way of life, and rejected "civilization" and perpetual growth. Because biocentrists developed an antipathy not only for anthropocentrism but for humanism, however, their outlook all too easily shaded into misanthropy. One writer in the *Earth First! Journal* – Christopher Manes, using the pseudonym Miss Ann Thropy – stated that the AIDS epidemic might help restore ecological balance by reducing population; Foreman said in an interview that the famine in Ethiopia might be beneficial; Abbey opposed immigration. Critics on the left appalled by such comments called Earth First! racist.

The most extensive rebuttal to Earth First!'s deep ecology came from Murray Bookchin, the anarchist who established the Institute for Social Ecology in Vermont in 1974. Bookchin had long polemicized against Marxism but he retained socialist commitment in his conviction that a liberated society would have to be "post-scarcity," based on communal management of resources and free participation of individuals in small-scale self-governance. He argued that deep ecology ignored the systemic roots of environmental crisis not in humanity per se but in the destructive dynamics of capitalist production and centralized state power. Deep ecology, in Bookchin's view, repeated the error of Thomas Malthus by supposing population pressure to be the principal danger. Environmentalists, he held, should take seriously workers' fears of unemployment due to limits on current production processes and explain how a different future – decentralized democratic communalism – offered better prospects. *Social* ecology took capitalism and its heedless growth imperative, not civilization in itself, to be the problem.

---

[29] Zakin, *Coyotes and Town Dogs*, 291.

When Bookchin and Foreman debated in New York City in 1989 they were, surprisingly, more in agreement than not. They converged in seeing mainline environmentalism as compromised and in seeing the traditional left as insufficiently committed to the earth. "I believe that the color of radicalism today is not red, but green," said Bookchin, deriding the "ecological illiteracy of so much of the conventional left." Worried by the discovery of a hole in the ozone layer and other indications of a mounting planetary crisis, ecoradicals of all sorts saw an urgent need to go to the root, to move back toward the margin, to shock and provoke from outside.[30]

SILENCE = DEATH was the slogan found on small stickers posted all over New York and San Francisco, printed in white letters against a black background below a pink triangle, the symbol that those categorized as "homosexual" had been forced to wear in Nazi concentration camps. Here was yet another 1980s claim to survival against exterminism, another campaign of in-your-face, do-it-yourself protest addressing matters of biological urgency. When AIDS first manifested itself in 1981, the *New York Times* headline read "Rare Cancer Seen in 41 Homosexuals," but scientists soon determined it was a virus transmissible by bodily fluids shared through intravenous drug use, blood transfusions, and virtually any form of sexual activity. Profoundly debilitating, AIDS weakened victims' immune systems and left bodies vulnerable to fatal infections and cancers. The resultant death toll sparked a new turn in sexual politics, which would also see a massive feminist debate about sexuality, freedom, and pornography.

From 1983 to 1985, gay men debated the bathhouses, sensual playgrounds that had flourished with the advent of gay liberation, making sex possible with many anonymous partners. Given AIDS, some saw the baths as a menace to the gay community's collective health. Others saw them as spaces that, like bedrooms, should be immune from regulation. While denial of the ramifications of the AIDS crisis was a factor in some defenses of the bathhouses, sex radicals were at bedrock refusing to relinquish their newfound freedom. Many gay male sex radicals were deeply suspicious of a state that still criminalized homosexuality in some places and a medical profession that until recently pathologized homosexuality. The still-precarious status of gays and lesbians in American society

---

[30] *Defending the Earth: Debate between Murray Bookchin and Dave Foreman*, ed. David Levine (Montreal: Black Rose Books, 1991), p. 68.

in the 1980s – out, proud, but not yet accepted – was indicated by the Democratic national convention in 1980, when the sole gay rights speech, touted as a breakthrough, came in an untelevised time slot. Reagan called homosexuality "an abomination" and "an alternative lifestyle which I do not believe society can condone." The AIDS crisis brought hysterical calls on the right for quarantining all virus bearers – or even all gays. Gays and lesbians felt their freedom and progress were in jeopardy. In 1986, the New York City council passed its first gay rights bill; eleven days later the Supreme Court in *Bowers v. Hardwick* ruled that a Georgia man arrested for fellatio with another man in his own bedroom had not had his privacy rights violated.[31]

As health officials shut down the baths, bringing the early debates to an end, the unbearable sight of lovers and friends wasting away prompted an eruption of new gay protest directed against the health establishment and Reagan administration for their inaction and indifference. As the death toll from AIDS neared 30,000 Americans by the end of the decade (50,000 by 1995), SILENCE = DEATH provided a rejoinder to those who concluded, as moralizing conservatives implied, that *sex* equals death. The movement resolved not to return to the closet or celibacy but to compel medical action to counter the epidemic. A February 1987 Disease Control and Prevention conference of professional gay leaders and health experts in Atlanta was disrupted by Marty Robinson, earlier a founder of the Gay Liberation Front and Gay Activist Alliance, and Michael Petrelis, a brash 26-year-old "person with AIDS," who called themselves the Lavender Hill Mob and wore concentration camp uniforms bearing the pink triangle. "We're dying!" shouted Petrelis.[32]

The AIDS Coalition to Unleash Power (ACT UP), formed in New York City the following month by Robinson, Petrelis, novelist Larry Kramer, and others, would reshape the health crisis. ACT UP's refusal to accept the AIDS holocaust revived confrontational street politics among gays and lesbians, and its young members in advertising, the arts, and public relations produced stunning graphics. Within two weeks of its founding, ACT UP held its first protest at which 250 people in Manhattan's Financial District burnt in effigy the commissioner of the Food and Drug Administration for delaying approval of new AIDS drugs and assailed pharmaceutical

[31] Reagan quoted in Dudley Clendinen and Adam Nagourney, *Out for Good: The Struggle to Build a Gay Rights Movement in America* (New York: Simon and Schuster, 1999), p. 421.

[32] Clendenin and Nagoury, *Out for Good*, 545.

corporations for exorbitant prices. The plague radicalized gays and lesbians. ACT UP campaigned for free needle-exchange programs so that
impoverished intravenous drug users would be protected; for universal
health care; and for explicit safe-sex education about proper use of con-
doms and rubber dams to prevent viral transmission without repressive
constraints on sexuality. Begun by gay white men, ACT UP was joined
by women (particularly lesbians, aware that rising homophobia threatened them too) and people of color. A statement approved by more than
300 New York ACT UP members drew connections between "the major
issues of our day: racism, sexism, disablism, homophobia, economic dis-
franchisement, homelessness, and unequal access to decent health care,
among other issues." ACT UP rallied 230 people to stage a "same-sex
kiss-in" at St. Vincent's Hospital, where incidents of antigay violence had
occurred. "Your gloves don't match your outfits!" they shouted at police
officers who wore protective yellow gloves when arresting them at the
White House gates on June 1, 1987. ACT UP had an electrifying effect
by compelling larger research budgets, hastening action, and converting
an epidemiological disaster into a turning point in American sensibility,
an empathic basis for greater social acceptance of homosexuality.[33]

A parallel debate over sexuality roiled feminism in the 1980s. Feminism was no longer a mass movement, but substantial turnouts could still
be mounted to oppose New Right efforts to close abortion clinics. Most
women by the 1980s worked outside the home, whether because they
were single or to compensate for the stagnation of family incomes. Social
spending cuts, increased divorce rates, and pay inequity led to what social
scientists began to call a "feminization of poverty," particularly among
women of color, but most women rejected the New Right's solution of
a return to the traditional male-headed family, telling pollsters a strong
women's movement was still needed. The language itself altered as "stew-
ardess" was replaced by "flight attendant," "fireman" by "firefighter."
Feminists created women's studies programs in universities (with socialist
feminism retaining influence) and at the national level where a liberal feminist lobby consolidated. Radical feminism and cultural feminism thrived
at the community level, and it was there that a tremendous argument
broke open over pornography.

Feminists such as Andrea Dworkin, onetime New Leftist and author
of *Woman Hating* (1974), argued that pornography inculcated fantasies

[33] "Exchange," *The Nation*, 20 March 1989, pp. 377–378; Clendenin and Nagoury, *Out
for Good*, p. 558.

of total male power, contributing to women's exploitation, including rape, battery, and child sexual abuse. Dworkin first organized protests in New York against the violent film *Snuff* in 1976, helped form Women Against Pornography (WAP), and wrote *Pornography: Men Possessing Women* (1979). In 1980 Dworkin supported Linda Lovelace, star of *Deep Throat*, the first porn movie to reach mass audiences, after she revealed that her former husband had coerced her during the filming. Defining pornography as "the sexually explicit subordination of women, graphically depicted, whether in pictures or in words," Dworkin joined with legal scholar Catherine MacKinnon to draft legislation that would permit women to sue porn traffickers for damages under federal civil rights law. The Minneapolis city council passed their ordinance in 1984 with broad feminist support and with one of its leading sponsors being a Republican councilwoman opposed to the Equal Rights Amendment (ERA). Minneapolis's mayor vetoed the measure for civil libertarian reasons, but a revised version became law in Indianapolis, Indiana – again with both feminist and conservative backing. The Supreme Court struck down the Indianapolis statute on First Amendment grounds in 1986, but a few months later Attorney General Edwin Meese's Commission on Pornography endorsed additional constrictive measures. In 1987, Dworkin published *Intercourse,* characterizing all heterosexual sex as "the fundamental expression of male rule over women" – either to keep "the prostitute incarcerated in a ghetto hellhole of sexual subservience" or "the wife used, controlled, sexually subservient in the home."[34]

Other radicals saw in such efforts not radicalism but a dangerous convergence of feminism and the Moral Majority. Ellen Willis, writing in the *Village Voice* as early as 1979, observed that antipornography laws would likely be turned against speech and eroticism women found affirmative – an argument echoed by gay and lesbian activists and civil libertarians who predicted the legislation would be used by philistines against erotic art or in the AIDS panic to suppress explicit same-sex education. The Feminist Anti-Censorship Taskforce cautioned against puritanism and generalities about women and pornography, cultivating terminology such as "sex workers" to free those involved in the industry from moralizing opprobrium or the presumption that they are necessarily victims. Some feminists sought to improve health care and working conditions in the sex industry. The first woman-made erotic magazine, *On Our Backs* (its title a witticism at the expense of the older feminist newspaper *off our*

---

[34] Andrea Dworkin, *Intercourse* (London: Secker and Warburg, 1987), pp. 165, 167.

backs) appeared in San Francisco in 1984. Created by a group of lesbian and bisexual women, *On Our Backs* espoused a "sex-positive" philosophy, celebrating orgasm without denying that danger and pleasure could collide in women's lives, and refusing to be judgmental about consensual sadomasochism that many feminists had opposed as it flourished among gay men. Susie Bright, a former revolutionary socialist, typified the *On Our Backs* feminists who, like ACT UP, saw sexual freedom as the real radicalism. By decade's end, a politics of free expression had largely won out among young feminists and radicals, but misogynistic pornography and the physical abuse it depicted would forever be a target of feminist cultural criticism.

How could common political cause be wrought between feminists and Arab Americans, labor diehards and environmentalists, farmers and AIDS militants? It seemed improbable, but a strong electoral attempt was made by the Rainbow Coalition of Rev. Jesse Jackson, a former aide to Martin Luther King, Jr., and head of Chicago's Operation PUSH. The Rainbow, as metaphor, was a double entendre. One dimension was race. "The American flag is red, white, and blue," Jackson told the Democratic National Convention in 1988, "but America is red, white, black, brown, and yellow – all the colors of a rainbow." The other meaning was political, a "rainbow coalition of the rejected," as Jackson called it, that included all those left out of the political process: farmers, the unemployed, blue-collar workers, the disabled, students, the elderly. From disarmament to economic justice, from nuclear weapons to Central America, from green to lavender to red, a congeries of causes and constituencies blended in the Rainbow. This umbrella of alliance gave the Jackson campaigns of 1984 and 1988 a radical sheen, as did his pointed criticism of the Democratic establishment for reacting to Reagan's triumph by pushing a "centrist" approach designed to win back suburban and Southern white voters by distancing the party from "special interests" such as unions – an approach Jackson excoriated as a concession to corporations and yuppies at the expense of the poor.[35]

The Rainbow expressed the left's sentiments for racial equality while – equally importantly – offering a way to heal its internal racial divides. The political left was still a mainstay of antiracist groups such as the National Anti-Klan Network (after 1985 called the Center for

35 David Moberg, "On the Road with Jackson in Iowa," *In These Times*, 20–26 January 1988, pp. 6–7.

Democratic Renewal) and Political Research Associates, crucial centers for monitoring far-right organizations such as the Aryan Nations. At the same time, race remained a profound separator even within the left. An Urban Environment Conference in New Orleans in 1983 met to discuss the relation between industrial toxins and race, and a black-led community group there in 1989 conducted a protest march through the "cancer alley" of petrochemical installations abutting black neighborhoods, but the national environmental groups remained overwhelmingly white. Workplaces remained relatively segregated (Chicana in Watsonville, California, white in Austin, Minnesota) making the goal of interracial labor solidarity difficult to attain even though the working class and ranks of labor unions, as *Labor Notes* editor Kim Moody wrote, were "more black and brown" than the population on average. Feminism, too, often expressed professional white women's interests primarily, despite counterdevelopments such as the formation of Kitchen Table: Women of Color Press launched by Audre Lorde, Barbara Smith, and Cherrie Moraga in 1980. Even solidarity with Central America and South Africa occasioned divisions. Sandinista Nicaragua's mistreatment of the Miskito Indians had divided the American Indian Movement (AIM), one factor in a factionalism that left many Indians "walking around AIM-lessly," as joked Jimmie Durham, an organizer who turned from political action to work in painting and poetry. Even as South African divestment lit up college campuses, black students often felt that white students dominated. Students of color at Yale, for example, sought a "constituency-based" steering committee guaranteeing them half the positions so as to combat white voices crowding others out.[36]

The gravitational center of the Rainbow was in black politics. In the 1980s, black unemployment was twice the national average, the drug trade boomed, and numbers on relief rose while the purchasing power of welfare and food stamps declined. The election of Harold Washington as Chicago mayor in 1983, a left-social-democratic upset against the city's white-dominated, business-oriented Democratic machine, showed the potential for black-led coalition politics. In black radical circles, nationalism and Marxism both remained influential, but the Rainbow was a more typical formation, drawing together virtually all

---

[36] Kim Moody, *An Injury to All: The Decline of American Unionism* (London: Verso, 1988); Jimmie Durham, "Those Dead Guys for a Hundred Years," in *I Tell You Now: Autobiographical Essays by Native American Writers* (Lincoln and London: The University of Nebraska Press, 1987), p. 164; Matthew Countryman, "Beyond Victory: Lessons of the Divestment Drive," *The Nation*, 26 March 1988, pp. 406–9.

strands of black organizing. One or two contrarian voices aside – Adolph
Reed faulted the Rainbow as "black elites' opportunistic conceptualiza-
tion of politics" – the Rainbow attracted black nationalists, socialists,
and left-liberals. It was endorsed by the National Black United Front and
its staff included freedom movement veterans Jack O'Dell and Rev. C. T.
Vivian.[37]

In 1984, few constituencies outside of blacks supported Jackson's campaign. The National Organization for Women, the Freeze, SANE, Citizen
Action, the AFL-CIO, and the Democratic Socialists of America (DSA)
quickly endorsed the presumptive nominee, Walter Mondale, a Minnesota liberal who had been Carter's Vice President and who selected
a woman, Geraldine Ferraro, as running mate but remained hawkish on
foreign policy. The Rainbow's only other basis of support was among far-
left radicals, including such "new communist" organizations as Line of
March and the League of Revolutionary Struggle, as well as the CPUSA.
Such radicals saw the Rainbow as a way to reconnect with the black
masses and fight Reaganism, seeing work in the Democratic Party not as
"inherently accommodationist" but as "maturation" beyond the spontaneous leftism of the sixties.[38]

Jackson argued that his involvement in the political process would
increase black registration and turnout, especially in the South, and boost
the number of black elected officials and the Democratic vote so as to help
defeat Reagan. "Only the South can liberate the nation," Jackson argued.
"The reactionary South is blocking the national progressive arteries –
and the blocked arteries have given America a stroke." He went beyond
New Deal liberalism in calling for reparations for slavery, supporting an
independent Palestinian state, endorsing the Freeze and ERA, advocating
single-payer health care, and arguing that drug policy should emphasize
treatment, not punishment. Jackson won primaries in Louisiana, Virginia,
South Carolina, and Mississippi, took 21 percent of the nationwide primary vote, and carried such cities as Philadelphia. Holding only 8 percent
of the delegates, however, Rainbow forces could make little difference in
the Democratic platform, and Mondale subsequently lost to Reagan in a
49–1 state landslide.[39]

---

37 Adolph L. Reed, *The Jesse Jackson Phenomenon* (New Haven, Conn.: Yale, 1986),
    p. 87.
38 "The New Motion in Black Politics and the Electoral Arena," *Line of March* 15 (Spring
    1984), pp. 16–17, 60.
39 David Moberg, "Jesse Jackson: A Catalyst for Left and Black Politics," *In These Times*,
    5–11 October 1983, p. 7.

One factor in Jackson's 1984 bid left lasting damage: his casual reference to New York City as "Hymietown," a blatant anti-Semitic slur. Jackson apologized, but the slip was disastrous for the Rainbow's claim of inclusiveness, and the alienation of white liberal and Jewish voters was so complete that a writer in Irving Howe's *Dissent* even blamed Jackson for Mondale's loss, claiming he "made it easier for whites to vote for Reagan as a means of resentment and denial." In the *Nation*, however, Andrew Kopkind and Alexander Cockburn drew an opposite conclusion, faulting an "Anybody but Reagan" logic for the choice of the uninspiring Mondale: "With hardly a backward – or forward – look, the bulk of the surviving American left has blithely joined the Democratic Party center, without the will to inflect debate, the influence to inform policy or the leverage to share power." Failure to embrace Jackson, they held, had brought disaster: "Once again, racism destroyed the promise of a populist, progressive, internationalist coalition within the Democratic Party.... The only way the left can work within the Democratic Party is to act without it. That is, the future of the party will be determined by the development of forces operating on its margins or beyond its boundaries."[40]

By 1988, the Rainbow was prepared for a much broader, left-populist campaign. Jackson had spent the intervening years shoring up his progressive credentials by championing the Central America and South African solidarity movements, walking union picket lines, and taking part in civil disobedience. The Democratic field lacked a front-runner but included Asia-bashing protectionist Richard Gephardt and high-tech "Atari Democrats" such as Gary Hart of Colorado and Michael Dukakis of Massachusetts. Most on the left shared Manning Marable's sense of the Rainbow as "a social protest movement against Reaganism," an electoral counterpart to the kind of coalition-building evident when the exiled African National Congress representative Fred Dube spoke to striking Hormel workers in Austin, Minnesota, and Local P-9 sent a delegation to the 1987 Washington antiintervention and antiapartheid rally.[41]

DSA pirouetted to endorse Jackson in 1988. Barbara Ehrenreich wrote in the *New Republic* that he represented an important break from the right-wing monopoly on the language of populism and class. Michael Harrington called the Rainbow an "interracial coalition based on

---

[40] Jeremy Larner, "Four More Years," *Dissent*, Winter 1985, p. 9; Andrew Kopkind and Alexander Cockburn, "The Left, the Democrats, and the Future," *Nation*, 21–28 July 1984, pp. 1, 42, 44.

[41] Manning Marable, "Mandate for Leadership," *Nation*, 27 February 1988, p. 254.

principled opposition to injustice and class rule and in favor of a social democratic alternative." Irving Howe still rejected Jackson because of his criticism of Israel, while his *Dissent* co-editor Michael Walzer was even colder: "If we are looking for a leader, even for a speaker, we need to look for someone else." From revolutionary socialist quarters came different objections. The Detroit-based Marxist group Solidarity expressed "keen appreciation for what is different and inspiring about this candidacy and the Rainbow Coalition" but held that remaking the Democratic Party "into a party that can speak for our concerns is a tragic illusion" since "corporate capital finances and directs its policy-making apparatus and defines the limits of its debate." Most socialists, however, supported the Jackson campaign, including not only DSA, the Communist Party, and the Marxist-Leninist lineup from 1984, but former Trotskyist Peter Camejo and his North Star Network, former Citizens Party candidate Barry Commoner, and the National Committee for Independent Political Action headed by attorney Arthur Kinoy.[42]

In 1988, the Rainbow campaign focused on the most disadvantaged: the homeless, small farmers, the black poor, the disabled, the unemployed, those without health care. Jackson censured corporate tax cuts as producing plant closures, not supply-side reinvestment, and in a rhyming diction connected service cuts to social pathology and rising incarceration rates, asserting, "Head Start and day care are cheaper than welfare and jail care." Jackson won eleven primaries and caucuses, including Michigan, Vermont, and Delaware, in the most successful national-level black candidacy to date. His "common ground" theme, however, sealed a pledge to support the ultimate Democratic Party candidate, who turned out to be Dukakis, a technocrat afraid to embrace what his opponent Vice President George Herbert Walker Bush called "the L-word." Dukakis lost badly, carrying only ten states.[43]

By the end of the 1980s, social movements could show some successes and had spawned a new wave of radical contributions to culture, including Tracy Chapman's "Talkin' 'Bout a Revolution" (1988) and Public

---

[42] Michael Harrington, "A Case for Jackson," *Dissent*, Summer 1988, p. 264; Irving Howe, "A Mixed Response," *Dissent*, Summer 1988, p. 267; Michael Walzer, "Why Not Jackson?" *Dissent*, Summer 1988, p. 268; Joanna Misnik, ed., *The Rainbow and the Democratic Party – New Politics or Old? A Socialist Perspective* (Detroit, Mich.: Solidarity, 1988).

[43] Andrew Kopkind, "Is Jesse the Great White Hope?" *Nation*, 26 December 1987–2 January 1988, p. 791; Jackson, quoted in Bruce J. Schulman, *The Seventies* (Cambridge, Mass.: Da Capo, 2001), p. 71.

Enemy's "Fight the Power" (1989). Even a new radical periodical, *Z* magazine, appeared on the scene. The cumulative effect, however, never quite added up. The Rainbow Coalition had always been two things: a manifestation of the spirited social movements of the day and a personal vehicle for Jackson, who wanted no structure making him accountable to his base; in the end the Rainbow was beholden to Jackson rather than the other way round. His decision to disband it after 1988 left his most ardent supporters without any clear direction forward. Those who hoped the Rainbow would eclipse the Democratic Party, as Jack O'Dell predicted, were left without a pole around which to organize and fight even within the Democratic Party. In the aftermath of the Jackson campaigns, neither a restored liberalism nor a revived radicalism would exist as a foundation for activism in the decade to come. The death of Huey Newton in a crack cocaine deal in 1989 seemed symbolic of a more general disintegration. Across the 1980s, radicalisms had cropped up, exerted a check on abuses, and won clusters of recruits who helped a left to survive, but they never achieved a full-bore radicalization, that mounting force of protest that starts to rattle the nerves of the elites that hold power in property, government, and culture.

The year 1989, the two hundredth birthday of the French Revolution, turned out to be an epochal milestone in its own right as world-changing transformation swept Eastern Europe. A crucial precondition was Mikhail Gorbachev's ascension four years earlier to head the Soviet Union. Recognizing the Soviet economy's decrepitude, Gorbachev initiated *glasnost* (openness) and *perestroika* (restructuring). He took unilateral disarmament measures and pushed arms reduction talks with Reagan to enable resources to be diverted to more productive investments. That such reform from above might inadvertently detonate revolution from below first became plain in Poland, where Round Table discussions in 1989 between the Communist government and the outlawed Solidarność labor union resulted in permission for Solidarność to organize as a political party. In June parliamentary elections, Solidarność won 99 percent of those seats the Round Table made open to free competition (totaling 35% of the lower house). When those astounding results led in August to formation of a non-Communist coalition government headed by Solidarność, it became the first opposition in a Communist country to take power democratically. That same spring, another democracy movement arose among students in the People's Republic of China. Tens of thousands camped out in Beijing's massive Tiananmen Square under banners

calling for free speech and a free press. On June 4, the very day of Solidarność's first electoral victories, Chinese authorities commenced a military assault on the Tiananmen demonstrators, killing hundreds if not
thousands. If Tiananmen denoted tragedy, Poland signified potentiality.
Outpourings of citizens that autumn upended the Communist regimes in
Hungary, Czechoslovakia, Bulgaria, Romania, and East Germany. The
jubilation of November 9, as thousands poured over the Berlin Wall,
was the epitome. With amazing suddenness, what had seemed permanent
vanished – and with it the Cold War. In contrast to 1956 in Hungary or
1968 in Czechoslovakia, the USSR did not intervene to abort the process,
in large part because of Gorbachev's worldview and because the Soviet
state was stretched thin from falling revenues given declining world oil
prices and from the failed invasion of Afghanistan.

In a way, Eastern Europe's toppling of obsolete dictatorships vindicated the left, showing wholesale social change still possible through
nonviolent popular protest, a process that the Czech dissident leader
Václav Havel called a "Velvet Revolution." Most American radicals had
long criticized the Soviet Union. During an earlier New York forum called
to protest the initial suppression of Solidarność by the Polish military in
1982, writer Susan Sontag had declared that Communism was but "the
most successful variant, of fascism," or "fascism with a human face."
A subsequent vigorous debate in the *Nation* included the magazine's
Europe correspondent, Daniel Singer, who cautioned against a "cheap,
fashionable equation between Marx and the barbed wire," but Singer –
a Rosa Luxemburg admirer opposed to both capitalism and Stalinism –
was equally critical of the bureaucratic model, evoking the dream of "a
classless society of equals, of immediate producers taking their destiny
into their own hands, of the vanishing division of labor and the withering
state." That same year, the Campaign for Peace and Democracy/East and
West was founded by Joanne Landy, a Free Speech Movement veteran
and "third camp" socialist who rejected Soviet-bloc claims to represent
"actually existing socialism."[44]

Radicals such as Singer and Landy were, however, disappointed by the
outcome of 1989. They had favored *glasnost*'s liberalization of thought
but objected to moves under economic *perestroika* to privatize state prop-
erties. In admiring the Polish working-class movement of 1980–81 and
the Soviet miners' strikes of 1989, they hoped bureaucratic state power

[44] Sontag and Singer, in "Communism and the Left," *Nation*, 27 February 1982,
pp. 229–238.

would be replaced by workers' power; the monolithism of single-party rule by democracy; despotism and absolutism by socialism and freedom, East and West. As the tidal wave restored capitalism to the former Soviet satellite states of Eastern Europe, the region's dissidents, who for decades had spoken in the idiom of a more genuine socialism, seemed instead to echo Margaret Thatcher and her dictum on behalf of the capitalist system: "There is no alternative." Landy found herself depressed by the former dissidents' embrace of a "shock therapy that allowed the *nomenklatura* to reclaim privileged positions in the new order and left working people without governmental power."[45]

It is fitting that '89 is '68 upside-down. Revolution was in the air in 1989, but as an agency to establish parliamentary rule and competitive markets, the very social model '68ers had faulted as exploitative and inegalitarian. In "The End of History," published in a neoconservative journal that summer, Francis Fukuyama saw "the triumph of the West, of the Western idea, . . . in the total exhaustion of viable systematic alternatives to Western liberalism." Left-wing intellectuals found it easy to deride Fukuyama since his phrasing seemed to echo "end of ideology" talk in the fifties, when similar assumptions of settled order were quickly upended by New Left dissent, but this time something had indeed changed profoundly. The system born of 1917 had always had a double-sided quality in its effect on global radicalism; on the one hand, its contortion into a dreary bureaucratic system had debased the moral integrity of the socialist movement, but at the same time its very existence demonstrated that capitalism was not the only option available, suggesting that other more democratic possibilities yet untried might be possible.

With the Cold War rendered all but moot by the events of 1989, old pacifist visions of hammering missiles into ploughshares seemed newly realistic, causing some to dream of a "peace dividend" or NATO's dissolution. Such talk vanished after the Pentagon invaded Panama in December 1989, to unseat the once-U.S.-supported dictator Manuel Noriega. Further demoralization came by way of revolutionary Nicaragua. The Iran-contra scandal, rather than producing Reagan's impeachment, had actually redounded to the right's benefit as contra backer Lieutenant Colonel Oliver North appeared before Congress in televised hearings in 1987, becoming a patriotic hero despite his admitted criminal flaunting of

---

[45] Joanne Landy, quoted in an interview with her and Tom Harrison, "Regretting the Region's Right Turn," *Huffington Post*, 30 April 2013, http://www.huffingtonpost.com/ john-feffer/regretting-the-regions-ri_b_3187802.html.

Congressional will while at the National Security Council. In 1990 came the electoral defeat of the Sandinistas by publisher Violeta Chamorro, a product of considerable CIA dollars and Nicaraguans' fatigue from the war and the economic crisis fostered by the U.S.-imposed trade and loan embargo. The Sandinistas, in abiding by their pluralism, disproved the idea that revolutionary socialist regimes would never allow free elections or a peaceful, democratic transition of power, but their rejection at the polls deflated the Central America solidarity movement, which wilted. The ending of racial apartheid in South Africa began in 1990 with Nelson Mandela's release from prison and would culminate in his ascension to the presidency, developments to which radical divestment activists had contributed from afar. What would dominate post-1989 developments, however, were the newly global capitalist market and American superpower supremacy, which would work in simultaneity to return radicalism to the margins.

7

What Democracy Looks Like, 1990 to the Present

When Winona LaDuke, an Ojibwe from Minnesota, attended the Fourth United Nations Conference on Women in Beijing, China, in 1995 along with tens of thousands of others, she urged adoption of the Declaration of the Rights of Indigenous Peoples. At the China gathering to represent the Indigenous Women's Network, LaDuke was long familiar with global endeavors. She had joined the International Indian Treaty Council after hearing Cherokee organizer Jimmie Durham speak during her first year at Harvard. "There's no such thing as an Indian problem," Durham had said. "It's a problem with America." Impressed by Durham's view that American Indians' fate was inseparable from that of aboriginals world-wide, LaDuke had traveled to speak at age eighteen, in 1977, to a UN conference in Geneva, Switzerland. After time spent researching corporate uranium mining on Navajo land in New Mexico, which she called "radioactive colonialism," she moved in the 1980s to Canada, where she assisted a Cree campaign against a vast hydroelectric development project at James Bay. Long before Winona LaDuke arrived in Beijing, indigeneity and globality to her were one and the same.[1]

From Chico Mendes, defender of native Amazonian rubber-tappers, to Rigoberta Menchú, Guatemalan human-rights proponent, indigenous voices had won global recognition in the prior decade. In 1992, protests throughout the Americas marked the five hundredth anniversary

---

[1] *The Winona LaDuke Reader* (Stillwater, Minn.: Voyageur Press, 2002), p. 209; Marjorie Rosen, "Friend of the Earth," *People*, 28 November 1994, http://www.people .com/people/article/0,,20104531,00.html; Sonya Paul and Robert Perkinson, "Winona LaDuke," *The Progressive*, October 1995, pp. 36–40.

of Christopher Columbus's arrival, calling his legacy one of conquest, slavery, and genocide. Then came New Year's Day 1994, when Mayans in Chiapas in southernmost Mexico launched a Zapatista Army of National Liberation on the day of implementation of the North American Free Trade Agreement (NAFTA). "Zapatista" paid homage to Sandinista, with Mexican icon Emiliano Zapata as substitute hero. Subcomandante Marcos, the Zapatistas' spokesperson, created a wholly new genre of communiqué. In an urbane prose bathed in Mayan allusion, he mocked the top-down politics of the traditional Latin American left, his self-deprecating title "Subcomandante" signifying subordination to the "collective and democratic leadership" of Chiapas's Indians. "We are gauche, stammering, well-intentioned," he wrote. "We have not come to lead you, we have not come to tell you what to do, but to ask for your help." No longer would Mexico's marginal be silenced: "Does the country want Chiapan oil, electrical energy, natural resources, labor, in short, the life blood of Chiapas, but not the opinions of the indigenous people of Chiapas about the future of the country?"[2]

LaDuke would visit Chiapas, but she had her own base camp amid the pine trees and lakes of her father's birthplace, the White Earth Indian Reservation in northern Minnesota. Her mother, born Betty Bernstein, was raised in the Bronx, daughter of immigrant Eastern European Jews active in the Popular Front left who sent her to Wo-Chi-Ca summer camp, where she met Paul Robeson and Pete Seeger and came to love painting; in her twenties she spent three years studying mural art in Mexico, meeting Diego Rivera and David Siqueiros. On returning to Manhattan, she met a visiting native rights activist by the nickname "Sun Bear" – Vincent LaDuke. In 1959, their child Winona was born in East Los Angeles while Sun Bear worked as an Indian extra in Hollywood westerns. When they divorced five years later, Betty LaDuke moved with her daughter to Ashland, a small town in southern Oregon, to teach art. Growing up there, Winona LaDuke felt like an outsider, both as Indian and Jew. No one invited her to the prom – a sign, she later concluded, of unspoken racism. After excelling at high school debate, she resolved to defy low expectations by applying to Harvard.[3]

[2] *Shadows of Tender Fury: The Letters and Communiqués of Subcomandante Marcos and the Zapatista Army of National Liberation* (New York: Monthly Review Press, 1995), pp. 84, 107, 175, 228; Subcomandante Marcos, "The Hourglass of the Zapatistas," in *A Movement of Movements*, ed. Tom Mertes (London and New York: Verso, 2004), pp. 7–8.

[3] Betty LaDuke, telephone interview with Christopher Phelps, 15 February 2014.

In 1982, LaDuke "came home" with degree in hand to White Earth as high school principal. Poverty had caused an Anishinaabe exodus to Minneapolis–St. Paul and other cities, and less than one tenth of the reservation's original 837,000 acres of 1867 remained in Indian hands, much of it lost to speculators and logging companies after it was broken into individual allotments in 1887. A federal treaty rights settlement controversy pitted LaDuke against White Earth's all-male tribal council, whose development strategy revolved around a casino and timber clear-cutting. The council proved corrupt, and its leaders were convicted for bid-rigging, but further obstacles remained. "The Indians will get the land back when hell freezes over," one state representative said.[4]

Similar white attitudes had sparked creation of the American Indian Movement in 1968, with White Earth Ojibwe Clyde Bellecourt as its first chairman. LaDuke's novel *Last Standing Woman* (1997) had a fantasy scenario of an armed occupation at White Earth reminiscent of AIM, but her own organizing style was not as centered on confrontation as sixties male-dominant Indian radicalism. In 1988, LaDuke put $20,000 from a human rights award toward founding the White Earth Land Recovery Project, which recovered 1,400 acres of Indian land. She struggled with the local all-white Nature Conservancy when it bought 400 acres and gave it to the state of Minnesota, not White Earth, and she proposed return of the federal Tamarac Wildlife Refuge, created by forcible removal of Anishinaabe families in the 1930s. While learning Ojibwe, LaDuke fostered sustainable economic development in wild rice cultivation, organic maple syrup harvesting, and a natural seed library, including 850-year-old squash seeds found in a clay pot in an archaeological dig.[5]

Because of her belief that the U.S. government was "largely illegal," LaDuke never voted before 1996 and 2000, when she accepted Ralph Nader's invitation to be his running mate on the Green Party ticket. She respected Nader for authoring a very early 1956 law review article on Indian treaty rights and welcomed the campaign as an opportunity to combine issues. As a mother of three, LaDuke thought the mainline feminist movement correct on abortion rights but mistaken in failing to give equal weight to justice and the environment. "Women should be rioting" about breast cancer, she said: "the disease gets overly personalized, and all of the toxic dumping and environmental destruction that cause

---

[4] Peter Ritter, "The Party Crasher," *City Pages*, 11 October 2000, http://www.citypages.com/2000-10-11/news/the-party-crasher/.

[5] Peter Ritter, "The Party Crasher."

it get ignored." She pressed environmentalists to support Indians' right to subsistence harvesting of salmon and whales and advocated unilateral withdrawal of all U.S. forces abroad. Yet she called herself "pretty politically conservative," justifying that claim by her reverence for the Creator and traditionalist efforts to protect wild rice against genetic modification and thousand-year-old trees from being made into phone books. Her organizing, LaDuke said, was sustained by Anishinaabe spirituality's respect for future generations: "What we all need to do is find the wellspring that keeps us going, that gives us the strength and patience to keep up the struggle for a long time."[6]

In 1991, the longtime left-wing intellectual James Weinstein argued that the Soviet Union's collapse, which completed the changes begun in 1989, had brought an end to "the long detour" by which American radicalism was led astray by the Bolshevik heritage and harsh disputes about it. No longer tainted by Communist authoritarianism, the left could resume its struggle for radical democracy. The remark proved prescient since democracy did animate protest movements in the years that followed. From protest against the World Trade Organization at Seattle in 1999 to massive outpourings against war with Iraq in 2003 and the Occupy Wall Street movement of 2011, perhaps the most frequently heard chant was, "This is what democracy looks like!" That slogan celebrated the festival of the streets, suggested a commonality of diverse causes, and directed a defiant taunt upward at government tribunals and corporate boardrooms.

For radicals facing barren years, the aspiration for a deeper democracy afforded, in Subcomandante Marcos's expression, a sustaining self-image of being a "majority-which-disguises-itself-as-untolerated-minority." In the decades following the collapse of Communism, radicals operated on the margins of the society as market and virtue were taken to be synonymous, capital accumulation exploded in new technologies and exotic financial instruments, and vast divides in income and wealth yawned. A new degree of fatalism took hold in American life as the disciplining functions of insecure employment, low wages, and increased consumer and student debt, the gutting of labor law to employer advantage, the

---

[6] Ritter, "The Party Crasher"; Paul and Perkinson, "Winona LaDuke"; *The Winona LaDuke Reader*, p. 244; Jay Walljasper, "Celebrating Hellraisers: Winona LaDuke," *Mother Jones*, January/February 1996, http://www.motherjones.com/politics/1996/01/celebrating-hellraisers-winona-laduke.

loss of free time to long working hours, and a jaded popular culture produced a corrosive cynicism that undermined belief in the viability of common action leading to an alternative future. For much of the period American radicalism struggled to stay alive. "The only starting-point for a realistic left today is a lucid registration of historical defeat," wrote Perry Anderson in 2000 in the *New Left Review*.[7]

American radicalism after 1990 saw a pattern in which occasional, sudden, impressive bursts of protest momentum would occur, only to dissipate rapidly. Episodic upsurges occurred during each presidency: under Bill Clinton (1993–2000), the left lay largely dormant until movements against capitalist globalization erupted in the administration's final years; under George W. Bush (2001–2008), immense public outpourings against the administration's obvious moves toward invasion of Iraq virtually came to an end once war actually began; and under Barack Obama (2009–present), discontent over enrichment of the few at the expense of the many was expressed in the Occupy Wall Street movement of 2011, which disappeared from view almost as rapidly as it had materialized, and then a "Black Lives Matter" movement in 2012–2015 to object to vigilante and police shootings of unarmed black suspects. In between these encouraging flourishes of protest, melancholia tended to settle over the once-utopian left as radicals whose calling had always been to signify promising new worlds to come were often compelled to bear bad portents, whether scientific findings about global warming, staggering levels of incarceration, or exposures of pervasive electronic surveillance by the national security state.

The left since 1990 has rallied around hope for a more vibrant democracy – diverse in constituencies, bottom-up, egalitarian, communitarian, open-ended, and more robust than what liberal society offers – pitched against both the corporate organization of the dominant society *and* earlier hypercentralized models of the left. A "horizontal" or "network" conception of the left has prevailed. While admirably democratic in intention, this conception is so loose and ephemeral that it leaves little behind once the spirit flags, the resulting vacuum being filled by NGOs ("nongovernmental organizations," originally a United Nations term now widely used to describe nonprofit groups), which are driven by staffs, boards, and funders rather than by self-governing memberships, producing an unintended undemocratic effect. Meanwhile, the strength of anarchist sentiment in

---

[7] *Shadows of Tender Fury*, p. 214; Perry Anderson, "Renewals," *New Left Review*, n.s., 1 (January/February 2000), p. 12.

direct-action circles has often inhibited the formulation of demands on the state. Nevertheless, the left since 1990 has held to common themes and values under the broad aegis of democracy and sustainability, shown deeper appreciation for identity differences, given voice to widespread apprehensions about corporate power and inequality, identified capitalism as a social order in need of radical reform or replacement, kept a commitment to racial justice, and brought labor back to the center of vision even as unions have continued their steep decline. Radicals have not, however, succeeded in meeting the mainstream-margin challenge: presenting a vision for the future that many can imagine to be realizable, even as it dramatically differs from the existing order of things, and winning over publics to that vision. How to reach broad audiences, how to build lasting democratic structures beyond face-to-face meetings, remain challenges for a radical left that has found itself producing bursts that suddenly capture public attention, only to disperse, struggling between these eruptions to make a coherent force out of what has become a left indefinite in shape.

At the beginning of the 1990s, the radical left in the United States entered a great slump. President George Herbert Walker Bush, a Senator's son who had served as CIA director and Reagan's vice president, claimed victory on two fronts in 1991: the Persian Gulf War and the Cold War. When Saddam Hussein, Iraq's dictator, launched an invasion of tiny neighboring Kuwait, calls for American intervention were met by an ardent protest movement demanding "No Blood for Oil." Not predicated on sympathy for Saddam, this protest movement reflected worry over a repeat Vietnam-style quagmire and suspicion of the motives of a president who had made millions in the Texas oil industry. Since Kuwait was a semifeudal emirate, U.S. involvement could not be justified on democratic grounds, but Saddam's tyranny and annexationism limited the brief protest wave's appeal to the wider public. After the U.S.-led coalition's mission to repel Iraq from Kuwait was rapidly accomplished, the Bush administration encouraged Iraqis to overthrow Saddam, resulting in catastrophe for Shiites and Kurds who rebelled, only to be ruthlessly suppressed. For the next decade, the Iraqi people suffered under a U.S.-imposed economic embargo that merely stiffened Saddam's hold on power.

Dissolution of the Soviet Union in 1991 sealed "end of history" assumptions that socialism was dead. No one better personified this image of a fossilized left than Gus Hall, aged head of the Communist Party USA (CPUSA), who had supported Soviet bureaucratic hardliners opposed to *glasnost* and *perestroika* and was revealed to have received $40 million in Soviet assistance between 1970 and 1991, with zero effect in broadening the party's influence. In 1991, the CPUSA split asunder, those no longer accepting Hall's leadership leaving to form the Committees of Correspondence, complemented by *CrossRoads* (1990–1996), a periodical issued from remnants of the new communist movement, which had almost completely collapsed after 1989. The end of the *Guardian* newspaper, which closed up shop in 1992 after being published since 1948, capped that declension. It became difficult to speak of a socialist movement at all as the word "revolutionary" seemed to become the property of tiny sects and as more than one erstwhile Leninist passed from democratic centralism to Democratic centrism. As for social democracy, it mourned the deaths of its most eloquent American expositors, Michael Harrington (in 1989) and Irving Howe (in 1993), while facing a serious structural paradox. The Soviet Union, social democracy's great competitor, had withered away, but its very existence had provided an incentive to European states to grant their working classes concessions. Without the Cold War, "the market" became the vogue, typified by Tony Blair in Britain, whose Labour Party, once a fortress of social democracy, repealed the clause committing it to socialism.

Bush's unparalleled poll ratings following the Gulf War vanished in the 1990–1991 recession when corporate "downsizing" (then a new word) cost millions of white-collar positions. In South-Central Los Angeles, rioting broke out in the spring of 1992 after the acquittal of white police officers videotaped a year earlier beating a black motorist. The L.A. riots resulted neither in new liberal programs nor a radicalization of the kind similar rebellions sparked in the sixties – even though the death toll exceeded that of the fiery Detroit upheaval of 1967. Instead the 1992 election saw William Jefferson Clinton, centrist governor of Arkansas, emerge as Democratic Party frontrunner without opposition from the party's left. Inside the Republican Party, Pat Buchanan mounted a proudly "paleoconservative" primary race, while in the general election Texas billionaire Ross Perot ran as an independent favoring deficit reduction and opposing a free-trade agreement with Canada and Mexico. Clinton prevailed over Bush with a mere 43 percent plurality, less than Dukakis gleaned in his defeat four years before, a victory made possible by Perot siphoning off 19 percent of the votes. The Democratic victory put an end to a long period of Republican residence in the White House – the GOP won five of six presidential elections from 1968 to 1988 – and Democrats secured massive majorities in Congress, leading some liberals to perceive an ending of the Reagan era presided over by the first sixties-generation president, with one enthusiast at *Dissent* calling Clinton "a stealth social democrat."[8]

It was wishful thinking. Clinton came as advertised: a "New Democrat" of the Democratic Leadership Council (DLC). Underwritten by Merrill Lynch, Microsoft, Dow, Raytheon, Occidental Petroleum, and other corporations, the DLC emphasized "opportunity" and "responsibility" rather than justice or equality, placed labor unions and other "special interests" at arm's length, and catered to suburban voters and wealthy backers. After his lifting of the ban on homosexuality in the military met a storm of right-wing opposition, Clinton backtracked, resulting in a "don't ask, don't tell" policy under which more gay and lesbian personnel were discharged than ever. When First Lady Hillary Rodham Clinton presided over health care reform planning, the administration sidelined the single-payer universal Medicare solution preferred by the left in favor of "managed competition" by corporate insurers – with even that proposal, in the end, abandoned. A 750,000-strong NOW-led "March for Women's Lives" in 1992 prompted President Clinton to make abortion-clinic obstruction a federal crime, but the most sweeping pieces of legislation he signed, such as NAFTA and a $30 billion tough-on-crime measure, fit with longstanding Republican objectives.

Despite pursuing policies that marked him as a corporate centrist, if not conservative, Clinton enraged the right, which excoriated him as a draft-dodging, pot-smoking, woman-chasing, baby-boomer radical. As the National Rifle Association, the Christian Coalition, and talk radio host Rush Limbaugh stoked fires of anger, Republicans took back both the House and Senate in 1994 for the first time in forty-six years. This volatility in American politics, combined with a centrist-corporate consensus in the main parties, made the landscape difficult to read. Arguably, with the South a Republican stronghold, the "realignment" strategy of purging the Democratic Party of its Dixiecrat wing had been accomplished; the result, however, did not fulfill the hope of 1960s realignment socialists that one party of labor and popular interests would line up neatly against another party of "conservatism and big business, the militarists and nationalists, the stand-patters." Instead, labor was on the ropes, business logic guided both parties, and the ideological polarization was asymmetrical: the right waged full-bore assault while its targets

---

[8] Harold Meyerson, "The Election: Impending Realignment?" *Dissent*, September 1992, p. 145.

hesitated even to be called liberal. Looking ahead to 1996, Clinton's advisor Dick Morris urged him to practice "triangulation," showing independence from liberals while trading deals with Republican House Speaker Newt Gingrich of Georgia. In signing the Welfare Reform Act in 1996, Clinton eliminated the six-decade-old New Deal program Aid to Families with Dependent Children (AFDC) and set rules forcing poor people off welfare rolls. The Defense of Marriage Act (DOMA) barred same-sex couples from federal benefits and allowed states to refuse recognition of same-sex marriages from other states. That November, unprecedented campaign fundraising helped Clinton defeat both Republican Bob Dole and a second Perot bid. "The era of big government is over," Clinton stated in his 1996 State of the Union address, persuading many left-liberals and the few remaining radicals that they faced a bipartisan corporate consensus, a view reinforced as Clinton signed legislation in 1999 deregulating the financial sector by repealing the New Deal's Glass-Steagall measure separating commercial from investment banking.[9]

New debates over foreign policy erupted among left-leaning intellectuals during Clinton's presidency, especially over the Balkans. After the Soviet Union's breakup, ethno–national–religious conflicts flared in the former Yugoslavia between Eastern Orthodox Serbs, Roman Catholic Croats, and Bosnian Muslims. With Bosnia-Herzegovina's capital of Sarajevo besieged and reports of Serbian rape and "ethnic cleansing" of Bosnians, many liberals began to advocate "humanitarian intervention" to stem genocide's return to Europe. Indeed, U.S. military intervention acquired a luster among liberals greater than at any time since the Vietnam War, attracting even feminist Ellen Willis and onetime Trotskyist Christopher Hitchens, a *Nation* columnist who condemned the "Slavo-fascism" of Serbian leader Slobodan Milošević. Initially U.S.–NATO policy in 1992–1995 imposed an arms embargo on all Balkans belligerents, but because Bosnian Muslim forces were weak, the radical left argued the embargo merely enabled anti-Muslim genocide, calling for lifting the embargo while still opposing Pentagon intervention. Noam Chomsky continued as the most prominent critic of American foreign policy, joined by *New Left Review* and others who opposed U.S. interventions on anti-imperialist grounds. Few radicals denied or downplayed Serbian barbarity, most arguing instead that the abusive practices of U.S.-backed states – including NATO member Turkey's oppression of the Kurds – showed that

---

9 *A Way Forward: Political Realignment in America* (New York: Socialist Party-Social Democratic Federation, 1960).

the sole remaining superpower was motivated not by human rights but by strategic interest. The Rwandan genocide of Hutus against Tutus in 1994, far bloodier than that in the Balkans, had not brought editorials in the *New York Times* or *Dissent* calling for military intervention, these critics noted, perhaps because NATO's credibility was not on the line in central Africa as it was in Europe. In 1998–1999, NATO undertook high-altitude bombing campaigns against Serbia for its suppression of Albanians in Kosovo. Radical skepticism of militarism cast as humanitarianism included criticism of a 1998 Clinton-ordered cruise missile attack on a Sudanese pharmaceutical factory mistakenly thought to manufacture chemical weapons; the resulting loss of medicine caused untold deaths from malaria and tuberculosis. Such pointed debates over morality and American power would be reprised, with many of the same antagonists, in polemics over "Islamo-fascism" after September 11, 2001.[10]

As national politics became largely a contest between hard right and center, it seemed that the radical left had lost its way. Radicalism was consigned – and, increasingly, resigned – to marginality while the right showed impressive vigor in what Pat Buchanan termed "a cultural war" against "radical feminism," "abortion on demand," and "homosexual rights." Here was a paradox reminiscent of the 1950s: at the very moment of the radical left's disintegration, conservatives tarred liberalism as radical, a trope that would be perfected on Fox News, founded in 1996 and soon to replace CNN as the nation's top-ranked cable news network.[11]

The right's anxiety that it was losing culturally even as it gained politically had some basis. "Multiculturalism" expressed a new consensus accepting of diversity in race and ethnicity. A postsixties disposition toward personal freedom in sexual relationships had taken hold, with divorce, extramarital cohabitation, and varied sexual orientation all more widely accepted. Even as Limbaugh blasted "feminazis" and "liberal elites" in Hollywood and universities, fundamentalist preachers from Jim Bakker to Jimmy Swaggart found it difficult to resist the hedonistic temptations they condemned from the pulpit. When President Clinton was exposed for having engaged in a sexual dalliance with a White House intern, he was condemned in a prurient report by a Republican

---

10 Hitchens quoted in Maria Ryan, "Bush's 'Useful Idiots': 9/11, the Liberal Hawks, and the Cooption of the 'War on Terror,'" *Journal of American Studies* 45 (2011), p. 675.
11 Buchanan quoted in James T. Patterson, *Restless Giant: The United States from Watergate to Bush v. Gore* (New York: Oxford University Press, 2005), p. 252.

independent counsel and impeached by the Republican-controlled House in 1998 but held onto his presidency, acquitted by the Senate. Polls found most Americans did not believe that his perjury to protect his marriage qualified as one of the "high crimes and misdemeanors" the Framers intended as grounds for removal.

In the "culture wars" of the 1990s – struggles over affirmative action, arts funding, media coverage, campus hate speech, and science and history education – actual radicals, not just imaginary ones, did play a part in pushing back against the right. *Angels in America* (1992), a dramatization of AIDS by Marxist playwright Tony Kushner, won a Pulitzer Prize, while two self-described Marxists at Harvard, biologists Stephen Jay Gould and Richard Lewontin, were prominent defenders of evolutionary biology against creationist "intelligent design." To an extent, however, the culture wars transpired *within* the left, as left-liberals Todd Gitlin in *The Twilight of Common Dreams* (1995), Michael Tomasky in *Left for Dead* (1996), and Richard Rorty in *Achieving Our Country* (1998) aimed their fiercest fire leftward, blaming irresponsible radicals for a balkanizing "identity politics" that fragmented movements for social change. In answer to their call for a revived reformist patriotism and redistributive class politics, historian Robin D. G. Kelley called such an approach economistic and rebutted the "idea that class, unlike race, gender, or ethnicity, constitutes the only basis for 'true' progressive politics – one that unites rather than divides." Certainly there were many forms of identity politics, some parochial and others more generous. Often the narrowest forms of identity politics, moreover, were espoused by conservatives, not radicals. Minister Louis Farrakhan, the openly patriarchal, homophobic, probusiness leader of the Nation of Islam, espoused militant black separatism. His "Million Man March" of 1995, the largest black march of the decade, was built around inward-looking individual responsibility, its values very different from the black protest activity that spurred American radicalism from the 1940s to the 1980s.[12]

The abatement of black social justice movements by the 1990s was a result of multiple factors, not only the advances of black conservatism. Black radicals ascribed the loss of organizing idealism to the fatalism left by government repression, the rash of heroin and crack cocaine in the 1970s and 1980s (with middle-class white addicts better able to afford recovery and less harshly policed), and the decoupling of the black

---

[12] Robin D. G. Kelley, *Yo' Mama's Disfunktional! Fighting the Culture Wars in Urban America* (Boston: Beacon, 1997), p. 11.

professional-business class from the urban poor. In *Beyond Black and White* (1995), Manning Marable argued that capital disinvestment from central cities, cuts to welfare and social spending, and the expansion of an underground urban economy of guns and drugs, combined with a consensus of black nationalists and integrationists both favoring "symbolic representation" of black faces in high places, created both an illusory degree of racial integration and a kind of quarantine isolation of the black poor. For that "underclass," the racial divide still worked to preclude interracial action on working-class grounds. At the same time, new awareness had been fostered by radical inroads into intellectual culture. It became common in academic life to see "race" placed in quotation marks, portrayed as a "social construct" or viewed through the lens of "whiteness" – all reflective of modes of perception originating out of earlier radical challenges to the arbitrary and shifting forms of racialism. Nevertheless, efforts to revive black radical organization in the 1990s through instruments such as the Black Radical Congress remained at the margins.

Occasional radical developments did issue from the swirl of the culture wars. One was reclamation of the word "queer," before then a slur. Queer Nation burst on the scene at New York's 1990 Gay Pride march, armed with its chant, "We're Here! We're Queer! Get Used to It!" Its manifesto expressed outrage at AIDS deaths and gay bashing while criticizing materially comfortable gays and lesbians for their conventional gender presentation and casting of gay rights as a privacy matter. The practice of "outing," or exposing closeted celebrities in sports, politics, and entertainment, appalled many who saw it as a violation of individual control over one's identity, but queer nationalists held the closet oppressed everyone's "freedom to be public"; in their view, tearing down that closet by any means necessary was the only way to overcome "heterosexism." Invoking the sexual radicalism of early gay liberation ("we are an army of lovers"), Queer Nation proclaimed, "You as an alive and functioning queer are a revolutionary." Older gay radicals recoiled from the word "queer," just as many older black radicals disliked hip-hop references to "niggaz," but Queer Nation's name recalled the nationalist trends among people of color of an earlier period, while "Queers Bash Back" (a slogan more rhetorical than acted upon) recalled Black Power's armed self-defense. The manifesto denounced straight liberals who "never stick their necks out to keep us alive."[13]

---

[13] "Queers Read This," June 1990, http://www.actupny.org/documents/QueersReadThis .pdf.

Despite parallel projects such as Lesbian Avengers and "Riot Grrrl" punk, Queer Nation chapters collapsed, transgender writer Susan Stryker noted, "under the weight of their own internal contradictions – 'queer,' after all, means 'diversity,' whereas 'nation' implies 'sameness.'" Nonetheless, queer politics helped change American language with an embrace of what was conventionally strange, thus helping give expression to a continuum of sexual and gender orientations, including transgender and bisexual identities, beyond the male-centric, same-sex connotations that had settled over the word "gay." The acronym LGBTQ – Lesbian, Gay, Bisexual, Transgender, Queer – entered the mainstream in coming decades. Queer thought would continue to exhibit tensions between aims of equality and difference, justice and diversity, but by legitimating those who declined to assimilate and by defending identity as an infinite expressive canvas, queer advocates offered an implicit counterpoint to the perception that a focus on "identity" only augured disunity among rigidly defined different groups. As the 1990 Queer Nation manifesto declared (in a tacit jibe at the mainline gay Human Rights Campaign), "Being queer means leading a different sort of life. It's not about the mainstream, profit-margins, patriotism, patriarchy or being assimilated. It's not about executive directors, privilege and elitism. It's about being on the margins, defining itself." This bracing claim revealed a central dilemma. Radicals' willingness to be outsiders enabled a bucking of conformist pressure in inhospitable times, but too strong an embrace of outsider status threatened to cut stigmatized groups off from larger, inclusive alliances. From Chiapas came one suggestion of how the infinity of identities might cohere. "Marcos is gay in San Francisco, black in South Africa, Asian in Europe, Chicano in San Isidro, Anarchist in Spain, Palestinian in Israel," wrote the Zapatista Subcomandante. "Marcos is all the minorities who are untolerated, oppressed, resisting, exploding, saying 'Enough.'"[14]

What the news media was calling economic "globalization," the seamlessness of worldwide trade and investment following the fall of the Berlin Wall, was resisted from the outset by protesters, but the "antiglobalization" label placed on them was a misnomer, for radical and left-liberal critics opposed not a world economy but market fundamentalism: the assumption that markets, if left to their own devices, best solve virtually

---

[14] Susan Stryker, "Queer Nation" (2004), *glbtq: an encyclopedia of gay, lesbian, bisexual, transgender & queer culture*, http://www.glbtq.com/social-sciences/queer_nation.html; *Shadows of Tender Fury*, 214.

all social problems. Wall Street, corporate America, and the economics discipline all foresaw a world of perfect competition, a utopia of rational actors buying and selling, their decisions constituting "votes" that empowered individuals while allocating capital sagely. Free-market ideology, with its mantra to privatize and deregulate, placed under suspicion all taxes, regulations, and public spending. To radicals "the market" was an abstraction that concealed a set of economic relations of ownership, class, and power in a profoundly unstable system. Doug Henwood's *Left Business Observer* and book *Wall Street* (1997), Robert Brenner's special issue of *New Left Review* on "The Economics of Global Turbulence" (1998), and Thomas Frank's *One Market Under God* (2000) all provided astute criticisms of what Frank called "market populism," the claim that markets would set everyone free. "If globalization means anything," said Ellen Meiksins Wood at the very apex of Wall Street's bull market in the late 1990s, "it means increasing contradictions in capital, including the intensification of competition."[15]

Ecoradicalism constituted one ongoing challenge to such market dogmas. It contested anyone's "right to strip our forest and leave nothing," since "the forest belongs to the ages," in the words of Judi Bari, a leader in the fight to save northern California's two-thousand-year-old redwoods. Against free-marketeers seeking limitless economic growth, ecoradicals called for sustainability and stewardship. Nowhere was the clash sharper than in California's Humboldt and Mendocino counties, where a tie-dyed, marijuana-growing hippie culture long coexisted with a flannel-shirt, rural logging culture. In 1986, Maxxam, a Texas-based conglomerate led by Charles Hurwitz, used Wall Street junk-bond financing to effect a hostile takeover of the family-owned Pacific Lumber Company, which for many decades practiced responsible forestry via selective cutting and principles of "sustained yield." To meet its new debt obligations, the company began clear-cutting giant redwoods, sparking Earth First! to organize marches, lawsuits, and tree sits in a last-ditch campaign to preserve the primordial coastal rainforest – especially a vast stand that Earth First! christened Headwaters Forest.

At the center of the drama was Judi Bari, who brought many changes to Earth First! in the 1990s. A red-diaper baby whose Italian and Jewish parents had once been Communists, she opposed the Vietnam War as a student in Maryland, organized rank-and-file wildcats in the grocery and postal sectors in the 1970s, and then moved to the West Coast to work as a

[15] "An Interview with Ellen Meiksins Wood," *Monthly Review* 5:1 (May 1999), p. 86.

FIGURE 7.1. Judi Bari infused the radical environmental group Earth First! with eco-feminist perspectives and sought an alliance of workers and environmentalists against the destruction of ancient redwood forests in Northern California. © *BRANT WARD/San Francisco Chronicle/Corbis.*

carpenter. Outspoken, hot-tempered, sometimes abrasive, Bari was principled, funny, and gutsy. By the 1990s she was a prominent champion of two trends in ecoradicalism: ecofeminism and a "worker-environmental alliance." Earth First!, because of its Southwestern roots, had a macho, beer-guzzling, cowboy-booted culture, but a more hippie-feminist style evolved in its northern California chapter, where Bari, her sidekick Darryl Cherney, and others sought alliances with millworkers and loggers. Small bands of ecoradicals could not win alone, they argued, particularly given industry attempts to brand environmentalists job-killers. When Bari sat down with loggers for breakfast at a local diner, they asked, "Are you communists?" "No," she replied. "I'm much more radical. Communists only want to redistribute wealth in society; we want to have an entirely new society that's based on achieving a stable state with nature instead of exploiting the earth." She viewed destruction of the earth as rooted in patriarchal violence, while criticizing the "utter lack of class consciousness by virtually all of the environmental groups," holding that "all value derives from labor and the earth," and arguing "profits are gained by not paying workers the true value of their labor and by taking from the earth without replacing what's taken."[16]

In 1990, Earth First! organized Redwood Summer, modeled on Mississippi Freedom Summer of 1964. The plan was for thousands of youth to come to northern California for civil disobedience and to promote a Forests Forever state ballot measure that autumn. While building support for Redwood Summer, Bari was challenged at a public event in Oregon by Gene Lawhorn, a Roseburg millworker who urged her to renounce tree-spiking, saying it drove a wedge between workers and environmentalists. She immediately did so, and all of Earth First! in northern California and southern Oregon followed suit. Consequently, Dave Foreman resigned from the group he created, saying Earth First! was supposed to be "a wilderness preservation group, not a class-struggle group." Bari was not averse to monkeywrenching; she took delight whenever logging equipment "self-combusted" at night. But she concluded that tree spiking, which endangered workers' lives, had to be forsaken if a coalition was to be built to preserve the ancient redwoods. On May 24, 1990, an explosion tore through Bari's car seat in Oakland, disfiguring her and nearly ending her life. The FBI and Oakland police arrested her and Cherney, alleging they were carrying a bomb for terrorist purposes, a charge subsequently disproven. The legal and health complications sapped Bari and cast a pall over Redwood Summer, with Forests Forever going down to defeat. Never the same, Bari died of cancer seven years later, her slander suit against the government successful only after her death. The redwoods struggle spurred creation of a 7,000-acre Headwaters Forest Reserve in 1999, and the environmental–labor alliance envisioned by Bari and Lawhorn would undergird the WTO protests in Seattle.[17]

---

[16] Christine Keyser, "No Compromise in Defense of Mother Earth: An Interview with Earth First! Activist Judi Bari," *woman of power* 20 (spring 1991), p. 48; Judi Bari, *Timber Wars* (Monroe, Maine: Common Courage Press, 1994), p. 24; Stephen Talbot, "Earth First! What Next?" *Mother Jones*, November/December 1990), pp. 76–77.

[17] Dave Foreman and Nancy Morton, "Good Luck Darlin'. It's Been Great" (1990), in *The Earth First! Reader: Ten Years of Radical Environmentalism*, ed. John Davis (Salt Lake City, Utah: Peregrine Smith, 1995), p. 264. The Bari bombing's perpetrator has never

The fight over NAFTA in 1994 produced new labor–environmental linkages – in the Citizens Trade Campaign, for example – but also showed the decline of union clout. The measure, which would create a free market from Canada to Mexico, passed Congress despite Democratic control of both houses, and was signed by Clinton over union objections that it would inflate the trade deficit, cost jobs, destroy U.S. manufacturing, and depress wages. Labor's parlous state was indicated by the masthead of *Labor Notes*, which called for "putting the *movement* back in the labor movement." The economy expanded in the 1990s as the stock market boomed, budget surpluses materialized, and the new Internet prompted talk of a "New Economy" free of the business cycle and yielding perpetual growth. Yet income and wealth gains were quite limited for most Americans, in contrast to the prosperity that lifted all boats from 1945 to 1973. Many were compelled to take "McJobs" of the kind described in the novel *Generation X* (1991): "Low pay, low prestige, low benefits, low future." Old nostrums to "organize" could seem hollow in an era when the National Labor Relations Board, as Thomas Geoghegan observed in *Which Side Are You On?* (1991), "almost operates to prohibit" union success.[18]

Yet a new generation of labor leaders was on the rise. In 1991, Ron Carey, a reformer backed by Teamsters for a Democratic Union (TDU), won election to the Teamsters presidency. He presided over a stunning 1997 strike victory against United Parcel Service (UPS) that saw 10,000 part-time jobs converted into full-time positions with benefits. In a disheartening turn, Carey soon resigned in a financial impropriety scandal, but other changes were afoot. In 1995, Lane Kirkland, the plodding AFL-CIO president, resigned and was replaced by John Sweeney, head of one of the few growing unions, the Service Employees International Union (SEIU). Bill Fletcher, a black socialist, became the new AFL-CIO education director. Meanwhile, campus teach-ins – the first taking place at the University of Oregon on May Day in 1992 – gave impetus to hopes that a

---

been identified. She suggested that the FBI, timber companies, or right-wing mill hands may have tried to assassinate her, but others say she privately suspected her ex-husband, a onetime Stanford radical who denies responsibility. See articles from the *Anderson Valley Advertiser* at http://theava.com/bari.html and Stephen Talbot, "The Mysterious Death of Judi Bari," *Salon.com*, 23 May 2002, http://www.salon.com/2002/05/23/judibari/. On Lawhorn and Bari, see Bari, *Timber Wars*, p. 69, and Lawhorn, e-mails to authors, 16–18 February 2014.

[18] Douglas Coupland, *Generation X* (1991; London: Abacus, 1992), p. 5; Thomas Geoghegan, *Which Side Are You On? Trying to Be for Labor When It's Flat on Its Back* (New York: Farrar Straus, 1991), p. 4.

thirties-style labor-left coalition might revive again, the most-publicized one occurring at Columbia University in 1996, with Sweeney speaking along with Betty Friedan and Cornel West, attended by 1,700. Labor radicals were often skeptical, however: bureaucratic union structures, they said, made a displacement of business unionism unlikely, even as the AFL-CIO promoted "Union Summer" internships and an Organizing Institute. United Students Against Sweatshops (USAS), founded in 1998, campaigned against the raw exploitation that had reemerged in the garment industry in states such as New York, California, and Texas and in countries such as Indonesia, demanding universities buy logo apparel from shops whose wages and conditions were approved by an independent watchdog. Tony Mazzocchi and other left-wing unionists launched Labor Party Advocates in 1996 to advocate independent political action given Clinton-era Democrats' failure to defend labor, but the Labor Party never took wing, uncertain about whether or when to begin running candidates. Despite reformist stirrings prompted by radicals, unions were mostly inert, defensive, and declining.

Chiapas provided an electrifying contrast. At the very moment of NAFTA implementation, Subcomandante Marcos urged all "the excluded" – "the indigenous, youth, women, homosexuals, lesbians, people of color, immigrants, workers, peasants" – to challenge "the globalization of misery" by building a new "international of hope." As Mexico deployed 15,000 troops to suppress the Zapatista rebellion, the rebels ceded control of the seven towns they had seized and retreated into the rainforests, never to take state power. But that was part of their charm. Soon the rest of the left in the Americas was celebrating resistance to what Marcos's communiqués – in a phrase initially unfamiliar in English – called "neoliberalism," namely the reversion to nineteenth-century free-trade nostrums, the gutting of public expenditures on social needs, the maintenance of elite power, and the harsh application of punitive law at the same time.[19]

The Zapatista resistance helped accelerate a new worldwide sensibility strongly critical of dominant global economic priorities. Despite their hard-won independence from colonial rule, many so-called developing countries, particularly in Africa and Latin America, had suffered immiseration since the 1970s. Even as growth in the "Asian tigers" of South Korea, Taiwan, Hong Kong, and Singapore shattered Third World

---

[19] "First Declaration of La Realidad for Humanity and Against Neoliberalism" (1996), in *Zapatista Encuentro* (New York: Seven Stories, 1998), pp. 13–19.

stereotypes, most underdeveloped countries became entangled in debt, often racked up in World Bank-funded projects that enriched a tiny stratum of the population without improving the lives of most. Subsequent high rates of interest meant that debt repayments vastly exceeded loan amounts, the resultant state fiscal crises causing currency crises. Rescue by the International Monetary Fund (IMF) invariably compelled "structural adjustment": selling off public assets and industries to private interests, opening borders to trade and investment, and adopting austerity budgets, including eliminating subsidies that enabled the poorest to buy staples.

The staffs of humanitarian groups such as Doctors without Borders (Médecins Sans Frontières), Oxfam, or Human Rights Watch soon became concerned. Such NGOs were not radical but sought to ameliorate disease, hunger, lack of clean water, and women's low status. NGO staffers began to take note of a spate of spontaneous strikes, protests, and food riots in the 1980s against structural adjustment measures from Bolivia to Nigeria, particularly the outpouring in Caracas, Venezuela, in 1989, against public transportation price increases. These NGO dissenters started to charge that global financial agencies such as the IMF and World Bank were deepening poverty rather than reducing it. These critics were insiders, not outsiders; schooled in economic theory, they worked for organizations based in the richest nations. Their dissent was therefore in a register distinct from insurgent groups such as the Zapatistas, lending a touch of sophistication and technical expertise to the opposition that challenged the chorus of market exuberance. Remarkably, their message was not so far removed from that of Fidel Castro, who told a gathering of a group of 133 underdeveloped nations in Havana in 2000 that the image of "globalization" as a single planetary ship masked a reality analogous to "the terrible slave trade": "Eighty-five percent of the passengers on this ship are crowded into its dirty hold, suffering hunger, disease, and helplessness."[20]

NGOs, to be sure, came in many different forms. The World Economic Forum, meeting annually in Davos, Switzerland, celebrated the market. Others tilted leftward, including Global Exchange, a consortium based in San Francisco that emerged out of the Central American solidarity movement and was convened in 1988 to encourage "fair trade," assuring decent prices to small-scale producers of the underdeveloped world. From more technical quarters came the Development Group for Alternative

[20] Fidel Castro, "We Either Unite or We Die," in *Democratizing the Global Economy*, ed. Kevin Danaher (Monroe, Maine: Common Courage, 2001), p. 75.

Policies (the Development GAP, or D-GAP), whose acronym played on the gap between global North and South. A grouping of heretics within the policy establishment who came together early, in 1976, D-GAP promoted local, usually small-scale, poverty-fighting initiatives rather than massive development projects such as hydroelectric dams. Initially seeking to persuade decision makers in institutions such as the U.S. Agency for International Development (USAID), D-GAP policy wonks by the 1990s found themselves gadflies, assisting other NGOs in opposition to the very institutions they once sought to influence.

A few prominent NGOs emerged from "the global South" – a designation that increasingly vied with "Third World" to describe the world's lesser-developed countries. Here the revolutionary argot spoken by Castro waned after 1991, not only because of the collapse of the Soviet Union and imposition of "shock therapy" in Eastern Europe but because of market reforms in China and Vietnam and privatizations implemented by the African National Congress (ANC) after it took power in South Africa. A key voice of radical dissent was the Filipino intellectual Walden Bello, who studied at Princeton at the height of New Left radicalism. In opposing "World Bank development models and other patterns of domination" he grew convinced "these couldn't simply be challenged at the national level" and by the early 1990s joined with colleagues from India, Thailand, Korea, and Japan to establish a Bangkok-based institute called Focus on the Global South.[21]

While policy experts suggested that World Bank and IMF "development" was really a mode of extraction, popular movements mounted resistance. Poor villagers in India, their homes threatened by inundation in the Narmada River Valley, opposed construction of a giant dam underwritten by the World Bank. In the teeth of severe repression, including shootings, arrests, and torture, the Save Narmada Movement, much of it woman-led, created so much dissent that the World Bank withdrew its funding from the project in 1993. Considerable protest focused on trade, since leveling trade barriers seemed less a recipe for freedom and growth than a means of market access and domination by multinational corporations. The Landless Workers Movement (MST) in Brazil opposed what João Pedro Stedile called "the monopolization of world agricultural trade by the multinational corporations" – seven major conglomerates

---

[21] Walden Bello, "The Global South," *A Movement of Movements: Is Another World Really Possible?*, ed. Tom Mertes (New York: Verso, 2004), pp. 49–56.

including Monsanto, a firm selling genetically modified seeds – and began to talk of "food sovereignty."[22]

In 1994, the 50 Years is Enough Network was established by D-GAP, Global Exchange, Oxfam, Friends of the Earth, Greenpeace, the Environmental Defense Fund, and other groups – some 35 NGOs in all. The name referred back to 1944, when at the end of the Second World War the United States met with allies at Bretton Woods, New Hampshire, and established a dollar-centered world currency system with two new institutions geared to facilitating trade: the IMF to provide emergency loans to countries encountering monetary or fiscal problems, thus threatening trade breakdowns, and the World Bank to fund development sustaining worldwide demand. In 1949, a third leg was added to Bretton Woods when dozens of countries reached a related General Agreement on Tariffs and Trade (GATT) with the aim of steadily reducing tariffs, a process that by 1986 took the form of an "Uruguay round" that was the context for the creation of the European Union (EU) in 1993 and NAFTA in 1994. By 1995, GATT had become the World Trade Organization (WTO). Firmly led by the most powerful G-7 nations (the United States, Britain, France, Germany, Italy, Japan, and Canada), the WTO negotiated "free trade" rules and established judicial procedures whereby member states could be fined or sanctioned for any national policies violating free-trade standards.

What worried many NGOs was the way such rules were impinging on national policies concerning the environment, labor, and other areas. The United States, for instance, had prohibited importation of tuna caught with nets that also trapped and killed dolphins and banned the use of shrimp nets that killed large sea turtles, but other countries challenged the regulations before a WTO tribunal as barriers to trade. The same danger existed for Europe's banning of genetically modified food products from the United States. Critics argued that the WTO was establishing private ownership rights where there should be none, as when U.S. agribusiness sought proprietary rights for seeds that it wished to patent and sell at protected prices – although the seeds were a common, natural resource. Rather than promote freedom in trade, critics argued, the WTO was a centralized body imposing a single, uniform, neoliberal way the whole world over, all to benefit the world's most powerful economic interests. The naked intrusiveness of this global capitalism accounts for the surprise

---

[22] Mertes, *A Movement of Movements*, p. 43.

vogue, on its 150th anniversary, of Marx's *Communist Manifesto*, with its talk of a bourgeoisie using cheap commodities to batter down all Chinese walls. As Verso Books reissued the book in 1998, a crowd of 900 filled Cooper Union in New York for a "Manifestivity" of readings from the text by Amiri Baraka, Wallace Shawn, and Tony Kushner, among others.

The 50 Years is Enough Network assailed the World Bank and IMF as "profoundly undemocratic," called for moratoria on massive dam projects and logging in primary forests, and demanded cancellation of all outstanding debt owed to the agencies by "severely indebted low income countries," an aim that would also be the focus of Jubilee 2000, a parallel NGO coalition originating out of the United Kingdom. A genuine momentum was mounting, if still below the sight of most Americans transfixed by rocketing share prices on the stock market. Outliers were becoming involved. In Arcata, California, the obliteration of small shops by low-wage, antiunion giants such as Wal-Mart led Paul Cienfuegos, a veteran of the 1970s antinuclear movement, to question corporate personhood, the Supreme Court's interpretation of the Fourteenth Amendment giving corporations untrammeled rights in managing property. "By what authority do they even *exist*?" asked Cienfuegos. When Arcata was offered Measure F on its ballot in 1998, establishing a committee "to ensure democratic control over corporations conducting business within the city," it passed by a two-thirds majority. Meanwhile, the Zapatistas raised the slogan *¡Ya Basta!* – "Enough!" – to neoliberal globalization. In 1998, *¡Ya Basta!* admirers from 71 countries met in Geneva to establish People's Global Action (PGA), a "horizontal" network that promptly called for mass protests at the third ministerial meeting of the World Trade Organization scheduled for Seattle, Washington, from November 28 to December 2, 1999.[23]

As organizations from more than eighty countries converged on Seattle, from the Indigenous People's Biodiversity Network to the Rainforest Action Network, the bulk of the 40–50,000 protesters hailed from the United States, where use of e-mail and websites made Seattle the first major demonstration organized via the Internet. The Earth Island Institute had brought hundreds of giant sea turtle costumes for demonstrators

[23] "Platform of the U.S. '50 Years is Enough' Campaign" (1994), http://www.library.ohiou .edu/indopubs/1994/05/10/0006.html; Cienfuegos, quoted in Paul Kingsnorth, *One No, Many Yeses: A Journey to the Heart of the Global Resistance Movement* (New York: The Free Press, 1993), pp. 279, 281.

to wear, the Institute's 80-year-old founder David Brower joining with Steelworkers district leader David Foster to focus criticism on corporate baron Charles Hurwitz, given his controlling interests in the Pacific Lumber Company *and* antiunion Kaiser Aluminum. Workers and ecoradicals linked arms, upholding banners stating, "Turtles and Teamsters – Together at Last!"

The day of most intense action, planned for months in advance, was Tuesday, November 30, the WTO's intended ceremonial opening day. Early in the morning protesters from the developing world marched from one direction, students from the other, in a symbolic convergence of global North and South. Simultaneously, thousands organized by the Direct Action Network and trained in nonviolent civil disobedience by the Ruckus Society converged on Seattle's city center. They implemented a complex operation in which different affinity groups took responsibility for sections of the city map, blocking all traffic at intersections by making human barriers using lock-down techniques fashioned from thick plastic pipes, metal chains, and carabiners. By mid-morning, Seattle was ensnarled, WTO delegates were unable to reach the Convention Center, and the opening assembly was cancelled. A giant AFL-CIO rally at Memorial Stadium attended by 50,000, meanwhile, heard Leroy Trotman of the Barbados Workers Union declare, "This demonstration is not a demonstration of United States. It is a demonstration of all working-class people all over the world: rich country, poor country, white country, black country – all country!" It was adding up to be one of the most impressive shows of labor–environmental alliance, global North–South unity, and nonviolent civil disobedience in American history. Seattle's chief of police told the *Seattle Times*, "There were those saying they would shut down the city of Seattle, and they managed to do that today."[24]

Two other features, however, took greater prominence in news coverage. The first was the chaos as Seattle police, outnumbered and outmaneuvered, did not respond with orderly arrests but instead applied "pain compliance" in the form of pepper spray, a chemical poison, against the locked-down protesters. The bulk of repressive force fell on young activists – although uninvolved passersby, too, were caught in the gas clouds and roundups. The second aspect dominating news coverage was a small number of self-described anarchists – many of whom had emanated

[24] *This is What Democracy Looks Like*, dir. Jill Friedberg and Rick Rowley (2000; Big Noise Films); David Solnit, *The Battle of the Story of the Battle of Seattle* (Edinburgh; Oakland, Calif.; Baltimore, Md.: AK Press, 2009), p. 6.

FIGURE 7.2. A demonstrator against the World Trade Organization in Seattle, Washington, in 1999 wears a protective mask and bears the American flag to symbolize the democratic right to dissent after police gassed demonstrators. *Colleen Cummins.*

from a militant ecoradical milieu in Eugene, Oregon – comprising a "black bloc," dressed in black, their faces masked, who smashed windows at outlets such as Starbucks, NikeTown, the Gap, Key Bank, and Bank of America. The black-bloc tactic, first used by Germany's "autonomists" in 1986, was barely known in the United States before Seattle, but the window-smashing dominated the national news that night. Portrayed as "violence," the property damage would eclipse the Direct Action Network's success in shutting down the WTO nonviolently. News anchors now called it "The Battle of Seattle." Seattle's mayor, anticipating President Clinton's impending visit to address the WTO, declared a state of emergency, called in the National Guard, and set up a 25-block "no-protest zone." Protesters retorted by chanting the words of the Constitution: "Peacefully Assemble!" but rubber bullets, truncheons, and stun guns were deployed and more than 600 arrests were made that week. At the WTO's official proceedings, talks collapsed as Third World delegates, stirred by the action in the streets, refused to accept unfavorable terms.

As the tear gas cleared, it seemed a new movement had been born, remarkable for its mass dimensions, disruptive capacity, and ability to combine labor concerns with the "new social movements," from queer to ecoradical. Acridity was left by the black-bloc intervention, however. Some of its members argued they had targeted "corporate private property," not personal property, because it is "infinitely more violent than any action taken against it." Property destruction's morality, however, was not the issue for the black bloc's critics so much as its tactical and strategic wisdom in this instance. All the protesters in Seattle revered the French farmer José Bové for his dismantling of a McDonald's with his tractor, but most loathed the black bloc's window-smashing that day. "It was so obviously and critically the wrong time and place," wrote a Seattle radical who declared himself an anarchist but repudiated the black bloc. "Fifty thousand of us – mostly young, mainly self-identified anarchists – had an important and irretrievable part of our stunning, historic victory snatched away by the property damage tactics of a relative handful of tunnel-visioned fools." Barbara Ehrenreich nevertheless held that the rock-throwing did not "demonstrably 'ruin' the Seattle protests" but had "probably doubled the media attention, with most press accounts carefully distinguishing between the fifty thousand rock-less protesters and the twenty or so window-smashers." Other critics focused on the black bloc's disrespect for democratic planning. "With five days of WTO meetings to choose from," one close observer wrote, "I thought it was petulant of the Seattle black bloc to insist on holding their action on the same day as the blockade, despite requests from the Direct Action Network that they not do so."[25]

Seattle accelerated an already rising interest among youth in anarchism, an outlook opposed to authority and domination. Not since the period stretching from the Haymarket explosion in the 1880s to Emma Goldman in the 1910s had anarchism exerted such attraction. Before Seattle, it had already been stirring, a result of young radicals' rejection of both Communism and Clinton's compromises. The anarchist revival was apparent in the early 1990s in Love & Rage, an intellectually precocious group with a strong antiracist focus, at the surrealist-inflected Kerr Publishers

[25] ACME Collective, "N30 Black Block Communiqué," in *The Battle of Seattle: The New Challenge of Capitalist Globalization*, ed. Eddie Yuen, George Katsiaficas, and Daniel Burton Rose (New York: Soft Skull Press, 2001), pp. 117–118; Geov Parrish, "Imagine," in *The Battle of Seattle*, pp. 121–123; Barbara Ehrenreich, "Anarkids and Hypocrites," in *The Battle of Seattle*, pp. 100–101; L. A. Kauffman, "Who Are Those Masked Anarchists?," in *The Battle of Seattle*, p. 128.

of Chicago, and in the small remnant of the Industrial Workers of the World (IWW). Anarchism's many versions, from individualist-libertarian to anarchosyndicalist, left its principles murky – whether, for instance, it opposed *illegitimate* authority or *all* authority, *liberal-representative* democracy or *all* democracy. The new anarchism, heavily based in the punk scene and its posture of alienation, showed little continuity with the strain of anarchopacifism prominent from the 1940s to the 1960s. If anything, as Seattle showed, it was accompanied by a return to tactics favored by the ultra-left of the 1960–1970s, partly influenced by a polemical Ward Churchill essay on "pathological pacifism" that claimed pacifism was white and middle-class despite the Gandhi–Rustin–King legacy. Still, many whose aim was a society free of coercion and domination were frustrated by the black bloc's refusal to commit to action agreements and abide by majorities' preferences at demonstrations. Attempts to suppress strategic debate on such questions by speaking of a "diversity of tactics," some believed, amounted to license to act however one pleased, even if it placed the disabled, children, the elderly, and other vulnerable parties at risk.

At its best, the new interest in anarchism spread salutary notions of mutual aid, autonomy, and rule by direct producers; warned against undue reliance on charismatic leadership; and defended do-it-yourself, associative action in distinction to NGO, think tank, party-oriented, and nonprofit, professional-dominated models. Anarchist theory and analysis, however, tended to rely on recitations of stock ideas, leaving Marxism to generate the more serious analyses capable of puncturing capitalism's self-image. It was as if there had been a bifurcation, with street protest culture trending toward anarchism while radical theory and analysis remained largely Marxist. Many in coming years would suggest a need for a synthesis, but anarchism's carte-blanche opposition to government could appear to socialists simply an upside-down version of right-wing libertarianism, while anarchists harbored a built-in bias against the "authoritarian" or "reformist" left. Some of anarchism's most venerable exponents, such as Murray Bookchin and Noam Chomsky, grew impatient with its more puerile forms in the 1990s, refracted through the fun-house mirrors of a corporate media fixated on property destruction. Bookchin began calling himself "communalist," a word ugly enough to make him its only proponent, while Chomsky observed, "As a result of centuries of popular struggle there is a minimal welfare system that provides for poor mothers and children. That's under attack.... Anarchists can't seem to understand that they are to support that. So they join with the ultra-right in saying, 'Yes, we've got to minimize the state,' meaning put more power into the hands of private tyrannies which are completely unaccountable to the public and purely totalitarian."[26]

The much broader milieu to emerge out of Seattle was a global justice coalition – or what writer Naomi Klein, a Canadian, was calling "a movement of movements." To her and others, denying any expectation of overarching unity was a positive attribute, since too strong an insistence on a common program hearkened back to an older penchant for a "party line." The new metaphor was "network," wide-ranging coalition-building without fixed rules and with maximum flexibility, all alliances being dissoluble and recombinant. In something like the "strength of weak ties" – the idea that low demands on conformity help sustain solidarity – the multiplicity of overlapping commitments would provide conditions under which forces for change could grow in numbers and affiliations. "Horizontalism" would soon be a term used to describe this kind of montage. In its original use by Argentinian workers who seized disused factories in the economic crisis after 2001, *horizontalidad* meant self-management of production, but in North America and Europe horizontalism became a vague blanket term for a predilection against all hierarchy. Sometimes predicated on the immediacy of direct assemblies, given to suspicion of representation and expertise of all kinds, its consequent contingency and amorphousness was a source of both strength and weakness, contributing greatly, as did anarchism proper, to the period's characteristic quality of a left that was indefinite, a left episodic.

The electoral complement of Seattle was the Green Party presidential candidacy of Ralph Nader, a liberal lion whose rupture with the Democratic Party gave his bid a system-questioning character. An icon of regulatory liberalism ever since his book *Unsafe at Any Speed* (1965) resulted in Great Society legislation requiring seat belts, head restraints, and other safety features the auto industry had long resisted, Nader was credited for other significant legislation, including the Clean Air Act. Sounded out for the vice-presidential nomination by McGovern in 1972, he said he wished to work *on* government, not *in* it. Only an "invasion from Wall Street" in the 1980s and 1990s made him run for office in protest.[27]

[26] Noam Chomsky, "Anarchism, Intellectuals, and the State" (1996) in *Chomsky on Anarchism* (Edinburgh; Oakland, Calif.; and West Virginia: AK Press, 2005), pp. 212–213. On anarchism and Marxism, we draw on the insights of Nikil Saval, "Cheerleaders for Anarchism," *Dissent* (summer 2013): 121–127.

[27] Justin Martin, *Nader: Crusader, Spoiler, Icon* (New York: Basic Books, 2002), p. 226.

Nader first ran in New Hampshire in 1992 to promote a "none of the above" ballot option to allow voters to demand new slates of candidates. In 1996, he allowed the Green Party to enter his name for president, but only in 2000 did he and Winona LaDuke run avidly, seeking a 5 percent tally that would result in millions of dollars in federal matching funds for the Greens. In spring 2000, that seemed obtainable. Nader was polling at 7 percent nationally and was on the ballot in forty-three states, raising more than $8 million despite refusing all interest-group money. The Democrats nominated Al Gore, Clinton's vice president and a New Democrat whom Nader hoped to bend leftward. At the Democratic National Convention, Gore did strike a "for the people" stance against big oil, pharmaceuticals, and insurance, but by autumn was back to a wooden centrism. Gore viewed the IMF, World Bank, and WTO just as favorably as his Republican opponent, George W. Bush, the governor of Texas, son of the former president and a self-defined "compassionate conservative."

Nader was anticorporate but objected to neither capitalism nor competition, seeking to restore them in trust-busting fashion. Despite his exclusion from the televised presidential debates by the private commission that ran them, millions responded to his message that the Democratic and Republican parties were "Pepsi vs. Coke, GM vs. Ford, aspirin vs. Tylenol," differing only in "the velocity with which their knees hit the floor when big business comes knocking on the door." Stadiums filled for Nader "super-rallies," culminating in a sold-out event at New York City's Madison Square Garden with Eddie Vedder of Pearl Jam, comedian Bill Murray, filmmaker Michael Moore, and actors Tim Robbins and Susan Sarandon. Other liberals worried Nader would be a "spoiler," handing the election to the Republicans. The *New York Times* called his campaign "self-indulgent." Historian Sean Wilentz drafted a letter signed by many *Dissent* writers that said Nader was "never a champion of women's rights" and was waging "a wrecking-ball campaign – one that betrays the very liberal, humane, and progressive values it claims to uphold." Todd Gitlin called Nader's bid "a parochial fantasy" that could tip the election to Bush, who would owe political debts to "the fundamentalists, the union-busters, the South Carolina Confederate flag-fliers." John B. Judis, once a founding editor of *Socialist Revolution,* disparaged the "destructive role" of a "Manichean left" that "elevates the struggle with corporations into an apocalyptic conflict between good and evil."[28]

---

[28] Roger Simon, *Divided We Stand: How Al Gore Beat George Bush and Lost the Presidency* (New York: Crown, 2001), p. 300; Ruth Conniff, "It's Not Easy Being Green,"

Nader was Arab American, LaDuke Native American, and they counted among their black endorsers Cornel West, Randall Robinson, and Danny Glover, but the prevalence of white youth among Nader supporters led journalist Eric Alterman to hold, "This nascent leftist movement has virtually no support among African Americans, Latinos, or Asian Americans." The race between a corporate Republican and a corporate Democrat, however, lacked appeal to a growing number of the disenchanted, since neither Bush nor Gore, as Barbara Ehrenreich wrote, proposed "to end poverty, abolish the death penalty, restore the progressive income tax, or bring the U.S. military budget into line with those of our most powerful enemies – Cuba and North Korea," whose expenditures were a fraction of the Pentagon's. Sixties veterans Joanne Landy and Jesse Lemisch circulated a letter signed by 373 intellectuals and artists who objected to "the two-party big-business alliance that funds the presidential elections and excludes Nader" and to "unleashed corporate power" with its "barbarizing impact on health care, the environment, welfare, distribution of income, criminal justice, media, publishing, civil liberties, workplace safety, education, and privacy." The *Nation* advised "strategic voting" – casting a ballot for Nader except in swing states where the Bush–Gore match was too close to call.[29]

What ensued was an extraordinary mess. Gore won the nation's popular vote, but the Electoral College hinged, in the end, on the uncertain results in Florida, where on election night the major networks called the race first for Gore, then for Bush. Gore conceded by telephone, then reversed himself, since Florida law required a recount in very close elections. Democrats thought a recount would favor Gore since counting machines in largely black counties had failed to detect any presidential vote despite dimpled chads on tens of thousands of punch-card ballots. The top Florida elections official was a Republican who sought to block the recount, citing lack of uniform standards for determining voter intentions. Republican congressional staffers flown in from Washington halted the recount in heavily black Miami-Dade County by staging an outburst many saw as physical intimidation. The Florida Supreme Court, laden with Democrat-appointed jurists, ordered the recounts resumed,

The Progressive 64 (August 2000), p. 12; "Mr. Nader's Misguided Crusade," *New York Times*, 30 June 2000; "The Nader Letters," *Salon*, 6 November 2000, http://www.salon.com/2000/11/06/letters_7/; John B. Judis, "Seeing Green," *New Republic*, 29 May 2000, p. 26.

29 "The Nader Letters." Eric Alterman, "Not One Vote!" *Nation*, 13 November 2000, p. 12; Barbara Ehrenreich, "We Are Certain to Elect a Scumball," *Progressive* 64 (April 2000), p. 13.

but on appeal, the U.S. Supreme Court's Republican majority halted them with finality, thus resolving the national election in Bush's favor.

Many liberals blamed Gore's defeat on Nader, who had received 97,488 votes in Florida, where Bush was, according to the count that the Supreme Court legitimized, ahead by only 537. Had Nader withdrawn before Election Day, Gore in all likelihood would have won, but Green campaign supporters believed Nader was being made a scapegoat for a flawed process. As Nader supporter Adolph Reed put it, "Republicans blatantly stole the White House." In any case, Gore had failed to carry either Clinton's home state of Arkansas or his own home state of Tennessee. To Manning Marable, Gore was "largely responsible for his own defeat" since he did not give progressives any reason to think of him as anything other than "the pro-death penalty, pro-globalization, pro-corporate poster boy of the Democratic Leadership Council," To unrepentant Nader voters the outcome merely confirmed Nader's arguments about an archaic winner-take-all electoral system in need of replacement by proportional-representation or instant-runoff procedures for voting. "Are they seriously going to blame us for this?" asked a Nader backer in Oregon. "They sold people out, and they're paying for it."[30]

Unfazed by the Bush inauguration, the global justice movement – still labeled "antiglobalization" by the news media – continued to organize, finding its analysis of capitalism's instability and unreliability confirmed as the "dot-com" stock market bubble burst. "They label us 'anti,'" said Lori Wallach of Public Citizen. "We have to shake off the label. We're *for* democracy, *for* diversity, *for* equity, *for* environmental health." A movement consensus was emerging in favor of stronger labor and environmental standards, subordination of trade agreements to popular sovereignty, defense of "the commons" (shared life-giving resources, from water to seeds to public forests) against corporate attempts to claim them as private property, and a more egalitarian distribution of wealth and power the world over. After Seattle, police agencies infiltrated protest groups and monitored e-mail lists, diminishing the element of surprise, but protests continued at global elite summits. Tens of thousands turned out for protests in Washington, D.C., against the World Bank and IMF

---

[30] Adolph L. Reed, Jr., "Get Off the Defeatist Cycle," *Progressive* 65 (February 2001), p. 18; Manning Marable, "Gore's Defeat: Don't Blame Nader," *Synthesis/Regeneration* 25 (Summer 2001), http://www.greens.org/s-r/25/25-03.html; Greg Kafoury, Portland lawyer, quoted in Ruth Conniff, "After the Rollercoaster Ride," *Progressive* 64 (December 2000), p. 11.

in April 2000; in Prague against the World Bank and IMF in September 2000; in Quebec City, Canada, at the Free Trade Area of the Americas meeting in April 2001; and in Genoa, Italy, at the meeting of the G-8 in July 2001. Many had begun to doubt the value of this ritualized summit-hopping and called for more local organizing. One vital new venue for strategizing was the World Social Forum (WSF) inaugurated in February 2001 at Porto Alegre, Brazil. The electoral success of the Latin American left, from Brazil's Workers Party to Venezuela's president Hugo Chávez, drew tens of thousands from Europe and Latin America to Porto Alegre, seeking a grand counterpoint to the World Economic Forum at Davos, Switzerland, under the slogan endorsing alternative futures of social justice, "Another World *Is* Possible."[31]

This global justice momentum came to an abrupt halt on September 11, 2001, when al Qaeda (Arabic for "The Base"), a network led by a wealthy Saudi national and Islamist named Osama bin Laden based in Afghanistan, crashed two hijacked commercial airliners into the World Trade Center and one into the Pentagon, killing a total of almost three thousand people, nearly all of them civilians. As Americans struggled in grief and anger to make sense of these events, the Bush administration pushed the USA PATRIOT Act through Congress, significantly increasing government powers of search and surveillance, and then rapidly launched two wars, one against Afghanistan, the other against Iraq. The rightward lurch of world politics bewildered those bent on global justice. One Bolivian farmer proposed that the partisans of Porto Alegre convey "a culture of life against a culture of death," with terrorism and capitalism on one side, economic justice and democracy on the other. Such a vision proved exceedingly difficult to maintain in a world polarized between George W. Bush's neoconservative-led United States and bin Laden's theocratic obscurantism.[32]

Given the anger and grieving as bodies were dug from the rubble at Ground Zero at the World Trade Center in New York, only muted objection from some radical quarters could be heard against the U.S. invasion of Afghanistan, where the ultraconservative Islamic fundamentalist Taliban held power, forbidding women from seeking education, banning television, destroying ancient Buddhist monuments, and allowing al Qaeda a base of operations. In an address to Congress, Bush explained the September 11 attacks by saying of the Islamist conspirators, "They hate

---

[31] Wallach quoted in Kingsnorth, *One No, Many Yeses*, p. 221.
[32] Bolivian farmer, quoted in Kingsnorth, *One No, Many Yeses*, p. 79.

our freedoms." The Taliban and bin Laden, however, had emerged out of the anti-Communist *mujahedeen* sponsored as "freedom fighters" by the Reagan administration in the 1980s against the Soviets in Afghanistan, making the terrorist attacks, actually, a powerful case of "blowback," the holy warriors who helped defeat one superpower turning on the other. The most visible critic of bombing Afghanistan in retribution for the September 11 attacks was Noam Chomsky, whose 9/11 (2002) became a surprise bestseller. Chomsky ascribed "9/11" to "a reservoir of bitterness and anger over U.S. policies in the region," particularly support for authoritarian Arab regimes, sanctions on Iraq after the Gulf War with their terrible toll on civilians, and blanket support for Israel in its occupation of the Palestinian territories. One bin Laden grievance, he noted, was that after the Gulf War American troops were stationed permanently in Saudi Arabia, home to Mecca, revered birthplace of the prophet Muhammad.[33]

To American conservatives, such an analysis amounted only to apologetics for terrorism, rather than an attempt to comprehend the source of rage in the Muslim world. They denounced as treason such remarks as Chomsky's assertion that "in much of the world the U.S. is regarded as a leading terrorist state, with good reason." Other radicals observed that the states that most underwrote Islamist extremism were ostensible American allies such as Pakistan and Saudi Arabia: Pakistan's intelligence service had sponsored the Taliban, fifteen of the nineteen September 11 hijackers were Saudis, bin Laden was the son of a wealthy Saudi building contractor, and the Saudi monarchy subsidized a Wahhabi version of Islam that was ultraorthodox and a seedbed of fundamentalist rage. As the Bush administration struck against the Taliban "rogue state" in Afghanistan, disdaining UN authorization, voices urging that the attacks be treated as a crime deserving of international police action to arraign the perpetrators in court were barely audible. To be sure, the critics' reservations only revealed further quandaries: exactly who or what could exercise such international police powers? A few radicals commented on wider strategic interests underlying the intervention, such as the pipeline the oil corporation Unocal sought to develop in Afghanistan in the 1990s. "At base, this war will be fought to set the boundaries of U.S. and Russian

[33] "President Bush Addresses Nation," *Washington Post*, 20 September 2001, http://www .washingtonpost.com/wp-srv/nation/specials/attacked/transcripts/bushaddress_092001 .html; Noam Chomsky, 9/11 (New York: Seven Stories Press, 2002), p. 13.

influence in Central Asia," wrote James Ridgeway in the *Village Voice,* and to "carve up the oil and gas resources of the Caspian Sea."[34]

Given the massive security failure of September 11, one might well imagine a public backlash. In the early months of his presidency Bush had been preoccupied with domestic priorities, such as his proposed $1.6-trillion tax cut, a measure that reduced the top marginal rate on the wealthiest taxpayers from 39.6 to 35 percent, but few Americans knew that he had been warned explicitly by intelligence officials about the threat, as in the Presidential Daily Briefing of August 6, 2001: "Bin Laden Determined to Strike in U.S." As Bush vowed retribution after September 11, his approval rating shot up, reaching a staggering 90 percent by year's end as the Taliban's capital of Kabul fell. That victory bounce carried over decisively into the 2002 elections, when Republicans regained control of the Senate and widened their House majority. Not since Herbert Hoover had Republicans controlled the House, Senate, and presidency as they would from 2003 to 2007. As a result, the American left's policy scope was reduced to nil. Even the most sophisticated journalistic accounts, which acknowledged that Islamists such as the al Qaeda militants saw themselves as seekers of justice, dubbed the September 11 attackers "radicals" – fostering terminological confusion since the attackers were actually theocratic reactionaries with aspirations thoroughly at odds with the egalitarianism and inclusiveness characteristic of historical radicalism.

Still, the largest demonstration against war in all of history occurred on February 15, 2003, as some 10 million took part in hundreds of cities from London to Paris, Rome, and New York. The protesters attempted to forestall what they considered a brazen, imperialist misadventure that targeted Saddam Hussein's Iraq as a "terrorist" fount. From the beginning, Bush had framed the response to September 11 expansively, not as a campaign against al Qaeda but a "war on terrorism," a "monumental struggle between good and evil," or a "crusade" (a word disastrously received in the Muslim world). Even though both bin Laden and Afghan Taliban leader Mullah Omar had escaped into the mountains, leaving the stated mission in Afghanistan incomplete, the Bush administration was bent on achieving authority in the Persian Gulf. Bush declared an "axis of evil" in his 2002 State of the Union address comprised of Iraq, Iran, and

---

[34] Chomsky, *9/11*, p. 23; James Ridgeway, "The God of Fossil Fuels," *Village Voice*, 9 October 2011, http://www.villagevoice.com/2001-10-09/news/the-god-of-fossil-fuels/.

North Korea, though the three states had no clear connection. A ranking based on threat of "weapons of mass destruction" – chemical, biological, or nuclear – would likely have placed North Korea at top and Iraq at bottom, but the war drums beat for Iraq. As the administration began to speak of "preemptive war," Sen. Edward Kennedy said it would mean a "twenty-first century American imperialism that no other nation can or should accept." Nonetheless, Congress – including the Democratic-controlled Senate – voted overwhelmingly in October 2002 to accord the President authority to wage war against Iraq. By 2003, 72 percent of Americans believed Saddam had been involved in the September 11 attacks, although no evidence of that existed; in fact, his Ba'athist dictatorship, being Arab nationalist and secular, had suppressed Islamism in Iraq. In March 2003 the Iraq War was launched in a barrage of "shock and awe."[35]

The militaristic neoconservatives who held sway in the White House and the Pentagon justified the war in democratic terms, claiming that Saddam's tyranny would be supplanted by a new Arab democracy. Some commentators at the time suggested that because a few leading neoconservatives had been Trotskyists in their youth, this stated democratic mission traced back to Leon Trotsky's idea of "permanent revolution," but that charge both obfuscated Trotsky's ardent opposition to capitalist war and muddied the differences between radicalism and conservatism. More importantly, it missed the point that neither democracy nor national security motivated the neoconservatives as much as imperial calculus. Several neoconservatives, including Vice President Dick Cheney, had been architects of a 1992 Defense Planning Guidance document during the first Bush administration that called for the United States to pursue unipolar world dominance, blocking all rival regional powers. That, together with the attractiveness of Iraq's vast oil reserves and a palpable sense of unfinished business left over from the 1990–91 Gulf War's failure to unseat Saddam, best explains the Iraq War that toppled Saddam.

Far from opposing the Iraq War, American liberals supplied much of its most effusive democratic gloss. The "liberal hawks" – intellectuals such as Paul Berman, George Packer, and Michael Ignatieff – pitched the Iraq War as a Good Fight much like the Second World War. Casting

35 Bob Woodward, *Plan of Attack* (New York: Simon and Schuster, 2004), pp. 92, 178, 194, 203; Seymour Hersh, *Chain of Command: The Road from 9/11 to Abu Ghraib* (London: Allen Lane, 2004), pp. 212, 230, 234; Bob Woodward, *Bush at War* (London: Pocket, 2003), pp. 45, 94, 100.

U.S. forces as liberators rather than conquerors, accepting administration claims that Iraq was stocked with weapons of mass destruction, and equating Saddam's Ba'ath Party with Islamism and Nazism were common tropes among Democratic politicians such as Senator Hillary Clinton of New York and writers such as Bill Keller, Thomas Friedman, and Judith Miller at the *New York Times,* David Remnick at *The New Yorker*, and Peter Beinart at the *New Republic*. What little criticism of the war existed in such quarters was purely about its execution. The liberal hawks – espousing a line of thought that could be traced back through Cold War liberalism to the Wilsonian idealism of the First World War – had first surfaced in debates over humanitarian intervention in Bosnia in the 1990s but registered more visibly after September 11, when writers at *Dissent* demanded that the left embrace patriotism and Paul Berman held Islamist terrorism to be a new totalitarianism. Fine distinctions were possible; Todd Gitlin, David Rieff, Michael Bérubé, and Michael Walzer found casus belli in Bosnia, Kosovo, and Afghanistan but not Iraq. But this "democratic left" and the liberal hawks joined in excoriating anyone to their left. *Dissent* suggested after September 11 that those questioning the "war on terror," such as Chomsky and Edward Said, were bin Laden appeasers. Christopher Hitchens said opponents of the Iraq War did not consider Saddam to be so bad. *New York Times* columnist Friedman spoke of "antiwar activists who haven't thought a whit about the larger struggle we're in." Punching back at such jibes, historian Tony Judt, a social democrat, would brand the liberal hawks "Bush's Useful Idiots" for failing to realize that the Iraq intervention was really about the U.S. pursuit of "martial dominance."[36]

"The World Says No to War," proclaimed a giant banner in New York City on February 15, 2003. Those who held out against the war were either skeptical of the evidence for Iraq's possession of weapons of mass destruction (WMD, or "weapons of mass deception," as a joke would later put it); considered the Bush administration a proxy for the oil industry ("Go Solar, Not Ballistic," read one San Francisco demonstrator's sign); objected to what Norman Mailer called "the desire to have a huge military presence in the Middle East as a stepping-stone to taking over the rest of the world"; or simply thought the danger posed

---

[36] Thomas L. Friedman, "Big Talk, Little Will," *New York Times*, 16 August 2006, http://www.nytimes.com/2006/08/16/opinion/16Friedman.html; Tony Judt, "Bush's Useful Idiots," *London Review of Books*, 21 September 2006, http://www.lrb.co.uk/v28/n18/tony-judt/bushs-useful-idiots.

by Saddam's regime was already adequately contained, wishing to give UN inspectors more time to determine the facts about alleged WMD stockpiles. Few thought protest would stop the war. "This government is going to do what they are going to do regardless," a 22-year-old student marching in Washington said. "But at least by coming we can try to make sure that people in other countries know that all Americans are not down with this war."[37]

After the onslaught that toppled Saddam's regime, on May 1, 2003, Bush landed on a U.S. aircraft carrier off the California coast and stood before a giant banner stating "Mission Accomplished." The claim of victory was premature. Iraq descended into a maelstrom of insurgency as discharged Ba'ath military personnel, Islamist militants from around the region, and nationalists of both the Sunni and Shi'a ethnoreligious groups within Iraq organized a violent resistance that drew on popular disaffection as the occupiers failed to provide enough electricity or jobs. Use of improvised explosive devices (IEDs) and suicide bombings against American troops escalated, confirming fears that an invasion would feed, not dampen, terrorism. But in the United States, the giant crowds of anti-war demonstrators melted away even as the streets of Baghdad, Fallujah, and Basra ran with blood between 2003 and 2007, with thousands of American losses and hundreds of thousands of Iraqis dead or wounded.

Why no protest crescendo against the Iraq War on the scale of that for the Vietnam War? It would be facile to blame that on the blunders of radicals themselves – though indeed, foolishness on the left gave right-wing Fox News plenty of fodder for assailing radical protest. Bill Ayers, promoting a memoir of his Weatherman days, had the extraordinary misfortune to be profiled in the *New York Times* on the very morning of September 11, 2001, saying, "I don't regret setting bombs. I feel we didn't do enough." One day later, Ward Churchill outrageously condemned the dead of the twin towers as "the little Eichmanns" (that is, complicit in U.S. war crimes abroad). Prompted by that kind of grandstanding, reporters scrutinized Churchill's career and debunked his claim to Indian ancestry; he was dismissed from the University of Colorado for plagiarism, in what a jury later ruled violated his academic freedom. Furthermore, big

[37] Robert D. McFadden, "From New York to Melbourne, Cries for Peace," *New York Times*, 16 February 2003, http://www.nytimes.com/2003/02/16/nyregion/threats-and-responses-overview-from-new-york-to-melbourne-cries-for-peace.html; "Thousands Converge in Capital to Protest Plans for War," *New York Times*, 19 January 2003, http://www.nytimes.com/2003/01/19/us/threats-responses-rally-thousands-converge-capital-protest-plans-for-war.html; Norman Mailer, *Why Are We At War?* (New York: Random House, 2003), p. 52.

demonstrations against the Iraq War were organized by ANSWER (Act Now to Stop War and End Racism), front group of the Workers World Party, a neo-Stalinoid sect that supported Saddam Hussein and admired North Korea. "9/11 Truthers," meanwhile, claimed that U.S. government insiders had leveled the World Trade Center.[38]

But such inanities paled next to the war itself. Weapons of mass destruction were never found in Iraq. Massive tax cuts and two wars under the Bush administration caused the national debt to balloon. Revelations of abuses cascaded: indefinite detention of prisoners at Guantanamo Bay; assassination by predator drones of alleged terrorists on the ground in Iraq, Afghanistan, and Pakistan, amounting to summary execution without judicial proceedings; the U.S. military's torture of prisoners at Abu Ghraib near Baghdad; and CIA "waterboarding" of terror suspects. In opposition arose plenty of instances of creative, rational radicalism: the antiwar coalition United for Peace and Justice (UfPJ); Medea Benjamin's Code Pink, with feminist inflection; Iraq Veterans Against the War; *Nation* columnist Katha Pollitt's advocacy on behalf of the Revolutionary Association of the Women of Afghanistan; the efforts of U.S. Labor Against the War (USLAW) to support beleaguered Iraqi unions against neoliberal privatizations during the occupation; Michael Moore's scathing indictment of the Bush administration in *Fahrenheit 9/11* (2004), the top-grossing documentary of all time; and journalist Jeremy Scahill's exposés of military contractor Blackwater USA. Cornel West's *Democracy Matters: Winning the Fight Against Imperialism* (2004) sold 100,000 copies. Howard Zinn, a radical pacifist ever since his days as a Second World War bombardier, wryly compared war to crack cocaine: "War doesn't solve fundamental things. It's like crack. Really, war is like a fix. You get high on war: 'We won, we won.' And then you are down on the ground again, you need another fix, you need another war. Why do you think we've had war after war? . . . Expansion, power, economics, business."[39]

Large-scale antiwar protests, however, failed to persist. Radicals often explained the muted dissent after the mammoth antiwar demonstrations

---

[38] Dinitia Smith, "No Regrets for a Love of Explosives: In a Memoir of Sorts, a War Protester Talks of Life With the Weathermen," *New York Times*, 11 September 2001, http://www.nytimes.com/2001/09/11/books/no-regrets-for-love-explosives-memoir-sorts-war-protester-talks-life-with.html. Ward Churchill, "'Some People Push Back': On the Justice of Roosting Chickens," *Pockets of Resistance*, September 2001, http://www.kersplebedeb.com/mystuff/s11/churchill.html.

[39] Zinn quoted in *You Can't Be Neutral on a Moving Train*, dir. Deb Ellis and Denis Mueller (2004).

of February 15, 2003, by blaming the corporate media, whose subservience to the Bush government certainly played a part. More important
was the nature of the war. In Iraq, unlike Vietnam, there was no draft.
With fewer boots on the ground, American casualties were nowhere near
as extensive. The shadowy Iraqi opposition, shot through with Ba'athists
and al Qaeda, provided no revolutionary inspiration as had the Vietnamese guerrillas. The contrast in political conditions was also salient.
Opposition to the Vietnam War was inspired by the black freedom movement that had flourished throughout the ten years prior to escalation in
1965, an uplifting example of effective mass dissent. By the twenty-first
century, in contrast, the scene was more desolate, Seattle being virtually the sole major example of protest in the prior decade. A few socialist
organizations persisted, including the International Socialist Organization
with its Haymarket Books, but the dominant activist culture was anarchistic, contingent, one of loose-limbed "networks." The attenuation of
long-term *organizing,* which could establish an enduring infrastructure
like that which the union movement provided for some decades after the
Great Depression, left a vacuum of institutional forms that could focus
public disquiet about the Iraq War and connect it to analysis, program,
and action. Instead, the two-party system was taken as the sole horizon
of possibilities for dissent. In spite of his past as Vietnam War veteran
and objector, Senator John Kerry, the Democratic candidate for president
in 2004, had voted for the Iraq War. His "equivocal and diffuse" statements about it, one young radical wrote, were not at all "in line with the
antiwar movement's message," and outside of that slack electoral effort,
there was no room for "all the energy the left once had – for example,
the massive, worldwide demonstrations before the war hit."[40]

September 11 could, on the other hand, be politicizing. One who was
shocked into awareness was Rachel Corrie, a young native of Olympia,
Washington. Despite her feeling that there was "something escapist"
about "espousing radical politics" at her hometown Evergreen State College, she traveled after graduation to join the International Solidarity
Movement in the Palestinian territories during the second *intifada* of
2000–2005. She concluded that in Gaza "all means of survival is cut off"
by Israel, backed by the United States and the "global power structure."
Writing to her mother, she described the Israel-Palestine conflict as one

---

[40] Arthur Liou, "To the Left," in *Letters from Young Activists: Today's Rebels Speak Out,*
      ed. Dan Berger et al. (New York: Nation Books, 2005), p. 168.

part of "a very large-scale problem with a widening disparity of wealth and power, a problem with increasingly private control over matters of public interest, basically a very large-scale problem with democracy." On March 16, 2003, while engaged in civil disobedience to block an Israeli Defense Forces bulldozer from destroying a Palestinian home, Corrie was run over and killed at age 23.[41]

The cause for which Corrie gave her life provides one example of how, even under George W. Bush, marginal views could reach wider mainstreams. Once-taboo criticisms of Israel gained traction because of worries that injustices toward Palestinians were fanning Islamism. On April 20, 2002, the largest demonstration for Palestinian rights until then in American history drew 50,000 to Washington. Meanwhile, students, many of them Jewish, began pushing American universities to divest from companies doing business with Israel. "We don't support suicide bombings," said one member of Students for Justice in Palestine, responding to charges of conciliating the intransigent Hamas group in the occupied Palestinian territories or Hezbollah in Lebanon, "but we believe that there is a difference between the violence born out of desperation and the systematic state violence of Israel." The Boycott, Divestment and Sanctions movement spearheaded by the U.S. Campaign to End the Israeli Occupation arose. At the same time, questions about the viability of any sovereign Palestinian entity given extensive Israeli settlements in the West Bank and Gaza led Edward Said to drop the once-thought-radical call for a two-state solution (returning to the aspiration for a democratic secular state in Palestine for Jews and Arabs alike), while Bush embraced it.[42]

The Republican juggernaut suffered an electoral rout in 2006, when Democrats took back the House, Senate, and most state legislatures and governorships, including socialist independent Bernie Sanders' advance to representing Vermont in the U.S. Senate. That came only two years after the Republican sweep of 2004, when pundits thought "morals" voters, their turnout boosted by state ballot measures against same-sex marriage, would determine all future elections. That religious constituency's power turned out to be overrated, counterbalanced in 2006 by the "netroots" of MoveOn, Truthout, The Huffington Post, and other liberal or left-leaning websites. A pushback against the Christian right had occurred, one aspect

---

[41] *Let Me Stand Alone: The Journals of Rachel Corrie* (London: Granta, 2008), pp. 243, 275, 280.

[42] Liza Featherstone, "The Mideast War Breaks Out on Campus," *Nation*, 30 May 2002, http://www.thenation.com/article/mideast-war-breaks-out-campus.

being the "new atheist" challenge to theocratic Christianity and Islam from writers who polemicized against religion in the name of science and reason. Rather than derogate others' faiths, however, most radicals and liberals – even most atheists – preferred to argue for secularism, including religious freedom and separation of church and state. A simultaneous challenge to the right came on sexual moralism. If queer radicals saw same-sex marriage as bourgeois, in conventional politics it still seemed radical. Jason West, a 26-year-old Green Party member elected mayor of New Paltz, New York, in 2003 conducted same-sex marriage ceremonies until blocked by court order. The turnabout was sensational; within a decade, mainstream support for same-sex marriage seemed irreversible.

The change of 2005–2006 also resulted from two other critical developments, both pointing to the enduring role of the racialized subaltern in generating dissent. First, Hurricane Katrina's devastation of the Gulf Coast in August 2005 laid bare fault lines of race and poverty as footage streamed across television screens of African Americans trapped in flooded New Orleans. The ineffectuality of Bush-appointed federal emergency officials provided a reminder of just how vital the basic functions of government stigmatized by conservatives really were, while responses of mutual aid showed popular capacities to promote social justice. Second, one million immigrants marched on May 1, 2006, in major American cities. The marchers demanded that the Senate table a Republican bill passed by the House proposing to militarize the U.S.–Mexican border with a 700-mile fence and make it a felony to be in the United States without proper papers or to aid such felons – thus criminalizing the families, friends, and clergy of those immigrants who lacked official papers or were "undocumented." The right wing associated such "aliens" with terrorism, claiming "border security" was under threat. Liberals saw that as xenophobic, while radicals viewed it as also a corollary of neoliberalism: NAFTA had hit Mexico with competition from U.S. agribusiness and pushed millions of peasants off the land, causing unprecedented job-seeking migration to the United States. Seeking a pathway to documentation and citizenship, immigrant marchers chanted *Aqui estamos y no nos vamos* and *Hoy marchamos, mañana votamos* ("We're here and not going away," "Today we march, tomorrow we vote") in Los Angeles, Chicago, New York, and elsewhere. On a "Day Without Immigrants," they stayed away from work to illustrate their critical roles in low-paying jobs as maids, day laborers, busboys, childcare workers, and the like.

Bush, who spoke Spanish, had enjoyed unusually high Latino support in his presidential races, but the Republican right's antiimmigration push alienated the voting bloc, helping account for the GOP defeat in the 2006 midterm elections. "Everyone's an immigrant here," a Puerto Rican hotel doorman told a reporter. "The only real American is the Indian."[43]

Initially, neoliberalism had seemed to be about starving the state – slashing social expenditure, privatizing services, and cutting taxes, regulations, and tariffs – but border patrolling, the PATRIOT Act, and the Pentagon's wars disproved theories that globalization was eroding the powers of the nation-state. Actually, radicals realized, it was creating a leviathan, with prisons a case in point. The number of American prisoners rose from 200,000 in 1970 to almost two million by 2000, mostly black or Latino and under 40 years of age, largely because of mandatory sentencing for repeat felony offenses, even if nonviolent. Mumia Abu-Jamal, a radical found guilty of murdering a policeman who became a cause célèbre of death penalty opponents – whose agitation resulted in the commutation of his death sentence – wrote that "corrections" and "penitentiaries" were meaningless words since prison was "a second-by-second assault on the soul, a day-to-day degradation of the self, an oppressive steel and brick umbrella." The "prison-industrial complex" became a focus for Angela Davis, herself a former inmate, who lamented imprisonment as "the response of first resort" to "homelessness, unemployment, drug addiction, mental illness, and illiteracy." The "automatic attribution of criminal behavior to people of color," she said, fed a highly profitable sector sustained by privatization, corporate-run prisons, and use of prison labor when "what we need is . . . new health care, housing, drug programs, jobs, and education." If prison abolitionism, proposed by anarchist Paul Goodman after Attica in 1971 and now a slogan of young agitators, struck many as utopian, radicals did raise awareness that the United States was jailing more of its population than any other society; drew connections between the "war on drugs" and "war on terror"; mainstreamed marijuana decriminalization; and dramatized what legal scholar Michelle Alexander termed a "New Jim Crow" (just as Latinos called Arizona and Alabama's harsh new antiimmigrant laws "Juan

---

43 Amy Shannon, "Mobilizing for Political Power: Immigrant Marches and Their Long-term Impacts," *Voices of Mexico,* no. 78 (2007), p. 29; Benita Heiskanen, "A Day Without Immigrants," *European Journal of American Studies* 4 (2009), Document 3. http://ejas.revues.org/7717.

Crow"). Counterterrorism, radicals warned, was criminalizing dissent, with mandatory sentences for wilful property damage resulting in long prison sentences for Earth Liberation Front members classed as "ecoterrorist" for their rash firebombings, although none of them had injured anyone.[44]

In autumn 2008, economic and political ruptures put a coda on the Bush administration and demarcated a new period. First came collapse in late August of Lehman Brothers, a major Wall Street firm, and the stock market crash in October, precipitating the worst economic crisis since the Great Depression. Then came election in November of Barack Hussein Obama as President. With Bush's public approval at 25 percent, the vote for the Democratic nominee represented a final repudiation of Bush's policies, from the Iraq War to the free-falling economy. Also decisive was the adroitness of the senator from Illinois, a onetime community organizer on Chicago's South Side with a Harvard law degree. The son of a Kenyan immigrant, raised in Indonesia and Hawaii by his Kansan mother, Obama broke the White House color line, a landmark in black and American history. He benefited from being an early critic of the Iraq War, having spoken out against it as an Illinois state legislator in 2002 while Hillary Clinton, his main Democratic primary opponent, and John McCain, the Republican candidate, voted for it as senators.

In desperation, his opponents accused Obama of radicalism, using guilt by association. His South Side Chicago pastor, Rev. Jeremiah Wright, had given a fiery sermon after 9/11 citing "state terrorism against the Palestinians and black South Africans" and shouting (in an echo of Malcolm X), "America's chickens are coming home to roost!" Even more controversial was a "God damn America" sermon of Wright's on social injustice. Obama repudiated Wright's remarks in a speech on race in Philadelphia, although another Wright congregant told a reporter, "I wouldn't call it radical. I call it being black in America." Then there was Bill Ayers, "unrepentant domestic terrorist," as Sarah Palin, McCain's running-mate, took to calling him. The former Weatherman had once hosted a coffee for Obama in his run for the Illinois statehouse, but Obama breezily waved

---

[44] Mumia Abu-Jamal, *Live from Death Row* (New York: Avon, 1995), pp. 64–65; Angela Davis, "Masked Racism: Reflections on the Prison Industrial Complex," *Colorlines*, 10 September 1998, http://colorlines.com/archives/1998/09/masked_racism_reflections_on_the_prison_industrial_complex.html; Michelle Alexander, *The New Jim Crow* (New York: New Press, 2010).

away Palin's claim that he was "palling around" with Ayers, calling him "somebody who engaged in detestable acts 40 years ago, when I was 8."[45]

In actuality Obama was no radical, although the lilt of his cadence seemed to distil the rhetoric of past social movements and his idealism could suggest larger intentions. Nor was he a black candidate of the Jesse Jackson stamp, his cool élan instead suggesting the supersession of ardent racial identity. Obama ran on a centrist promise to overcome Bush-era partisanship. Once elected, he turned to the economy. The financial crisis – brought on by highly leveraged Wall Street firms creating sub-prime mortgages and bundling them as asset-backed securities – called into doubt the investment banks' supposed raison d'être, the shrewd and efficient allocation of capital. Radical criticism of excessive risk-taking and obscene executive pay abounded, the most indelible line being Matt Taibbi's depiction of the leading Wall Street bank Goldman Sachs as "a great vampire squid wrapped around the face of humanity, relentlessly jamming its blood funnel into anything that smells like money." The sub-sequent economic freefall – foreclosures, bankruptcies, joblessness, and reduced hours and wages – seemed to demand a rupture with delusions of a self-correcting market. Many Obama supporters pined for a new New Deal.[46]

Obama, however, declared himself a DLC-style "New Democrat" and his policies proved largely continuous with Bush on economic grounds. Neither he nor Bush adhered to free-market purism; it was the Bush administration, angering purists on the right, that first bailed out "too big to fail" banks rather than allow market discipline to take its toll, a program Obama continued. Both focused on stabilization of the system at the top. Both drew on seasoned Wall Street personnel, with Obama hiring Timothy Geithner and Lawrence Summers, acolytes of Bill Clinton's

---

[45] Brian Ross and Rehab Al-Buri, "Obama's Pastor: God Damn America, U.S. to Blame for 9/11," ABC News, 13 March 2008, http://abcnews.go.com/Blotter/DemocraticDebate/story?id=4443788&page=1; Michael Cooper, "Palin, on Offensive, Attacks Obama's Ties to '60s Radical," *New York Times*, 4 October 2008, http://www.nytimes.com/2008/10/05/us/politics/05palin.html?_r=0; Michael Grynbaum, "In Struggling Ohio Town, Palin Again Invokes Ayres," *New York Times*, 9 October 2008, http://thecaucus.blogs.nytimes.com/2008/10/09/palin-ohio/; Scott Shane, "Obama and '60s Bomber: A Look Into Crossed Paths," *New York Times*, 3 October 2008, http://www.nytimes.com/2008/10/04/us/politics/04ayers.html?_r=1&.

[46] Matt Taibbi, "The Great American Bubble Machine," *Rolling Stone*, 9 July 2009, http://www.rollingstone.com/politics/news/the-great-american-bubble-machine-20100405.

Treasury Secretary Robert Rubin, who had written the legislation deregulating the financial sector. Both Obama and Bush racked up massive
deficits, Bush's in 2008 larger than any of Obama's. Both increased military spending. Both expanded health care coverage in ways benefiting
private companies, Bush by a Medicare prescription drug benefit, Obama
by passing insurance industry-approved mandatory health insurance coverage. (The hysterical attack on "Obamacare" as "socialist" – even totalitarian – patently misconstrued what was in fact a market-based model
first hatched by the Heritage Foundation and enacted on the state level
by Massachusetts Republican Gov. Mitt Romney in 2006.) In *New Left
Review,* Peter Gowan wrote that while the global system was "legitimated
by free-market, laissez-faire or neoliberal outlooks, these do not seem to
have been *operative* ideologies for its practitioners, whether in Wall Street
or in Washington." The order is really, Chomsky said, a "state capitalist"
system in which profit is privatized while risk is socialized.[47]

The broad policy consensus among elites for government intervention
to save the major financial institutions prompted some, noting the variance of that policy from laissez-faire precepts, to suppose that "We Are
All Socialists Now," as stated a *Newsweek* cover in 2009. The Great
Recession could certainly make it seem that reality was compelling a radicalization, as when economist and Nobel Prize winner Paul Krugman
wrote, "If you haven't been radicalized by recent events, you haven't
been paying attention." Obama, however, was no socialist, nor would
his two terms as president see a sustained revival of American radicalism.
Pressure from below and the left would have been required to compel the
new administration to offer a "new New Deal," but the left and labor
were weak. If unions were a social-democratic bloc within the Democratic Party, they were a badly attenuated one; Obama declined even to
pursue a labor-backed Employee Free Choice Act that would thwart the
tactics of intimidation and obstruction that employers used to prevent
unionization of their employees. Obama's "stimulus" fell hundreds of
billions short of what liberal economists, Krugman included, advocated.
Many of Obama's campaign supporters initially looked to him to act
for them, while the right wing, determined to frustrate his every move,
fomented a "populist," mostly white, revolt against "socialism." Radicals
saw these Tea Party fulminations as a demagogic and well-bankrolled

---

[47] Peter Gowan, "Crisis in the Heartland," *New Left Review*, n.s., no. 55 (January-
February 2009): 20; Chomsky, *Class Warfare: Interviews with David Barsamian*
(Monroe, Maine: Common Courage, 1996), *passim.*

"Astroturf" (phony grassroots) movement, but the right-wing thunder allowed Republicans to take back the House in 2010. Together with the Supreme Court of Republican Chief Justice John Roberts, the House blocked or weakened many Obama aims, including repeal of the Bush tax cuts, although the health insurance measure survived in reduced form.[48]

At the national level, Republicans faced difficulties. They appeared to have lost the culture wars, Obama having opened the military to gay, lesbian, and bisexual personnel in 2010 and voters in three states having approved same-sex marriage, while Wisconsin elected an open lesbian to the U.S. Senate in 2012. Key demographic constituencies – unmarried women and people of color – voted disproportionately Democratic, tilting prospects against the Republicans since birth rates indicated whites would soon become a minority in the United States. The right-wing media exerted considerable power, capable of a setup, for example, that destroyed the once-vibrant, black-led Association of Community Organizations for Reform (ACORN) in 2009. Republicans had an edge over Democrats among big donors, and at the state level Republican governors used the Great Recession to justify cuts to social expenditure and removal of union protection for public sector workers, leaving radicals dumbfounded to discover that the government's answer to the 2008 crisis of neoliberalism appeared to be more neoliberalism.

In 2011 came the only significant popular charges from the left in the Great Recession. In the cold days of February in Wisconsin came the first salvo, mass rallies in Wisconsin to prevent Republican governor Scott Walker's "budget repair" measure from stripping public-sector workers' unions of bargaining rights. Not long before, the Arab Spring had taken shape in Cairo's Tahrir Square, inspiring hopes of democratic revolution through the region. Wisconsin's statehouse soon filled with teachers, social workers, and nurses and their families, students, and supporters, and a hundred thousand filled Madison's streets, but despite the ebullience of the demonstrators, Republicans pushed through the bill. By May, complementary outpourings in Europe replaced Wisconsin as the center of reverberation. A debt crisis derived from the financial collapse had caused youth unemployment to spike, and that along with severe government austerity measures brought demonstrations of "indignant citizens" into public squares from Spain to Greece.

---

[48] Paul Krugman, "Phony Fear Factor," *New York Times*, 8 August 2013, http://www .nytimes.com/2013/08/09/opinion/krugman-phony-fear-factor.html?_r=0>.

"Arab Spring, European Summer, American Fall": So read one protester's sign during Occupy Wall Street. The largest protest development of the Obama years, "Occupy" began September 17, 2011, as protesters took over Zuccotti Park in lower Manhattan, soon to be followed by Occupy outcroppings all around the world. Occupy's most common chant – "We are the 99%!" – was a succinct expression of class and democracy, positioning the vast social majority against the top "one percent" of income earners who had more than doubled their share of the nation's wealth over the prior three decades. In Zuccotti Park's daily General Assemblies, Occupiers conversed, breaking speakers' statements into fragments relayed in successive echoes so that the thousands present could hear what was being said in the absence of electrified PA systems. "Twinkling" finger tips expressed applause to avoid interruption. Facilitators rotated to foil any kind of concentrated authority in the movement, and a modified-consensus formula required 90 percent acceptance for any action measure to be adopted. Most of these techniques were innovations of prior direct-action movements – the "people's mic," for example, had been used at the Battle of Seattle. Occupy welcomed anyone, and participants ranged from libertarian conservatives to liberals. At its core, however, were radicals, especially anarchists. Occupy showed every strength and weakness of the network style. Freewheeling and egalitarian, Zuccotti Park boasted a kitchen, a free medical clinic, a People's Library, and the *Occupy Wall Street Journal*. Yet the General Assemblies were more attentive to internal problems of Occupy's functioning than to formulating explicit demands on the power structure, as many occupiers scorned even the suggestion of developing a definite political program. Occupy Oakland sponsored a one-day "general strike" that shut down the Port of Oakland, and Occupy Portland entered banks in protest, but Occupy Wall Street as a whole caused barely a ripple in the functioning of capital, nor did it advance political demands about foreclosure policy, bailouts for the rich, a Robin Hood tax on financial speculation, or any other measure that might check Wall Street's power. When authorities nationwide, in coordination with Homeland Security, shut down the Occupy sites before winter set in at the end of 2011, the movement had produced no change in Wall Street's functioning.[49]

Two years later, one radical disgruntled by the Obama "placebo" and in despair about the looming climate crisis wrote, "One looks in vain

[49] Writers for the 99%, *Occupying Wall Street: The Inside Story of an Action that Changed America* (New York: OR Books, 2011), p. 53.

FIGURE 7.3. "This is What Democracy Looks Like": Occupy Wall Street protestors in 2011 form themselves into human numerals to signify the vast majority of the population distinct from the wealthiest 1 percent, at Freedom Plaza, Washington, D.C. Chip *Somodevilla/Getty Images.*

across this vast landscape of despair for even the dimmest flickers of real rebellion and popular mutiny, as if surveying a nation of somnambulists. We remain strangely impassive in the face of our own extinction."[50] Every radical had surely felt precisely the same way from time to time, for it is a classic expression of the defining condition of marginality. Beneath the calm, however, was it possible to discern signs of simmering opposition? On May 1, 2012, tens of thousands marched in New York City, reviving the old radical tradition of May Day. That September, Chicago teachers went on strike in defense of the public sphere. In 2013, recurrent demonstrations on "Moral Mondays" were launched in North Carolina by a black-led coalition against the drastic antidemocratic and austerity measures of the Republican-dominated legislature; socialist Kshama Sawant was elected to the city council in Seattle; and the Democrat Bill de Blasio, once a Sandinista supporter, replaced a Republican mayor in New York. The new periodical *Jacobin* typified youthful

[50] Jeffrey St. Clair, "The Silent Death of the American Left," *CounterPunch* (24–26 May 2013), http://www.counterpunch.org/2013/05/24/the-silent-death-of-the-american-left/.

interest in socialism, which polls found more popular than capitalism among Millennials. System-questioning political economy revived, with Marx's relevance cited even in the conventional press. The gunning down of Trayvon Martin in Florida in 2013 by a would-be vigilante and police killings of Michael Brown in Missouri and Eric Garner in New York in summer 2014, all of them unarmed black men, saw marches and protests against racism under the banners of "Black Lives Matter," "Hands Up, Don't Shoot," and "I Can't Breathe." The largest climate-change march in history came in September 2014, when 300,000 filled the streets of Manhattan. In 2015 came the electoral victory in Greece of the radical left-wing coalition Syriza in opposition to European austerity.

Clearly, the Great Recession, racial disparities, economic inequality, and environmental deterioration continued to generate discontent and resistance even as the surveillance state continued unabated under Obama, monitoring cellphone and Facebook communication. But radicals had proven better at cresting with occasional bursts of quickening popular enthusiasm than at making sustained inroads into American politics. If new layers of youth had come to see capitalism as unstable, destructive, and inequitable, how to connect that observation to imaginative political practice, how to challenge the established order and offer plausible visions of a better future that popular movements can bring into being – in other words, how to move from margin to mainstream – remained opaque.

Conclusion

Radicalism's Future

Radicalism becomes invisible, paradoxically, in its victories. When the Americans with Disabilities Act (ADA) was signed into law in 1992 by Republican President George Herbert Walker Bush, few thought back to Helen Keller, the socialist and early deaf advocate. Few remembered the bohemian radical Randolph Bourne, who penned the pathbreaking essay "The Handicapped" in 1911. Few recalled the "Rolling Quads," a band of sixties-era Californian quadriplegics led by Ed Roberts who repurposed power wheelchairs meant for hospital use and took them out into the streets, showing up en masse at a Berkeley city council meeting in 1969 to demand that the city cut ramps in its five-inch curbs, making the city's sidewalks wheelchair-accessible for the first time. Few recalled Black Panthers bringing soul food to the disabled occupiers of the San Francisco offices of the Department of Health, Education, and Welfare in 1977. But disability rights were won by a mosaic of such alliances, which mobilized people facing a range of adverse conditions, from multiple sclerosis to cerebral palsy. In 1988, protests broke out at Gaulladet University, a federally chartered institution serving the deaf since 1864, to demand appointment of its first deaf university president, with thousands signing "Deaf President Now" and marching on Congress, successfully. Two months later, the ADA was introduced in Congress. In 1990, members of Americans Disabled for Accessible Public Transit (ADAPT) abandoned their wheelchairs for a "crawl-up" of the Capitol steps to demand access as a right, each carrying a scrolled Declaration of Independence. Once objects of disgust or pity, the disabled had overcome stigma and shame to imagine a world of access and wrest a transformation that affected resource allocations, not just sensibilities – changing, in fact, the very physical design of American life.[1]

Although the radical left has occupied very few positions of high office in American politics since the Second World War, it has had a catalytic role in American life. Dwight Macdonald once distinguished liberals who see themselves as "the left opposition within the present society" from radicals who seek a new society altogether. If radicals have not obtained a wholly new society on the scale some have dreamt, the past seven decades have in many instances seen a mutually reinforcing dynamic at work, with radicals pushing for sweeping, previously unthinkable alterations until liberals – or even conservatives, once the outré passes into the ocean of common sense – enact reforms. "How does progress occur?" asked the octogenarian British socialist Tony Benn. "To begin with, if you come up with a radical idea, it's ignored. Then if you go on, you're told it's unrealistic. Then if you go on after that, you're mad. Then if you go on saying it, you're dangerous. Then there's a pause and you can't find anyone at the top who doesn't claim to have been in favor of it in the first place."[2]

Radicals face the perpetual challenge of how to devise the tactics and strategies to help make revolutionary prospects become reality. Because radicalism by its very nature must permit a place for the audacious, the heterodox, the "unacceptable" and "impossible," because it must find ways to jolt the existing order out of complacency, the radical left has not always behaved well – or even in its own best interest. There have been moments when radicals have formed the proverbial circular firing squad, with particular radicals' rhetorical excesses, tactical errors, moral deficiencies, and foolish delusions sending the whole lot straight back to the margins, wholly without public appeal or effectiveness. Such a tendency was manifest long before Weatherman or the black bloc in Seattle. "I am as radical now as ever," Walt Whitman told a friend, "but I am not asleep to the fact that among radicals as among the others there are hoggishnesses, narrownesses, inhumanities, which at times almost scare me for the future."[3]

[1] Joseph P. Shapiro, *No Pity: People with Disabilities Forging a New Civil Rights Movement* (New York: Three Rivers Press, 1994), and correspondence from Ed Roberts's bother Mark Roberts, 5 and 6 November 2013, and Ed Roberts's Berkeley attendants, Damon Tempey (4 November 2013) and Sidney Berger (4 November 2013).

[2] Dwight Macdonald, "Thomas for President?" *politics*, October 1944, p. 278; Stephen Moss, "Tony Benn: 'All political careers end in failure. Mine ended earlier than most,'" *Guardian*, 27 October 2013, http://www.theguardian.com/politics/2013/oct/27/tony-benn-labour-ralph-miliband.

[3] Horace Traubel, *With Walt Whitman in Camden* (New York: D. Appleton, 1908), p. 24.

Exclusive focus on radical misfires and misdeeds, however, can be mis-leading. One observer, having traded an absolutism of the left for an abso-lutism of the right at the end of the 1970s, stated, "Hatred of self, and by extension one's country, is the root of the radical cause." America-haters, self-haters: these are epithets that the right typically throws at radicals. Time and again American radicalism has accomplished the reverse, how-ever, serving to assist in the rejection of self-hatred and encourage the self-assertion and pride needed to wrest greater American freedoms: con-sider Winfred Lynn fighting for his country while contesting the Jim Crow Army, Malcolm X chiding Harlemites to celebrate their natural hair, the American Indian Movement drumming and dancing at Wounded Knee, HIV-positive men pinning pink triangles to their chests, Mexican immi-grants announcing themselves as undocumented, women defending abor-tion clinics, same-sex lovers embracing the term "queer," or the Rolling Quads taking to the streets. Insofar as radicalism challenges the self, it calls for broader horizons, higher standards of conduct, deeper sensitiv-ities, a more capacious sense of humanity, and a willingness to sacrifice for others, dispositions motivated by a profound desire to change self and society for the better. Radicals, disinclined to accept any country just as they find it, have often been critical of American society and taken inspi-ration from abroad. In certain cases, including the Communist Party's subordination to the Soviet Union, they have shown woefully insufficient skepticism about the models other societies have on offer, but after the 1950s no one foreign state held sway over any significant segment of the U.S. left. Countries such as Cuba, Vietnam, and Nicaragua sought interaction and solidarity but did not try to control or organize the left in the United States. The internationalism of the American left is therefore primarily the story of a generous recognition of a common humanity. The radical left is in no way a pure moral community, to be sure, but radicals have often acted as the conscience of the society, attentive to the excluded, the oppressed, the exploited, the destitute, the powerless, the homeless, the disparaged, the hated, and the hard-pressed, seeking to win wider acceptances and fundamental equalities.[4]

Following the high point of the cascading radicalizations that ran from the 1950s through the 1970s, American political history shows two seem-ingly antithetical trends: one conservative, toward growing inequality, weakened unions, and an emphasis on private, market relations as a way of life; the other liberalizing, toward greater participation by women and

[4] Frank Browning, "The Strange Journey of David Horowitz," *Mother Jones*, May 1987, p. 28.

people of color in most aspects of social, economic, and political leadership and a dramatic easing of sexual proscription to make gay and
lesbian identities more legitimate. Some historians explain this discrep-
ancy by holding that the sixties wrought a cultural revolution that will not
be reversed, while a political and social revolution against capitalist standards was never really in the cards. In this view, a new American society
emerged during and after the 1970s whose behavioral norms are far freer
than those of the mid-twentieth century. Insofar as the agenda of racial,
gender, and sexual liberalization first gestated on the fringes of the radical
left, radicals may be said to have succeeded in their cultural aspirations if
not their political and economic vision of egalitarian-democratic collec-
tivity. A related argument suggests that the sixties not only brought about
much greater latitude for personal self-definition but also a more "democratic" society – a participatory civil society marked by a wide range of
organizations devoted to advocacy, dissent, and involvement in policy-
making in areas such as women's rights, environmentalism, community
development, and healthcare reform.

The genuinely reactionary trends in our time, however, include the
consolidation of the news media and other economic sectors under corporations decidedly top-down in structure, the drafting of much state
and federal legislation by corporate lobbyists, a degree of polarization
in wealth and income that exceeds that of Europe's historically more
hierarchical societies, anxiety-inducing insecurity in employment, an erosion of the limited "social safety net" established in the New Deal and
Great Society years, the stubborn persistence of racially linked poverty
and gender divisions in jobs and income, the vulnerability of children to
violence and poverty, and prisons bulging such that critics have begun
to describe the United States as a "mass incarceration" society. Successes
over several decades in extending respectability and belonging to women,
people of color, gays and lesbians, the disabled, and other once blatantly
disparaged groups have been impressive, but they are incomplete and
cannot be separated from other signs of a country turning ever less egalitarian and democratic. The remarkable opening of access to many new
demographic categories has coexisted with growing class differentiation
and stratification. A sharp divide among black women now exists, for
instance, between a poor, underemployed group and highly educated,
well-paid professionals. Furthermore, while middle-class black women's
salaries now equal those of white women with comparable education and
jobs, unemployment among young black men has risen catastrophically,
as have rates of imprisonment. Combined household income and asset

levels for African Americans and Latinos lag far behind those of white families; in fact, they shrank further in the wake of the 2008 economic crisis, deepening the color divide.

There is, therefore, a profound difference between *liberalizing* social relations, in the sense of widening the bounds of acceptable behavior and extending access to achievement for individuals of diverse groups, and *democratizing* and *equalizing* social relations. The trends toward growing social and economic inequality, persistent racial discrepancies, the hollowing out of the public sphere by powerful private influence, the collapse of provision for the common welfare, the crisis of many urban neighborhoods and schools, and the punitive ethos of massive incarceration: all indicate a less democratic society. These phenomena are interrelated, for how can gains in liberalized social relations and rights be genuinely secure as democratic social principles are reversed? What does it mean that anyone of any color can sit in the front of the bus, for example, or that it contains a wheelchair lift, if buses, heavily used by the working poor and elderly, now come with much less frequency and at greater cost to riders because of privatizations and cuts to public transit budgets? The George W. Bush years saw violations of civil liberties and human rights at home and abroad that showed the vulnerability of rights-oriented trends in American life. At the same time, undemocratic trends in social relations result in an ever more skewed access to opportunity. Private networks and associations deliver education, credentials, connections, reputations, jobs, and career advancement to the economically privileged, all under a façade of "meritocracy," eating deeply into the practical gains won in liberalized chances for individual mobility by members of oppressed or persecuted groups. Ultimately, securing the cultural liberations of the past four decades will depend on changing the social and economic course to better democratize American life.

The divergence between liberalizing and democratizing trends in American life is echoed in the fate of two strong traditions in the radical critique of capitalism. One is the artistic critique of bourgeois culture – of the stifling and puritanical conformity required by a capitalist order devoted to money-getting and subservience to the boss – in favor of personal autonomy, creativity, and experimentation. The other is the social critique of poverty, exploitation, and selfish greed in favor of equality, security, solidarity, and cooperation. The modern left dating from the nineteenth century was committed to both critiques. In our time, the artistic one has been partly co-opted by the claims of business culture that bureaucratic controls have lessened in corporate life as a world of flexibility has opened up for talented individuals who can chart their own life courses. At the same time, the social critique has been shunted outside of mainstream public discourse – until the radical agitation known as the Occupy movement helped draw attention back to worsening inequality. After all, how meaningful is the promise of "creative fulfillment," the opposite of alienation and conformity, if vast numbers of people are excluded from achievement and security in the closed world of high-flown career connections? Rather than letting the powers that be get away with claiming to represent the promise of individuality, a radical left needs to refurbish its capacity to link real personal liberation with the struggle for social equality, common welfare, mutual aid, and collective action.

The challenge facing the radical left in the United States is to synthesize these dimensions of desire for a better future, to speak to interest *and* solidarity, to a society both liberated *and* democratic, one of personal freedom *and* social equality. This is, at the same time, a challenge of margin *and* mainstream. There has always been a strain between the self-conscious preservation of a rebel's consciousness, which puts the radical left at the margins from the outset, and the pursuit of those broader realms of popular opinion and pathways that may lead to social transformation. The very vitality of a radical left has always depended on this dialectic, the struggle to hold both perspectives at once, largely by imagining how the present reveals the potential for a more appealing future. Yet the ability to maintain such a balance has been increasingly difficult in the long period since the Second World War, when the accumulation of modern horrors made it difficult for many radicals to maintain conviction in the reality of future possibilities – what the left had traditionally understood as "progress." Ever since Auschwitz and Hiroshima, doubts about the inexorability of progress, or even its virtues, have accompanied the development of the radical left, making for a radical sensibility different from that of prior generations. The earlier conviction that a better world was foreseeable and coming provided a potent reason for revolutionary commitment, enabling radicals to bear marginality and uphold staunch opposition while they also proposed programs for a different way of life they believed would ultimately appeal to a broad democratic constituency.

The kind of disenchanted new radicalism pioneered by Dwight Macdonald's *politics* in the 1940s planted many of the seeds of doubt about the promise of progress, about the viability of visions of the future that socialists, communists, and anarchists had long cherished. Since then, there has always been a significant note of pessimism in ideologies of the radical left – a stance that may express antagonism to the present status quo but requires balancing by some measure of redemptive hope if radical motivation is to be sustained. Nonetheless, both the organized socialist left and independent radicals, including anarchists and pacifists, ended up contributing to the left-revival program that sprouted in the late 1950s and contributed to the great radicalization that reached its apogee in the years of the late 1960s and early 1970s. Since then, especially since the end of the 1980s, the breach between margin and mainstream has grown much deeper, as radical activists, by necessity or choice, embraced marginality as a principle for resisting the normality of the going system.

Many manifestations of radical activism in the most recent period have self-consciously stood on the *edge* of society, speaking from "outsider" vantage points. These trends might be compared to the terrain occupied by slave resisters and abolitionists in the nineteenth century, when small communities of rebels were scattered on the outskirts of society as "maroons" who periodically ventured forth and discovered allies in the center of society. Working alliances among rebels and dissenters tended to be impermanent, coming and going, and converging again in new combinations. It was a mode of operation that John Brown hoped to activate with his daring raid on Harpers Ferry, Virginia, intended to spark a general slave rebellion and that Wendell Phillips helped to articulate by imagining a fusion of concerns from abolitionism to labor. An analogous politics is the working sensibility of those protest forces today who have seen in disparate campaigns for global social justice a "movement of movements." Such a politics has a latent potency, for while Brown's raid failed, it remained a climactic symbolic event that helped spark a civil war that brought Emancipation after decades of agitation under severe public opprobrium. On the other hand, resisters may very well remain scattered and isolated, stranded in their dreaming and unable to affect the course of events. If radicals have worried over cooptation – the famous "sell-out" that sacrifices principle for accommodation – an equal danger exists of encapsulation in small, irrelevant, ineffectual, sealed-off quarters.[5]

The socialist-feminist historian Sheila Rowbotham has observed that there is no easy answer to how you carry yourself in a world you want to change radically. There certainly is no pat formula, despite

[5] On the significance of "maroon" politics in the nineteenth century, see Steven Hahn, "'Slaves at Large': The Emancipation Process and the Terrain of African American Politics," in Hahn, *The Political Worlds of Slavery and Freedom* (Cambridge, Mass.: Harvard University Press, 2009).

the perpetual tendency of small left-wing sects to proclaim they possess just that. Recent styles of radicalism emphasize the virtues of pluralism, flexibility, and lack of coercion, imagining radicalism as a loose and shifting confederation of causes and groups. This premise is informed by a desire to supersede the drawbacks of past radical practice typified by Old Left teleology, rigid discipline, ideological dogmatism, and schismatic factionalism. The New Left, likewise, was framed as just such a way out. Yet it experienced many of the same traits, as seen in the fracturing of SDS between authoritarian leaderships, the entrenched combat between black "cultural nationalism" and "revolutionary nationalism," the insistence on "the correct line" among 1970s Maoists, or the tearing down of prominent leaders accused of "elitism" in the radical women's movement. Since the new period that opened in the 1990s, the demand to do away with all that has become more insistent than ever, resulting in calls to maximize the multiple facets of dissent along with decentralization and looseness in coordination. At its best this ethos signifies a valuably ecumenical and bottom-up view of radicalism. Less desirable are its extremity of localism, rigid dislike of anything suggesting "universalism" or common goals for diverse constituencies, evasion of the problem of organization, and disinclination to submit tactical options to democratic decision. Any prospects for the radical left to burgeon again will require the crafting of open and inviting institutions that can serve as lasting platforms and resource centers capable of sustaining social criticism, vocal dissent, public protest, agitation, and movement-building over time. The unions and parties that once fulfilled these functions no longer do. Finding substitutes for those older structures – fashioning new forms suited to new times – remains a challenge for any radical left to come.

Here indeed lies a paradox: Insofar as the radical left, combining the perspectives of margin and mainstream, awaits those exceptional moments of history when formerly outlandish ideas of change suddenly gain unaccustomed access to a wide audience and thus make transformation possible, it also needs to cultivate a respect for organization. The ability to recognize the spontaneous breakthroughs that no one can anticipate, to respect the insurgent forces that may suddenly appear out of nowhere, and to respond quickly to changing events requires also experience, perspective, training, associations, and preparedness of the kind long-running organizations best provide.

Above all, the left of our time suffers from a loss of conviction in the kinds of positive visions of the future that once enabled radicals to keep the perspectives of margin and mainstream together in tension with each other. Socialism, communism, national liberation, and similar large-scale objectives of midcentury, however amorphous, gave adherents the semblance of a definite goal worth striving for, the suggestion of a new future just visible on the far line of horizon. The socialist vision of equality and common ownership was, according to T. J. Clark, wedded to the spirit of "modernism" in the arts, for it meant "the turning from past to future, the acceptance of risk, the omnipresence of change, the malleability of time and space." That future-oriented expectation, with its goal of a "democratic commonwealth," to use the old language, has largely been lost. The "movement of movements" of our time has had difficulty fashioning a rough consensus of a new world to come – and has even actively resisted the attempt, given its antipathy for common platforms. The definite end held in view by socialism (and modernism in Clark's view) may not suffice for today's world and today's activists, but if the radical left is to revive, it will depend on fashioning some new and more plausible image of a future society worth striving for, something more specific and motivating than "Another World is Possible."[6]

At present, a negative futurity, dystopian and apocalyptic, threatens to overwhelm the radical imagination: one of frightening climate deterioration leading to food and resource scarcity, of police states crystallizing within the hollowed-out shell of corporate-dominated democracies, and of an extreme capitalism even more ruthless, in which the top one percent of people own 46 percent of the world's wealth, with the United States as most skewed among all nations.[7] To prevent or dislodge such outcomes will require adopting a cold realism and facing such probabilities squarely, but dreadful warnings of catastrophes to come will not do. Worsening conditions will not automatically produce radicalizations, for they are perfectly capable of generating right-wing authoritarianism. Resources of hope are needed, offering a future orientation that identifies constituencies and roads forward, seeking to involve wide circles of others well beyond the present delimited colonies of radical maroons. Any socialism – if that is the name by which the ideal survives – must reflect egalitarian, democratic, and social values while not forsaking the

[6] T. J. Clark, *Farewell to an Idea: Episodes from a History of Modernism* (New Haven, Conn.: Yale University Press, 1999), p. 10.

[7] Kim Hjelmgaard, "Oxfam: Richest 1% own nearly half of global wealth," *USA Today*, 20 January 2014 <http://www.usatoday.com/story/news/world/2014/01/20/davos-2014-oxfam-85-richest-people-half-world/4655337/>.

liberalizing "rights revolution." That suggests, then, a libertarian socialism inclined to decentralization but valuing organization, suspicious of
the strong state but unafraid to undertake assertive political engagement,
and clearly democratic in its decision making, a politics that might well
be forged out of the resources provided by present left-of-center social
movements and the forces of radicalism already loosely informed by such
an ethos.

In the early twenty-first century, the radical left in the United States
is at low ebb, in part as a consequence of its many successes. Even as
radicalism has upended one pattern of bigotry and maltreatment after
another, clearing away broad swathes of discrimination, oppression, and
exclusion, the pockets of the radical left that still persist in seeking to
transform the structures of the world economic order and class structure
have once again been sent back to the margins. The sixties breakthrough,
from the black freedom movement to the New Left, flourished during
what in retrospect appears a golden age of American capitalism when
economic boom, rising living standards, and Cold War avowals of American democracy fed rising popular idealism. Although the objective bases
for economic and class grievance have only multiplied ever since, radicalism from 1990 onward has seemed a spent force despite episodic tremors
from Seattle to Occupy. Perhaps the seemingly chronic inability of radicalism to catch hold in our time signals the permanent defeat of a radical
left whose primary remaining objectives are those that cut most deeply
against a highly individualistic American political culture deeply imbued
by capitalist logic and assumptions. That political culture, however, has
been compelled, at times, to allow enactment of many measures, including Social Security, Medicare, and Medicaid, that are not individualistic
and has preserved them across even the neoliberal era, precisely because
they are in fact deeply and widely valued. The economic instabilities and
anxieties of the present may be occasioning new longings for common
and humane economic measures, still beneath the surface, particularly
since the history of modern radicalism going all the way back to the turn
of the nineteenth century has shown a sinuous wave-like character, here
collapsing, there catching on in surges.

If some currently obscure sources of opposition emerge to raise new
banners of radical change, then radicalism's recent history of sterile
marginality may come to look very different. The strength of the political
right and superficiality of present-day policy debates would then appear as
surface trends masking something else rumbling below, from the depths.
If history shows anything, it is the great danger of conceiving of history's

course as fixed. No precise future is inevitable, but a return of radicalism in new form and vibrancy would not be a complete surprise. The storehouse of past radicalisms may provide creative inspiration, although the real yield will surely derive from innovations yet to come. As Albert Camus wrote, in equally bleak circumstances, we would do well to appreciate that "*a* future, if not *the* future, remains a possibility."[8]

---

[8] Albert Camus, *Neither Victims Nor Executioner* (1945; Berkeley, Calif.: World Without War Council, 1968), p. 5.

Acknowledgments

This book has two points of origin: in conversation about the history of radicalism that we two began a quarter century ago in Eugene, Oregon, where we first met as teacher and student; and in Cambridge Essential Histories series editor Donald Critchlow's request for a book covering a long arc in the history of the left, from the 1940s to the present.

We have benefited not only from the extensive historical literature already written on left-wing radical social movements since the Second World War but also from narratives by and conversations with first-hand participants in many of the social movements and radical political currents described here. The list of colleagues, professional acquaintances, political allies, and personal friends who have helped us understand the history of the radical left in the United States over many years would be too long to tabulate, but you know who you are.

The text was improved enormously by the expert judgment of our editor at Cambridge University Press, Deborah Gershenowitz. Nelson Lichtenstein supplied a deft reading of the manuscript as referee for Cambridge, and we were also fortunate to receive further comments on all or part of prior drafts by Michael Carriere, Eric Crahan, Donald Critchlow, K. A. Cuordileone, Joanne Landy, Kim Moody, Linda Nicholson, Daniel Pope, and Alan Wald. Comments by audiences and hosts at institutions where we presented versions of this material (University of Birmingham, University of Maryland, Washington University in St. Louis, and University of Michigan) shaped our thinking about the recent history of left-wing radicalism; we would like to thank in particular Carl Davidson, Arthur Eckstein, Richard Flacks, Andrea Friedman, James Gilbert, Julie

Greene, Casey Hayden, Scott Lucas, James Maffie, Angela Miller, and Mary Helen Washington.

The University of Nottingham granted a Dean's Fund leave. At Washington University in St. Louis and the University of Michigan, Aaron Bekemeyer, Justine Fernandez-Gatti, Dmitry Galkin, and Noah Glaser provided invaluable research assistance. A treasure trove of historic left-wing books, magazines, and pamphlets was given to us personally by Professor Emeritus of Mathematics William M. Boothby of Washington University. Gregory L. Parker of the Eisenberg Institute for Historical Studies, University of Michigan, obtained illustrations and permissions. Production at Cambridge University Press was expedited by Dana Bricken, Diane Aronson, and the rest of the wonderful staff. Jim O'Brien supplied the index and saved us from a host of small errors.

Needless to say, the authors alone are responsible for the book as a whole and whatever its shortcomings may be. Finally, we thank our families for their love and support.

Bibliography

General

Bell, Daniel. *Marxian Socialism in the United States*. Ithaca, NY, 1996.

Buhle, Mari Jo, Paul Buhle, and Dan Georgakas, eds. *Encyclopedia of the American Left*, 2nd ed. New York, 1998.

Cobble, Dorothy Sue. *The Other Women's Movement: Workplace Rights and Social Rights in Modern America*. Princeton, NJ, 2004.

D'Emilio, John. *Lost Prophet: The Life and Times of Bayard Rustin*. Chicago, IL, 2003.

———. *Sexual Politics, Sexual Communities: The Making of a Homosexual Minority in the United States, 1940–1970*. Chicago, IL, 1983.

Gore, Dayo F., Jeanne Theoharis, and Komozi Woodard, eds. *Want to Start a Revolution? Radical Women in the Black Freedom Struggle*. New York, 2009.

Danielson, Leila. *American Gandhi: A. J. Muste and the History of Radicalism in the Twentieth Century*. Philadelphia, 2014.

Isserman, Maurice. *The Other American: The Life of Michael Harrington*. New York, 2000.

Kazin, Michael. *American Dreamers: How the Left Changed a Nation*. New York, 2011.

McCarthy, Timothy Patrick, and John McMillian, eds. *The Radical Reader: A Documentary History of the American Radical Tradition*. New York, 2003.

Wolf, Sherry. *Sexuality and Socialism: History, Politics, and Theory of LGBT Liberation*. Chicago, IL, 2009.

Zaretsky, Eli. *Why America Needs a Left: A Historical Argument*. Cambridge, 2012.

War and Peace, 1939–1948

Cochran, Bert. *Labor and Communism: The Conflict That Shaped American Unions*. Princeton, NJ, 1977.

Dellinger, David. *From Yale to Jail: The Life Story of a Moral Dissenter.* New York, 1993.

Denning, Michael. *The Cultural Front: The Laboring of American Culture in the Twentieth Century.* London, 1996.

Duberman, Martin Bauml. *Paul Robeson: A Biography.* New York, 1988.

Gilmore, Glenda Elizabeth. *Defying Dixie: The Radical Roots of Civil Rights, 1919–1950.* New York, 2008.

Horowitz, Daniel. *Betty Friedan and the Making of The Feminine Mystique.* Amherst, MA, 1998.

Isserman, Maurice. *Which Side Were You On? The American Communist Party During the Second World War.* Middletown, CT, 1982.

Klehr, Harvey. *The Heyday of American Communism: The Depression Decade.* New York, 1984.

Klein, Jennifer. *For All These Rights: Business, Labor, and the Shaping of America's Public-Private Welfare State.* Princeton, NJ, 2003.

Lichtenstein, Nelson. *The Most Dangerous Man in Detroit: Walter Reuther and the Fate of American Labor.* Urbana, IL, 1995.

Lipsitz, George. *A Rainbow at Midnight: Labor and Culture in the 1940s.* Urbana, IL, 1994.

Markowitz, Norman D. *The Rise and Fall of the People's Century: Henry Agard Wallace and American Liberalism, 1941–1948.* New York, 1973.

Sumner, Gregory. *Dwight Macdonald and the politics Circle.* Ithaca, NY, 1996.

Wald, Alan M. *The New York Intellectuals: The Rise and Decline of the Anti-Stalinist Left from the 1930s to the 1980s.* Chapel Hill, NC, 1987.

———. *Trinity of Passion: The Literary Left and the Anti-Fascist Crusade.* Chapel Hill, NC, 2007.

Weigand, Kate. *Red Feminism: American Communism and the Making of Women's Liberation.* Baltimore, MD, 2001.

All Over This Land, 1949–1959

Biondi, Martha. *To Stand and Fight: The Struggle for Civil Rights in Postwar New York City.* Cambridge, MA, 2003.

Drucker, Peter. *Max Shachtman and His Left: A Socialist's Odyssey through the "American Century."* Atlantic Highlands, NJ, 1994.

Faderman, Lillian. *Odd Girls and Twilight Lovers: A History of Lesbian Life in Twentieth-Century America.* New York, 1991.

Friedman, Andrea. *Citizenship in Cold War America: The National Security State and the Possibilities of Dissent.* Amherst, MA, 2014.

Haynes, John Earl, and Harvey Klehr. *Early Cold War Spies: The Espionage Trials That Shaped American Politics.* New York, 2006.

Isserman, Maurice. *If I Had a Hammer...: The Death of the Old Left and the Birth of the New Left.* New York, 1987.

Lieberman, Robbie. *The Strangest Dream: Communism, Anticommunism, and the U.S. Peace Movement, 1945–1963.* Syracuse, NY, 2000.

Meyerowitz, Joanne. *Not June Cleaver: Women and Gender in Postwar America, 1945–1960.* Philadelphia, 1994.

Mollin, Marian. *Radical Pacifism in Modern America: Egalitarianism and Protest.* Philadelphia, 2006.

Morris, Aldon. *The Origins of the Civil Rights Movement: Black Communities Organizing for Change.* New York, 1987.

Ransby, Barbara. *Ella Baker and the Black Freedom Movement: A Radical Democratic Vision.* Chapel Hill, NC, 2003.

————. *Eslanda: The Large and Unconventional Life of Mrs. Paul Robeson.* New Haven, CT, 2013.

Rosengarten, Frank. *Urbane Revolutionary: C. L. R. James and the Struggle for a New Society.* Jackson, MS, 2008.

Schrecker, Ellen. *Many Are the Crimes: McCarthyism in America.* Boston, 1998.

Smith, Richard Cándida. *Utopia and Dissent: Art, Poetry, and Politics in California.* Berkeley, CA, 1995.

Starobin, Joseph R. *American Communism in Crisis, 1943–1957.* Cambridge, MA, 1972.

Storrs, Landon R. Y. *The Second Red Scare and the Unmaking of the New Deal Left.* Princeton, NJ, 2013.

Sugrue, Thomas. *Sweet Land of Liberty: The Forgotten Struggle for Civil Rights in the North.* New York, 2008.

Wald, Alan M. *American Night: The Literary Left in the Era of the Cold War.* Chapel Hill, NC, 2012.

Washington, Mary Helen. *The Other Blacklist: The African American Literary and Cultural Left of the 1950s.* New York, 2014.

Wittner, Lawrence S. *Resisting the Bomb: A History of the World Nuclear Disarmament Movement, 1954–1970.* Stanford, CA, 1997.

A New Left, 1960–1964

Arsenault, Raymond. *Freedom Riders: 1961 and the Struggle for Racial Justice.* New York, 2006.

Barber, David. *A Hard Rain Fell: SDS and Why It Failed.* Jackson, MS, 2008.

Carson, Clayborne. *In Struggle: SNCC and the Black Awakening of the 1960s.* Cambridge, MA, 1981.

Cohen, Robert. *Freedom's Orator: Mario Savio and the Radical Legacy of the 1960s.* Oxford, 2009.

Frost, Jennifer. *An Interracial Movement of the Poor: Community Organizing and the New Left in the 1960s.* New York, 2001.

Gaines, Kevin. *American Africans in Ghana: Black Expatriates and the Civil Rights Era.* Chapel Hill, NC, 2006.

Gitlin, Todd. *The Sixties: Years of Hope, Days of Rage.* New York, 1987.

Gosse, Van. *Where the Boys Are: Cuba, Cold War America, and the Making of a New Left.* London, 1993.

Kelley, Robin D. G. *Freedom Dreams: The Black Radical Imagination.* Boston, 2002.

Le Blanc, Paul, and Michael D. Yates. *A Freedom Budget for All Americans: Recapturing the Promise of the Civil Rights Movement in the Struggle for Economic Justice Today.* New York, 2013.

Marable, Manning. *Malcolm X: A Life of Reinvention*. New York, 2011.

Miller, James. *"Democracy Is in the Streets": From Port Huron to the Siege of Chicago*. New York, 1987.

Payne, Charles M. *I've Got the Light of Freedom: The Organizing Tradition and the Mississippi Freedom Struggle*. Berkeley, CA, 1995.

Rossinow, Doug. *The Politics of Authenticity: Liberalism, Christianity, and the New Left in America*. New York, 1998.

Sale, Kirkpatrick. *SDS*. New York, 1973.

Swerdlow, Amy. *Women Strike for Peace: Traditional Motherhood and Radical Politics in the 1960s*. Chicago, 1993.

Tyson, Timothy. *Radio Free Dixie: Robert F. Williams and the Roots of Black Power*. Chapel Hill, NC, 1999.

The Revolution Will Be Live, 1965–1973

Bardacke, Frank. *Trampling Out the Vintage: Cesar Chavez and the Two Souls of the United Farm Workers*. London, 2011.

Braunstein, Peter, and Michael William Doyle, eds. *Imagine Nation: The American Counterculture of the 1960s and 1970s*. New York, 2002.

Burrough, Bryan. *Days of Rage: America's Radical Underground, the FBI, and the Forgotten Age of Revolutionary Violence*. New York: Penguin, 2015.

Carmichael, Stokely, with Ekwueme Michael Thelwell, *Ready for Revolution: The Life and Struggles of Stokely Carmichael (Kwame Ture)*. New York, 2003.

Countryman, Matthew J. *Up South: Civil Rights and Black Power in Philadelphia*. Philadelphia, 2006.

Duberman, Martin. *Stonewall*. New York, 1993.

Echols, Alice. *Daring to be Bad: Radical Feminism in America, 1967–1975*. Minneapolis, MN, 1989.

Evans, Sara. *Personal Politics: The Roots of Women's Liberation in the Civil Rights Movement and the New Left*. 1980.

Fraser, Ronald, et al. *1968: A Student Generation in Revolt*. New York, 1988.

Jay, Karla. *Tales of the Lavender Menace: A Memoir of Liberation*. New York, 1999.

Joseph, Peniel. *Waiting 'Til the Midnight Hour: A Narrative History of Black Power in America*. New York, 2006.

Kornbluh, Felicia. *The Battle for Welfare Rights: Politics and Poverty in Modern America*. Philadelphia, 2007.

Maeda, Daryl. *The Chains of Babylon: The Rise of Asian America*. Minneapolis, MN, 2009.

Moraga, Cherrie, and Gloria Anzaldúa, eds. *This Bridge Called My Back: Writings by Radical Women of Color*. Watertown, MA, 1981.

Moser, Richard R. *The New Winter Soldiers: GI and Veteran Dissent During the Vietnam Era*. New Brunswick, NJ, 1996.

Muñoz, Carlos, Jr. *Youth, Identity, Power: The Chicano Movement*. London, 1989.

O'Reilly, Kenneth. *"Racial Matters": The FBI's Secret File on Black America, 1960–1972*. New York, 1989.

Smith, Paul Chaat, and Robert Allen Warrior. *Like a Hurricane: The Indian Movement from Alcatraz to Wounded Knee.* New York, 1996.

Varon, Jeremy. *Bringing the War Home: The Weather Underground, the Red Army Faction, and Revolutionary Violence in the Sixties and Seventies.* Berkeley, CA, 2004.

Wells, Tom. *The War Within: America's Battle over Vietnam.* Berkeley, CA, 1994.

Anticipation, 1973–1980

Berger, Dan, ed. *The Hidden 1970s: Histories of Radicalism.* New Brunswick, NJ, 2010.

Breines, Winifred. *The Trouble Between Us: An Uneasy History of White and Black Women in the Feminist Movement.* New York, 2006.

Brenner, Aaron, Robert Brenner, and Cal Winslow, eds. *Rebel Rank and File: Labor Militancy and Revolt from Below during the Long 1970s.* London, 2010.

Brown, Elaine. *A Taste of Power: A Black Woman's Story.* New York, 1992.

Elbaum, Max. *Revolution in the Air: Sixties Radicals Turn to Lenin, Mao and Che.* New York, 2002.

Epstein, Barbara. *Political Protest and Cultural Revolution: Nonviolent Direct Action in the 1970s and 1980s.* Berkeley, CA, 1991.

Gottlieb, Robert. *Forcing the Spring: The Transformation of the American Environmental Movement,* rev. ed. Washington, D.C., 2005.

Rosen, Ruth. *The World Split Open: How the Modern Women's Movement Changed America.* New York, 2000.

Shilts, Randy. *The Mayor of Castro Street: The Life and Times of Harvey Milk.* New York, 1982.

Springer, Kimberly. *Living for the Revolution: Black Feminist Organizations, 1968–1980.* Durham, NC, 2005.

Thompson, Heather. *Whose Detroit? Politics, Labor, and Race in an American City.* Ithaca, NY, 2001.

Woodard, Komozi. *A Nation within a Nation: Amiri Baraka (LeRoi Jones) and Black Power Politics.* Chapel Hill, NC, 1999.

Over the Rainbow, 1981–1989

Brenner, Johanna. *Women and the Politics of Class.* New York, 2000.

Brisbin, Richard A., Jr. *A Strike Like No Other Strike: Law and Resistance during the Pittston Coal Strike of 1989–1990.* Baltimore, MD, 2002.

Bronstein, Carolyn. *Battling Pornography: The American Feminist Anti-Pornography Movement, 1976–1986.* New York, 2011.

Chase, Steve, ed. *Defending the Earth: A Dialogue between Murray Bookchin and Dave Foreman.* Montreal, 1991.

Duggan, Lisa, and Nan D. Hunter, eds. *Sex Wars: Sexual Dissent and Political Culture.* New York, 1995.

Foley, Michael Stewart. *Front Porch Politics: The Forgotten Heyday of American Activism in the 1970s and 1980s.* New York, 2013.

Manes, Christopher. *Green Rage: Radical Environmentalism and the Unmaking of Civilization.* Boston, 1990.

Merchant, Carolyn. *Radical Ecology: The Search for a Livable World.* New York, 1992.

Moody, Kim. *An Injury to All: The Decline of American Unionism.* London, 1988.

Reed, Adolph. *The Jesse Jackson Phenomenon.* New Haven, CT, 1986.

Smith, Christian. *Resisting Reagan: The U.S. Central America Peace Movement.* Chicago, 1996.

Wittner, Lawrence S. *Toward Nuclear Abolition: A History of the World Nuclear Disarmament Movement, 1971 to the Present.* Stanford, CA, 2003.

What Democracy Looks Like, 1990 to the Present

Arias, Arturo, ed. *The Rigoberta Menchú Controversy.* Minneapolis, MN, 2001.

Danaher, Kevin, ed. *50 Years Is Enough: The Case Against the World Bank and the International Monetary Fund.* Boston, 1994.

Ewen, Alexander, ed. *Voice of Indigenous Peoples: Native People Address the United Nations: With the United Nations Draft Declaration of Indigenous Peoples Rights.* Santa Fe, NM, 1994.

Heaney, Michael T., and Fabio Rojas. *Party in the Street: The Antiwar Movement and the Democratic Party after 9/11.* New York, 2015.

Klein, Naomi. *Fences and Windows: Dispatches from the Front Lines of the Globalization Debate.* New York, 2002.

_____. *This Changes Everything: Capitalism versus the Climate.* New York, 2014.

Kunkel, Benjamin. *Utopia or Bust: A Guide to the Present Crisis.* London, 2014.

Martin, Justin. *Nader: Crusader, Spoiler, Icon.* Cambridge, MA, 2002.

Mertes, Tom, ed. *A Movement of Movements: Is Another World Really Possible?* London, 2004.

Ramírez, Gloria Muñoz. *The Fire and the Word: A History of the Zapatista Movement.* San Francisco, CA, 2008.

Shepard, Benjamin, and Ronald Hayduk, eds. *From ACT-UP to the WTO: Urban Protest and Community Building in the Era of Globalization.* London, 2002.

Taylor, Astra, et al. *Occupy! Scenes from Occupied America.* London, 2011.

Writers for the 99%. *Occupying Wall Street: The Inside Story of an Action That Changed America.* Chicago, IL, 2011.

Yuen, Eddie, Daniel Burton Rose, and George Katsiaficas, eds. *The Battle of Seattle: The New Challenge to Capitalist Globalization.* New York, 2001.

Index

Page numbers in italics refer to illustrations.